Martinis, Girls and Guns

Fifty Years of 007

Martinis, Girls and Guns

Fifty Years of 007

Martin Sterling and
Gary Morecambe

ROBSON BOOKS

First published in Great Britain in 2002 by Robson Books, 64 Brewery Road, London N7 9NT

A member of **Chrysalis** Books plc

British Library Cataloguing in Publication Data
A catalogue record for this title is available from the British Library.

ISBN 1 86105 555 2

Typeset by SX Composing DTP, Rayleigh, Essex
Printed by Mackays of Chatham Plc, Chatham, Kent

Picture Credits:
The authors are grateful to Sir John Morgan for his contributions.
George Lazenby photo courtesy of Kobal Collection/Danjac/Eon.
David Niven photo courtesy of Kobal Collection/Columbia/Famous Artists.
Sean Connery photo courtesy of Kobal Collection/United Artists.
Roger Moore photo courtesy of Kobal Collection/Eon/United Artists.
Timothy Dalton photo courtesy of Kobal Collection/Eon/Keith Hamshere.
Pierce Brosnan photo courtesy of Kobal Collection/Eon.

Martin dedicates this book to

BLANCHE

5 May 1990–8 November 2001

A truly loyal and beautiful friend who lay at his feet during the writing of the first three and a half chapters but who could not stay around for the remaining ones. Sleep well, my darling.

Authors' note

To prevent any confusion, we have made a distinction between the titles of Ian Fleming's James Bond novels and the films Eon Productions have made of those titles. Throughout the text, we have written Fleming's titles in capitals (MOONRAKER) and the film titles in italics (*Moonraker*). The titles of the James Bond novels written by Robert Markham (Kingsley Amis), John Gardner and Raymond Benson are also written in capitals.

All opinions expressed in this book are our own and must not be regarded as reflecting the beliefs or opinions of Robson Books, Eon Productions, Glidrose Publications, the Ian Fleming Trustees or any other individuals or organisation.

Contents

Acknowledgements

This book is the culmination not just of many – some of those closest to us will claim *too* many – nights in the cinema and at home in front of the TV screen watching the adventures of James Bond, but over twenty years of our discussing James Bond with those most closely associated with the phenomenon. Prominent among those we have had cause to be thankful to in talking to us about 007 over the years are: the late Albert 'R' Broccoli (a true gentleman in every sense of the word), Michael Wilson, Barbara Broccoli, Roger Moore, Timothy Dalton, Pierce Brosnan, the late Desmond Llewelyn, Lois Maxwell, Dame Judi Dench, Samantha Bond, the late Terence Young, Lewis Gilbert, John Glen, David Arnold, Michael Apted, Jonathan Pryce, Peter Janson-Smith, Caroline Bliss, Tim Rice, the late Maurice Binder, Peter Lamont, Patrick Macnee, Valerie Leon, Christopher Lee, the late Peter Hunt and Graham Rye. We should also like to apologise to the cast and crew of several Bond movies for hanging around their sets. We had permission to be there – honest, we did!

Of particular help over the years have been John Parkinson, Anne Bennett, Meg Simmonds, and the late Amanda Schofield, who was taken far too early and whose gorgeous smile is greatly missed by everyone who knew her.

There are so many other people we wish to thank for their help in the writing of this book. For his unstinting and invaluable help in providing background research, the film historian Chris Boxall. For her support, Joan Morecambe. For her editorial skills, Dorothy Twist. For his provision of accommodation in London, David Coupe. For her continued support of all our literary endeavours, our own special Bond girl, Jennifer Luithlen. And for making this project so enjoyable, Jeremy, Jo, Anthea, Kate and everyone at Robson Books.

But we reserve our deepest gratitude to Sir John Morgan whose contribution to this book – drawing, as it does, unselfishly, on private memories of his relationship with Ian Lancaster Fleming, first as a friend and then as Fleming's stepson-in-law – gives the book a dimension and veracity which would have been impossible otherwise.

Introduction

In January 1952, former Lieutenant-Commander Ian Fleming of His Majesty's Royal Navy sat down at his Jamaican house, Goldeneye, and began writing his first James Bond novel, CASINO ROYALE. Exactly ten years later, in January 1962, Eon Productions began filming *Dr. No* in Jamaica, which was released in October 1962 and ultimately proved to be the first in what was to become the most successful series in movie history. And on Monday, 14 January 2002, Eon Productions began principal photography on *Die Another Day*, their twentieth James Bond film and the fourth to star Pierce Brosnan as 007. Thus 2002 marks the fiftieth anniversary of the creation of James Bond, and the fortieth anniversary of the establishing of the most enduring movie franchise of all time.

'James Bond has the stuff of immortality in him,' observed the late Anthony Burgess in 1987. 'If one of the tasks of the artist is to enhance life, then no one can deny Ian Fleming the title of artist. As for James Bond, he will be with us indefinitely – a near-immortal, less than Shakespearean but a model neo-Elizabethan, a hero we need.'

James Bond *is* an icon. Yet his survival is intriguing. The world is a very different place from the spring of 1952, when Fleming wrote CASINO ROYALE. The British Empire has gone. The British way of life, which took a thousand years to mature, has been debased and devalued in less than a decade. The United Kingdom has been filleted into disparate regions by self-serving politicians. And the British themselves have been all but subjugated by Brussels.

But the guardian of the Free World, on film at least, is still Her Majesty's Secret Agent 007. James Bond may be 'a sexist, misogynist

1

dinosaur' and 'a relic of the Cold War' but, in a world that is changing as bewilderingly quickly as ours, it's good to know that there is still the tough and resourceful 007, who answers to a boss called M and who flirts with a secretary called Moneypenny. Bond has become a dependable fairy story for grown-ups.

The fiftieth anniversary of the creation of James Bond is an apposite time to tell the story of the James Bond phenomenon. Relying less on critiques of individual Bond novels or films, we have decided instead to write the definitive history of the Bond character from the moment Ian Fleming sat down to write CASINO ROYALE in 1952 right up to the first day of principal photography on *Die Another Day* in 2002. *Martinis, Girls and Guns* is not intended specifically for James Bond anoraks, although we hope it appeals to both the dedicated and casual 007 fan: rather, it is the ultimate history of a unique literary and cinematic icon.

The James Bond story is fascinating and involves a whole cast of larger-than-life characters. Apart from the actors who have played Bond – Sean Connery, George Lazenby, Roger Moore, Timothy Dalton and Pierce Brosnan – the story features extraordinary individuals such as Ian Fleming himself, the legendary producer Albert R (Cubby) Broccoli, Noël Coward and even President John F Kennedy. It's story of how a fictional character, who was essentially one man's wish-fulfilment fantasy (Fleming once said each new Bond book was 'the next instalment of my autobiography'), completely eclipsed his creator. It's the biography of a latter-day St George set against the changing social mores of Western society. And it's the story of the ongoing battle of the Bond copyright holders continually to reinvent the character to keep him relevant while remaining faithful to Ian Fleming's original concept.

Martin Sterling, Gary Morecambe, 2002

001: The Man with the Golden Typewriter

'Bond reflects the times he lives in. We live in violent times, we all have to accept that.'

Ian Fleming, 1963

'I know there are some who would deny that Ian Fleming practised the literary art,' wrote Anthony Burgess in 1987. 'They are the aesthetic snobs who will not grant that the Sherlock Holmes stories are literature either. But the definition of literature as the exploitation of language to the end of giving enlightened pleasure certainly applies to what Conan Doyle and Ian Fleming tried to do. Neither wished to be Balzac or Henry James: each concentrated on a fairly low genre and perfected it. And both, as Shakespeare did, believed that fiction (drama or narrative) should be about well-defined characters in interesting situations.'

Burgess did not compare Fleming to Conan Doyle lightly, for there is much that unites the two writers. Not least the fact that they both created characters who not only eclipsed their creators but also found a far wider fame beyond their progenitor's works. One does not need to have read a Conan Doyle story to know the names Sherlock Holmes or

3

Dr Watson; similarly, people who've never read an Ian Fleming thriller know precisely who James Bond 007 is, and that he has a licence to kill.

Kingsley Amis went even further. Reviewing Fleming's last Bond novel, THE MAN WITH THE GOLDEN GUN, published posthumously in April 1965, Amis wrote, 'Ian Fleming was a good writer, occasionally a brilliant one. His gifts for sustaining and varying action, and for holding down the wildest fantasies with cleverly synthesized pseudo-facts, give him a place beside long-defunct entertainer-virtuosos like Jules Verne and Conan Doyle, though he was more fully master of his material than either of these. When shall we see another?'

Amis and Burgess were surely right: Ian Fleming *was* one of the twentieth century's finest novelists, but you'd never get the literati to admit to that. Had Ian Fleming been alive today, his name would never have appeared on the Booker shortlist – although, since that pretentious and self-indulgent annual prize has long since ceased to interest anyone outside Hampstead or Islington, maybe that's no bad thing.

It must be said, however, that Fleming himself did nothing in his public quotations about his books to encourage critics to take him seriously: 'I write for warm-blooded heterosexuals in planes and trains'; 'Bond is a cardboard booby'; 'My books are piffle'.

But Fleming was sending himself up deliberately. And his books certainly weren't piffle. Few writers have exploited so assiduously the wish-fulfilment fantasies of the British people at a specific time in their history. Fewer still have written more compellingly about the world under the sea, of gambling, or of the sensual pleasure of the good things in life.

When Ian Fleming began writing the Bond books, the British people faced enormous social changes. Rationing was ending; consumerism beginning; neuroses about communism and the bomb were in the ascendancy. And, above all else, Britain was having to adjust to her diminishing global relevance.

Ian Fleming's genius was to create in James Bond a character who was, according to Raymond Mortimer in the *Sunday Times* in 1963, 'what every man would like to be and what every woman would like between her sheets', anchor him in the new postwar world order and, by sheer force of convincing prose, launch Bond on a series of genuinely thrilling, frankly absurd, adventures. Fleming's *coup de théâtre*, however, was in ensuring that, although Bond's exploits were wildly fantastic, they never went beyond the possible. Fleming was also a visionary. Sir Hugo Drax's planned destruction of London from the air with a nuclear missile; Auric Goldfinger's poisoning of the water supply around Fort Knox with chemical agents and his smuggling into the USA of a nuclear bomb; and Ernst Stavro Blofeld's waging biological warfare on England: all of these seemed utterly fantastic, absurd even, when Fleming devised them. After the horrific terrorist attacks on the World Trade Center on 11 September 2001 and the subsequent panics about terrorists' ability to wage biological and chemical warfare on the civilised world, it was horribly apparent that what Fleming had envisaged was all-too possible.

On 7 October 2001, less than a month after those devastating attacks, the *Sunday Times* called Osama Bin Laden 'an Ernst Stavro Blofeld for our times'. Bin Laden was, according to their editorial, 'straight out of an Ian Fleming story, a twisted millionaire mastermind, holed up in an Afghan hideout, protected by the poorest people on earth and spreading terror across the globe with the aid of encrypted orders, secret bank accounts and cells of fanatical followers.'

Americans seemed to agree. In the weeks immediately following the outrage in New York, there was a surge of interest in Ian Fleming's Bond novels. 'Bond novels are flying off the shelves at American book stores,' wrote the *Sunday Times* journalist Roland White on 7 October 2001. 'Of course,' he added, 'what the public craves in all this is a real-life James Bond to tackle Bin Laden.'

Many people assume that the film series produced by Eon Productions, starting with *Dr. No* in 1962, has been the most important catalyst in establishing James Bond as the cultural phenomenon we know today. While the films have undoubtedly promoted the 007 brand far beyond anything Fleming himself might have imagined, their glittering success should not be allowed to obscure the fact that Fleming's Bond books were established as a major cultural force before the films began. So important were the books by 1958 that Paul Johnson felt compelled to attack Fleming in a scathing – and frankly rather hysterical – article for the *New Statesman*, in which he described DR. NO as 'without doubt, the nastiest book I have ever read'. And it's a sobering thought that, on the eve of the assassination of President Kennedy in November 1963, JFK himself was reading an Ian Fleming James Bond novel – as was Lee Harvey Oswald.

James Bond could have been created by no one other than Ian

Fleming. He knew from an early age that his life was never going to be conventional and, indeed, throughout his adult life he actively craved an unconventional life. His closest friends described him variously as 'charming', 'relaxed', 'suave', 'cool', 'strange' and 'puzzling', but, in fact, no one ever knew Ian Fleming definitively. Mainly this was because of his habit of not only choosing his friends carefully – he abhorred people who bored him – but compartmentalising them and then revealing only one facet of his character to them. Family and friends knew him *individually* and John Pearson, his first biographer, has suggested, in that sense, he ran his life precisely like a spy, not letting even his closest friends know everything about him. 'You never could anticipate how Ian would behave,' recalled one of his many girlfriends from the 1930s. 'In a shipwreck I simply don't know whether he would go off in the first lifeboat, or go down with the ship. In the war, if the Germans had invaded and Ian had turned out to be a great Quisling, I would never have been surprised. He was totally unpredictable.'

Nonetheless, a consensus of sorts *did* emerge from the testimonies of all those who thought they'd known him best. It's a portrait of a man who, despite his Anglo-Scottish background, was very English in everything apart from his approach to sex; an adventurer whose sometimes appalling treatment of women did nothing to prevent his ability to seduce any woman he wanted; and a man whose unerring ability to fulfil his fantasies meant he could be anybody he aspired to be.

'I knew Ian for twenty years,' wrote Donald McCormack in a letter to Martin Sterling in 1991. 'Both in the Navy (I was in Combined Operations) and in journalism. For twelve years I was in an office next door to his and saw him daily. It was really exciting working for him: one could always expect surprises. Once I got a cable saying he would like me to meet "an amiable rogue of Spanish extraction" in the Hotel Minzah at Tangier. No name, no indication as to why I should see this chap or what it was all about, or even how I could identify him. What it amounted to was "yours not to do or die, but to reason why". And God help you if you didn't. One never queried back with Ian: one just plunged in at the deep end.'

Above all else, Fleming's intimates were all agreed that James Bond was Ian Fleming's idealised version of what he, himself, would have liked to have been.

'James Bond was his creator in a way that Tarzan or Sherlock Holmes or Billy Bunter clearly weren't theirs,' wrote Philip Larkin in 1981. 'It was Fleming who smoked seventy cigarettes a day, who wore dark blue Sea Island cotton shirts and loved scrambled eggs and double portions of orange juice for breakfast; Bond was a kind of *doppelgänger* sent out to enact what Fleming himself had never achieved.'

Ian Fleming was the grandson of the wealthy Scottish banker Robert Fleming, a self-made man who'd begun working in a jute factory in Dundee but whose enterprising drive had seen him establish the prestigious banking firm Robert Fleming & Company. Ian's father was Valentine Fleming, who became a lawyer and then entered Parliament as a Conservative MP before he was thirty. Valentine married Evelyn St Croix in 1906 and they had four sons between 1907 and 1913, of whom Ian, born in Mayfair on 28 May 1908, was the second.

Although Robert Fleming had moved south to London and bought a monstrous, darkly panelled house called Joyce Grove near Nettlebed in Oxfordshire, the Flemings never forgot – nor were any of their offspring ever *allowed* to forget – their Scottish roots. The Flemings were a clan relocated to Oxfordshire and the family's leisure preoccupations, fishing for salmon and shooting at grouse, were almost a caricature of Scottish *nouveau* nobility.

Ian, a rebel from the moment he could express himself, was the only one of Valentine's sons not to conform. He was a wilful, moody, difficult boy who, as John Pearson wrote, took against porridge at the age of four and emptied it over the top of the nursery wardrobe; and who at five objected to dumplings, which he put down the lavatory. When it became apparent they would not flush away, he tried to force them down with one of the weights from a grandfather clock, shattering the pan: the dumplings remained intact. Yet such was his overriding charm, even then, that everyone – his parents, his grandfather, even his harassed nannies – adored him. Ian's brothers, the elder Peter and the younger Richard and Michael, were true Flemings, but Ian, who would always like to do his own thing, seemed to dislike intensely everything his family liked and held dear. He was, without a doubt, the black sheep of the Flemings; paradoxically, his family seemed to love him all the more for it.

Ian's brothers all took after their father more than their mother. Typically, Ian was much more like Eve than Valentine, although it must be noted, as Raymond Benson – who has recently assumed the mantle of steering James Bond's literary adventures – points out, Ian did inherit Valentine's 'pride, patriotism, geniality and intelligence'. Valentine must also have had a streak of adventure that his career as a lawyer and politician and his general, somewhat stolid, day-to-day demeanour disguised, because Eve was anything but the conventional wife for an Edwardian gentleman.

With an ancestry of Irish, Scottish and Huguenot origins, and as a direct descendant of John of Gaunt – or, at least, that's what she claimed – Eve was an exotic, beautiful, demanding, sometimes frightening woman; 'an acknowledged prima donna used to getting her own way as very beautiful, very rich women usually do', according to John Pearson.

Eve was every bit as much a rebel as Ian was – although she was devoted to Valentine no matter how much she was prepared to stand up to him – and there can be no surprise that Ian, who was quite unlike the other solidly Scottish Flemings, was drawn to his mercurial, challenging, beautiful, violin-playing mother.

Being so alike, however, meant that Eve and Ian clashed frequently, and there was much amusement in the Fleming family when Ian began writing the Bond books and christened 007's boss 'M': 'M' was the nickname with which Ian, like his brothers, addressed Eve, and the occasionally difficult relationship between Ian and Eve, underwritten by an unspoken but solid mutual respect and affection, was the blueprint for the fictional rapport between James Bond and M.

Ian was six years old when the Great War began and just a week short of his ninth birthday when his father Valentine, who'd already distinguished himself by winning the DSO, was killed by a shell on 20 May 1917. Valentine's friend and colleague Winston Churchill wrote Valentine's obituary in *The Times*. Praising Valentine's 'lovable' and charming personality', Churchill continued, 'He was one of those younger Conservatives who easily and naturally combine loyalty to party ties with a broad liberal outlook upon affairs and a total absence of class prejudice. He was a man of thoughtful and tolerant opinions, which were not the less strongly or clearly held because they were not loudly or frequently asserted.'

Naturally, Valentine's death devastated his widow and four sons, although Valentine's harsh will – which guaranteed Eve a generous income only for as long as she remained a widow – was somewhat at odds with the 'liberal, thoughtful' tolerance of the man profiled in the hagiographical obituary Winston Churchill had written. Nevertheless, as the shock of Valentine's death receded, Eve did not feel any bitterness towards her husband's ensuring she would most likely never remarry. Quite the reverse, since she promoted her late husband as a model of masculine virtue and urged her sons to pray every night that they might be allowed to grow up to be as good as their father.

Eve was not above using the spectre of their father to bring her sons into line. Andrew Lycett has written of her using Valentine's memory 'as a psychological weapon to beat her sons'. And Valentine had given her a more practical weapon to keep them all in check. His will had provided a trust fund for his children and their families but there was a catch: Eve had the power to disinherit any of her sons if she so wished. So the Fleming boys grew up with an emotional dichotomy. When they behaved, their mother was loving to, and relaxed with, them. But, if they ever dared to disobey her, Eve's emotional blackmail knew no bounds. She left them in no doubt that they were betraying not only their mother and noble family but the ghost of their dead father as well.

Of all Valentine's sons, it was Ian who was always going to be the one who found it hardest to live up to the image of the hero cut down in his inestimable prime. It's always impossible to compete with a ghost – particularly a spectre as immaculately preserved in death as Valentine Fleming had been – and the rebel Ian was the son with the greatest potential to disappoint Eve.

Interestingly, Ian would always keep a copy of his father's *Times* obituary, signed by Churchill, hanging on a wall wherever he lived. He had it on his bedroom wall in his house in 16 Victoria Square, which he bought with his wife Ann in 1953, and given the sadomasochistic vein that characterised both the Flemings' marriage and Fleming's own personal obsessions, it might be said that even in middle age Ian Fleming was flogging himself with his dead father's memory.

All four Fleming boys went to Eton, where there was always pressure on them to deliver, and this was particularly hard for Ian, since Peter, scarcely a year older, was so brilliant academically that he was once described as 'the most successful schoolboy there has ever been'. John Cork, of the Ian Fleming Foundation, suggested in an illuminating 1995 article that everything seemed to be conspiring against Ian at this time: 'The knowledge of Ian's late father's looming wealth and Ian's lack of access to it was bound to make the young Fleming feel disinherited, and the elusive Fleming fortune and the high achievements of Valentine and Peter seem to have put a chip on Ian's shoulders.' Cork has further argued that it was Ian's failure to live up to Valentine and Peter that made him determined to forge his own identity, away from the Fleming family norm, and to be applauded for his own success.

Peter's success at Eton certainly seems to have fuelled Ian's rebelliousness: his failure to match his brother's outstanding achievements made him all the wilder, to the extent that he was bordering on the delinquent. Fortunately, this was offset somewhat by Ian's prowess on the sports field. The young Ian Fleming was a magnificent and distinguished athlete and was Victor Ludorum in successive years – 1925 and 1926 – a feat achieved only once subsequently in Eton's history. In the description of the author for the jacket of the first edition of CASINO ROYALE, which Fleming wrote himself, he is revealing – perhaps more revealing than he intended – about this achievement: 'Like his brother Peter – a more famous author – he was educated at Eton, where he was Victor Ludorum two years in succession, a distinction only once equalled – presumably, he suggests, by another second son trying to compensate for a brilliant elder brother.'

One lasting legacy of Ian Fleming's time at Eton was his broken nose, sustained when he collided with Henry Douglas-Home (the brother of the future prime minister) head-on during a football game. The injury was so bad that a small copper plate had to be inserted in the bridge of his nose and the plate was the cause – or so he always believed – of the blinding headaches he was to suffer for the rest of his life.

On another occasion, Ian's continued contempt and disregard for Eton's rules had led to his being scheduled to be beaten yet again. The timing of the beating clashed with the school cross-country race. Ian applied to the headmaster to be beaten a quarter of an hour earlier so that it would be over in time for him to run the race. He was beaten so savagely that blood was seeping through his white shorts as he ran: 'his shanks and running shorts stained with his own gore', as his friend Paul Gallico later described it vividly. Nevertheless, Ian gritted his teeth against the pain and was second in the race. Many have interpreted this incident as triggering Ian's later determination to expose James Bond to all manner of sadistic torture.

Despite Ian's athletic success at Eton, his time there was a profound disappointment, particularly to his mother. For his part, Ian *loathed*

Eton, and his last year was characterised by his indifference to academic achievement – he knew he could not compete with Peter and so didn't even try – and a marked deterioration in his behaviour. Finally, there was trouble with a girl and it was generally agreed between the school and Ian's mother that he should leave a term early to avoid the scandal of his having to be expelled.

Eve Fleming decided that Ian should become an army officer like his father and virtually insisted that he attend the Royal Military College at Sandhurst to undergo officer training. One can understand her reasoning: surely the *only* way in which Ian Fleming would ever live up to his father now was in becoming a soldier like him. However, if she had expected the regime at Sandhurst to knock the rebelliousness out of her son, she was to be severely disappointed.

Eton, with its beatings and hierarchy, had been bad enough, but compared with Sandhurst it was a model of relaxed liberalism. The first term at Sandhurst was deliberately tough, aimed at processing privileged schoolboys into a set of loyal, unquestioning killing machines. Adherence to discipline was all and the slightest infringement of Sandhurst's rules was dealt with severely and mercilessly. It was not the environment in which Ian Fleming was ever likely to thrive; and, although there is evidence that he did, for a very short while at least, attempt to conform when he arrived in the autumn of 1926, he soon realised that he was not equal to the struggle and simply decided not to try. 'He could do really well if only he would realise that as he is at Sandhurst he might just as well make the best of what is, to him, a bad job and settle down,' wrote his commanding officer, somewhat wearily, in the spring of 1927. But Ian had become more determined than ever to do his own thing: he'd been bridling against his family's expectations almost from birth and he was damned if he would now allow Sandhurst's absurd discipline – at least, *he* regarded it as absurd – to dictate how he ran his life.

Ian Fleming left Sandhurst in September 1927, without taking an officer's commission. Officially, the reason given for his leaving Sandhurst was that he had been caught out after curfew once too often. In later years, Fleming attempted to romanticise his reasons for leaving by saying that the mechanisation of the British army dismayed him. 'I didn't become a soldier because they suddenly decided to mechanise the Army and a lot of my friends and I decided that we did not want to be glorified garage hands,' he claimed in an interview shortly before his death in 1964.

But the truth about Ian Fleming's departure from Sandhurst – revealed by Andrew Lycett in 1995 – was more sordid. Let down by a girlfriend with whom he'd wanted to spend the evening, Ian had driven to London one night in a fit of pique to 'find myself a tart'. He found that tart and enjoyed a brief moment of passion. But it left him with rather more than he had bargained for: a dose of the clap.

Eve Fleming was furious with him and this time her anger knew no bounds. At the same time, she looked after all the practicalities by booking him into a nursing home for treatment and contacting Sandhurst to tell them he had been taken ill and requesting that they allow him to take a term off.

While Ian was treated for his gonorrhoea, Eve reconsidered the situation. At Eton and now Sandhurst, Ian had proved, to her at least, that he was beyond mere rebelliousness. Eve was convinced that he was bordering on the schizophrenic. In this, she may not have been exaggerating as much as one might think since Dr Joshua Bierer, a retired Harley Street consultant psychiatrist, claimed in February 1983 to have assessed the young Ian Fleming's state of mind in 1927. 'He was the classic psychopath,' Dr Bierer was quoted as saying. 'I suggested he should begin writing because the thoughts of a mind as brilliant as his should be shared. That, very simply, is how James Bond was born. He was the fantasy figure which kept his creator sane.'

Whatever the validity of Dr Bierer's claims – and it must be noted Fleming did not actually create James Bond until 1952 and somehow managed to remain sane during the intervening quarter of a century – Eve Fleming believed that, having been humiliated yet again by his behaviour, she could not risk further scandal by having Ian return to Sandhurst. She therefore insisted on his resigning his commission in September 1927. Whatever relief he will have felt at this, it must have been tempered by his knowing that he was doing so at his mother's express instructions.

In some desperation, Eve turned to an unusual source for help. She had heard of a private school in the Austrian town of Kitzbuhel, which was run by an idealistic couple, Ernan Forbes Dennis and his wife, the novelist Phyllis Bottome. What they had established in Kitzbuhel was, essentially, a finishing school where the wealthy could send any of their children who had behavioural problems.

Ian Fleming thrived under the influence of Forbes Dennis and his wife. In contrast to Eton and Sandhurst, which in his mind seemed to exist solely to repress his character, he *loved* the environment they had created, which complemented his character perfectly. He had the freedom to ski and to drive and to flirt with the local girls – most of whom found him compellingly irresistible – and also found the motivation to study hard to become fluent in French and German. In stark contrast to Ian's reports from Eton and Sandhurst, Forbes Dennis was able to write to Eve Fleming after his first six months at Kitzbuhel, 'Ian's qualities are considerable. His general intelligence is above average; he has imagination and originality, with the power of self expression. He has excellent taste; a love of books, and a definite desire both for truth and knowledge. He is virile and ambitious; generous and kind-hearted.'

It is no exaggeration to say that Ian Fleming truly found himself in Kitzbuhel because he had the space and the freedom to create his own sense of identity without the spectre of his father intimidating him or the shadow of his older brother eclipsing him. His fellow students knew only of Ian himself, and to them he was civilised, good-looking, witty and supremely debonair.

Of course, Fleming's time at Kitzbuhel could not have passed without some trauma, and this came when he met a Swiss girl called Monique Panchaud de Bottomes. He had numerous affairs and three regular girlfriends during his first year in Austria and his amorality when it came to sex was notorious. 'Ian was quite ruthless about girls,' recalled one of his girlfriends from this time. 'Women were all a bit of a joke for Ian, a treat to enjoy but not to make any sort of fuss about afterwards. Of course, in those days this was a very unusual attitude to find in an Englishman, but it was very normal in Vienna. Ian seemed to get the idea straight away and he behaved exactly as any young Viennese with his looks and his means would have expected to behave.'

Monique, though, was different. She was the first girl with whom he truly fell in love and they became 'sort of engaged', as Ian put it.

Ian was quite convinced his mother would approve of Monique. But Eve did not approve and insisted Ian break with her. She reminded Ian, yet again, of her trump card: she would disinherit him if he did not do as she demanded. 'If there's one thing we have arguments about more than sex, it's money,' he bemoaned to a friend at this time. Reluctantly, Ian broke up with Monique and, emotional trauma notwithstanding, it was a trying time because there was trouble with Monique's father, a powerful landowner, who threatened legal action. The whole affair dragged on for months and Ian was humiliated by it. When it was over, Ian told friends he was resolved to be even more ruthless with women from then on and to treat love 'like a glass of champagne'. 'I'm going to be quite bloody-minded about women from now on,' he said. 'I'm just going to take what I want without any scruples at all.'

There was, however, an interesting footnote to his relationship with Monique. In his penultimate novel, YOU ONLY LIVE TWICE, published in 1964, Fleming revealed that James Bond's mother was a Swiss woman called Monique Delacroix, while his father, Andrew Bond, was Scottish. James Bond was a unique personal creation and Ian Fleming once joked that 'each new Bond book is the next instalment of my autobiography', but, in making Bond the son of a Scottish father and a Swiss mother called Monique, he was drawing directly from his own life. Even more piquant was the fact that the fictional Mrs Bond's maiden name of Delacroix was very similar to Fleming's own mother's maiden name of St Croix Rose.

One of the most important things Ian Fleming learned at Kitzbuhel was how to write creatively. In this, he was encouraged by Phyllis Bottome and he very quickly and instinctively became a fine writer. Phyllis had had her first novel accepted when she was just seventeen and had achieved great acclaim with her 1926 novel *Old Wine*. When Fleming himself was similarly established, he wrote to her, 'Looking back, I am sure that your influence had a great deal to do with the fact that I became a successful writer. I also remember clearly writing a rather bizarre short story for you which you criticized kindly and which was, in fact, the first thing I ever wrote.'

In 1931, Fleming sat for the Foreign Office exam, having decided on a career in the Diplomatic Service. He was bitterly disappointed to be placed 25th out of 62. Ironically, his lowest marks were for his English essay.

It was a humiliating experience and he would always later play it down by telling friends that he had come seventh but only five were accepted. He then turned to journalism, joining Reuters, the international news agency, at the age of 23. He was to serve with them for four years in London, Berlin and Moscow.

Ian Fleming learned his trade as a journalist very quickly and he enjoyed himself enormously. 'Reuters was great fun in those days,' he said. 'A very good mill. The training there gives you a good straight-forward style. Above all, I have to thank Reuters for getting the facts in my books right.'

In 1933, Fleming was sent to Moscow, where – his athletic prowess at Eton notwithstanding – he was truly to distinguish himself for the first time in his life. Unlike many of his fellow journalists, Fleming enjoyed Moscow and quickly added fluent Russian to his command of French and German. He liked the ordinary Russian people he met and became fascinated by the tactics of the secret police, the OGPU. 'They were everywhere,' he said in an interview in 1963, when discussing how his time spent in Russia had influenced his Bond books. 'And it was through my interest in them that I learned about SMERSH who had been set up by Stalin to do his dirty work. They were okay as the villains for a while until Khrushchev closed them down, but always a bit restricting because, being the real thing, there was always only so far I could go with them in a fictional sense. So I invented SPECTRE to give me the freedom of invention I needed for the more recent books.'

Fleming had been sent to Moscow to help cover one of Stalin's show trials, when six British and several more Russian engineers who were employed by the Metropolitan-Vickers Electrical Company were arrested for crimes against Soviet Russia. The accused were alleged to have sabotaged machines and installations at building sites and factories. Like most of his colleagues, Fleming was convinced the trial was a fraud but he, himself, came out of it extremely well. Despite being considerably younger and certainly less experienced than the other press veterans who'd descended on Moscow – the arrest of the six Britons had caused an international outcry – Fleming wrote some of the most vivid accounts of the trial. He had, by this time, developed a natural instinct for journalism: in particular, he seemed to know just what people wanted to read and how to present it in a stylish and urbane manner far in advance of his years.

Fleming never forgot what he witnessed at the Metro-Vickers trial and he was particularly taken by a beautiful Russian girl called Anna Kutusova, who was the lover of one of the accused British engineers,

Leslie Thornton. Kutusova was originally arrested on suspicion of being involved in the spying but she eventually gave evidence against Thornton. Fleming was entranced by her and made no secret that she was the inspiration for Tatiana Romanova when he wrote FROM RUSSIA WITH LOVE 23 years later.

In a typical example of Fleming's chutzpah, he decided to try for a scoop while he was in Moscow. Stalin always ignored interview requests from foreign journalists but that did not deter Fleming, who wrote to the Soviet dictator with just such a request. To his surprise, he received a handwritten letter in reply: 'It was badly typed on a mixture of Cyrillic and Roman keys and addressed to "Micter Fleming". Sometimes I think I will give it to Sotheby's to auction because I have long since ceased to dine out on it because of the anticlimax. For when I tell people I have a personal letter from Stalin they ask, "What does it say?" and I have to reply, "Sorry, I cannot see you, J. Stalin."'

Even his leaving of Russia was typically Fleming. Having seen Russian contraceptives in a chemist's shop in Moscow, he wondered if they were made of the same latex as in Britain. So he bought a packet just prior to leaving Moscow to have them tested back home in Britain. 'You've never seen anything like the face of the Russian customs officer when he went through my case,' laughed Fleming. 'He took the contraceptives out of the packet one by one and held them up to the light. I'm sure he was convinced they must have contained secret messages.'

On his return from Moscow, Fleming was interviewed by several agents who claimed to be from the Foreign Office. They questioned him at length about his impressions of and experiences in the Soviet capital.

Despite his success with Reuters, Fleming had discovered that journalists actually earned very little money, and when his grandfather died in August 1933, leaving no money in his will for his grandchildren, Fleming believed his financial situation was rocky, despite his being a member of a very rich family indeed. The problem was that the Fleming family fortune could not be accessed by Ian until his mother died or remarried. Neither option seemed likely to happen in 1933 and Fleming felt cheated by this impasse which, he felt, limited his options and lifestyle.

Of course, Fleming's sense of deprivation was not shared by everyone. Compared with those of many of his contemporaries, Fleming's life was not exactly one of unremitting hardship. Gerald Coke, a close friend during the 1930s, once commented, 'The odd thing about Ian is that he really had everything he could possibly have wanted – looks, brains, enough money and position. Yet he was never satisfied. He always behaved as if he were permanently deprived.'

In October 1933, Ian Fleming resigned abruptly from Reuters and joined the City banking firm Cull and Company as a stockbroker. After two years, he moved to Rowe and Pitman, where he remained a junior partner, in name at least, until 1945.

Banking bored Ian Fleming to death and he was once described as 'the world's worst stockbroker'. He had a penchant for entertaining clients at the Savoy, but the day-to-day business of finance held no appeal for him whatsoever. His friend Hilary Bray – whose name Fleming appropriated for ON HER MAJESTY'S SECRET SERVICE – said many years later, 'Ian wouldn't have a chance of getting away with life at Rowe and Pitman today as he did in the days when he was there. He was accepted on the old boy basis because of his connections with Robert Fleming. Nowadays he would have to learn a great deal of Stock Exchange laws and the technique of finance, but then he was virtually able to write his own part.'

His new career did, however, afford him the opportunity to gain some independence and he began living in Belgravia, at the suitably gothic 22B Ebury Street, part of an ancient converted temple where Sir Oswald Mosely had once lived. Here he carved out what he considered the perfect life for himself, and what others regarded as the life of a philanderer. 'Whenever I saw Ian towards the end of his time in the City, he gave the impression of being a playboy businessman with all the money and all the friends he could possibly want,' Cyril Connolly told John Pearson. 'I met him once in Brook Street. He was wearing a blue suit and an Eton Ramblers tie and his appearance was so absolutely correct that it made me think of someone out of a Wodehouse novel.'

During this time, Fleming established *Le Cercle gastronomique et des jeux de hasard* – The Circle of gastronomy and of games of chance – which was a group of similarly minded old Etonians who dined and played bridge together, and Fleming's creation of it seemed to epitomise, for many, the impression that he was an aimless playboy of little ambition. In this, Ian Fleming was hardly helped by the continued success of his older brother, Peter.

Having had to endure Peter's reputation as 'the most successful schoolboy there has ever been' throughout his years at Eton, Ian now had somehow to come to terms with Peter being described as 'the most promising man in England'. Peter had become a traveller and writer and his first book, *Brazilian Adventure*, had been a bestseller when published in 1933. By the mid-1930s, Peter had become something of a folk hero and, just as had been the case throughout his life, Ian Fleming always found himself on the wrong side whenever comparisons were made between the two brothers. Those closest to Ian knew that he found such comparisons absolutely devastating and, however much he might pretend to enjoy his reputation as the black sheep of the Flemings in public, he developed quite a complex about it in private. His feelings of inadequacy were mitigated only by his knowing that Peter himself did not encourage any comparisons. Indeed, the two brothers were devoted to each other.

True to the resolution he'd made after the humiliating break-up of his engagement to Monique, Fleming had developed a ruthless attitude towards women during the 1930s and he achieved, as John Pearson noted, 'a fearsome reputation'. His appetite for sex was remarkable and his complete lack of guilt about anything he did sexually wholly un-English.

'Women have their uses for the relief of tension,' Fleming once wrote. 'And for giving a momentary relief from loneliness. The only time people are not alone is just after making love. Then the warmth and languor and gratitude turn them into happy animals. But soon the mind starts to work again and they become again lonely human beings.'

Women with whom he became involved were liable to get hurt if they tried to become too involved emotionally. This did, of course, put some off, but his looks, compounded by the broken nose – sinister to some, intriguing to others – and his air of diffidence attracted many more. 'He struck me as being terribly complex,' said one former girlfriend, 'and that is always exciting. He was like one of those children's play-blocks with a different picture on each side, and you never knew which side you would come across when you met him.' Another recalled, 'When I first saw him, I felt that there was something of the wild animal about him, something restless and uncaged and untrappable.'

Despite his many affairs and casual sexual flings, there were two women who remained constants in Fleming's life from the 1930s onwards. One of these was a very good-looking society girl called Muriel Wright. Pert, vivacious and bright, Muriel was one of the first girls of her class ever to take up modelling as well as being one of the leading polo players of the time. Her father had been an MP with Valentine Fleming and had served as a high sheriff of Derbyshire. Her niece later married Major Ronald Ferguson, whose daughter, Sarah Ferguson, married Prince Andrew and became Duchess of York in 1986.

Fleming and Muriel met in the summer of 1935 in Kitzbuhel and their relationship became sexual immediately. The association was not welcomed by either family. Muriel's relatives regarded Fleming as a cad; Fleming's thought Muriel scatty and bohemian. Muriel's brother, believing Fleming to have treated his sister very badly on one occasion, journeyed from the family home at Yeldersley Hall in Derbyshire and turned up at Ebury Street brandishing a horsewhip with which he proposed to thrash Fleming. Fleming, having got wind of this, side-stepped a brother's ire by promptly taking himself and Muriel off to Brighton for the weekend.

There is no doubt that Muriel was treated like a slave by Fleming: she seemed eager to be his doormat and Fleming obliged by wiping his feet on her. Their affair was to stagger on for nine years until Muriel, who had become a dispatch rider during wartime, was killed during an air raid in 1944, when a flying piece of masonry flew in through a window and hit her on the head. Fleming – who had last seen her when he instructed her to collect two hundred of his special cigarettes from Morlands – had to identify the body. He was racked with guilt at the way he had treated her and became sentimental about her, even to the point of wearing her bracelet on his keyring. 'The trouble with Ian,' noted one cynical friend at the time, 'is that you have to get yourself killed before he feels anything.' A poignant reminder of Muriel was discovered in 2001, when three dusty family albums turned up in an Oxford antique shop. The anonymous buyer told the *Evening Standard* in July 2001, 'I came across them quite by accident while browsing through some books. I just saw these faces and wondered who the people in the photographs were. I thought I could trace them. It was all done purely out of interest.

'The albums had a name on them – Violet Wright – which meant nothing to me at the time and a house – Yeldersley Hall – which I discovered is about ten miles south of Ashbourne. The albums were probably thrown out during a house clearance but it turns out they had quite a history.'

The history displayed in the albums was that of the Wright family between 1915 and 1935, and included six photographs of Muriel, as well as several of her brother, Fitzherbert, the man who had threatened to horsewhip Fleming.

The albums were auctioned at the Bloomsbury Book Auctions in September 2001 and, given that there is always tremendous interest in anything to do with Ian Fleming and James Bond, the sale elicited massive media attention.

The other constant woman in Fleming's life from the mid-1930s, and the woman who would become Mrs Ian Fleming in 1952, was a very different lady from Muriel Wright. Beautiful, wily, opinionated, outspoken and cutting in her wit, Lady Ann O'Neill – wife of Shane, the third Baron O'Neill – was unlike Fleming's usual women in almost every way. At one dinner party she had patiently listened while all the men present told the story of how they'd had their first woman, at the end of which she said, 'All right, now I'll tell you how I had *my* first woman!'; at another party she had asked one famous gay man, in front of all the other guests, 'Tell me, why *are* you a homosexual?'

Fleming found Ann maddening, alluring and fascinating and knew that she threatened the symmetrical life he'd carefully created for himself. Theirs was the attraction of opposites and they enjoyed a sadomasochistic relationship, even to the extent of Fleming binding her and whipping her. 'I loved cooking for you and sleeping beside you and being whipped by you and I don't think I have ever loved like this before,' Ann wrote to Fleming once they had commenced their affair behind Shane's back. 'I hope you are safe at home and missing your black bitch and I long for you even if you whip me because I love being hurt by you and kissed afterwards.'

'Ann was the kiss of death for any man with whom she came into contact!' wrote Donald McCormack in a letter to Martin Sterling in February 1991. 'She was the kind of woman whom all men should avoid marrying. Ian knew this, yet, surprisingly, he capitulated.' Sir John Morgan, who married Ann's daughter, Fionn, concurs: 'Ann was a difficult person. A very complex person. Quite often horrendous.' (See Appendix 1, 'Ian Fleming Remembered'.)

The relationship between Ian Fleming and Ann O'Neill was passionate, stormy and intense. Both loved its illicit nature and although Ann did not want to hurt Shane – who was a solid and dependable father to their two children, Raymond and Fionn – she could not resist Fleming, whose melancholic moodiness presented her with a challenge. She also had no illusions about him. 'It really is extraordinary,' she once cabled him from New York, 'but I cannot be in any major city in the world for more than a day without meeting some woman with whom you have had carnal relations.' Fleming reciprocated her sexual liberalism by cheerfully accepting Ann's simultaneous affair with Esmond Harmsworth. Esmond was heir to the *Daily Mail* and became Viscount Rothermere on his father's death in 1940. His affair with Ann predated her sexual relationship with Fleming. Ann's marriage was dangerously crowded, although the acceptance of the status quo by Fleming, Rothermere and her husband Shane was remarkably liberal and admirable in its way.

Ann was the society hostess *par excellence* and among her intimates she could count Noël Coward – who later became more Ian's friend than hers, much to Ann's chagrin – Cyril Connolly, Cecil Beaton, Somerset Maugham, Evelyn Waugh, Peter Quennell and Sir Isaiah Berlin. Since Ann was notoriously more comfortable in the company of men than women, she had far fewer female friends, although she was friendly with Loelia, Duchess of Westminster (whose first name Fleming appropriated for James Bond's secretary – Loelia Ponsonby – in the early Bond novels) and Lady Diana Cooper.

Ian Fleming's life in the second half of the 1930s was, in many ways, wasted. He was a rootless playboy, overshadowed by his brilliant, bestselling older brother, who flitted from affair to affair, breaking hearts with indifference, and who was undeniably bored by his career. All that changed in 1939 as war with Germany became inevitable.

Ever since his return from Moscow and the Metro-Vickers trial, Ian Fleming had been 'watched'. In March 1939, his lengthy absence from journalism notwithstanding, Fleming took temporary leave of Rowe and Pitman to report, ostensibly for *The Times*, on the British Trade Mission to Moscow. While his fluency in Russian and his previous reporting experience in Moscow for Reuters *might* explain why *The Times* thought he was the ideal man for the job, it seems unlikely they had no more suitable reporter on their staff than a stockbroker whose last journalistic experience had been six years earlier. The fact that Fleming's observations about security at the Kremlin and Russia's intentions in any war – 'Russia would be an exceedingly treacherous ally who would not hesitate to stab us in the back the moment it suited her,' he wrote – were read more avidly at the Foreign Office than by the editor of *The Times* belies the real nature of his trip to Russia that spring.

Many years later, both Moscow Radio and *Pravda* stated that Fleming had been on a spying mission for British Intelligence, and Sefton Delmer, who was covering the Trade Mission for the *Daily Express* and who worked closely with Fleming for those few days, believed the Russians were right.

Whether or not Ian Fleming *had* been spying for British Intelligence, it was certainly true that he'd scarcely settled back at his desk at Rowe and Pitman when he was summoned to a lunch at the Carlton Grill on 24 May with Admiral John Godfrey, newly appointed Director of Naval Intelligence (DNI).

Godfrey's predecessor as DNI in World War One, Admiral 'Blinker' Hall, had advised the new DNI that he had relied on the talents of a remarkable PA, who'd acted as his eyes and ears in the department. This PA, unencumbered by a military mindset, had been an Old Etonian stockbroker named Claud Serocold. Hall advised Godfrey to find a similar original thinker in the same mould at once.

Godfrey's search brought him to Ian Fleming and he offered him the job as his deputy in the forthcoming war, which everyone now believed was inevitable. And so, on 26 July 1939, Ian Fleming was appointed lieutenant in the Royal Naval Volunteer Reserve. His duties went far beyond what the term 'PA' might suggest, since Admiral Godfrey was determined to involve Fleming in every aspect of the Naval Intelligence Division (NID). 'From the beginning my idea was that I would tell Ian everything,' Godfrey said. 'So that if anything happened to me there would be one man who would know what was going on. He could ensure the continuity of the department. I also used him a lot to represent me on important routine interdepartmental conferences.'

This meant that Lieutenant Fleming, operating out of Room 39 in the Admiralty's building in Whitehall, was involved in all of NID's intelligence gathering. He had access to all the secret data on the cracking of codes, the interrogation of spies, the interpretation of aerial reconnaissance, the monitoring of radio traffic and, especially important, the infiltration of Allied agents in Occupied Europe. Fleming's rare ability blossomed with Godfrey's support and he was eventually promoted to the rank of commander. He was an officer of rare contacts – Ann O'Neill's own unique contacts were, of course, also open to him and he used them without compunction – and he liaised brilliantly with the MI6 director (known by the codename 'C'), the other naval departments and, perhaps most significantly of all, with US Naval Intelligence in Washington.

Fleming's war provided him with the best platform for his unique talents. Compelled to work within a regime of military discipline, he found that his rebellious streak – not to mention his tendency to become bored – was reigned in. The war *forced* Fleming to concentrate on the job in hand and he relished it. His was an important role, a *vital* role, in the British war effort, one that many people, both at the time and subsequently, failed to recognise because of his tendency to downplay the very real work he was doing. As both a fixer and an ideas man, Fleming was ideally suited to the task of Godfrey's PA: he was a man who had spun elaborate plots to enliven his life prior to the war and now he was able to do so quite legitimately as he tossed out idea after idea as how to enrage and bamboozle the Nazis.

Fleming's sense of fun and adventure, coupled with the fundamentally adolescent make-up he was never to lose, might have seemed anathema to the senior officers in NID but the reverse was true. Fleming's flair for the bizarre, his ability to approach a problem from a wholly unexpected angle, led to his being very highly regarded by top brass, although junior officers were less enamoured: they nicknamed him 'the Chocolate Sailor' because of what they regarded as his 'cushy number' sitting behind a desk and because of his perceived freedoms.

It's certainly true that Fleming himself saw little active service, though this was largely due to Admiral Godfrey's overruling his going on missions, something that Fleming himself found constraining at times. Nevertheless, he *was* sent to Paris on a mission early on during the war. While he was there, France began to fall and Fleming, like everyone else, had to flee. When he arrived in Bordeaux, where everyone had congregated, he found a somewhat chaotic situation. Putting himself in charge, Fleming sorted the situation out, which, among other things, involved coordinating the evacuation of King Zog of Albania. The last night he was there, on the eve of the fall of France, Fleming and a fellow officer dined at the best restaurant in town. The proprietor, realising the game was up and that everything was crumbling, went down to his cellar and brought up his finest bottle of wine. With chaos approaching, Ian Fleming calmly sat in the best restaurant he could find, drinking the finest wine he had ever drunk – it was a gesture worthy of James Bond. On another occasion, Fleming flew with Godfrey to Washington for talks with their opposite numbers in US Naval Intelligence. It was prior to the attack on Pearl Harbor and, therefore, America's joining the war. Fleming and Godfrey, in plain clothes, flew to Washington via neutral Portugal. What happened next illustrated not only Fleming's penchant for the offbeat gambit, but also how it could sometimes go wrong. 'On our first night in Lisbon we met up with some of our secret agents,' recalled Fleming. 'They told us that if we wanted to see some of the Nazi agents we'd find most of them gambling in the casino at Estoril. I suddenly had the brilliant idea of taking on these Germans at the tables and stripping them of their funds, thus making a small dent in Nazi funds. So I sat at one of the tables and I bancoed one of the Germans once and lost. I bancoed again, and lost again. I bancoed him for a third time and I was cleaned out. I'm afraid patriotism wasn't enough and it wasn't a very successful exploit.

'But it was this real-life escapade that I used as the basis for the big gambling scene in CASINO ROYALE.'

Other Fleming ideas were to prove more fruitful. It was his initiative that duped Hitler's deputy, Rudolph Hess, into flying to Scotland in 1941. Fleming's disinformation, which included playing on Hess's known obsession with astrology, led the Nazi deputy leader to believe he would be met by a British underground movement, led by influential members of Britain's social elite, when he landed in Scotland on 10 May 1941. Instead, Hess was arrested and spent the rest of his life after the war in Spandau Prison, West Germany. Fleming liaised with J Edgar Hoover in Washington and with the notorious William Stephenson – the spymaster known as 'Intrepid' – in New York. He also wrote several memos to George William 'Wild Bill' Donovan, discussing how Donovan should set up the OSS – Office of Strategic Services – the forerunner of the CIA. For this service, Fleming later received a .38 police Colt revolver from the American government engraved with thanks – 'For Special Services'.

Fleming also assumed command of a group of specialist commandos who were sent on specific intelligence missions behind enemy lines, sending back their intelligence to Room 39. Known as 30 Assault Unit – or, more informally, as 'Ian's Red Indians' – they were trained by Fleming, who also planned their missions, although he did not accompany them on any dangerous adventures.

Contrary to the impression that Fleming enjoyed the war – 'I had great fun,' he claimed; 'I worked around the world and got involved in a lot of escapades which were exciting at the time' – he would not escape the inevitable sadnesses that war brought. He had to send men on missions from which they never returned and, having lost his father in World War One, he now lost his younger brother, Michael, in its successor when he died of wounds sustained at Dunkirk in a prisoner-of-war camp. Michael's death *did* have an impact on him, which many people around him noticed.

Despite the war – or maybe *because* of it – Fleming's off-duty hours were still characterised by his insouciant womanising. His affairs with Ann O'Neill – whom he was still sharing with Viscount Rothermere – and Muriel (until her death) continued unabated. But there were many others. Ian Fleming was never seen without a woman by his side: if he felt like a woman, he simply had one, treating love, as he had vowed more than a decade before, like a glass of champagne.

Even so, Ann O'Neill remained the woman to whom he was most devoted – if his feelings towards her could be so distinguished – and their relationship was complex to say the least.

When Shane O'Neill was killed in action in Italy in 1944, Ann was staying at Rothermere's house at Ascot. Ann and Rothermere were practically living together, although she knew she didn't really love him and was irritated by his reluctance even to talk of their future. With deep irony, Fleming was visiting Ann at the house when the telegram arrived informing her of her husband's death. 'Death is the best revenge,' she remarked to Fleming, almost suggesting Shane had got himself killed to pay her back for her adultery.

Ann had a choice of lovers whom she could marry. There was the very rich and grand Viscount Rothermere, who was reluctant to divorce his own wife, or Ian Fleming. Believing marriage was anathema to Fleming, who never wanted to have his freedom inhibited, Ann plumped for Rothermere, whom she knew she really didn't love any more. But she confided to friends that she would never have married Rothermere if Fleming had asked her to marry him. 'The night before I married Esmond,' Ann wrote, 'I dined with Ian, and we walked and walked in the park. He said several times "I want to leave some kind of mark on you"; if he had suggested marriage I would have accepted.'

Ann married Rothermere on 28 June 1945, but the new Lady Rothermere did not break off her affair with Fleming. 'It makes absolute sense,' commented one caustic acquaintance. 'She's marrying Rothermere and Ian's round the corner in his flat.'

A few months before Ann's marriage, Fleming had gone to an Anglo-American conference in Jamaica with his old Etonian friend Ivar Bryce. Fleming had never been to Jamaica before and what he found when he arrived there was a completely unspoiled Caribbean paradise, which had been all but untouched by the war. Fleming fell in love with Jamaica at once and he told his friend Ivar Bryce, 'When the war is over, I'll never spend another winter in England.'

Fleming bought a patch of land on the north shore of Jamaica – somewhere he knew he would feel utterly alone in the world, and where he could indulge his passion for snorkelling – and built a house there. He christened it Goldeneye, after a joint NID/SOE operation in Gibraltar masterminded by Fleming himself in 1941, and it was built to his own Spartan specifications. He wanted to live with nature and, consequently, Goldeneye made no concessions to comfort: there was no glass at the windows, no air conditioning and not even any hot-water plumbing. The first tenant to rent the house. Noël Coward, was appalled and famously likened it to a municipal clinic – 'Goldeneye, nose and throat' – although this did not prevent Coward building his own Jamaican home nearby shortly afterwards.

After the war ended, Fleming was offered a job as foreign manager with Kemsley Newspapers, owners of *The Times* and the *Sunday Times*. He accepted, *provided* it was written into his contract that he would have three months' holiday – January, February and March – every year. These were the months he would set aside for Goldeneye and this regime never altered from 1946 until his death in 1964, so his pledge to Ivar Bryce never to endure another English winter held good for the rest of his life.

Fleming's journalism for Kemsley Newspapers was outstanding, and he excelled at travel and adventure features. He joined the noted French archaeologist Norbert Casteret on an exploration, and went diving with Jacques-Yves Cousteau. He also pulled off the coup of getting Somerset Maugham, who had always refused to allow any newspaper to serialise his work, to agree to the *Sunday Times* running a series of articles Maugham had written about the 'ten best novels in the world'. Fleming was also asked to take over the writing of the 'Atticus' column in the *Sunday Times* in 1953; this was a singular honour but he accepted only on the understanding that nothing he wrote for the column would be altered in any way.

If Fleming's postwar professional life seemed settled, his personal life was as complicated as ever. Ann's marriage to Lord Rothermere had done nothing to dampen her passionate relationship with Fleming and – telling her friends that Rothermere was 'as remote as the north pole' – she found herself desperately in love with him.

For his part, Fleming was still fascinated by her. Perhaps he felt he was reaching for the unattainable: Ann was a challenge and that's what fuelled his own passion. Certainly, she was the one woman he had loved but hadn't left, and it was remarkable that he could tell her, just a couple of years short of his fortieth birthday, that she was the first woman he had spent a whole night with.

In January 1948, Ann went to stay with Fleming at Goldeneye for the first time. She later told her closest friends that these were the happiest weeks of her life. Alone with Fleming, apart from daytime chaperones such as Noël Coward, Ann found Goldeneye enchanting. She would not always do so: a decade or so later she would come to loathe the place because it represented the heart of the Bond business she detested and because Fleming's long-time mistress, Blanche Blackwell, lived just up the coast.

But in 1948, Ann noticed only Goldeneye's lush tropical backdrop – the perfect setting for her romance with Fleming. Perhaps inevitably, the holiday resulted in her becoming pregnant by Ian. She eventually gave birth, prematurely, to a baby girl who lived for only a few hours.

Rothermere was, understandably, furious and forbade Ann from seeing Fleming again for at least six months. Fleming and Ann did actually consider this, but then realised they would never be able to agree to it in the sure knowledge they would break their pledge the minute Rothermere's back was turned.

Ann returned to Jamaica in January 1949, assuring Rothermere that she was staying at Noël Coward's house. But she was incapable of discretion and word soon leaked back to Rothermere that Ann was staying with Fleming at Goldeneye.

The messy triangle dragged on for another couple of years but, by 1951, Ann had had enough and decided she wanted to be with Fleming. Late in 1951, Fleming and Ann travelled to Goldeneye to await Ann's divorce coming through. By mid-January 1952, Ann knew she was again pregnant by Ian and, despite his terror of the obligations of marriage, Fleming realised he finally had to accept responsibility for the first time in his life and marry Ann as soon as her divorce was final.

Those early weeks of 1952 were extremely stressful for both Ann and Fleming. Ann, who was a gifted watercolourist, alleviated the pressure somewhat by painting. Fleming, eager to find 'something to take my mind off the shock of getting married for the first time at the ridiculous age of 43', decided to sit down and write a novel. And so, on the morning of 15 January 1952, Ian Fleming went for his customary swim, had breakfast and then shut himself inside Goldeneye with a ream of finest-quality typing paper he had recently bought in New York and his old Imperial portable typewriter to begin work on CASINO ROYALE.

He would joke in later years that writing CASINO ROYALE had been the equivalent of digging a large hole in the garden just for the sake of it. But, not for the first time, Ian Fleming was being disingenuous. The decision to write CASINO ROYALE was not as spontaneous as he later insisted it was.

He had often remarked to friends – both before the war and during it – that he intended to buy himself a patch of land somewhere away from England, build himself a house and then 'write the spy novel to end all spy novels'.

Well, he had the house; and, whatever personal reasons had made him reach the decision, he judged that the time was now right to try to fulfil the second part of his prophecy. It was time for Ian Fleming to write that spy novel.

002: The Name's Bond

> 'I never intended James Bond to be a particularly likeable person, which makes me wonder a bit about the real motives of people who treat him like a cult.'
>
> Ian Fleming, 1963

On 25 March 1952, Ian and Ann Fleming flew from Jamaica to New York, en route for London. They had been married for less than a day, the ceremony having taken place in the magistrate's office at Port Maria. Noël Coward's long-time companion and secretary, Cole Lesley, and Coward himself were the only witnesses.

On the way to New York, Fleming knew that his life had changed irrevocably. He had a wife; he was about to become a father for the first time; and in his briefcase he had the 60,000-word manuscript of CASINO ROYALE, the first James Bond book.

He'd completed CASINO ROYALE exactly a week earlier, on 18 March, and it was the easiest book he was ever to write. Completed in two months, it had been written without notes, without prior research and with an energetic enthusiasm that, even in its uncorrected state, sang out from every page. Fleming remarked:

> James Bond came out of thin air. He was a compound of all the secret agents and commandos I met during the Second World War when I was personal assistant to the Director of Naval Intelligence.
>
> My job got me right into the heart of things, even the most

secret affairs. No one could have wished for a more exciting or interesting war. And it was all the things that I heard and learned about secret operations that finally led me to write about them in a disguised way and with James Bond as the central character.

The odd thing is that I don't think about Bond as a 'character' at all. I didn't intend that he would have any characteristics, except to be a blunt instrument in the hands of the British government. He's a cipher. What's happened over the years is that he has become a 'character' largely exaggerated in the public mind.

The paradox is that I quite deliberately made him rather anonymous. This was to enable the reader to identify with him. People have only to put their own clothes on Bond and build him into whatever sort of man they admire. If you read my books you'll find that I don't actually describe him at all.

This was not altogether true, since James Bond was, essentially, Ian Fleming daydreaming in the third person. Bond was Fleming's idealised version of the man he would have liked to have been: tough, resourceful, a man of action, and a man whose uncompromising freedoms were, unlike the newlywed Ian Fleming, unthreatened by marriage or tedious domesticity. However accurate the critic Raymond Mortimer's assertion was about Bond's being 'what every man wants to be and what every woman wants between her sheets', it was certainly true that Bond was what *Ian Fleming* wanted to be. And, in CASINO ROYALE, Fleming drew more heavily on his own experiences and attitudes than in any other novel. While his third book, MOONRAKER, remains the most personal of Fleming's books in its detail – not least because it is set in Fleming's London as well as in and around Dover, his favourite part of England – CASINO ROYALE's narrative draws on secret missions Fleming read about, and was involved in, during his time in NID.

Sent by M to Royle-les-Eaux in northern France, James Bond is instructed to take on Le Chiffre at the gaming tables. A Soviet agent, Le Chiffre has appropriated Russian funds to finance his outside activities. Desperate to recoup the money so he can repay the Russians, Le Chiffre is trying to win it at baccarat. Bond's mission is to clean him out and thus make a big dent in Soviet funds that would, otherwise, be channelled by Le Chiffre into a communist trade union. Bond defeats Le

Chiffre, only to find himself at the mercy of the villain in a breathtakingly violent torture scene.

The basic plot was, of course, a reworking of Fleming's own, disastrous, attempt similarly to blow a hole in Nazi funds at the gaming table in Portugal in 1941; but other elements were inspired by the war as well. For instance, Fleming explained that his inspiration for the Double-0 number – the licence to kill – in Her Majesty's Secret Service came from top-secret reports he handled during the war at NID, all of which were prefixed with a 00 number at the beginning of hostilities.

'Although this was later changed for security reasons, it stuck in my mind and I decided to borrow it for Bond to make his job sound more interesting and provide him with a licence to kill,' explained Fleming. 'Of course, in real life any spy may need to kill and probably will, quite irrespective of whether he is authorized to do so.'

Interestingly, the author Peter Haining has argued that Fleming, an admirer of Rudyard Kipling, might have been influenced by Kipling's short story entitled '007', which was in his collection *The Day's Work*, published in 1898; while Sir John Morgan has yet another theory on the origins of the number 007 (see Appendix 1, 'Ian Fleming Remembered'.)

CASINO ROYALE is an extremely violent and a surprisingly cynical book. The shortest of all the novels Fleming was to write – with the exception of the atypical and controversial THE SPY WHO LOVED ME nine years later – CASINO ROYALE sees James Bond actually questioning the work he does as 'a blunt instrument' of the British government. Recovering from what, even fifty years on, remains arguably the most harrowing torture scene in spy fiction – a naked Bond is forced to sit on a cane chair with its seat cut out, while his exposed genitals are assaulted by a carpet-beater – Bond allows his cynicism to take over as he wonders who are the heroes and who are the villains.

He points out that the kind of Conservatism prevalent in 1950s Britain would have 'damned near' been called Communism fifty years earlier and that had he been an agent then he would have been ordered by M to go and fight *that*. History moves very quickly, Bond observes, and heroes and villains consistently change sides.

Earlier in CASINO ROYALE, Bond is even disparaging about his Double-0 number. In later books, Bond is proud to be a Double-0: when, in YOU ONLY LIVE TWICE, it looks like M is taking Bond out of the Double-0 section, Bond threatens to tender his resignation, rather than lose his licence to kill. But in CASINO ROYALE his attitude to the Double-0s is almost ambivalent. He says it's fairly easy to gain a Double-0 number if you're prepared to kill. That's all the meaning it has and he believes it's nothing to be especially proud of.

Although Bond would question aspects of his work in subsequent novels, he would never again voice such profound doubts about the *essential* rightness of what he was doing. The passages in CASINO ROYALE in which Bond has these doubts are a stand-out in the entire series and many critics have commented that they are at odds with the image of Bond as Her Majesty's finest secret agent – and with Ian Fleming's perceived patriotism. But in one interview Fleming once let slip that he, himself, shared Bond's doubts.

'Bond's got his vices obviously,' said Fleming. 'And some virtues like patriotism and courage – although I'm not sure how much of a virtue they are.'

Fleming's attitude to women is also laid bare in Vesper Lynd, the first of James Bond's conquests in the series. In having Bond think to himself that 'the conquest of her body, because of the central privacy in her, would each time have the sweet tang of rape', Fleming offends our sense of decency today; but the prevailing social mores of half a century ago allowed him to get away with his silly adolescent fantasy. Bond also regards Vesper, a fellow agent, as 'a nuisance'; and, although he subsequently falls deeply in love with her, the revelation that she's a double-agent, which causes her suicide, hardens his heart: 'The bitch is dead now' is Bond's last line in the book.

Bond is not the humourless nonentity in CASINO ROYALE some critics have suggested. But he *is* shadowy and characterless in the book. Far from being the result of any deficiency on Fleming's part as a writer, this was *precisely* what Fleming set out to achieve in creating his 'blunt instrument'. And in appropriating his hero's name from a book he kept at Goldeneye – the author James Bond's *Birds of the West Indies* – Fleming stayed true to his brief: 'I wanted the simplest, dullest, plainest-sounding name I could find. James Bond seemed perfect.'

Bond is barely described at all in CASINO ROYALE. Vesper Lynd reflects after their first meeting that he's 'very good-looking' and he reminds her of Hoagy Carmichael. Apart from her thinking there's something cold and ruthless about him, that's about all we get except for details about what Bond likes to eat and drink – the famous martini 'shaken, not stirred', makes its debut here – and that his car, 'one of the last four-and-a-half-litre Bentleys', is his only personal hobby.

Obviously, Fleming had to flesh out Bond's character in subsequent novels because 007's coldness in his debut could not be sustained throughout what became a series of twelve full-length novels and two collections of short stories. But it is *precisely* Bond's essential anonymity that works so well in CASINO ROYALE, and the reason why some of Fleming's friends – most notably Raymond Chandler – insisted he never wrote a better book, much to Fleming's chagrin.

Inured as we are in the twenty-first century to random acts of violence and the casual slaughter of thousands of innocents by mindless terrorism, it seems odd that the violence in CASINO ROYALE should retain its capacity to unsettle; and yet the horror of the carpet-beater scene lingers in the memory of anyone who's read it. Although Fleming would gradually tone down the violence as the series progressed, cruelty remained an essential ingredient of his books and was always one of the main criticisms levelled against him. SEX, SNOBBERY AND SADISM was the headline of Paul Johnson's infamous tirade against Fleming in the *New Statesman* in 1958, in which Johnson accused Fleming of promoting 'the sadism of a schoolboy bully'. But Fleming defended himself eloquently.

'The fact of the matter is that Bond reflects the times he lives in,' he argued in 1963. 'We live in violent times, we all have to accept that. It's been said that I invented all the cruelties and brutalities to which Bond is subjected. But let me tell you, some terrible things were done to secret agents in the last war. I *know* that. And anyone who's been involved in the Secret Service in recent years certainly won't agree such things are made up. I wouldn't like anyone to think Bond enjoys killing people. He doesn't. It's part of his job and he gets on with it.'

Despite CASINO ROYALE being the first of the Bond books, it only partially established the Fleming formula. It is flawed structurally – the Secret Service story is over two-thirds of the way through the novel – and the lack of planning by Fleming prior to his writing the book *does* show through.

Furthermore, Bond's mission is hardly in the same league as his preventing the nuclear annihilation of London he accomplished in MOONRAKER just two years later, or his thwarting of the assault on Fort

Knox in GOLDFINGER, so the later books tended to eclipse the original in the public consciousness.

And while it's true CASINO ROYALE introduces M, Miss Moneypenny and Chief of Staff Bill Tanner – all series regulars – as well as CIA agent Felix Leiter, who appeared in five subsequent Fleming novels, both heroine and villain are atypical Fleming creations. Far from being a criminal mastermind, Le Chiffre is a glorified embezzler, albeit a particularly sadistic one, who's nothing more than a senior SMERSH agent. Subsequent Fleming villains might have been backed by Russia – such as Mr Big and Sir Hugo Drax – but they controlled their own private armies and were the instigators of their own nefarious plots. Fleming, who was obsessed with the misuse of absolute power, was to create some corking villains after CASINO ROYALE, but Le Chiffre has no real power except over various smaller SMERSH agents. He's an employee, an agent of the other side, just like Bond. Fleming was to use this idea just once more in a full-length novel. Le Chiffre is the progenitor of Emilio Largo in THUNDERBALL (1960). Just as Le Chiffre is an employee of SMERSH, so Largo is an executive of SPECTRE. Although Largo is the character with whom Bond comes into conflict in THUNDERBALL, he is *not* the main villain of the book: that is Ernst Stavro Blofeld. Thus Largo can be seen to be a reworking of Le Chiffre.

The duplicitous Vesper Lynd is as compelling as any of her successors – so successfully has she got under his skin that Bond weeps when he finds her body – but Vesper remains a traitor at the end. She may have fallen in love with Bond but she does not revert to the side of right and virtue and commits suicide as the only way out of her dilemma. While subsequent Fleming heroines are often associated with the villains at the outset – Solitaire, Tiffany Case, Tatiana Romanova, Pussy Galore and Domino – they all switch to Bond's side eventually and shelter under his protection. Vesper does not and she stands alone in the series of Bond novels.

Interestingly, however, while Vesper was not a blueprint for Fleming's later heroines, she did inspire double-dealing secondary female characters in the film series. Miss Taro in *Dr. No*, Helga in *You Only Live Twice* and, particularly, Fiona in *Thunderball* – none of them Fleming characters with the exception of Miss Taro (mentioned fleetingly in DR. NO) and all of whom do not switch sides after making love to Bond – were clearly inspired by Vesper. And Vesper did at least establish the Bondian tradition that any woman getting too emotionally close to Bond was liable to die.

Speaking many years after CASINO ROYALE had been published and James Bond established, Fleming, with his usual diffidence, tried to play down his excitement at having completed his first novel. 'When I got back to London I did nothing with the manuscript,' he claimed. 'I was too ashamed of it. No publisher would want it and if one did I would not have the face to see it in print.'

Having lived so long in the shadow of his vastly more famous, and seemingly more talented, brother Peter, Fleming can, perhaps, be excused his nervousness at letting anyone read CASINO ROYALE, lest he leave himself open to ridicule. And, if one were to take at face value the fact that it was nearly two months before he mentioned the manuscript to anyone (on 12 May 1952), one might even buy his comment that he was 'too ashamed of it'. But, as usual, Fleming was giving his idealised version of events. A better gauge of his enthusiasm for CASINO ROYALE in May 1952 is the fact that on the 17th he bought a custom-made gold-plated typewriter – from the Royal Typewriter Company in New York at a cost of $174 – to correct the manuscript.

Five days earlier, he had lunched with his friend William Plomer at the Ivy in London. Fleming had known Plomer, a poet and novelist, from the early 1930s – ever since, in fact, he had sent him a fan letter. Plomer, who had also worked briefly with Fleming in NID during the war, was now a reader for the publisher Jonathan Cape.

During the lunch, without preamble, Fleming said to Plomer, 'How does one get cigarette smoke out of a woman once you've got it in?' Plomer had barely time to register this bizarre conversational gambit before Fleming added, 'One can't use "exhales" and "puffs it out" just sounds silly.'

'My God,' said Plomer, the penny dropping. 'You've written a book.'

Plomer asked to read it and, although this was precisely what Fleming had intended all along when inviting Plomer to the Ivy, he always persisted with his charade that Plomer practically had to drag the manuscript from him.

'I'm ashamed of it,' Fleming wrote in his covering letter to Plomer when he submitted CASINO ROYALE. He claimed he had had the idea that he could write a thriller with half of his mind, and simply wrote 2,000 words a day to prove to himself he could. He said he didn't read it through as he wrote it and was appalled on doing so when he got back to England. 'After riffling through this muck you will probably never speak to me again,' Fleming concluded. 'For God's sake don't mention this dreadful oafish opus to anyone else.'

Plomer had known Fleming too long to pay any attention to his mock humility, and read CASINO ROYALE in one sitting. Excited by it beyond belief, he ignored Fleming's strict instruction to show it to no one else and sent it to Jonathan Cape's other reader, Daniel George. George's now-famous letter reply to Plomer was dated 14 July 1952:

My dear William,

I sat up till 1.20 last night. 'Casino Royale' made me sit up. It was so exciting that I could persuade myself that I was back at the old baccarat table, and the vodka and caviar were so delicious that I tolerated the abominable condition of the typescript.

Both Plomer and George recommended publication – after some revision – although Jonathan Cape himself was not overly impressed by the book, and only a quiet word from Peter Fleming himself persuaded him to publish it. 'Peter's little brother has written a book,' Cape confided to intimates. 'It's not up to scratch but I'm publishing it because he's Peter's brother. But he's got to do much better if he's going to get anywhere near Peter's standard.' In fairness, it must be pointed out that Cape had, hitherto, published little in the way of suspense thrillers and was not, himself, an aficionado of the genre.

Having been disparaging about CASINO ROYALE initially, Fleming now worked hard on the revisions of the book, and he completed them in August, just days after Ann had given birth to their son, whom they christened Caspar. He was particularly keen to get all the factual details right in his book. Partly this was because of his journalistic background; but it was also a prescient realisation that Bond's adventures would not seem quite so absurd if they were anchored in some kind of reality. Thus, it was at this stage that silly errors in the original manuscript, such as his calling Bond's gun a .28 Biretta instead of the correct .25 Beretta, were amended.

The last three months of 1952 were a frenzied period in the life of Ian

Fleming. In the midst of his and Ann's having Caspar christened – with Noël Coward and Anthony Eden's wife Clarissa numbered among the godparents – and their moving to a splendid Regency house, 16 Victoria Square, Fleming, who had pretended to William Plomer he was ashamed of the book, now began preparing the way for the launch of James Bond and his new life as a bestselling author with gusto.

Privately convinced CASINO ROYALE would be a bestseller, Fleming tried to persuade Jonathan Cape to print an initial run of 10,000 copies, an unheard-of print run for an unknown first author. He also tried to get the wily publisher to agree to royalty terms far beyond what even an established writer might earn. Cape baulked at most of Fleming's suggestions but Fleming himself was cheerfully unfazed. 'I hope you won't find any of these suggestions unreasonable,' he wrote to Cape. 'I am only activated by motives of (a) making as much money for myself and my publishers as possible out of the book; and (b) getting as much fun as I personally can out of the project.'

Clearly anticipating he would earn big money from CASINO ROYALE, Fleming bought a small, defunct theatrical agency, Glidrose Productions (later changed to Glidrose Publications), to offset the tax on the earnings from CASINO ROYALE. He signed over all rights, film and serial rights excepted, to the company, of which he and Ann became directors.

Fleming had already sounded out his old friend Ivar Bryce about potential American publishers – 'I'm not being vain about this book,' he claimed, 'I'm simply trying to squeeze the last dirty cent out of it' – and had asked Kemsley Newspapers' Hollywood correspondent, 'what sort of sums do the big studios pay for a novel by a writer who is not yet established?' And, without shame, he tried to marshal the support of friends whose testimonials might prove useful in publicity. One of these was Paul Gallico, to whom he sent a copy of the corrected manuscript.

When Gallico wrote back, Fleming couldn't have been more delighted. 'The book is a knockout,' believed Gallico. 'I thought I had written a couple of pretty fair torture scenes in my day, but yours beats everything I have ever read. Wow! It goes in for frankness and detail far beyond any American-type thriller and could have a big sale. Get out of that office kid and write, because you can.'

Nor was Gallico just playing the part of the loyal friend: he offered to tell his own Hollywood agent about the book because, 'here is a rib-snorter which would make a marvellous movie. No one has *ever* had the bright idea to couple gambling with espionage and economic sabotage and this gimmick would film marvellously.'

Buoyed up by the new life as a bestselling author he believed was now his for the taking, Ian Fleming stared the new year of 1953 with greater confidence than at any other time of his life. His three months' annual holiday at Goldeneye stretched ahead of him and he knew precisely what he was going to do during it. He had been advised by several friends to write a second book before CASINO ROYALE could be savaged by the critics, and that was what he was going to do. James Bond would live twice, and make his second appearance in a book initially called THE UNDERTAKER'S WIND, but, eventually, titled LIVE AND LET DIE.

LIVE AND LET DIE is a much longer book than CASINO ROYALE but, so confident was Fleming in the first months of 1953, it actually took him less time to write the first draft than had CASINO ROYALE.

Fleming's second book marked a profound shift in gear from his first. CASINO ROYALE had been an *instinctive* book: Fleming had simply drawn on events from his own past, albeit heavily romanticised, and inserted James Bond in his own place. From LIVE AND LET DIE onwards, the reverse was true. Fleming used Bond as the vehicle to give him a free hand in exploiting his own imagination and bizarre fantasies. Many of his own obsessions and interests would continue to feature of course – LIVE AND LET DIE is partly set in Jamaica and uses voodoo, a subject that fascinated Fleming, as a plot device – but the difference was that from now on Ian Fleming viewed everything through James Bond's eyes.

After 1953 Fleming's books would always, according to himself, 'go beyond the probable, but never beyond the possible'; and, as he had intuitively worked out when writing CASINO ROYALE, achieving this meant that the fantasies had to be anchored in some kind of reality. For Fleming, this meant thorough research to ensure he got his *technical* details right. He would research his books with assiduity beforehand and, as far as possible, he would always try to experience Bond's world for himself: smoking the excessive number of cigarettes Bond smoked; scuba-diving in the Caribbean; driving fast; living hard. In later years, with the middle-aged Fleming suffering from drinking too much alcohol and smoking too many cigarettes, his striving to keep up with his fictional alter ego, who was forever in his mid-thirties, created severe health problems. But in January 1953 this was not an issue for Fleming, who, believing 'tough men are very rare', still thought of himself as a tough man.

Midway through January, en route for Jamaica, Fleming and Ann arrived at New York and boarded the *Silver Meteor* train to St Petersburg in Florida – a journey James Bond and Solitaire were also to take in LIVE AND LET DIE. In St Petersburg, Fleming researched a worm factory, which would also feature in the book, before he and Ann flew to Jamaica from Tampa.

LIVE AND LET DIE is a terrific book, and moves with a violent speed that, perhaps, Fleming never quite again achieved. If CASINO ROYALE had been a very European take on the thriller genre, LIVE AND LET DIE takes Bond to the heart of the American thriller: New York. Sent by M to investigate the possibility that gold coins from a seventeenth-century pirate treasure hoard have been salvaged and are being used to finance SMERSH operations in America, James Bond comes up against a black gangster, Mr Big, who operates out of Harlem. Having rescued the mysterious, telepathic Solitaire from Mr Big's organisation, and working again with the CIA agent Felix Leiter, Bond follows Mr Big's trail to St Petersburg and then to Jamaica for their final confrontation.

LIVE AND LET DIE perfected the Fleming formula. James Bond is a more rounded character; the violence is as sadistic as in CASINO ROYALE but slightly more stylised; and what many critics have described as 'the Fleming Sweep' – the sheer verve with which the original Bond novels motor – is evident here for the first time. In Solitaire and Mr Big, Fleming also realised his ideal heroine and villain respectively for the first time.

Mr Big is the first of the truly splendid Fleming villains. Omnipotent and powerful, Mr Big is able to run what is, effectively, a private army in Harlem, seemingly untouchable by the FBI. But then, as Bond's CIA buddy Felix Leiter observes, Mr Big has the best protection of all – fear. If Fleming treats some of the minor characters in Mr Big's all-black organisation somewhat patronisingly, Mr Big is written with respect. Mr Big is a highly intelligent operative: he may be financing SMERSH operations in New York but he is no mere lackey of the Russians like Le Chiffre.

Fleming portrays Mr Big as the all-powerful father figure to Bond's helpless little boy. This is a theme Fleming returned to again and again with his villains, particularly Sir Hugo Drax, Dr No, Auric Goldfinger and Ernst Stavro Blofeld: all of these villains are intellectually superior to Bond and regard the British agent, initially, as a minor nuisance. Ian Fleming, of course, had always lived in the shadow of his brother Peter's perceived greater intellect; and Ann Fleming delighted in cultivating the friendship of the alleged 'elite', many of whom openly mocked Ian Fleming's books. Thus James Bond's eventual victories against the supposedly superior villains – a tough man and blunt instrument of the British government (as Fleming had once been himself) defeating cerebral supremacy – can be interpreted as Ian Fleming's own fantasised revenge on the world.

Tee-Hee, a relatively minor villain in LIVE AND LET DIE, is another important character in the Bond canon in that he is the first of Fleming's henchmen really to stick in the mind. Le Chiffre, who was himself a glorified henchman in CASINO ROYALE, had had his own henchmen but they were all pretty colourless, as are most of Mr Big's other operatives in LIVE AND LET DIE. But Tee-Hee, who bursts into a falsetto giggle when ordered by Mr Big deliberately to break the little finger on Bond's left hand, stands out. Fleming would develop the role of the secondary villains in later books: Krebs in MOONRAKER; Wint and Kidd in DIAMONDS ARE FOREVER; Rosa Klebb and Grant in FROM RUSSIA WITH LOVE; Irma Bunt in ON HER MAJESTY'S SECRET SERVICE/YOU ONLY LIVE TWICE; and, unforgettably, Oddjob in GOLDFINGER. The Eon Film series would develop the concept still further, sometimes using Fleming's characters but more often inventing their own, some of whom actually eclipsed the main villains in some of the films: Fiona in *Thunderball*; Jaws in *The Spy Who Loved Me* and *Moonraker*; and May Day in *A View To A Kill*.

The other important Bondian theme to be established in LIVE AND LET DIE was Fleming's obsession with the undersea world. His description in Chapter 19 of Bond's nocturnal swim in the Caribbean to attach a limpet mine to Mr Big's yacht is one of the most atmospheric passages to be found anywhere in Fleming's works; Bond's horrified realisation that he's suddenly surrounded by sharks and barracuda in a feeding frenzy, because Mr Big's lieutenants are throwing offal into the sea above him, is a masterstroke. Fleming's description of the under-water world in LIVE AND LET DIE is superb and he returned to this theme again in THUNDERBALL.

Again, the violence in LIVE AND LET DIE is shocking, although the beating of Bond's testicles and his near castration in CASINO ROYALE were not surpassed. The deliberate breaking of Bond's finger by Tee-Hee, however graphically described, could scarcely compete; while Mr Big's keel-hauling of Bond and Solitaire was, perhaps, a shade too fantastic truly to unsettle readers.

Nonetheless, Fleming's cruel streak manifested itself in his ruthless treatment of Felix Leiter. The real-life worm factory Fleming had visited in St Petersburg in January 1953 became a cover for Mr Big's Florida operations in the novel, and came complete with a hidden shark tank accessed by trapdoor. Lured to the trapdoor by the Robber, another of Mr Big's henchmen, Leiter falls victim to the shark, losing an arm and half of one leg. When Bond investigates the worm factory he, in turn, kicks the Robber into the shark pool via the same trapdoor. These horrific passages – rendered more effective by Fleming's describing them so matter-of-factly – inspired the shark pools seen in the Bond films *Thunderball* and *Live And Let Die* and were used virtually as described in the controversial 1989 Bond movie *Licence To Kill*. Despite being less graphic than Fleming's original, Leiter's ordeal in the shark pool led to *Licence To Kill* earning the movie series' first 15 certificate; an indication of the power, still, of Ian Fleming's writing.

The first draft of LIVE AND LET DIE was completed by March 1953 and Fleming returned to London, where, on 13 April, CASINO ROYALE – its dust jacket of bleeding hearts having been designed by Fleming himself – was published to reviews that were as good as he might have wished. The *Spectator* believed the book was, 'lively, most ingenious in detail, on the surface as tough as they are made and charmingly well-bred beneath, nicely written and – except for a too ingeniously sadistic bout of brutality – very entertaining reading.' The *Observer* urged its readers, 'Don't miss this. A sort of Peter Cheyney de luxe, with everything of the very best and most expensive.' And John Betjemen for the *Daily Telegraph* believed, 'Ian Fleming has discovered the secret of narrative art which is to work up to a climax unrevealed at the end of each chapter.' Simon Raven, who would write additional dialogue for *On Her Majesty's Secret Service* in 1969, was less sure, lamenting 'the clumsy ending and also the torture scene, which is really too monstrous to be excused even by its ingenuity'; but *The Times Literary Supplement* had no doubts, saying 'Mr Fleming has produced a book that is both exciting and extremely civilized.'

No sooner had Fleming read the reviews than he and Ann travelled to the South of France to join Jacques Cousteau, who was salvaging a Roman galley. Fleming, who was obsessed with buried treasure, was there, ostensibly, on behalf of Kemsley Newspapers to write three articles about the salvage work for the *Sunday Times*, but he also used the experience to revise LIVE AND LET DIE, which did, of course, already have a theme of buried treasure. Six years later he reused the treasure-hunt theme in THUNDERBALL, when SPECTRE's movement of stolen nuclear bombs is disguised by a bogus treasure hunt in the Bahamas led by Emilio Largo.

As far as Jonathan Cape was concerned, CASINO ROYALE was a tremendous success for a first-time novelist. The first print run of 4,750 copies had sold out by the end of May 1953 and Cape's publicity department was claiming that a copy of CASINO ROYALE had been sold every six and a half minutes the bookshops were open. But Fleming himself was disappointed by how little money, in his view, CASINO ROYALE was making him. 'It will just about keep Ann in asparagus over Coronation Week,' he complained.

The news from New York was even more depressing. Fleming's agents, Curtis Brown, had approached three publishers and had had three flat rejections. Doubleday just didn't like it; Norton believed it was a 'very English cross between early Ambler and Mickey Spillane'; while Knopf objected to the book's 'excesses'. Finally, Macmillan agreed to take the book and to publish it in early 1954.

Following the success of Fleming's three *Sunday Times* articles about the Jacques Cousteau salvage operation, Fleming appealed to the readers of the newspaper to send him details of other treasure hunts going on around the world. The one that appealed to him most he would then follow up. From the mass of replies he received, he chose Creake Abbey, near Burnham Thorpe in Norfolk, where legend held that monks had hidden a priceless stash of gold and silver to keep it from Henry VIII. The ensuing treasure hunt was a grave disappointment for Fleming and the three-man team from the Royal Engineers he'd assembled, who were testing out the Army's new mine detectors. 'In two days we dug up about thirty nails of different sizes, one frying pan, one mole-trap, one oil drum and about a hundredweight of miscellaneous scrap-iron,' wrote a rueful Fleming. 'Our jokes about twelfth-century sardine tins ceased at an early stage.'

Despite the disappointment of his foray to Norfolk, his choosing this treasure hunt above all others was significant: not only was Burnham Thorpe the birthplace of his hero, Lord Nelson, but he chose it out of all the readers' letters he'd received 'because of its spectral name'.

The origins of the criminal consortium SPECTRE, James Bond's opponents in Fleming's later books, would be hotly contested for forty years after their introduction in THUNDERBALL (1960), as we shall see. But it is worth pointing out at this juncture that the word 'spectre' was a favourite one of Fleming's; he loved the sound of, and the associations with, the word and it was one he used again and again in his speech and in his writings.

Thus, he liked Creake Abbey 'because of its spectral name'; in LIVE AND LET DIE, during Bond's swim to Mr Big's yacht, the wide sea fans 'waved spectrally' (Chapter 19); in DIAMONDS ARE FOREVER, the Spang Brothers' Wild West ghost town hideaway is named Spectreville, and is situated near a range of mountains called the 'Spectre Mountains'; and in FROM RUSSIA WITH LOVE the top-secret Russian deciphering machine, the bait to trap James Bond, is called the Spektor. Throughout Fleming's life and works, the word 'spectre' and its derivations appeared regularly, and certainly long before the plot of THUNDERBALL was conceived.

In the autumn of 1953, Ian Fleming began making notes for what would become MOONRAKER, his third Bond book, once he had completed revisions for LIVE AND LET DIE.

Despite many unusual aspects – it was the only full-length Bond novel or film to take place entirely in England and to have a scenario in which Bond does not make love to the heroine – MOONRAKER was to become the most important of Fleming's books in establishing many Bondian traditions.

Most importantly, MOONRAKER puts James Bond at the forefront of the British Secret Service's battle against the spectre of nuclear terrorism. Eight years on from Hiroshima and Nagasaki, Ian Fleming envisages a nuclear threat against Britain coming not from the Soviet Union but from the Moonraker, a weapon devised by the supposed patriot Sir Hugo Drax ostensibly for the very protection of the country. Drax, though, is a former Nazi and he plans revenge for the defeat of the Third Reich by nuking London on the Moonraker's first test flight.

By 1953, the nuclear threat was all-too apparent and Fleming, his finger on the pulse in intelligence matters as it ever was, sought to capitalise on prevailing fears. From MOONRAKER onwards, he would introduce nuclear themes, to a greater or lesser degree, throughout his works: in FROM RUSSIA WITH LOVE, Bond is on a committee discussing the defection of British spies to Russia and its implications for whether the Americans will be keen to share nuclear secrets in future; in DR NO, the titular villain's main scheme is the toppling of American missiles, sending them off course, causing them to crash in the sea so their warheads might be examined, and confusing their guidance systems into making them crash on Miami; in GOLDFINGER, Auric Goldfinger plans to blast open the bullion vault at Fort Knox with a nuclear warhead he has obtained at a cost of $1 million on the black market; and, in YOU ONLY LIVE TWICE, the Japanese Secret Service boss Tiger Tanaka shows Bond a deciphered Russian document, which discusses how the strategic dropping of a nuclear warhead on London and another on Aberdeen could wipe out Britain and Ireland completely. The Russians are planning to use the information to demand the removal of all American airbases from the United Kingdom and the nuclear disarmament of Britain itself (this scenario, a relatively minor plot point in YOU ONLY LIVE TWICE, formed a major part of the script of the 1983 Bond movie *Octopussy*, when a renegade Soviet general tried to force the disarmament of Europe by exploding a nuclear bomb on a USAF airbase and making it look like an accident). And, of course, the plot of THUNDERBALL revolves around the theft of nuclear warheads and the blackmailing of the Western powers.

Fleming ensured that the technical details in MOONRAKER were as accurate as possible. Nonetheless, the book marked a distinct move into science fiction and this, again, was an important step in the development of James Bond. With a plethora of technology, a hidden rocket base – actually, Drax's base wasn't hidden but its real purpose was – and a private army, MOONRAKER establishes several recurring themes that appear in subsequent Fleming novels, and even more so in the film series. Dr No's Caribbean hideaway, complete with private army and gadgets to interfere with American space hardware, and Blofeld's alpine fortress in ON HER MAJESTY'S SECRET SERVICE, again with private army and the technology to wage biological warfare, are just two examples of how Fleming reworked the ideas he first used in MOONRAKER.

But MOONRAKER also marked another departure for Fleming. Good though CASINO ROYALE and LIVE AND LET DIE were, Fleming shifted gear with MOONRAKER. There is less action in the book and, consequently, the book moves much more slowly. Instead, MOONRAKER is full of atmosphere and introspection: for the first time, James Bond is actually a *character*. We read about his home life, his working life when he is not on one of the special assignments suitable for a Double-0 agent, and the fact that he spent his weekends playing golf and his evenings gambling at Crockford's or making love 'with rather cold passion' to one of three 'similarly disposed married women'. This is Fleming's old life, his life prior to his marrying Ann. 'MOONRAKER was the most intriguing and profound novel Fleming had written,' as John Pearson has pointed out. From then onwards, the James Bond novels became a kind of subliminal autobiography of Fleming himself.

In January 1954, just as Fleming and Ann were preparing to fly to Jamaica for their annual three months' holiday, Sir Alexander Korda read an advance copy of LIVE AND LET DIE. Korda, the Hungarian-born British film producer and director, was then nearing the end of his life, but his reputation in the film industry remained awesome. Among his credits were *The Private Life of Henry VIII* (1932), *Things To Come* (1935) and *The Third Man* (1949), and he could rightly claim to have saved the British film industry in the early 1930s. Korda, who seems to have been the first producer to spot the cinematic potential of James Bond, thought LIVE AND LET DIE was a tremendous book. 'I couldn't put it down until I'd finished it,' he told Fleming. 'Then I gave it to my wife to read about midnight and she could not go to sleep until she'd finished the whole book.' Nevertheless, despite his enthusiasm, and his passing the book on to the directors Carol Reed and David Lean for their opinions, Korda cautioned Fleming that the book might not work as a film: 'The best stories for films are always the stories that are written for films.'

Excited by the prospect of a James Bond film – albeit made at Pinewood, not Hollywood – Fleming wrote to Korda, telling him his next book was an expansion of a story he'd had in his mind since the end of the war: 'A straight thriller, set in London and on the White Cliffs of Dover, and involving the destruction of London by a super V-2, allowing for some wonderful film settings in the old Metropolis idiom.' Whether this was the truth or not, only Fleming knew, although he did inscribe his own personal copy of MOONRAKER with the words: 'This was written in January and February 1954 and published a year later. It is based on a film script I have had in mind for many years.' Eventually, though, Korda decided not to follow through his initial enthusiasm for James Bond and eventually returned all Fleming's material with a polite note of rejection. CASINO ROYALE was published in the USA on 23 March 1954. The syndicated columnist and society writer Elsa Maxwell, a friend of Fleming's, gave the book a useful plug, telling her readers it was 'one of the most breathtaking thrillers I have ever read. Don't miss it.' But the actual reviews were nothing like as good as the British ones had been, and typical was that of Anthony Boucher in the *New York Times Book Review*, who believed Fleming 'pads the book out to novel length, leading to an ending which surprises no one but Bond himself'. Such reviews hardly helped and CASINO ROYALE practically disappeared without trace on its first printing in the US.

Just over two weeks later, on 8 March, LIVE AND LET DIE was published in great Britain and the reviews were, if anything, better than those for CASINO ROYALE a year earlier. *The Times Literary Supplement* was typical, stating that Ian Fleming was 'without doubt the most interesting recent recruit among thriller writers' and that he had fully maintained the promise of CASINO ROYALE. 'LIVE AND LET DIE', said the review, 'contains passages which for sheer excitement have not been surpassed by any modern writer in this kind.'

Fleming would have been amused by – as well as proud of – the fate of one of those first-edition copies of LIVE AND LET DIE. In 2001, 47 years after publication, a first-edition copy of the book was handed in among several other items in a plastic carrier bag to an Imperial Cancer Research charity shop in Edinburgh. Spotted by an eager volunteer, the book was eventually sold at Sotheby's for £5,287.

The spring and early summer of 1954 saw a flurry of activity in the burgeoning development of James Bond. In May, the Hollywood producer Gregory Ratoff paid $600 for a six-month option on CASINO ROYALE, with the additional promise of $6,000 when the film went into production. The same month, CBS paid $1,000 for the rights to do a one-hour live television adaptation of CASINO ROYALE. This wasn't bad going for a novel that had sold a measly 4,000 copies in the US.

A month later, Popular Library bought the US paperback rights to CASINO ROYALE for $2,625, although they insisted the title be changed to YOU ASKED FOR IT, because it was felt the American paperback-buying public wouldn't have a clue what 'Royale' meant. The dumbed-down tone of the marketing of YOU ASKED FOR IT when it was published in 1955 was obvious from the blurb on the back cover: 'If he hadn't been a tough operator, Jimmy Bond would never have risked a weekend with a woman who used her magnificent body to destroy him . . . But it was toughness that had landed Jimmy his job with the Secret Service – the job of smashing the ruthless Le Chiffre and his spy network – no matter how many women tried to stop him . . .'

The general tone of the blurb, not to mention James Bond's becoming 'Jimmy Bond', was somewhat at odds with Fleming's snobbery with violence that was contained within the covers. But Fleming was still disappointed with how little money the books had made thus far and this may account for his equivocation over MOONRAKER when he delivered the corrected manuscript to William Plomer at Jonathan Cape. 'It isn't much of a book,' he confided to a friend. 'But it should make a good film.' Fleming was being too hard on himself. If nothing else, the more introspective tone he had managed to put into MOONRAKER proved he was no mere hack repeating the same book over and over again. And, while MOONRAKER received more mixed reviews than had the first two Bond books, some significant voices believed Fleming had surpassed himself with it. Noël Coward confided in his diary on 23 January 1955 that he had read MOONRAKER and thought that it was the best he had done yet. While finding it far-fetched 'as usual' – though not, in his opinion, as much as CASINO ROYALE or LIVE AND LET DIE – there were fewer 'purple sex passages'. He wrote that Fleming's observation was 'extraordinary' and his talent for description 'vivid'.

On Thursday 21 October 1954, James Bond made his screen debut – played not by Sean Connery but by an American actor, Barry Nelson – when CBS transmitted their live, hour-long adaptation of CASINO ROYALE, the fourth in their *Climax* drama series, from Television City in Hollywood.

Many liberties were taken with Fleming's original, both to facilitate the running length and to make the programme more appealing to the American audience. Thus, James Bond became Jimmy Bond (as in YOU ASKED FOR IT), and was an American CIA agent. Similarly, CIA agent Felix Leiter became *British* agent Clarence Leiter, while Vesper Lynd was amalgamated with Rene Mathis, Bond's Deuxieme Bureau ally in the novel, to become Valerie Mathis, an agent for the Deuxieme Bureau. Furthermore, events are changed in the teleplay so that unlike in the novel, where Bond and Vesper fall in love *after* the main events at Royale-les-Eaux, Bond and Valerie had been lovers *previously*, with Valerie now dangerously involved with Le Chiffre. Interestingly, this scenario cropped up again, most successfully, in *Tomorrow Never Dies* in 1997, when Bond encounters Paris, with whom he was once deeply in love, who is now married to the villain Elliot Carver. Despite the changes and the obvious limitations of a live broadcast in the infancy of television, the adaptation *Casino Royale* still succeeds in capturing the essential flavour of Ian Fleming's first book. The sets are elegant and, for the time, look expensive, while the live broadcast is well directed and choreographed by director William H Brown. What is particularly significant is that the producers felt the need to introduce humour into the story. The introduction of one-liners into James Bond films has hitherto been credited to Terence Young, the director of the first Bond film, *Dr. No*, in 1962. The truth is that the production team of *Casino Royale* had identified the lack of humour in Fleming's earliest stories as a minus point eight years earlier.

As for Bond himself, Barry Nelson makes for a somewhat stolid 007, although he delivers his one-liners moderately well. Typical is his first encounter with Leiter after an attempt has been made on Bond's life:

LEITER: Aren't you the fellow who was shot?
BOND: No – I'm the fellow that was missed . . .

Linda Christian makes for a sexy and spirited Valerie Mathis, while Michael Pate as Leiter is an astonishingly hard-boiled British agent to be found on American television from this era. But the crowning glory of *Casino Royale* is Peter Lorre's Le Chiffre. Lorre turns in a performance of great subtlety, which underwrites his real menace beautifully. This is particularly telling in the scene where Le Chiffre tortures Bond into revealing where 007 has hidden the money won at the baccarat tables. Fleming's original excoriating torture scene in CASINO ROYALE could not be included for obvious reasons, but the substitution – Le Chiffre and his associates test the strength of a pair of pliers on Bond's toes while Valerie is forced to watch – is still pretty strong.

No record of *Casino Royale* was believed to have survived the live broadcast for more than thirty years until a kinescope – a recording made when a movie camera was placed in front of the TV monitor in the studio – was discovered in Chicago in the late 1980s by the film historian Jim Schoenberger. It was later released on video and, despite the sometimes appalling quality of the recording, proved to be of great interest to Bond fans worldwide, and a welcome addition to the Bond archive.

But *Casino Royale* was not a success on its original transmission. Audiences were indifferent and those few critics who did bother to review it were hostile: *Variety* believed Barry Nelson, Peter Lorre and Linda Christian 'drew laughs along the course by running with all legs off the ground'.

Its failure depressed Ian Fleming further: his initial excitement over the cinematic potential of James Bond had taken a severe knock. He was simply not earning the kind of money he had expected from the character. Nevertheless, he'd already got an idea for his next book, DIAMONDS ARE FOREVER, and spent several weeks travelling the USA with his friend Ernest Cuneo – a lawyer and one-time leading member of Roosevelt's inner circle whom Fleming had met during the war – to gather material for it.

DIAMONDS ARE FOREVER is the weakest of Ian Fleming's James Bond novels save for THE MAN WITH THE GOLDEN GUN, which was published posthumously and which Fleming had been unable to revise before his death.

DIAMONDS ARE FOREVER is not badly written – it moves more quickly than MOONRAKER; there are some tense scenes; Bond's character develops even further; the heroine, Tiffany Case, is one of Fleming's better-realised female characters (Bond ends up living with her in his London flat); and the gay henchmen, Wint and Kidd, are credible, nasty killers – but it never quite seems to work.

A major fault is that the main villains, the twin brothers Jack and Seraffimo Spang, are hardly in the same league as Mr Big or Sir Hugo Drax. Fleming seems to have been aware of this, which is why he has everyone from M to Felix Leiter repeating to Bond not to underestimate his foes. 'These Spangled boys are the tops,' warns Leiter, and suggests they're even more dangerous than SMERSH. The trouble is, Fleming never backs this up in the writing: the Spang brothers are never more than relatively minor gangsters – Wint and Kidd are certainly the more threatening characters in the book – who are indulging in a bit of diamond smuggling. For a man who saved London from nuclear annihilation by the Moonraker the previous year, Bond's assignment to shut down the Spangs' smuggling pipeline seems a comedown.

The locations, too, are a problem. The so-called Fleming Sweep, which had not been so much in evidence in MOONRAKER, returns with gusto in DIAMONDS ARE FOREVER. But the swift shift in locations – Africa, London, New York, Saratoga, Las Vegas, and a finale aboard the *Queen Elizabeth* – is often illogical. And James Bond simply does not belong in the vulgar setting of Las Vegas, something that was even more evident in the 1971 film version.

Perhaps the deficiencies in DIAMONDS ARE FOREVER were a sign of Fleming's own disenchantment with James Bond when he wrote the book at Goldeneye in the first two months of 1955. Certainly, his enthusiasm for 007 had waned for the first time since he'd begun work on CASINO ROYALE exactly three years earlier. He confided to his friend Hilary Bray that DIAMONDS ARE FOREVER 'has finally exhausted my inventiveness as it contains every single method of escape and every variety of suspenseful action that I omitted from my previous books.'

His mood was not helped by the publication of LIVE AND LET DIE in the US in January 1955, where it sold barely 5,000 copies ('Mr Bond will have to do better than this,' noted Fleming's American publisher, gloomily), nor by the mixed reviews for MOONRAKER when it was published in the UK three months later. Not even Gregory Ratoff exercising his agreement to buy the full rights to CASINO ROYALE for $6,000 – Fleming bought a Ford Thunderbird with the money – made him believe there was any future in James Bond.

James Bond may well have ended there and then in the late spring of 1955 had it not been for the burgeoning friendship between Fleming and Raymond Chandler. Chandler may have been burned out by then but he remained a hero of Fleming's and still had a deservedly formidable reputation in the literary world because of his seminal private eye, Philip Marlowe. Chandler had always refused to endorse other authors' books, but, after reading LIVE AND LET DIE, he made an exception in Ian Fleming's case.

Writing Fleming a letter, which he said could be used to help Fleming's publicity, particularly in the States, Chandler wrote that Fleming was probably the most forceful and driving writer of thrillers in England. He compared Fleming favourably with Peter Cheyney, whom he believed wrote one good book – *Dark Duet* – and another 'fairly good' one but whose pseudo-American tough guy stories bored Chandler. And Chandler believed Fleming was a much more accomplished writer than James Hadley Chase of whom he wrote caustically, 'the less said the better'.

Chandler would follow this up with a positive review for DIAMONDS ARE FOREVER, about which he wrote: 'The remarkable thing about this book is that it is written by an Englishman. The scene is almost entirely American, and it rings true to an American. I am unaware of any other writer who has accomplished this.'

Raymond Chandler's championing of the Bond books lifted Fleming's spirits during the summer and autumn of 1955, and the pessimism exhibited in his letter to Hilary Bray earlier in the year was noticeably absent when the actor Ian Hunter offered to buy the rights to MOONRAKER for Rank. Fleming demanded – and received – £10,000, explaining to his publishers, 'I have an idea that one of these days the film and television rights of James Bond and his adventures may be worth quite a lot of money and I hope you agree that there's no point in throwing them away.'

In July 1955, a friend at Scotland Yard invited Fleming to join him at an Interpol conference in Istanbul in his capacity as a journalist. Much of what Fleming experienced there, and many of the people he met, ended up in his fifth James Bond novel, FROM RUSSIA WITH LOVE.

The book would prove to be Fleming's most critically acclaimed novel of all; the one that can safely lay claim to being serious spy *literature*, rather than an entertaining thriller.

It would be notable for one other thing as well.

The apparent death of James Bond.

003: Cardboard Booby

'If one has a grain of intelligence, it is difficult to go on being serious about a character like James Bond. My books are straight pillow fantasies of the bang-bang, kiss-kiss variety.'

Ian Fleming, December 1959

'I would so love Ian to triumph over the sneers of Annie's intellectual friends,' Noël Coward confided in his diary on 23 January 1955.

It was the genuine concern of a friend who could see that, despite the critical acclaim Ian Fleming's Bond novels had attracted in Britain, his wife, Ann, and her intimate circle were dismissive at best about his achievement.

Fleming was hardly unaware of their disdain. On one occasion, arriving home unexpectedly early at Victoria Square, he had found Ann throwing a party for the usual suspects. Cyril Connolly, the critic and author, was reading passages aloud sarcastically from Fleming's latest book. Ann and her friends were laughing and joining in Connolly's mockery. Fleming was the only one not to laugh.

For the most part, Fleming was able to absorb the knocks and, with his usual public diffidence, even professed to understand why Ann and her friends poked fun at him. 'Probably the fault about my books is that I don't take them seriously enough,' he told Raymond Chandler, 'and meekly accept having my head ragged off about them in the family circle. You write "novels of suspense" whereas my books are straight pillow fantasies of the bang-bang, kiss-kiss variety.'

In more analytical moments, Fleming was able to pinpoint another problem: his detractors couldn't grasp that the Bond books weren't *quite* as far-fetched as they seemed. 'I invent the most hopeless sounding plots,' he told Georges Simenon, creator of Maigret. 'Very often they are based on something I have read in a newspaper. And people say, "Oh, this is all nonsense" – and then the Russians come along in Germany and shoot people with potassium cyanide pistols. I find constantly that the things I've read about in some obscure magazine or somewhere are always coming true in real life.'

Nevertheless, the truth is that the ragging not only hurt but triggered uncertainties within Fleming's mind. Thus, once he had completed DIAMONDS ARE FOREVER, his disappointment with the sales of his Bond books was matched with a nagging self-doubt. He wondered if he really was making a cracking fool of himself with Bond. Compared with what his brother Peter had achieved in *his* literary career, did the Bond books have any merit at all?

Allied to all this was a genuine concern that DIAMONDS ARE FOREVER really had exhausted his inventiveness.

'I intend to keep Bond spinning through his paces for as long as possible,' he confided to one friend, but then admitted that he felt he was running dry and was finding it increasingly difficult to find new ways of killing people. To Raymond Chandler, he was even more blunt: 'My talents are extended to their absolute limits in writing books like DIAMONDS ARE FOREVER,' he said. 'I am not short weighting anybody and I have absolutely nothing more up my sleeve.'

One fundamental problem was that Fleming's personal life was impinging upon his professional one. The Flemings' marriage was rocky, to say the least, and the physical side of it had all but died with the birth of their son, Caspar. There were many affairs on both sides – Hugh Gaitskell, the leader of the Labour Party, being one of Ann's notable conquests – and during the second half of the 1950s they pulled further apart, despite retaining a lingering affection for one another to the end of Ian's life.

Certainly, from around the time he wrote DIAMONDS ARE FOREVER, one of the main stumbling blocks in the Flemings' marriage was

Jamaica and Goldeneye. Ann came to loathe Goldeneye and insisted Fleming sell it. Fleming, who loved Goldeneye more than anywhere else in the world, refused. Since Goldeneye was where Fleming wrote each new Bond book every January and February, Jamaica also represented the heart of the Bond empire to Ann; and she openly admitted she despised everything to do with the vulgar world of James Bond. No wonder Noël Coward, witnessing the disintegration of their marriage, wondered wearily, 'Why do my friends delight in torturing each other?'

Fleming's domestic problems certainly didn't help resolve his dilemma over what to do about James Bond in the second half of 1955. While he had already more or less decided on the plot and theme of his next book, what would he do after that?

'I have a fifth book more or less in mind,' he told Al Hart, his American publisher, 'but after that, the vacuum is complete.' To William Plomer, he said he'd decided to 'rid myself of that cardboard booby'.

One of the root causes of Fleming's ongoing perplexity about Bond was, ironically, his friendship with Raymond Chandler. According to Sir John Morgan, Fleming admired Raymond Chandler more than any other living writer. Chandler's patronage was also invaluable and Fleming was very grateful for it. But Chandler was not a man to pull his punches and, despite the positive noises he made in his review of DIAMONDS ARE FOREVER, he left Fleming in no doubt that he believed MOONRAKER, which he called 'merely a spasm', and DIAMONDS ARE FOREVER marked a decline from CASINO ROYALE and LIVE AND LET DIE.

Chandler had not liked the development of Bond's character in MOONRAKER and DIAMONDS ARE FOREVER. He told Fleming he believed there was a degree of padding in DIAMONDS ARE FOREVER and worst – to Chandler at least – there were even pages in which James Bond thinks. A pointless activity, as the thoughts of such a 'blunt instrument' were superfluous. He was best, Chandler considered, when he was taking part in a lethal card game, when exposed to a 'dozen thin-lipped professional killers'. Chandler pleaded with Fleming not to become a 'stunt writer'; otherwise, he said, he'd 'end up no better than the rest of us'.

When Fleming arrived at Goldeneye in January 1956, he was determined to try to please Chandler by raising the literary standard of his fifth book, FROM RUSSIA WITH LOVE. There was also another reason: throughout the first half of 1956 Fleming vacillated between wanting to kill off Bond and soldiering on. So if FROM RUSSIA WITH LOVE really was going to be the last Bond book, Fleming rationalised when he began work on it, he wanted it to be the best.

Consequently, Ian Fleming took more trouble over writing FROM RUSSIA WITH LOVE than, perhaps, any book he ever wrote. The original manuscript was heavily revised, much more so than any of the others, and the ending ultimately changed. The care that Fleming took in writing the book shows because FROM RUSSIA WITH LOVE is, arguably, the Bond book richest in detail and characterisation.

Essentially, the plot of FROM RUSSIA WITH LOVE is very simple. SMERSH intends to assassinate James Bond and discredit the British Secret Service at the same time. Bond is lured to Istanbul to help a beautiful young Russian cipher clerk, Tatiana Romanova, defect. Her dowry is the top-secret Soviet decoding machine, the Spektor, which she says she will steal if Bond helps her. Neither M nor Bond is under any illusions that it might all be a trap, but the bait of the Spektor is simply irresistible.

Fleming drew heavily on his own experiences in writing FROM RUSSIA WITH LOVE. He set much of the action in Istanbul, where he had attended the Interpol conference in July 1955, and, of course, he had experienced the methods and morals of the Russian secret police at first hand during the Metro-Vickers trial in Moscow in 1933. As we have already seen, Fleming even based Tatiana Romanova on a Russian girl, Anna Kutusova, the lover of one of the accused British engineers, whom he'd witnessed at the trial. FROM RUSSIA WITH LOVE is perfectly structured and the lengthy finale on board the Orient Express, culminating in the brutal fight to the death between Bond and the SMERSH assassin Red Grant, ranks among the most thrilling passages – as well as overtly sexual – Ian Fleming ever wrote. Certainly he never again quite achieved the most perfect balance of action and characterisation he managed in FROM RUSSIA WITH LOVE. Bravely keeping Bond offstage until Chapter 11, Fleming takes his time in carefully building up the conspiracy against Bond in the first third of FROM RUSSIA WITH LOVE. This cranks up the tension unbearably.

For the first time, the reader is ahead of Bond. Bond may be wary of a potential trap but the reader *knows* he's walking into one; when Bond makes contact with Captain Norman Nash on the Orient Express in Trieste, he believes Nash is a fellow agent sent by M, but the reader *knows* it is Grant, coming aboard to complete the assassination conspiracy. The reader knows these things because Fleming has spent the first ten chapters explaining how the conspiracy will work in extreme detail. It is the care with which Fleming explains the plot against Bond that makes FROM RUSSIA WITH LOVE seem so credible and real.

Like the plot, the characters in the book are superbly realised. Bond is developed well, and the self-doubt and boredom he feels when we first meet him undoubtedly reflects Ian Fleming's own ambivalent feelings towards his 'cardboard booby' at the time FROM RUSSIA WITH LOVE was written.

The hideous Rosa Klebb – likened to the *tricoteuses* of the French Revolution – and Grant, the half-German half-Irish assassin who worked for Sinn Fein in Ireland and developed into a serial killer before defecting to the Russians, are both excellent villains. Raymond Benson rightly calls Grant 'Fleming's first seriously frighteningly psychotic'. But it is the character of Bond's ally and contact in Istanbul, Darko Kerim, that is Fleming's greatest accomplishment in FROM RUSSIA WITH LOVE. 'Vaguely gypsy-like', Kerim strikes Bond as looking like 'a vagabond soldier of fortune'.

Fleming based Kerim on Nazim Kalkavan, whom he met during the Interpol conference in Istanbul. Fiercely pro-British, the Oxford-educated Kalkavan was a shipowner and merchant who struck up an instant friendship with Fleming, of whom Kalkavan said, 'I have rarely met anyone in my life with so much warmth and with a personality so full of life.'

The feeling was mutual and, when Fleming writes of Bond's first encounter with Darko Kerim – Bond believes he has never before seen such vitality and warmth in a human face (he likens it to being close to the sun) and when he lets go of the 'strong dry hand' he stares back at Kerim 'with a friendliness he rarely felt for a stranger' – there can be no doubt that he is really writing of his own feelings on first meeting Kalkavan.

Rarely had Fleming met another man whose approach to life mirrored his own. On one occasion he jotted down – on official notepaper from the Turkish Criminal Police Commission – something that Kalkavan told him: 'I have always smoked and drunk and loved too much. In fact, I have lived not too long but too much. One day the Iron Crab will get me. Then I shall have died of living too much. Like all people who have known poverty, my chief pleasures are the best food, the best servants and changing my underclothes every day.'

Fleming may not have ever known poverty, but he understood Kalkavan's sentiments exactly. He, too, had always lived too much. As far back as 1946, when Fleming was only 38, an American heart specialist had written the following damning report after Fleming had consulted him:

> The patient admits to smoking seventy cigarettes a day and drinking at least a quarter of a bottle of gin. He is not seriously ill but during the last two months has complained of a constricting pain in the chest. He has slightly low blood pressure, the cardiograph shows an inverted T wave, but there are no important clinical symptoms of heart weakness. The above symptoms could all be the result of nicotine poisoning. I instructed the patient that the situation could not be improved by medication – only by will-power.

But Fleming took no notice. He had always taken good health for granted, although he was often tense and neurotic, and moderating his habits for health reasons was anathema to him.

'Tough men are very rare, particularly after forty, when nature and disease have dented them,' he once wrote. He liked to think of himself as a tough man but when he met Kalkavan he was heading towards fifty and not feeling in the best of health. Ian Fleming was also aware of the Iron Crab waiting for him. That was why he so admired Kalkavan's defiant words and why he put them into Darko Kerim's mouth almost verbatim.

Shortly after arriving back in London from Jamaica in March 1956, Fleming received an invitation from his old friend Ivar Bryce to join a scientific expedition to Inagua, a small island in the Bahamas. The expedition, led by Dr Robert C Murphy of the American Museum of Natural History, and Arthur Vernay of the Bahamas Flamingo Protection, was the first since 1916 to study the flamingo population.

Fleming found Inagua a bleak, unforgiving little island but it gave him a background for his next book. Less than a year later, Inagua would become Crab Key, Dr No's Caribbean hideaway; the flamingoes would become Roseate Spoonbills; and the marsh buggy Fleming had ridden on transformed into the 'Dragon Tank' with which Dr No frightens away inquisitive locals. The Bahamas would also become the main location for THUNDERBALL, four years later.

Not that Fleming was even sure there would *be* another Bond book when he took part in the expedition. Writing FROM RUSSIA WITH LOVE had drained him and he still wasn't sure that the books were worth all the effort.

The publication of DIAMONDS ARE FOREVER in April 1956 did nothing to convince him one way or another. Despite its being serialised in the *Daily Express*, the reviews were not quite what he had come to expect. While the *Birmingham Post* called it 'the best thriller of the season', other reviewers highlighted the novel's deficiencies.

Just as DIAMONDS ARE FOREVER was hitting the bookshelves, Fleming was introduced to the literary agent Peter Janson-Smith by Eric Ambler. Fleming was still disappointed by the sales of his books, particularly in the international market, and asked Janson-Smith to take over as his agent. It was a shrewd move, as Janson-Smith, one of that rare breed of efficient and trustworthy agents, secured a Dutch publisher for the Bond novels on his first day working for Fleming.

This was a good start. But Fleming was beginning to feel unwell. In fact, he hadn't been well since returning from Inagua and, for the first time in his life, failing health impacted on his life. The tough man could not pretend to be quite so tough any longer. A particular problem was his sciatica, which was especially painful. He was also suffering from a persistent cold and bouts of lethargy.

While Fleming had been away observing flamingoes in the Bahamas, Ann had been to a health clinic called Enton Hall, which was in Surrey. She now encouraged Fleming to spend some time there, too. Fleming agreed and booked himself into the clinic for ten days. There, he endured a strict regime, which allowed him just a glass of orange juice for breakfast and a bowl of soup for lunch. His sciatica was treated on a traction machine, which stretched his spine.

Despite himself, Fleming really rather enjoyed his week and a half at Enton Hall. Professionally it paid dividends, too. The first man he shared the steam bath with was Guy Welby, a goldsmith, whose enthusiasm for gold Fleming lapped up and later injected into GOLDFINGER; while Enton Hall itself became Shrublands, the health clinic to which M sends an out-of-condition James Bond at the start of THUNDERBALL.

Fleming even found a use for the traction machine that treated his sciatica: in THUNDERBALL, the SPECTRE agent Count Lippe sees an opportunity to kill Bond by sabotaging the traction machine to which a helpless 007 is strapped. It was a typical Fleming conceit: to turn something innocuous and commonplace into something fraught with danger and intrigue.

Like the American doctor whom Fleming had consulted in 1946, the doctors at Enton Hall advised him to cut down on his intake of alcohol and nicotine. The need to do so was much more pressing now, since they had discovered that his heart was already damaged. Typically, Fleming ignored their advice, however valid he privately admitted to himself it was. The underlying problem was that Fleming was beginning to feel his age – and he didn't like it. 'There are few things more disturbing than seeing your face in the window of a train or plane at night,' he believed. 'Riding beside you in the dark outside.'

Ian Fleming did not much care for the prematurely ageing man he now saw riding beside him in the dark outside and his continuing to drink and smoke to excess, against all reason or sense, was the only way he could defy mortality and, thereby, remain a tough man. Fleming returned home from Enton Hall towards the end of April feeling refreshed, but his dilemma about Bond was no nearer to being resolved. On 27 April he wrote to Raymond Chandler, again stressing that he didn't really think much about the Bond books and suggesting that he really should take them more seriously. Chandler's reply, dated 1 May, was uncompromising, telling Fleming he wasn't doing himself justice with Bond and that he ought to aim his sights higher. Chandler also reiterated his belief that Fleming had yet to write anything better than CASINO ROYALE.

This belief, which Chandler repeated again and again, was disheartening for Fleming. CASINO ROYALE had been an instinctive book which he'd written without notes or preparation. It was a trick he could never repeat. As far as Fleming was concerned, each new Bond book was becoming harder and harder to write. But what was the point if, as Chandler stressed, he'd done the best he was ever to do with Bond in CASINO ROYALE?

He wrote again to Raymond Chandler on 22 June 1956 and was particularly downbeat. Fleming said that he was getting 'fed up' with writing about Bond and that it had been particularly hard putting him through 'his tawdry tricks' in FROM RUSSIA WITH LOVE.

Another problem was that Fleming had developed serious doubts about FROM RUSSIA WITH LOVE while he'd been revising it. Although posterity would prove his fears groundless, Fleming somehow came to believe the book did not work. He admitted to William Plomer he was worried about 'staleness'. 'It's so difficult to communicate zest if it isn't there,' he complained before admitting, once again, of his 'waning enthusiasm for this cardboard booby'.

Although Plomer tried to convince Fleming, correctly, that FROM RUSSIA WITH LOVE was, if anything, the best Bond book he'd written thus far, Fleming insisted on making one major change to the novel's ending. Bond and Tatiana had enjoyed a romantic Parisian ending in the original manuscript, but, in the revised version, Bond is kicked by Rosa Klebb's poison-tipped shoe and, gasping for breath, pivots slowly on his heel and crashes 'headlong to the wine-red floor' in the very last line of the book.

Ian Fleming had done the unthinkable. He'd killed off James Bond. Or had he?

That last line of FROM RUSSIA WITH LOVE was deliberately ambiguous, much more so than when Conan Doyle had Sherlock Holmes and Moriarty toppling over the Reichenbach Falls in *The Final Problem*. And if Holmes could survive *that* – Conan Doyle had been forced to bring Holmes back from the dead by readers' demands – who was to say James Bond couldn't be resurrected sometime in the future?

Quite what Ian Fleming's intention was when he changed the ending to FROM RUSSIA WITH LOVE may never be known. It may have been a deliberate joke on his readers. Or perhaps the inveterate journalist in him knew that the apparent death of 007 would be a news story and would give a push to publicity when the book came out.

The most likely explanation, though, as Andrew Lycett has pointed out, is that Fleming was simply keeping his options open. If FROM RUSSIA WITH LOVE was successful and Fleming could find the enthusiasm to write another Bond book, then 007 could be resurrected. If not, he could lie where he'd fallen. It seemed the perfect solution to Fleming in the early summer of 1956.

Less than six weeks after leaving Enton Hall, Fleming fell ill again. This time it was kidney stones and the pain was even worse than that he'd suffered with his sciatica. A few days in the London Clinic did nothing to improve his mood – he admitted ruefully to one former girlfriend that 'all my malaises come from youthful overindulgences' – but there was better news when he came out of the clinic: an NBC producer, Henry Morgenthau III, approached Fleming to ask if he would be interested in writing a projected TV series provisionally called *Commander Jamaica*, an adventure series that was to be filmed on location in the Caribbean.

Fleming was enthusiastic and within two months had submitted a 28-page pilot script in which Commander James Gunn – Bond in all but name – investigates a secret island in the Caribbean where criminals are interfering with the guidance systems of American missiles launched from Cape Canaveral. As a cover for his activities, James Gunn poses as a member of a treasure hunt. This was, of course, a theme Fleming had previously used in LIVE AND LET DIE and he recycled the idea again in THUNDERBALL when SPECTRE'S moving of the stolen nuclear weapons is concealed by a bogus treasure hunt.

Commander Jamaica fell through at an early stage, probably because of the costs involved, but Fleming simply decided to use the script he'd written as the basis of his next book, DR NO. If nothing else, working on *Commander Jamaica* had convinced him that he must continue writing the Bond books.

There was nothing wrong in Fleming's recycling the *Commander Jamaica* script. It was his copyright and he could do what he liked with it. Had he but known it, though, he was setting himself a horrible precedent by doing so. He was to recycle scripts from aborted TV and film projects twice more in the next three years. Unfortunately, the third time he did so proved to be a disaster and led to a bitter copyright battle, which haunted the James Bond franchise until the year 2001. When he wrote to Henry Morgenthau III after the collapse of *Commander Jamaica* that 'the film and television world is a hell of a jungle', he could have no idea just how dreadfully prophetic his words actually were.

Around the same time, an American film producer called Albert R (Cubby) Broccoli became interested in filming one of the Bond books. 'It was an idea I'd had in the back of my mind for a long time,' recalled

Broccoli. 'James Bond appealed to me on several different levels. Fleming's character offered exciting scope for all the basics in screen entertainment: a virile and resourceful hero, exotic locations, the ingenious apparatus of espionage, and sex on a fairly sophisticated level.'

Convincing his then partner in Warwick Films, Irving Allen, however was not easy. Warwick Films had already enjoyed some success with films like *The Red Beret*, *Hell Below Zero* and *Cockleshell Heroes* but Broccoli felt the company needed a copper-bottomed hit. Allen agreed but he didn't believe James Bond would provide it. Broccoli eventually set up a meeting with Fleming and his agent but, when his first wife Nedra fell terminally ill with cancer, Broccoli was forced to leave the negotiations to Irving Allen. The meeting between Fleming and Allen did not go well: 'In my opinion, Mr Fleming,' Allen said, 'your books are not even good enough for television.' Consequently, Cubby Broccoli had to wait a few years more to produce James Bond for the big screen.

In deciding to carry on with the Bond books, Ian Fleming decided that any attempt to raise their literary standard was pointless. FROM RUSSIA WITH LOVE had taken a lot out of him – perhaps too much – and he remained uncertain that the effort had been worth it. Until he read the reviews, Fleming's doubts about the book persisted, and not even his American publisher Al Hart's enthusiasm could dispel them: 'The new one is far and away your best. FROM RUSSIA WITH LOVE is a real wowser, a lulu, a dilly, a smasheroo – it is a clever and above all sustained piece of legitimate craftsmanship.'

In a conscious, pragmatic and perhaps even slightly cynical response to Al Hart's enthusiasm, he openly stated his intention to write 'the same book over and over again' in future. Ignoring Raymond Chandler's opinion that he was capable of writing to a much higher level, Fleming decided to aim solely for what John Pearson has described as 'the best-seller stakes.'

Ironically, sticking to a Bondian formula finally liberated Ian Fleming's writing. His next two books, DR. NO, written in January and February 1957, and GOLDFINGER, written in January and February 1958, were not only two of his most inventive and successful books, but were also the easiest ones he ever wrote – easier, in many ways, than even CASINO ROYALE.

But then Ian Fleming was in much better spirits when he sat down to write DR. NO in January 1957. And that was because the Bondwagon had *finally* begun to gather momentum in the latter part of 1956.

DIAMONDS ARE FOREVER had been published in the US in October 1956 and, contrary to expectations, the reviews had been much better than usual, with even the *New York Times'* critic Anthony Boucher, a stern critic of Fleming, conceding that the author 'writes excellently'. Macmillan had also placed a clever ad in the *New Yorker*, which certainly upped Fleming's profile. It read, 'Gentlemen may prefer blondes, but blondes prefer Bond, who is back with his trusty Beretta on a new assignment for M, mixing it with mobsters at Saratoga and Las Vegas. A new lethal package by Ian Fleming $2.75 at your bookstore.'

But the main fillip came a month later when the British prime minister Sir Anthony Eden – exhausted by the recent Suez Canal debacle – and Lady Eden stayed at Goldeneye.

Exactly *where* a British prime minister could find rest away from the public gaze was a matter of conjecture within Whitehall until Lady Eden, a friend of Ann and godmother to the Flemings' son Caspar, thought of Goldeneye.

Anyone who stayed at Goldeneye could have told her that its basic facilities were hardly adequate for the Edens' needs, but neither Fleming nor Ann felt inclined to enlighten them. 'Like all the Flemings, Ian revels in discomfort,' Noël Coward had once said of Goldeneye, and he sent the Edens a basket containing champagne, pâté de fois gras and caviar on their arrival – 'anything I could see in fact that might mitigate the horrors I knew the poor dears were in for'.

Despite the hope that Goldeneye would afford the Edens plenty of rest away from the press, journalists besieged Fleming's house. This may not have been good news for Anthony Eden – who resigned anyway three weeks after returning to London from Goldeneye – but it was excellent publicity for Fleming. Even a potentially embarrassing story in the *Evening Standard* about the Edens being plagued by rats during their stay – a malicious rumour thought to have been initiated by Randolph Churchill – kept the story running.

The Edens' visit to Goldeneye was marvellous publicity for Ian Fleming and he was prepared to exploit it for all it was worth, which was considerable, as the sudden surge in sales of all his Bond books testified. As if that were not evidence enough, the *Daily Express* purchased the serial rights of FROM RUSSIA WITH LOVE for £3,000 – double what they'd paid for DIAMONDS ARE FOREVER just a year earlier – convincing him that everything he'd worked for was finally coming true.

Ian Fleming may have had no regard for Eden as a politician – he thought the handling of the Suez crisis had been a 'shambles' – but he had good reason to thank him for finally giving Bond the boost he needed. Nor was Anthony Eden the only politician Fleming would have to be grateful to for promoting Bond.

Burgeoning success reinvigorated Ian Fleming's writing. Despite domestic ructions at Goldeneye in January 1957 – the Flemings' marriage was particularly strained at this time – writing DR. NO was effortless compared with FROM RUSSIA WITH LOVE the previous year. The original manuscript was altered little before publication a year later, while Bond's conquest of Dr No had a delicious simplicity. Never before had Fleming's basic, ongoing theme of St George slaying the dragon been quite so obvious.

If Fleming's acceptance that the Bond formula was his books' strength was an important breakthrough for him, two other things became apparent around this time as well. First, he realised that he, himself, was Bond's best publicist and he began to camp up the Bond image in interviews and photo sessions for all it was worth.

Secondly, somewhat to his own amazement, he'd discovered that his books were enjoyed by an audience far beyond their target readership. Writing to CBS Television, he explained, somewhat superciliously, that in hardback his books were written to appeal to an 'A' readership, but that when reprinted in paperback the 'B' and 'C' classes also found them readable. 'One might have thought that the sophistication of the background and detail would be outside their experience and in part incomprehensible,' he added in a sentence only Ian Fleming could get away with.

Fleming resurrected James Bond effortlessly in DR. NO. Rene Mathis, Bond's French ally from CASINO ROYALE, who was with Bond when Rosa Klebb kicked him at the conclusion of FROM RUSSIA WITH LOVE, gave Bond mouth-to-mouth resuscitation to keep his lungs going until a doctor arrived. Luckily, the doctor had worked in South America and recognised the poison Klebb had used – how is never explained – and treated Bond accordingly.

As M comments, it was 'a chance in a million', and, while not quite a 'with-one-bound-he-was-free' cop-out beloved by Victorian melo-drama, it was not exactly plausible. Not that Bond fans complained in 1958 when DR. NO was published; nor, indeed, have they complained subsequently. 007 lived twice to fight on. And that was *all* that mattered. Holding Bond himself responsible for Klebb's almost killing him, M dispatches 007 to Jamaica to investigate an ostensibly open-and-shut case to humiliate him. British agent Strangways (a character from LIVE AND LET DIE) and his secretary have disappeared. Strangways had been working on a complaint from the Audubon Society about interference with a bird sanctuary on the island of Crab Key, off the coast of Jamaica. The owner of the island, Dr Julius No, has a mania for privacy and anyone who ventures to the island uninvited seems to have little chance of returning. Native Jamaicans refuse to go near the place because there's a 'dragon' loose on the island.

After several attempts on his life – including a poisonous centipede placed in his bed in one of Fleming's most brilliant blood-curdling passages – Bond and Cayman Islander Quarrel (who also appeared in LIVE AND LET DIE) sail to Crab Key to have a look around. There they encounter 'Girl Friday' Honeychile Rider, whose naïveté in the ways of the world is negated by her prodigious knowledge of the natural world.

Bond discovers that the 'dragon' is nothing more than a dressed-up marsh buggy equipped with a flame-thrower – via which Quarrel meets an horrific end – before he and Honeychile are captured by Dr No.

Wined and dined by No, Bond discovers that the not-so-good doctor is using Crab Key to interfere with American missiles launched from Turks Island. After the meal, Dr No uses Bond and Honeychile in experiments he is running into the nature of pain and endurance. Honey is stalked out in the path of Jamaican land crabs so that he can measure the length of time before they devour her. Bond, meanwhile, is put through an elaborate obstacle course Dr No has prepared, to see how long he will last: 'You will be the first dot on a graph. Something of an honour, is it not, Mr Bond?'

Naturally, Bond manages to survive the obstacle course, which culminates in a tussle with a giant squid. This passage is not only Fleming at his wildest but also gives the starkest indication of how he was now prepared to jettison the pursuit of high literary art in favour of vicarious thrills. The previous year Bond's fight to the death with Red

Grant aboard the Orient Express had been horribly believable in a way grappling with a squid can never be, although Fleming's writing somehow keeps the whole thing from seeming *too* absurd.

DR. NO is a fabulous but outrageous book and Fleming knew it. Honeychile Rider is one of his most appealing female characters, even if his description of her having a behind 'as firm and rounded as a boy's' prompted an impish Noël Coward to ask Fleming, 'Really, old chap, what *could* you have been thinking of?'; while Dr No himself, half Chinese, half German and with steel pincers for hands, is a gleefully unashamed reworking of Sax Rohmer's Fu Manchu.

Bond's character is again fleshed out well, and Fleming develops Bond's sense of humour much more. The love affair between Bond and Honeychile is particularly well handled. Bond's relationship with M is also developed well: for the first time there's real conflict between them – something the Eon film series would exploit – and the resentment Bond feels when M orders that Bond stop using his trusty Beretta and switch to the Walther PPK is palpable.

In reality, Fleming decided to change Bond's gun after receiving a letter in May 1956 from Geoffrey Boothroyd, a firearms expert, who criticised Bond's gun: the .25 Beretta was 'a lady's gun', Boothroyd claimed, 'and not a really nice lady at all'. A grateful Fleming even put Boothroyd into DR. NO as Major Boothroyd, 'the greatest small-arms expert in the world'. In the film series, Boothroyd also became 'Q', although they are separate characters in the original Fleming books.

With FROM RUSSIA WITH LOVE due to be published in April 1957, the *Daily Express*, which was serialising the book, approached Fleming with a proposition to turn James Bond into a cartoon strip. The offer meant he would be paid £1,500 per novel. Despite his own doubts, and the advice of William Plomer to reject the offer, Fleming went for the deal, provided he could keep some control over the strip. The *Express* agreed and promised to do a sterling job on the strip. They were as good as their word, for the James Bond strip, which subsequently ran for many years in the *Express*, was always well produced.

It was only when FROM RUSSIA WITH LOVE was published, bearing its distinctive cover drawn by Richard Chopping – a young artist discovered by Ann who would design most of the remaining Fleming hardback covers – that Ian Fleming could breathe a sigh of relief. Despite hearing rumours that Raymond Chandler did not like the book at all, Fleming could not ignore the glowing reviews. Calling Fleming 'the most readable and highly polished writer of adventure stories to have appeared since the war', the *Sunday Times* believed FROM RUSSIA WITH LOVE 'exerts the grip of some science-fiction monster almost from the first page. It adds the pleasures of a credible plot to the excitements of extreme physical violence.' *The Times Literary Supplement* said FROM RUSSIA WITH LOVE was 'Mr Fleming's tautest, most exciting and most brilliant tale'. And when FROM RUSSIA WITH LOVE was published a few weeks later in the US the American reviews were just as enthusiastic, with the *New York Herald Tribune* calling it 'the best thriller we have had since whatever you may admire most of the admirable Ambler'. The dissenting voice was Anthony Boucher in the *New York Times*, who reverted to form by calling FROM RUSSIA WITH LOVE 'a half-guinea dreadful'.

At the same time as FROM RUSSIA WITH LOVE was appearing in bookshops, Sir Percy Sillitoe, the former chief of the International Diamond Security Organisation, approached Fleming to write a series of articles for the *Sunday Times* about his outfit's attempts to thwart the international diamond-smuggling trade. The resulting articles were published in the *Sunday Times* in September 1957, and then again by Jonathan Cape in book form as THE DIAMOND SMUGGLERS in November 1957. Despite mixed reviews for the book, the Rank Organization, which still held the film rights to MOONRAKER, offered Fleming £13,500 for the film rights, although nothing ever came of this.

GOLDFINGER, which Fleming wrote on his annual break at Goldeneye in January and February 1958, is a further demonstration of the author's response to his burgeoning success and reputation. Despite some implausibilities – Auric Goldfinger's plan to rob Fort Knox is never quite believable, something that was remedied in the film version six years later – GOLDFINGER is the work of an artist at the height of his powers. Nowhere is this more apparent than the tense golf game between Bond and Goldfinger, which takes up chapters eight and nine. These twenty-odd pages could have marred the book: golf is usually of little interest to nongolfers. But the interplay between Bond and Goldfinger and the subtext – neither of them is *really* talking about golf – as each cheats the other is masterly.

GOLDFINGER is also, Raymond Benson suggests, a transitional novel, 'separating the early books from the later ones in that James Bond's character becomes increasingly obsessed with the mortal trappings of life'. While Benson is undoubtedly correct – the book opens in Mexico with Bond reflecting on the death of a man whom he has just killed – Bond is by no means obsessed with his own mortality in GOLDFINGER. Quite the reverse, since James Bond is at his most relaxed and humorous in the book. As tough and resourceful as ever, the Bond of Fleming's seventh full-length novel is also at his most rounded and developed.

Many people have attempted to suggest they were responsible for Bond's cinematic success by claiming they added humour to Fleming's original. But the truth is Fleming had done it for them in GOLDFINGER. Bond is dangerously sexy with a nice line in jokes in this book, and he also relies more on gadgets than ever before. He even gets behind the wheel of an Aston Martin for the first time – a DB III, rather than the famous DB5 from the films. Typical of Bond's humour in GOLDFINGER is when he has engineered a bump between the DB III and Tilly Masterton's Triumph. Examining where the Triumph's lamps and radiator grille have locked into the Aston Martin's rear bumper, he quips, 'If you touch me there again, you'll have to marry me.' It could have come out of the mouth of Sean Connery less than a decade later.

Although some have complained that there is little action in GOLDFINGER compared with the other Fleming Bond novels, the compensations are the development of Bond's character plus, in Auric Goldfinger and his mute Korean henchman Oddjob, the most outrageously successful villains of Fleming's entire output. If all that wasn't enough, Fleming even gives us Pussy Galore – his most blatant adolescent sexual fantasy – the tough lesbian gangster and associate of Goldfinger who is 'cured' and switches sides simply by meeting Bond.

'They told me you only liked women,' says Bond on the last page of GOLDFINGER. 'I never met a man before,' Pussy replies. One can almost sense the gleeful grin on Fleming's face as he wrote that exchange when one reads it today.

Fleming returned to London with the first draft of GOLDFINGER – which would be little altered – in time for the publication of DR. NO in March 1958. But now, for the first time, he found himself under attack from the chattering classes, presumably because he was becoming too successful for his own good and had therefore become a legitimate target.

First up was Bernard Bergonzi in *Twentieth Century*, who accused Fleming of 'vulgarity' and of 'sado-masochistic voyeurism'. Then the *Manchester Guardian* waded in, citing Fleming's 'advertising agency world' as being 'symptomatic of a decline in taste'. Most damning of all, though, was Paul Johnson's tirade in the *New Statesman*, published on 5 April 1958 under the now infamous title SEX, SNOBBERY AND SADISM. Johnson claimed DR. NO was 'the nastiest book' he had ever read and that he had had to 'suppress a strong impulse to throw the thing away'. He continued to read it, sacrificing himself on behalf of his readers, presumably, only because he claimed he 'realised that here was a social phenomenon of some importance'.

Johnson identified three basic ingredients in DR. NO that he claimed were all English and all unhealthy, as though the two were synonymous. These ingredients were: 'the sadism of a schoolboy bully'; 'the mechanical, two-dimensional sex-longings of a frustrated adolescent'; and 'the crude, snob-cravings of a suburban adult'.

Claiming Fleming 'deliberately and systematically excites and then satisfies the very worst instincts of his readers', Johnson believed 'Mr Fleming has no literary skill . . . but the three ingredients are manufactured and blended with deliberate, professional precision; Mr Fleming dishes up his recipes with all the calculated accountancy of a Lyons Corner House.' He even berated the *New Statesman* itself for calling Fleming's previous Bond book, FROM RUSSIA WITH LOVE, 'irresistible'.

Johnson's attack was way over the top and, in retrospect, can be regarded as absurd. If DR. NO really *was* the nastiest book he'd ever read, it's clear he needed to get out a bit more in 1958. And the only *truly* offensive snobbery was the intellectual arrogance with which Johnson, and others, sneered at Fleming and his readers. Ian Fleming may have been many things, but a bad writer he was not.

Other notable writers leapt to Fleming's defence. Simon Raven, reviewing DR. NO in the *Spectator*, wrote, 'Commander Fleming, by reason of his cool and analytical intelligence, his informed use of technical facts, his plausibility, sense of pace, brilliant descriptive powers and superb imagination, provides sheer entertainment such as I, who must read many novels, am seldom lucky to find.'

But controversy always sells and, if nothing else, the debate sparked by Paul Johnson's silly article created a buzz about DR. NO and it started outselling Fleming's previous novels. In America, where DR. NO was scheduled to be published in June 1958, *Time* reported the furore in Britain about the Bond books, and his publishers Macmillan used it to their advantage by promoting Fleming as a 'bad boy' writer.

Nevertheless, Fleming *was* stung by the attacks, which he felt, rightly, were most unfair. He even wrote to the *Manchester Guardian* crying foul.

Seven years later, Kingsley Amis, always Ian Fleming's stoutest defender, laid into Paul Johnson, without naming him, when reviewing the posthumous THE MAN WITH THE GOLDEN GUN, ironically for the *New Statesman*.

'To read some of [Fleming's critics], one would think that Bond's creator was a sort of psychological Ernst Stavro Blofeld, bent on poisoning British morality,' Amis mocked.

'An article in this journal in 1958 helped to initiate a whole series of attacks on the supposed 'sex, snobbery and sadism' of the books, as if sex were bad *per se*, and as if snobbery resided in a few glossy-magazine references to Aston Martin cars and Pinaud shampoos and what-not, and as if sadism could be attributed to a character who never wantonly inflicts pain.'

Amis claimed that it was obvious Fleming had taken the accusations against him very seriously because the violence in his books was scaled down in what he wrote after 1958. Amis believed that while some might regard this as a negative gain, others 'may feel that a secret-agent story without violence would be like, say, a naval story without battles'. With regard to the infamous 'sex' and 'snobbery', not to mention the mem-orable meals and the gambling for high stakes in the books, Amis argued that these, however 'unedifying', were vital elements of the 'unique Fleming world', and that the 'denaturing of that world in THE MAN WITH THE GOLDEN GUN' as well as sections of its immediate forerunners was a loss. He concluded by saying that, 'nobody can write at his best with part of his attention on puritanical readers over his shoulder'.

Immediately after DR. NO had been published, Fleming flew to the Seychelles to cover yet another treasure-hunt story for the *Sunday Times*. Although the trip was disappointing from a journalistic point of view, Fleming decided that he had to send 007 to the Seychelles at some point in the future. This was to be realised in his compelling short story, 'The Hildebrand Rarity', which, while not a Secret Service tale as such, brought Bond into contact with the appalling Milton Krest, perhaps the most boorish and bullying antagonist he ever faced.

From the Seychelles, Fleming flew to Italy to join Ann for a holiday before returning to London to discover CBS were offering him a sizable sum of money to write 32 episodes of a James Bond TV series over the next two years. Fleming agreed terms and began work immediately.

While Fleming was working on the drafts of the projected series, he also began discussing the possibility of making a James Bond film with his old friend from Eton, Ivar Bryce. Fleming and Bryce were, at heart, still Eton schoolboys when they were together, and in 1958 the idea of making a James Bond film together must have seemed like a fun, not to mention potentially profitable, lark. How serious Fleming actually was about the whole project, though, has always been open to question.

Bryce had recently begun working with a young writer and director called Kevin McClory, with whom he had set up Xanadu Productions. McClory, who had been an associate producer on Mike Todd's *Around the World in Eighty Days*, and who had worked with John Huston, was a young man of some apparent talent who was seemingly destined for greatness in the industry.

At the time Fleming and Bryce started talking about a Bond film in 1958, McClory was directing and producing *The Boy and the Bridge*, a sentimental piece of whimsy about a boy who, convinced he's committed a murder, hides in the ramparts of Tower Bridge. In addition to directing and producing, McClory also shared the writing credit with Geoffrey Orme.

Fleming met Kevin McClory in December 1958, when Bryce and McClory asked Fleming to watch a rough cut of *The Boy and the Bridge*. Afterwards, Fleming told them that he liked it but in private he professed to be much less impressed, citing its overt sentimentality as a major flaw. In this, he was not alone. Leslie Halliwell, for years the doyen of British film critics, believed 'this tiny fable adds up to very weak entertainment, despite inventive photography, because it has virtually no plot development'. Nevertheless, Fleming, perhaps urged on by Bryce, was happy to discuss the possibility of making a James Bond film with McClory, and McClory set about reading all the existing Bond books.

McClory became convinced that Ian Fleming's James Bond had

enormous cinematic potential and, as a keen oceanographer, he could not fail to appreciate the underwater scenes in LIVE AND LET DIE. But he was to make one suggestion that was to prove disastrous from Ian Fleming's point of view: instead of adapting one of the existing novels, McClory suggested he and Fleming collaborate on a new story for the screen. Fleming agreed but it was a decision he quickly came to regret. The collaboration was to lead to a bitter hearing at the High Court in November 1963 followed by nearly forty years of litigation. As recently as 1997, the lingering dispute led to a major legal wrangle between the giant Hollywood Studios MGM and Sony Pictures.

For Fleming, personally, it would be even worse. He had to suffer the humiliation of being accused of plagiarism in the 1963 court case, which left him 'shredded, absolutely shredded', according to Sir John Morgan. The 1963 case may even have shortened his life, for he was dead less than ten months after it ended with a settlement greatly to Fleming's disadvantage. Despite his already poor health prior to the court proceedings, many members of his family and friends were convinced that the stress of the case was what ultimately killed him.

At this juncture, we must make our own position clear. It would be wrong of us, not to mention extremely foolish, to challenge the outcome of the 1963 THUNDERBALL plagiarism case, and we have absolutely no intention of doing so. Whatever our private thoughts about the fairness, or otherwise, of its outcome and despite what we believe was the strength of Ian Fleming's case, this book is not the place to claim there was a miscarriage of justice. Nor is it the place to attempt to right any miscarriage of justice there may, or may not, have been.

The events of 1958–9 concerning THUNDERBALL and the creation of Ernst Stavro Blofeld and SPECTRE are confused and have been muddied by more than four decades of claim and counterclaim. The only people who *really* knew the truth of what was discussed in private between the four protagonists at the heart of the affair – Ian Fleming, Kevin McClory, Ivar Bryce and Ernest Cuneo – were the men themselves: and Fleming, Bryce and Cuneo (who died in 1964, 1985 and 1988 respectively) are no longer around to ask or, indeed, to defend themselves.

All we can do is attempt to explain as clearly, succinctly and, above all, as *objectively*, as we can what happened according to the facts known to us. And while it will become obvious we believe those facts support *our* belief that Ian Fleming acted honourably, if a little naïvely, throughout – and it is vital to remember that this was never disputed at the 1963 High Court hearing – it must not be inferred that we believe Kevin McClory, or anyone else, behaved *dis*honourably.

As Raymond Benson cautioned at the beginning of a lengthy article he wrote about THUNDERBALL for *007 Magazine* (Number 23, Winter 1990),

> The information presented in this article may or may not be accurate from a legal standpoint. I have simply related the stories as told to me by the various personnel involved, i.e., in interviews with Kevin McClory, Ivar Bryce and Ernest Cuneo conducted between 1982 and 1988.
>
> All sides told different versions of the THUNDERBALL history and each side never failed to refute the other. Nevertheless, it's a fascinating story – regardless of what the 'real' truth may be.

As writers, we, too, have been involved in creative script discussions for both film and theatre projects and, when ideas are being thrown around, it's often quite impossible to pinpoint precisely *who* the originator was. Furthermore, one of us can claim, quite legitimately, to have had ideas stolen by producers on two separate occasions and it's a sickening feeling. That's why clear, written agreements are always wise in creative collaborations, even between friends. If nothing else, the THUNDERBALL case remains an object lesson in that principle.

According to Raymond Benson, 'a more or less verbal agreement' existed between the three men that Ian Fleming would write an original screen treatment of the movie, which Ivar Bryce would produce and Kevin McClory would direct as well as co-writing the script; but, when Fleming flew to Jamaica for his annual holiday in January 1959, he pushed all thoughts of the proposed James Bond film to the back of his mind.

There was a good reason for this: his immediate problem was what he was going to do about a new book. 'I've really run out of puff,' he complained, yet again, to William Plomer. 'GOLDFINGER will really have to be the last full length folio on Bond. I shall never be able to give him 70,000 words again.'

Actually, Fleming had another five full-length James Bond novels to write but he had no desire to write one in January 1959. Fleming had been writing quite a bit about Bond throughout 1958 with the episodes he'd been drafting for CBS, and he really does seem to have had no appetite for writing another full-length novel at this time. He decided to write, instead, a compilation of Bond short stories. Four of these – 'From a View to a Kill', 'For Your Eyes Only', 'Risico' and 'The Hildebrand Rarity' – were all adaptations of draft scripts he had prepared for the proposed CBS series.

Again, just as he had adapted DR. NO from the aborted *Commander Jamaica* series, Fleming was perfectly entitled to do this. The stories were his, as were the characters of James Bond, M, Miss Moneypenny, et al. But, like DR. NO, this practice set him a dangerous precedent, which rebounded on him when he repeated it the following year. To these four short stories, he added a fifth – 'Quantum of Solace', described by William Plomer as 'very Maughamesque', to Fleming's delight – which he had written in the summer of 1958. All five stories were published under the umbrella title of FOR YOUR EYES ONLY in 1960, and if Jonathan Cape was a little disappointed not to have a full-length Bond that year, Eon Productions, producers of the film series, had cause to be grateful to the compilation in the 1980s: with all the available full-length novel titles used up, it gave them two more usable Fleming titles for the film series in *For Your Eyes Only* and *A View To A Kill* (the 'From' having been dropped for no reason from the original). Furthermore, 'Risico' and 'For Your Eyes Only' found their way, more or less intact, into the screenplay of *For Your Eyes Only*, while Milton Krest, the boor from 'The Hildebrand Rarity', made an excellent secondary villain in *Licence To Kill*.

Fleming returned to London in March 1959 in time for the publication of GOLDFINGER. All the critics noticed the change in Fleming's writing in the book and applauded Bond's three-dimensional character and developing humour. 'A new Bond has emerged from these pages: an agent more relaxed, less stagily muscular than of yore,' said *The Times*.

The critics were right. GOLDFINGER marked an important development in the James Bond story and its importance cannot be overstated. For one thing, Kevin McClory has argued that *he* encouraged Fleming to lighten up Bond for their proposed film. Indeed, he has gone much further in recent years by suggesting that the successful transfer of

James Bond from the pages of Ian Fleming's novels to Eon Productions' films series could have been made only by using ideas he, McClory, put forward in developing the proposed film with Fleming in 1959.

In Kevin McClory's most recent court battle for a cut of the Bond pie – an unsuccessful appeal in the United States Court of Appeals for the Ninth Circuit in 2001 – his counsel contended that 'McClory transformed the supposedly violent and alcoholic James Bond [*sic*] of the Fleming books into the movie character who is so beloved, recognisable and marketable, and that they [McClory and Spectre Associates Inc.] have a significant stake in the Bond movies.'

However, most critics and film historians agree that *Goldfinger*, the third Bond film, produced in 1964, is not only the definitive Bond film but also the blueprint of all the successive Bond films. So it is worth our pointing out that the elements that made *Goldfinger* definitive – Bond's wry insouciance; the larger-than-life Auric Goldfinger; the outrageously named Pussy Galore; Oddjob, the archetypal henchman with his deadly bowler hat; the assault on Fort Knox; the illegally acquired nuclear bomb; the girl painted in gold; the hints of kinkiness; and even the gadget-ridden Aston Martin – were *all* derived from Ian Fleming's source novel.

So if we accept that *Goldfinger* really is the definitive James Bond film and the true blueprint of the film series – and no one who knows anything about the subject seriously disputes this – then it surely follows that it was Ian Fleming himself, and no one else, who truly created the template for the cinematic James Bond in his seventh novel, GOLDFINGER.

And GOLDFINGER was written almost a full year *before* Ian Fleming met Kevin McClory.

Around the time of GOLDFINGER's publication, Fleming decided to change both his agent and publishers in the United States. He had been particularly unhappy with the way Curtis Brown had handled the film rights to his books in the States and he switched to the Music Corporation of America (MCA). The first thing MCA did was to buy back the film rights of MOONRAKER from Rank, which, rather stupidly, had done nothing with the property.

In the late spring and summer of 1959, Fleming talked some more about the proposed James Bond film with Kevin McClory, Ivar Bryce and Fleming's old friend, Ernest Cuneo. The meetings variously took place at McClory's home in London and Bryce's house at Moyne's Park in Essex.

Cuneo, ostensibly brought in by Bryce originally in a legal capacity, actually developed the first draft plot of the film. In a memo to Fleming dated 28 May 1959, Cuneo proposed a scenario in which a Russian agent was planning to explode a series of nuclear bombs on American bases. The scenario had a Soviet front company ordering a whole fleet of Bahamian boats with trapdoor hulls, which could take on board nuclear bombs without being seen.

Cuneo's idea of setting the film in the Bahamas was a pragmatic one because, as he explained to the others, they could make use of the Eady Subsidy Plan, the British government's long-running attempt to stimulate film production with complicated tax concessions. 'I told Ian that you would have the luxury of an inexpensive location, the benefit of Hollywood and very little tax burdens,' Cuneo told Raymond Benson.

Fleming was delighted with Cuneo's input, although he said the lack of a heroine was a flaw and, in a significant development, it *appears* he suggested that it might be a mistake to make the Russians as the villains because he felt the Cold War was thawing. In June 1959 there were signs this might be a real possibility: in February, the British prime minister Harold Macmillan had made a lengthy visit to Russia, where he had held talks with the Russian leader Nikita Khrushchev, while the US vice-president, Richard Nixon, was scheduled to visit Moscow and meet Khrushchev in July.

Fleming's suggestion seems to have been that Bond's adversaries should be an apolitical organisation called SPECTRE, which was an acronym for the Special Executive for Terrorism, Revolution and Espionage (this was later refined by Fleming into the Special Executive for Counterintelligence, Terrorism, Revenge and Extortion, which was far better).

But here we must sound another note of caution, because the question of just *who* suggested SPECTRE first has long been central to the later disputes about the THUNDERBALL case. Andrew Lycett makes a pretty convincing case for Fleming's having created SPECTRE (*Ian Fleming*, Chapter 12), but he adds that McClory remained adamant that SPECTRE was 'a cumulative idea', and the fruit of their joint discussions. Frankly, once the idea of using the Russians as villains had been discarded, the leap to using a criminal gang akin to the Mafia, which is what SPECTRE is, essentially, was pretty obvious. And what difference is there really in the setup of, and the methods used by, SMERSH and SPECTRE? Essentially, SPECTRE is nothing more than a privatised SMERSH.

As for the name of the organisation, the authors of this book are convinced the actual acronym SPECTRE *must* have been Fleming's own idea because of his own love of the word 'spectre', as we demonstrated in Chapter 2.

In fairness, we must point out that there is an alternative version of events. In Raymond Benson's article for *007 Magazine*, he states, presumably using information from Kevin McClory, 'From the beginning, the plot centred around the blackmailing of powerful nations by a group of bad guys threatening to use stolen atomic bombs.' According to this version, Fleming wanted to use the Russians as villains yet again, but the others argued that this was passé. Cuneo apparently suggested that the villains should be the Mafia before McClory came up with SPECTRE, an international terrorist group, which was run like a corporation.

Well, perhaps. Although the idea that Ian Fleming, the seasoned *Sunday Times* journalist and foreign editor, whose Jamaican house had been used by the former British prime minister and whose wife frequently entertained the leading political figures of the age at her endless parties, had to have the changing international and political landscape explained to him by *anyone* verges on the absurd.

In June and July, Fleming developed Cuneo's ideas into a 67-page treatment in which he introduced the villain, Emilio Largo, and the heroine, Domino. Doubts remain, though, as to just how committed Fleming really was to the project, and Andrew Lycett (*Ian Fleming*, Chapter 12) repeats Bond historian John Cork's assertion that Fleming was seemingly operating 'quickly and none too seriously'.

His interest waned somewhat more in July 1959 when McClory's *The Boy and the Bridge* opened to a drubbing from the critics, which presaged a pitiful performance at the box office. Despite assuring Ivar Bryce that he would write a full treatment of the film and would always be available to provide 'editorial and advisory services', Fleming was privately worried that Bryce and McClory were way out of their depth with the Bond film – and the critical and box-office failure of *The Boy and the Bridge* hardly reassured him. What made matters even more uncertain was that his new American agents were telling him of renewed interest in Bond from several major Hollywood studios.

Fleming also seems to have been genuinely concerned about both Bryce and McClory. He believed Bryce had lost an awful lot of money on *The Boy and the Bridge* and was loath to see his old friend lose another packet on the proposed Bond film. The projected budget of the Bond film was $3 million, which was a massive sum in 1959, and Fleming was daunted by the prospect of failure. 'We are a terribly amateurish crew playing around with your money,' Fleming told Bryce. 'I don't like either of these feelings.'

As for McClory, Fleming seems to have been worried that the young man, who was clearly talented and ambitious, might be trying to run before he could walk by taking on what was clearly going to be a huge project.

Private advice from MCA also influenced Fleming. They suggested that the film would require a much higher-profile director than Kevin McClory, whose sole directorial credit was the abysmal *The Boy and the Bridge*, to attract investors and stars. Laurence Evans of MCA was blunt: 'Really big stars will not be anxious to be produced and directed by a young man with only one film to his name, and that a film which has not found favour.'

In August, Fleming tactfully suggested to McClory and Bryce that they might approach Anthony Asquith as a co-producer. This did nothing to help relations between Fleming and McClory, which started to cool fast, particularly after Fleming returned home to 16 Victoria Square one day to find McClory had taken the house opposite – and that McClory's Thunderbird was parked alongside his own.

In September, Fleming took McClory to lunch and suggested they approach Alfred Hitchcock as director. This was not as fanciful as it sounds. Fleming had heard via MCA that Hitchcock had expressed an interest in the Bond books, and this makes sense when one considers that Hitchcock had just finished directing Cary Grant in the decidedly Bondian *North By Northwest*, and thirteen years earlier had directed *Notorious*, in which Grant had played a prototype James Bond called Devlin.

McClory agreed reluctantly to their approaching Hitchcock. Alas, to the regret of cineastes everywhere, the prospect of Alfred Hitchcock's directing a James Bond film never came to fruition. Hitchcock, while interested, turned the project down, presumably not wanting to share the profits with McClory and Bryce.

Hitchcock's rejection dampened Fleming's enthusiasm further and, by October 1959, he was, according to John Pearson, 'clearly becoming bored with the whole affair now'. This probably explains why he didn't demur when Kevin McClory brought in the veteran British screenwriter Jack Whittingham – among whose credits was the somewhat appropriate *Q Planes* (1939) – to do some work on the Bond script.

But by then Ian Fleming had other priorities: he was about to embark on a five-week trip around the world to write a series of articles for the *Sunday Times* about great cities. The resultant articles were published in the newspaper in 1960 and later in book form by Jonathan Cape as THRILLING CITIES. While in New York he wrote a short story called '007 in New York' – which was not published in Britain until it appeared in the *Sunday Times* in November 1999 – in which Fleming revealed the surprising fact that 'Bond had once had a small apartment in New York'.

When Fleming returned to London, he had little appetite to resume negotiations on the proposed Bond film. He was tired from his exhausting trip round the world and he started to wish he'd never become involved in the whole business. He was just looking forward to spending the first couple of months of the 1960s at Goldeneye, writing his new Bond book. If the film happened, fine; if it didn't, well, it couldn't be helped.

He could afford to be sanguine. It had taken him eight long years, but James Bond was finally established as a leading cultural icon.

There was not even any of his usual annual nonsense to William Plomer that he was written out, or had 'run out of puff'. The new Bond book was already fixed in his mind. Unfortunately, THUNDERBALL was to explode in his face.

004: The Men with the Midas Touch

'That couldn't be further from my idea of James Bond.
Everything was wrong: the face, the accent, the hair.'

Ian Fleming after meeting Sean Connery, 1961

It was not Ian Fleming's intention to defraud or cheat *anybody* when he wrote THUNDERBALL. He just wasn't that kind of man. And the strongest evidence of this was his dedicating THUNDERBALL to 'Ernest Cuneo, muse'. In other words, Fleming was crediting the man whom he *genuinely* believed to have been the progenitor of the THUNDERBALL plot.

But Kevin McClory and Jack Whittingham did not see it that way when they read an advance copy of the book in March 1961. As far as they were concerned, THUNDERBALL was based on the drearily titled *Longitude 78 West*, the latest screenplay based on the proposed Bond scripts and treatments that Fleming, Ivar Bryce, Ernest Cuneo, McClory and Whittingham had been discussing and which McClory had sent to Fleming at the end of 1959.

In January 1960, Kevin McClory travelled to Goldeneye to discuss *Longitude 78 West* with Fleming. Fleming told McClory that he wanted to hand over the script to his agents, MCA. He said that he and Ivar Bryce would recommend that McClory produce the film but, if MCA, or any interested studio, rejected the project on the basis of McClory's being the producer, then he felt McClory should step aside and allow the project to proceed with a new producer. Should that happen, Fleming believed it was up to McClory to sell himself to the new production team.

In taking this stance, Fleming was perhaps influenced by Ernest Cuneo's decision to do, what in Fleming's eyes at least, was 'the decent thing' by selling all of his interests in the script to Ivar Bryce for the sum of one dollar.

Ivar Bryce and Ernest Cuneo both admitted to Raymond Benson that the project just became too big for Bryce and Fleming to handle. 'They weren't filmmakers,' wrote Benson. 'They were boys inside men's bodies looking for a way to have fun and make money at the same time. Once they realized how much work it would really be, they both backed off.'

One of the many difficulties any objective reader has in understanding the complexities of the THUNDERBALL case today is appreciating just *what* Kevin McClory and Jack Whittingham – particularly Whittingham, who died in the late 1970s – brought to the party; although McClory certainly seems to have injected the doomed project with a certain enthusiasm and ability.

The problem is that THUNDERBALL, far from standing out from the other novels – which one would expect had it been the result of collaboration – is *pure* Ian Fleming. It's not merely that it sticks rigidly to Fleming's Bond formula, which he perfected in DR. NO and GOLDFINGER – Kingsley Amis said THUNDERBALL was 'full of the "Fleming effect"' – but that virtually every major incident and character in the novel would seem to be either recycled from previous Bond books or drawn from Ian Fleming's own life.

Thus, the characters of Bond, M, Moneypenny, May (Bond's housekeeper) and Felix Leiter were Fleming's; Emilio Largo is a rehash of Le Chiffre from CASINO ROYALE, as we examined in Chapter 2; Domino is an Identikit Bond Girl, with definite echoes of Solitaire from LIVE AND LET DIE (and her slight limp is a deformity on a par with Honeychile Rider's broken nose in DR. NO); the lengthy prologue at the Shrublands Health Farm, including Bond's ordeal on the traction machine, was based on Fleming's own recent stay at the Enton Hall Health Farm; SPECTRE No. 6's assassination of Count Lippe while he, in turn, is trying to kill Bond, is a direct steal of the SMERSH killing of Le Chiffre while he's torturing Bond in CASINO ROYALE; SPECTRE No. 6's method of carrying out that attack with a grenade ('twice the normal military size') in a crowded London street mirrors the method used by the 'Two Men in Straw Hats', the SMERSH agents who attempted to kill Bond with a bomb in a busy Royale-les-Eaux street in CASINO ROYALE; Largo's yacht, the *Disco Volante*, is merely a souped-up version of Mr Big's yacht, the *Secatur*, in LIVE AND LET DIE; and, while Mr Big is using the *Secatur* to find hidden treasure to finance his operations, Largo is using the *Disco Volante* as the base for a bogus treasure hunt as a cover for SPECTRE'S operation.

Blofeld's threat to nuke Miami is clearly inspired by Sir Hugo Drax's attempted nuclear annihilation of London in MOONRAKER and Bond even refers to his earlier case while searching for the stolen bombs with Leiter: 'Remember that Moonraker job I was on a few years back?'; Bond's duel with Largo over *chemin de fer* is a direct copy of his earlier battle with Le Chiffre in CASINO ROYALE; the three major underwater sequences are expansions of the similar scenes in LIVE AND LET DIE; Domino's switching to Bond's side having been initially involved with the villains follows the great tradition set by Solitaire, Tiffany Case, Tatiana Romanova and Pussy Galore before her; and the US Navy team's underwater ambush of the SPECTRE frogmen as they move the nuclear bomb into position is an aquatic retread of the US Marines' ambush of Auric Goldfinger's train, which is full of his personnel bringing the nuclear bomb with which they intend to blow off the doors of Fort Knox.

No wonder even Jack Whittingham, who sued Fleming for plagiarism, was forced to admit that 'Bond is very much Ian Fleming's personal creation.'

There is even less wonder at Fleming's bitterness about being accused of plagiarism, because THUNDERBALL was, essentially, an anthology of all the Bond books that had gone before. It was more exaggerated, perhaps, than any previous Bond book, maybe even more implausible, but it was still, nonetheless, an anthology of previous Flemingian/Bondian incidents.

So an objective reader might very well conclude that, if THUNDERBALL was, indeed, based directly on the screenplay *Longitude 78 West*, then *Longitude 78 West must* have drawn heavily on ideas culled from Ian

Fleming's earlier books, particular CASINO ROYALE, LIVE AND LET DIE, MOONRAKER, DR. NO and GOLDFINGER, all of which were written *before* Fleming had met Kevin McClory and Jack Whittingham. And, assuming he did reach that conclusion, our objective reader might then easily conclude further that, if Ian Fleming had plagiarised *anyone* in the writing of THUNDERBALL, it was, essentially, himself.

Is that why Fleming felt safe when he wrote THUNDERBALL? Did he, by dedicating the book to 'Ernest Cuneo, muse', believe he had done the honourable thing by crediting the one man in the enterprise whom he *genuinely believed* had contributed the only original material to the project? It would certainly explain Fleming's actions, which seem naïve otherwise. An affidavit on file in London, in which Fleming swore that the idea for THUNDERBALL came from Cuneo (who sold his rights in the property for a dollar, as we have seen), would seem to confirm this interpretation of events.

Furthermore, Ian Fleming does not seem to have believed the proposed film would ever happen in the first months of 1960, when he wrote THUNDERBALL. Indeed, by March 1960 he was even suggesting to Ivar Bryce that they 'wash [their] hands' of the whole project. His reasoning seems to have been that if the film *did* go ahead, then THUNDERBALL could be the book of the film; if it didn't, why should he lose a full-length Bond novel? He later argued that he believed everyone associated with the project understood, and had agreed, that that was the case. But McClory and Whittingham rebutted Fleming's claim.

What undermined Fleming's case were the elements in THUNDERBALL that could *not* be attributed directly to his previous Bond novels: essentially, these were the means of stealing the NATO nuclear bombs; SPECTRE; and Bond's nemesis Ernst Stavro Blofeld. Where these ideas originated was much less clear-cut.

SPECTRE'S stealing the bombs by hijacking a NATO plane in mid-flight *does* appear to have been suggested by McClory and Whittingham, something that Fleming never denied, although, even here, the germ of the idea may have been triggered by Ernest Cuneo's original treatment; but the origins of SPECTRE and Blofeld are much harder to pin down.

According to his website, Kevin McClory insists that 'SPECTRE first appears as a copyrighted-protected expression in the "McClory scripts" written in 1959 and progressed from there into the novel THUNDERBALL, which Ian Fleming had based on the "McClory scripts".

The SPECTRE organisation, and its chairman, Ernst Stavro Blofeld, and the "McClory scripts" continue to be properties owned by him and/or his companies.'

Nevertheless, just *who* first suggested SPECTRE remains unclear, as we have seen, and may now never be resolved definitively. As we showed in the previous chapter, Andrew Lycett has made a strong case for its having been Fleming's idea in response to Cuneo's first treatment; and, as we ourselves have demonstrated, 'spectre' was always one of Fleming's favourite words.

As for Blofeld, there can be no doubt that the character, as written in the THUNDERBALL novel, is, again, pure Ian Fleming: Ernst Stavro Blofeld is Mr Big, Sir Hugo Drax, Dr No and Auric Goldfinger revisited. Furthermore, Blofeld conducts his board meeting in THUNDERBALL much the same way as Colonel General Grubozaboyschikov, the head of SMERSH, conducts his departmental meetings in FROM RUSSIA WITH LOVE – hence our referring to SPECTRE as 'a privatised SMERSH' in the previous chapter.

According to Andrew Lycett, Fleming appropriated Blofeld's surname from a fellow member of his club, Boodles: one Tom Blofeld, who was a Norfolk farmer and also chairman of the Country Gentlemen's Association. Fleming was always using friends' and acquaintances' names in his books. His friend Hilary Bray turned up as Sir Hilary Bray in ON HER MAJESTY'S SECRET SERVICE; Bond travels under the name of 'Bryce' in LIVE AND LET DIE; and Ernest Cuneo begat Bond's taxi driver Ernest Cureo in DIAMONDS ARE FOREVER. Cuneo may also have inspired Blofeld's forenames – it is but a short leap from Ernest Cuneo to Ernst Stavro.

By any measure, then, Ernst Stavro Blofeld is a classic Ian Fleming creation, *as written* in THUNDERBALL, and Fleming certainly seems to have felt secure enough in his own mind about just *who* created the character, because he used Blofeld as his villain in ON HER MAJESTY'S SECRET SERVICE (1963) and YOU ONLY LIVE TWICE (1964), both of which were written *after* Kevin McClory's first legal action against him in March 1961.

But these arguments are academic. In the November 1963 court case, Fleming, under intense pressure and gravely ill, as we shall see, was forced humiliatingly to admit he had drawn on the McClory scripts in writing THUNDERBALL. On 14 November 1963 Fleming admitted through his solicitors, Farrer and Co., that:

1. The novel reproduces a substantial part of the copyright material in the film scripts or in one or more of them.
2. That the novel makes use of a substantial number of the incidents and materials in the film scripts.
3. That there is a general similarity of the story of the novel and the story as set out in the said film scripts.

It is surprising that neither Fleming nor his defence team thought to question to what extent – if any – the said film scripts had made use, uncredited, of a substantial number of incidents in the previous Fleming novels. But, by the time he made those admissions in 1963, Ian Fleming simply had no fight left in him.

That was not the case in March 1960, when Fleming, on his way back from Jamaica with the first-draft manuscript of THUNDERBALL in his suitcase, made a detour to Washington at the behest of the *Sunday Times*.

Fleming did not care much for Washington and was not looking forward to the trip. But, once he was there, his mood brightened considerably when his old friend Mrs Marion Leiter – whose name he had appropriated for his fictional CIA agent Felix Leiter – introduced him to the then Democratic presidential candidate-elect, Senator John Fitzgerald Kennedy. Kennedy was already a confirmed fan of Fleming's books and insisted that Fleming attend the small dinner party he and Mrs Kennedy were holding that evening.

And so, on the evening of 13 March 1960, Ian Fleming dined with the soon-to-be president – the man who would, arguably, prove to be the single most important supporter of James Bond in the USA.

During dinner, the vexed question of Cuba and Fidel Castro came up and Fleming's opinion was sought. Fleming put forward that the Americans were building up Castro too much and suggested that all their energies should be put into deflating and undermining him. With all the chutzpah of his days in Room 39 as a Naval Intelligence officer, Fleming put forward three suggestions, his tongue very much in his cheek.

He said that the US should send planes to scatter Cuban money all over Havana attached to notes that said it came with the compliments of the US government. He then said that US forces should conjure up some airborne religious symbols, a cross, perhaps, so that the religious

Cubans would forever be looking skywards. His final outrageous suggestion was that the US should drop pamphlets purporting to come from the USSR saying that the atmosphere around Cuba was radioactive because of American nuclear tests and that radioactivity settled particularly in long beards, making all bearded Cuban men impotent.

Fleming's audience was puzzled. 'How can that help?' asked JFK.

'The Cubans will all shave off their beards,' replied Fleming urbanely. 'And without bearded Cubans, there will be no revolution.'

JFK was delighted and, from that moment on, he and Fleming were firm friends. 'Kennedy was fascinated by Ian,' recalled a friend of both men. 'He was particularly fascinated by the line dividing Ian's real life from the fantasy life that went into his books. He often asked me how such an intelligent, mature, urbane sort of man could have such an element of odd imagining in his make-up.'

It was a friendship that became very important to Fleming once JFK had been elected and there is no doubt that he exploited his White House connections shamelessly afterwards. He certainly worked at the friendship, sending inscribed copes of all his books to JFK and other members of the Kennedy clan, particularly Robert Kennedy.

In December 1960, the Canadian producer Harry Saltzman took out a six-month option on all the existing and future Ian Fleming Bond novels, with the exception of CASINO ROYALE, the rights to which had already been bought by Gregory Ratoff. The option cost Saltzman $50,000 and THUNDERBALL was included in the deal because, at the time he made it, ownership of the property was not yet contested.

Harry Saltzman was born in Quebec in 1915 and ran away from home at an early age. He had found work in circuses and vaudeville and served both the Canadian Army and the RAF during World War Two. He almost certainly worked for the OSS in France during the war and even his own family remained for ever in the dark exactly to what extent he had taken part in clandestine operations.

Saltzman was a showman and extremely volatile. His rages were legendary but always short-lived and his desire always to shake things up meant that he was forever throwing out ideas. Colleagues always said that eight out of ten of Saltzman's ideas were crazy and unworkable – but two out of ten would always be brilliant.

After the war, Saltzman moved to Hollywood for a time and then to

London, where he became an independent film producer. His first film as producer was the unfunny comedy *The Iron Petticoat*, made in England in 1956 with an eclectic transatlantic cast of Bob Hope, Katharine Hepburn, James Robertson Justice and Robert Helpmann, of which one critic remarked, 'They seem amazed to find themselves in a comedy that has no humour and they go through the motions grimly, like children at dancing school, hoping it will all be over soon.'

After that, Saltzman formed Woodfall Productions with the director Tony Richardson and the playwright John Osborne and ushered in the short-lived (though not short-lived enough) 'kitchen-sink' school of British filmmaking, of which their depressing *Look Back In Anger* in 1959, based on Osborne's overrated play, was typical.

Saltzman always remained proud of what he'd achieved with films like *Look Back In Anger* and believed that Woodfall Productions' output had been seminal. But despite the personal joy the films had brought him, not to mention the critical plaudits, he made very little money from them and in late 1960 he was relatively poor. He knew he needed a string of solid commercial hits if he was to make any money in the film industry and saw Ian Fleming's Bond books as being ideal.

Finding backers once he had secured the option on the Fleming properties was another matter, however. Harry Saltzman was not a sensible man when it came to handling money, despite his business aspirations, and tended to spend whatever money he had. Potential backers were wary of his entrepreneurial skills.

While Harry Saltzman chased backers and distribution deals in the first two months of 1961, Ian Fleming took his annual holiday at Goldeneye to write his tenth James Bond book, THE SPY WHO LOVED ME. As with FROM RUSSIA WITH LOVE, Fleming had decided to experiment with THE SPY WHO LOVED ME. It is, according to Raymond Benson, 'an enigma . . . truly strange'. This is because Fleming tells the story in the first person from the point of view of the heroine, while James Bond doesn't actually enter the narrative until the last third of the book.

Vivienne Michel is by far the best of Fleming's female characters – well drawn, credible and a true victim who has found her own strength to confront life. There *are* lapses in Fleming's depiction of Vivienne. It is clearly, for instance, Fleming's voice we hear when, after Bond has made love to her for the first time, Vivienne writes that all women love semi-rape and love to be taken. When Bond makes love to Vivienne, she claims that it's his 'sweet brutality' against her 'bruised body' that makes the act 'so piercingly wonderful'. But, overall, his sustaining the female viewpoint throughout an entire novel was an astonishing achievement for a male thriller writer in 1961. Significantly, many women readers rated THE SPY WHO LOVED ME higher than any other Bond book. Male readers were less accepting, however, and THE SPY WHO LOVED ME caused Fleming major problems when it was published in the spring of 1962.

With the first draft of THE SPY WHO LOVED ME written, Ian Fleming returned to London in March 1961 to some fantastic news: on 17 March, *Life* magazine published a list of President Kennedy's favourite books. In ninth place was Ian Fleming's FROM RUSSIA WITH LOVE: it was incredible publicity, which sent Fleming's US sales through the roof overnight. Within weeks, he was the highest-selling thriller writer in the United States.

But, as always in Ian Fleming's life, just when things looked as though they couldn't get any better, they got a whole lot worse. On the same day that Fleming himself read the *Life* article, he heard that Kevin McClory and Jack Whittingham were seeking an injunction to block the publication of THUNDERBALL. McClory had got hold of an advance copy of the book and, seeing no credit to himself or Whittingham, he determined to have his day in court. In the event, he was to have *many* days in court.

McClory and Whittingham claimed that Fleming had infringed their joint copyright in *Longitude 78 West* by publishing THUNDERBALL because, they alleged, the book was based on the screenplay. This was a wholly unexpected bolt from the blue as far as Fleming was concerned, as he was utterly convinced he had done nothing wrong.

With THUNDERBALL's publication imminent, the petition for the injunction had to be heard very quickly. Thirty-two thousand copies of THUNDERBALL had already been sent to bookshops in Britain and abroad, review copies had been sent out to reviewers, and £2,000 already spent on publicity.

Mr Justice Wilberforce, hearing the case at the High Court on 25 March 1961, concurred with the representative from Fleming's publishers, Jonathan Cape, who insisted that the publication process of THUNDERBALL had gone too far to stop now. He agreed that

THUNDERBALL could be published as planned, but warned that his decision did not prejudice any action for breach of copyright McClory and Whittingham might take against Fleming.

Ian Fleming was devastated by the action McClory and Whittingham took against him and it's easy to understand his reasoning. *He* had created James Bond; *he* had written the books; and *he* had agreed to let McClory and Whittingham work with his characters and marketable hero on a film that, if successful, would have made them a lot of money. But the film hadn't happened and that wasn't *his*, Ian Fleming's, fault. It was unfortunate, but there it was. Why were they doing this to him now?

Fleming sank into a dark pit of melancholy after the injunction hearing and not even the enthusiastic reviews and increased sales enjoyed by THUNDERBALL could lift him out of it. He had had a profound horror of courtrooms ever since the Metro-Vickers trial in Moscow in 1933, and that, coupled with his failing health, did not auger well. Three weeks later, on 12 April 1961, Ian Fleming suffered a massive heart attack during a routine weekly conference at the *Sunday Times*.

Fleming's lifestyle surely contributed to his coronary but the strain of McClory's and Whittingham's action against him could hardly have helped. Fleming regarded plagiarism, rightly, as the worst accusation that could be made against any author and, in his case, he believed it was very unfair.

Fleming spent a month recovering in the London Clinic, where doctors advised him to cut down drastically on his smoking and drinking and to get plenty of rest. Typically, Fleming paid lip service to the advice but, once released from hospital, quickly came to loathe the diet he was put on, which eschewed his favourite sausages and butter-rich scrambled eggs.

As for resting, Fleming virtually ignored his doctors by starting to write a children's book, CHITTY CHITTY BANG BANG, while still recovering in the London Clinic. According to Sir John Morgan, Fleming based the book on a real Polish count who lived in Kent. 'He had this car he called Chitty-Chitty-Bang-Bang which he would drive frantically around the lanes of Kent near Bekesbourne,' says Sir John. 'That's where Ian got the original idea.' (See Appendix 1: 'Ian Fleming Remembered'.)

One of the lines in CHITTY CHITTY BANG BANG summed up Fleming's attitude to how one should live life: 'Never say "no" to adventures. Always say "yes". Otherwise you'll lead a very dull life.'

As Fleming began to feel better in the London Clinic, so his humour, too, recovered. He was particularly amused to learn that *The Times* had actually written his obituary and did everything he could to obtain a copy. His friends' varying advice on how to recover from a heart attack also made him laugh. The advice ranged from Noël Coward's suggesting Fleming be more spiritual, through Max Beaverbrook's insistence that strong liquor was the best medicine for the heart, right to Evelyn Waugh's advising him to get himself 'sucked off' gently every day. Brilliant though they were in their respective professions, it's clear Messrs Coward, Beaverbrook and Waugh were no loss to the medical profession. On leaving the London Clinic, Fleming recuperated first in Brighton, where he loathed sitting in bus shelters looking at the sea 'like some bloody old man', and then with Ann in France.

While the creator of James Bond pottered slowly around woodlands in Normandy, pausing often to look at birds' nests while leaning on a walking stick, the future of James Bond was quickly starting to take shape elsewhere.

Harry Saltzman's six-month option had almost expired and he simply hadn't been able to capitalise on it. It looked as though Saltzman's interest had been yet another false dawn for the cinematic James Bond. But then the writer Wolf Mankowitz introduced Saltzman to Albert R (Cubby) Broccoli.

Mankowitz was working on a script for Broccoli called *Arabian Nights Adventure*, but Broccoli was unenthused by the idea. Mankowitz understood and asked what Broccoli *really* wanted to do.

'I've always had this urge to film Ian Fleming's James Bond books,' Broccoli replied.

It was the same answer Broccoli had given his wife, Dana, a few days earlier when she had asked the identical question.

Mankowitz's response was blunt: 'Why don't you? Nobody else seems to want to make them.'

Broccoli explained how he had tried to get an option on the properties a couple of years earlier but how his then partner Irving Allen had scuppered the deal. 'Someone else has the options now,' said a rueful Broccoli.

'Yeah – Harry Saltzman,' said Mankowitz. 'But he hasn't been able to put a deal together and he only has about thirty days of the option left.'

Broccoli had never met Saltzman, but Wolf Mankowitz knew him and arranged a meeting between Broccoli and Saltzman the next day in Broccoli's office.

Albert Romolo Broccoli was born on 5 April 1909 and was the epitome of the American Dream. His Italian farming family had emigrated to the United States in the 1870s and had worked extremely hard to establish themselves. Two things were important to Broccoli from an early age: family and hard work. His mother instilled in him the belief that, if you worked hard enough, you could always achieve your dream. Given that Albert R Broccoli was instinctively a fine businessman, hard work was bound to pay off in the end.

Broccoli was particularly close to his cousin Pat de Cicco and it was de Cicco who gave Broccoli the nickname that stayed with him for ever: Cubby. Broccoli reminded his cousin of a then-famous cartoon character called Abie Kabibble. At first de Cicco called Broccoli 'Kabibble' but over the years it got shortened to 'Cubby'.

When Pat de Cicco became a Hollywood agent, he invited Cubby Broccoli to join him in Los Angeles. The first person Broccoli met on arriving at de Cicco's house was the neighbour – Cary Grant; the next night he met another of de Cicco's friends – Howard Hughes. Broccoli remained close friends with both men to the ends of their lives and both he and Cary Grant remained two of the handful of Hughes's trusted inner circle when the billionaire later lapsed into his bizarre reclusiveness.

Cubby Broccoli began his Hollywood career as a third assistant director at Twentieth Century-Fox but quickly became one of Tinseltown's top assistant directors. Perhaps the most memorable job he had at this time was working as Howard Hawks's assistant director on Howard Hughes's notorious western *The Outlaw*, the film that launched Jane Russell's career.

Broccoli married Gloria Blondell, sister of that fine comedienne Joan Blondell, but they divorced amicably in 1945. He then married his second wife, Nedra, in December 1951 and they moved to London when Broccoli set up Warwick Films with Irving Allen. Warwick Films' first film, *The Red Beret*, was a smash hit and quickly established

Broccoli and Allen as two of the first really successful independent filmmakers in England. Perhaps even more importantly, that first film utilised the talents of the screenwriter Richard Maibaum and the director Terence Young – two men who were to prove very important indeed in the story of James Bond.

Warwick Films thrived throughout the 1950s and Broccoli and Allen produced nearly twenty movies between 1953 and 1960. But Broccoli suffered personal tragedy too when Nedra died of cancer, leaving him a widower in his late forties with two small children to bring up. He found happiness again with Dana Wilson, an extremely beautiful actress and talented writer who had previously been married to Lewis Wilson, the screen's first-ever Batman. Cubby Broccoli married Dana on 21 June 1959; Cary Grant was Broccoli's best man. It had been a whirlwind romance but it was to lead to an enduring marriage. And Michael Wilson, Dana's son, hit it off with Broccoli immediately. This was important because Michael was to be another highly significant figure in the Bond empire in future years.

Despite renewed personal happiness, Broccoli's professional fortunes had taken a dip. He and Irving Allen had lost their shirts on a failed distribution company and had to finance their next movie, *The Trials of Oscar Wilde*, with their own money.

The Trials of Oscar Wilde was an artistic triumph. Written and directed by Ken Hughes, it starred Peter Finch, giving one of the finest performances of his career as Wilde, and a splendid supporting cast of James Mason, Lionel Jeffries and Nigel Patrick. Despite its facing competition from the simultaneous but vastly inferior biopic *Oscar Wilde* (an eerie foreshadowing of the Battle of the Bonds Broccoli would face in 1982–3), there was no doubt in the critics' mind which was the better film. 'The battle of the Wilde Ones is over with a clear-cut victory for *The Trials of Oscar Wilde*,' wrote the critic Margaret Hinxman. 'It is one of the finest film biographies I've ever seen.' Paul Dehn, the critic who turned screenwriter and eventually collaborated on the screenplay of *Goldfinger*, raved about Peter Finch's performance as Wilde. And the *Daily Express* believed *The Trials of Oscar Wilde* was 'a tremendous film. One of which the British film industry can, and should, be proud.'

But, in America, *The Trials of Oscar Wilde* fell foul of the absurd Legion of Decency, that ridiculous hotchpotch of self-appointed moralists and the religious right, whose approval distributors sought before they would take on a picture. And the Legion of Decency did not approve of *The Trials of Oscar Wilde*. In particular, they objected to an exchange in the courtroom between Oscar Wilde and Carson, the prosecution lawyer, and insisted it be cut:

CARSON: Mr Wilde – did you know this valet?
WILDE: Yes, I knew him.
CARSON: Did you give him a cigarette case?
WILDE: Yes, I gave him a cigarette case.
CARSON: Did you kiss him, Mr Wilde?
WILDE: Good heavens, no! He was too ugly!

Bravely, Cubby Broccoli refused to have the scene removed because he believed it would undermine not only the honesty of the picture, but his own integrity as a producer. But he discovered principles came with a high price tag: despite winning many awards around the world, *The Trials of Oscar Wilde* was relegated to the art-house circuit in the US. It was a financial disaster, which destroyed Warwick Films and left Cubby Broccoli virtually bankrupt. But he still had his contacts and, more importantly, his solid reputation in the business as a producer of probity.

He was, though, at a low ebb professionally when Wolf Mankowitz brought Harry Saltzman to see him. Having just ended one business partnership painfully, Cubby Broccoli had no intention of going into partnership again and was looking to Harry Saltzman to sell the option on the Fleming books to him. But Saltzman wasn't about to sell. He had the option, Broccoli had the connections: Saltzman insisted on a partnership. And so, somewhat reluctantly at first, Cubby Broccoli went into partnership with Harry Saltzman. They created two companies: Danjaq, which was based in Lausanne and held the film rights to the Bond books (the company name being a fusion of their wives' names – Dana Broccoli and Jacqui Saltzman); and Eon Productions, which would actually produce the Bond films. A myth persisted for many years that Eon was an acronym for 'Everything or Nothing' but Cubby Broccoli always denied it.

Broccoli and Saltzman took the Bond package first to Columbia Pictures, but Columbia had no interest in the property at all. Broccoli and Saltzman then flew to New York to meet with Arthur Krim, the chief executive of United Artists. Krim was very interested in the Bond package and in this he had, presumably, been influenced by his nephew David Picker, an enthusiastic fan of Fleming's books, who had, quite independently of Fleming's approach, also suggested to Alfred Hitchcock that he film one of the Bond novels.

Krim received Broccoli and Saltzman with his top executives – including David Picker – on 21 June 1961, and the United Artists Board agreed, there and then, to finance the first James Bond film for $1 million. After recoupment of their investment, United Artists would take 40 per cent of the profits, Broccoli and Saltzman 60 per cent. Despite their belief that James Bond would become popular, Broccoli and Saltzman could not know just how rich they would become within a matter of two or three years.

The partnership of Cubby Broccoli and Harry Saltzman was one of opposites. Saltzman was volatile, all over the place; Broccoli contained and focused. Saltzman would walk on set, lose his temper and storm off; Broccoli was much more one of the boys.

'I remember Cubby as the cuddly one and Harry as the tough one,' recalls Honor Blackman, who played Pussy Galore in *Goldfinger*. 'Although Harry did have a very dry sense of humour.'

'Harry liked to do six things at the same time or he became restless,' agrees Dana Broccoli. 'Cubby was quite different because he loved the project in hand.'

Remarkably, these two hugely different personalities shared a vision for James Bond and they continually sparked off each other.

'They were two opposing points of view reaching the same objective,' says David Picker. 'They both understood the Fleming books and they both understood the kind of films we wanted them to make. And they made them.'

Even after the partnership had inevitably fractured – although it lasted longer (fifteen years) than even Broccoli and Saltzman themselves could have imagined in June 1961 – Broccoli was able to say generously in 1978, 'I think we both contributed to the success of Bond through our ideas in the early films.'

With the backing of United Artists, Broccoli and Saltzman set to work immediately on the first Bond film. Bizarrely, *Thunderball* was chosen as Eon's first Bond film and Richard Maibaum, who had scripted or co-scripted several of Warwick's films previously for Cubby Broccoli, actually wrote a draft script. *Thunderball* was obviously an attractive property to Eon since it was the most recent Fleming bestseller, but, with the title in litigation with Kevin McClory's action against Ian Fleming still pending, the decision was made, sensibly, to switch to *Dr. No*.

Wolf Mankowitz and Richard Maibaum wrote a treatment that, when they read it, made Broccoli and Saltzman hit the roof. In 1989, Richard Maibaum recalled why:

> When Wolf and I began working on the script, we decided that Fleming's Dr No was the most ludicrous character in the world. He was just Fu Manchu with two steel hooks. It was 1961, and we felt that audiences wouldn't stand for that kind of stuff any more. So we decided that there would be no Dr No. There would be a villain who always had a little marmoset monkey sitting on his shoulder, and the monkey would be Dr No.
>
> We wrote about forty pages. Wolf and I thought it was marvellous, and we showed it to Cubby and Harry. Cubby was outraged, in his usual good-natured way. 'You've gotta throw the whole damn thing out. No monkey, d'you hear? It's got to be the way the book is!' He made a very strong point about it. Wolf withdrew. He just couldn't take it. Now I think about it, it was just a temporary collaborator's aberration.

Having endured the debacle with Kevin McClory and Jack Whittingham, not to mention recovering from his heart attack, Ian Fleming himself was intrigued by the film, but determined to keep his distance. Nonetheless, he submitted a fascinating thesis to Broccoli – 'with due humility Cubby' – which spelled out precisely the way *he* believed James Bond and the British Secret Service should be presented.

Fleming reminded Broccoli that James Bond is a 'blunt instrument wielded by a government department'. Professionally, Bond is 'quiet, hard, ruthless, sardonic, fatalistic' and displays the same qualities in his relationships with women, although Fleming allowed that 'he has a certain gentleness with them' and even allows that if a woman gets into trouble Bond is 'sometimes' prepared to sacrifice his own life to rescue them. 'But not always,' Fleming cautioned, 'and certainly not if it interferes with his job.' Fleming underlined in his memo that Bond likes gambling, golf and fast cars. Intriguingly, he insisted neither Bond nor M should ever endear themselves to the audience. 'They are tough, uncompromising men,' Fleming emphasised. 'And so are the people who work for and with them.'

Obviously, the key to the picture was the casting of James Bond – and both Broccoli and Saltzman were adamant that he must be played by a British actor. Cubby Broccoli's first thought was Cary Grant. Although by then an American citizen, Grant had been born in Bristol. Moreover, Broccoli knew through his friendship with Grant that the movie idol, then at the peak of his box-office power, was an acquaintance of Ian Fleming's and an aficionado of the Bond books.

Cary Grant would have certainly guaranteed *Dr. No*'s box-office success, but Broccoli knew more or less before approaching Grant that he wouldn't play the part. For one thing, the budget United Artists had allocated the film wouldn't cover Grant's fee (although had Grant come aboard, there's no doubt the studio would have upped the budget). For another, Grant himself pointed out he was too old: when the cameras started turning on *Dr. No* in Jamaica in January 1962, Grant would have just celebrated his 58th birthday.

Lastly, Cary Grant had never made a sequel in his entire career. He made it plain to Broccoli that, if he did do the film, he would sign for only one. Broccoli and Saltzman were looking to produce a series of Bond films – they hoped they might even manage a series of four or five films – and, if Grant made *Dr. No*, they would be faced with the same headache of finding a James Bond for the second one.

Broccoli and Saltzman asked Ian Fleming for his suggestions. Fleming put forward Roger Moore, whom he had been impressed by on television, and his friend David Niven. But Fleming's preferred choice, according to Sir John Morgan, was always a character actor called Edward Underdown (see Appendix 1: 'Ian Fleming Remembered'). Underdown – who actually appeared in the minor role of the air vice marshal in *Thunderball* – was a dependable, if somewhat stolid, actor who made his film debut in *The Warren Case* in 1934. Born in London in 1908 – the same year as Ian Fleming himself – Underdown was tall and thin and enjoyed a successful career as a jockey and steeplechase rider as well as an actor. His last film was *Tarka the Otter* in 1978 and he died in 1989. Fleming clearly saw parallels in Underdown's somewhat diffident, dour acting style with his idealised 'blunt-instrument' persona for Bond, but the author's enthusiasm was clearly not shared by Broccoli and Saltzman since there is no record that Underdown was ever considered for the role.

Harry Saltzman was more excited by Fleming's suggestion of Roger Moore, although Cubby Broccoli was concerned that he looked much too young. Ironically, a decade later, when they were recasting the part, Broccoli was more enthusiastic about Moore than Saltzman. Nevertheless, just *how* seriously Broccoli and Saltzman had been about using Roger Moore for *Dr. No* was made clear by Harry Saltzman, in an interview in 1972 during the filming of *Live And Let Die*: 'We originally planned to use Roger when we were making *Dr. No*,' he told a reporter. 'But he wasn't available. He was working on TV.' Patrick McGoohan was approached but he turned the part down on moral and religious grounds, as he did the part of Simon Templar in the TV series *The Saint* that same autumn for much the same reasons. James Fox, who was suggested to Broccoli and Saltzman, also rejected Bond because of his religious beliefs. Other big names – including the wholly inappropriate Trevor Howard and Michael Redgrave – were touted, plus a host of unknowns whose agents sent them up for the part. But neither Broccoli nor Saltzman was overly impressed by what he saw.

'I wanted a ballsy guy,' Broccoli said. 'I was sure we had to build on Fleming's 007, giving him a coarser shading. Just as menacing, but more overtly masculine, and with a touch of humour.'

While the search for a James Bond continued, Broccoli and Saltzman also had a headache finding a director for *Dr. No*. They approached Guy Green, who turned it down, as did Guy Hamilton. So did Ken Hughes, who Broccoli thought had done a fantastic job for him on *The Trials of Oscar Wilde*. Finally, Broccoli talked to Terence Young.

Young, who had previously directed *The Red Beret*, *Safari*, *Zarak* and *Tank Force* for Broccoli's Warwick Films, was a competent director but his work had not exactly displayed a surfeit of inspiration hitherto and neither Harry Saltzman nor United Artists wanted him for *Dr. No*. But Cubby Broccoli had his reasons: 'Terence had done good work for me before. He was well educated, had done war service and had a rapport with the higher echelons of the British establishment – all useful to bringing out the subtleties of the James Bond character. He also needed the money.'

In fact, Terence Young, who lived life to the full and spent as he earned, needed the money from *Dr. No* so badly that he insisted on being paid a lump sum to direct the picture rather than the salary plus percentage of the profits Broccoli and Saltzman were offering. Had Young accepted their offer of a share in the profits of *Dr. No*, his money problems would have been solved for the rest of his life and Cubby Broccoli, for one, was irked when, in later years, Terence Young claimed *he* had made Broccoli and Saltzman rich men.

Ian Fleming wasn't overly impressed with the choice of Young as the director of the first Bond film. He knew the director through their mutual friend Noël Coward. 'So they decided on you to fuck up my work,' he said to Young.

'Let me put it this way, Ian,' Young retorted. 'I don't think anything you've written is immortal yet. Whereas the last picture I made won a Grand Prix at Venice. Now let's start even.'

Young was even more scathing about Fleming's books to an interviewer some years later when looking back at *Dr. No*:

> We started rather flatly with *Dr. No*. And Fleming was a bit shy at first, though somewhat arrogant. But then he really was a superior sort of man. I think at first he was just afraid we were going to take the Mickey out of his book.
>
> But then I suppose I *didn't* really have a very clear conception of what I was going to do when I took on *Dr. No*. Fleming's original book was diabolically childish – like something out of a Grade B thriller. All Fleming's books are like that [*sic*]. He embellished them well, gave them a sophisticated veneer, but the stories themselves are infantile. The only way I thought we could do a Bond film was to heat it up a bit, to give it a sense of humour, to make it as cynical as possible.

Young – who was born in 1915 and whose years at Cambridge (where he excelled at rugby and tennis) and service with the Guards Armoured Division led many who worked on the early Bond pictures to believe *he* would have made the perfect James Bond – pressed for Richard Johnson to be cast as 007 when he began work on *Dr. No*. But Cubby Broccoli and Harry Saltzman had, quite independently, both come across an actor they thought perfect. His name was Sean Connery.

Thomas Sean Connery was the son of a truck driver and was born in Edinburgh on 25 August 1930. His was a deprived background and he'd worked as a milkman, a coffin polisher, labourer, cement mixer and a printer's devil after leaving school without qualifications at thirteen. At seventeen, he joined the Royal Navy but was discharged on medical grounds after just three years when he developed an ulcer. While in the Navy, he acquired the two tattoos on his arms – one read 'Scotland Forever', the other 'Mum and Dad' – which scores of makeup artists later tried desperately, and in vain, to camouflage in his movies.

Other remnants from his life in the Navy stood him in better stead – 'I ran while I was in the Navy and boxed and lifted weights,' he recalls – by giving him a marvellous physique, and he worked for a while as a male model at the Edinburgh School of Art.

Winning the Mr Scotland title in 1953, Connery represented Scotland at the subsequent Mr Universe contest – but came nowhere. He then joined the chorus in the original London production of *South Pacific*, where he was billed, for the first time, as 'Sean Connery'.

Connery's stage and television work developed through the 1950s. Perhaps his biggest breakthrough was his performance as a broken boxer in a live BBC TV production of *Requiem for a Heavyweight*, and he followed this with a BBC production of *Anna Karenina*, opposite Claire Bloom.

Connery's film roles were not exactly earthshattering in the late 1950s. He made his debut in *No Road Back* in 1955 and films such as *Time Lock* (1956) and *Hell Drivers* (1957) hardly did him any favours. So low was his film stock at this time that when he and another young aspiring actor by the name of Maurice Micklewhite went up for the same tiny part in producer Cubby Broccoli's 1956 movie, *How To Marry a Rich Uncle*, Maurice got the part. When Maurice had turned into Michael Caine and, like Connery, was a multimillionaire, he couldn't resist reminding Broccoli of this.

In 1957, Connery appeared in the director Terence Young's film *Action of the Tiger*. A desperately dull action melodrama, starring Van Johnson and Herbert Lom, *Action of the Tiger* was yet another mediocre movie on Sean Connery's CV. But, in Terence Young, he had at least established a rapport with the director who was to prove critical to his career less than five years later.

By 1961, Sean Connery had a burgeoning and impressive track

record on television and stage, but his film career had still, essentially, to catch fire. Even starring opposite the Hollywood star Lana Turner in the drippy romance *Another Time, Another Place* had not furthered his film career significantly.

Nonetheless, when the *Daily Express* launched a poll of its readers to find a suitable actor to play James Bond, Connery's name was well enough established for him to appear on the final list.

It was not the *Daily Express* poll that brought Connery to the attention of Broccoli and Saltzman, however, but a wonderful serendipitous coincidence.

Sean Connery had recently completed two films: *Darby O'Gill and the Little People*, a simple-minded Walt Disney whimsy with some fair trick effects; and *On The Fiddle*, a mild British RAF comedy in which he and Alfred Lynch played, respectively, a dim gypsy and a cockney wide boy.

Peter Hunt, who edited *On The Fiddle* – and who later edited the first five Bond movies and directed the sixth – recalled that the producer of the film, Benjamin Fisz, was a good friend of Harry Saltzman and suggested Connery would be a good candidate for the Bond role.

Simultaneously, in Los Angeles, Cubby Broccoli suddenly remembered Connery, to whom Lana Turner had reintroduced him, briefly, in London (Broccoli had no recollection of Connery from turning him down for *How To Murder a Rich Uncle*). 'He was a handsome, personable guy,' Broccoli recalled, 'projecting a kind of animal virility. He was tall, with a strong physical presence and there was just the right hint of threat behind that hard smile and faint Scottish burr.'

Broccoli immediately arranged for a screening of *Darby O'Gill and the Little People*. He didn't think much of the movie, but Connery stood out.

Nonetheless, Cubby Broccoli was a shrewd producer and he knew he was viewing Connery from a male perspective. But he knew that, if Bond was to be the kind of success he, Broccoli, believed he could be, the actor playing Bond *had* to appeal to women. So he asked his wife Dana to see the film as well.

Dana's reaction was unequivocal. 'That's our Bond,' she said. 'He's perfect.'

Broccoli and Saltzman were convinced they'd got their man. 'I liked the way he moved,' recalled Saltzman in 1966. 'And the fact that he had a lot of acting experience. He moves extremely well. There's only one other actor who moves as well as he does and that's Albert Finney. They move like cats. For a big man to be light on his feet is most unusual.'

Broccoli was even more illuminating:

Sean had the balls for the part. Put a bit of veneer over that tough Scottish hide and you've got Fleming's Bond instead of all the mincing poofs we had applying for the job.

Sean's looks and explicit body language cast him irresistibly as 007. I was convinced he was the closest we could get to Fleming's hero. The character was written as a semi-sadistic operator, well manicured but with a streak of mercilessness about him. The more I thought about Connery, the more he seemed to fit the image we had of James Bond.

Broccoli and Saltzman invited Connery to meet them at the office of No. 3 South Audley Street, just off London's Park Lane. For Connery it was, initially, just a question of going to talk about another job. He didn't really have any thoughts about playing James Bond, one way or another.

'I had only read two of Ian Fleming's books before filming began, and I wasn't all that in sympathy with the character,' says Connery. 'In fact, I thought to myself that I probably wouldn't even *like* Bond if I met him on the street.' He continues:

In fact, when I got to know Ian Fleming and was able to discuss Bond with him I found Fleming much more interesting than his writing. He was terrific company, with a tremendous knowledge of the world. He spoke German, French and Russian and told me all about the times when he was working for Reuters in Moscow.

He was a terrible snob. But once you got past that he was really a very nice guy; quite shy, very intelligent, highly original and most curious. But he had a snobbishness that he wrote into Bond in the novels. It was the lack of humour about himself and his situation which I didn't like about the character.

In truth, Sean Connery did not look much like *anybody*'s idea of James Bond when he first walked into Broccoli and Saltzman's office:

a brown open-necked shirt and suede shoes would have been anathema to 007. But the producers were already looking to broaden Bond's appeal somewhat and Connery, by general consent then a 'rough diamond', fitted their requirements of 'a sexual athlete who would look great in Savile Row suits' perfectly.

'It was never our intention for Sean to play Bond *exactly* as Fleming's original,' confided Cubby Broccoli. 'If we'd wanted that kind of character we might have considered Terence Young's suggestion of Richard Johnson, or David Niven.

'The whole point of having Sean in the role, with his strong physical magnetism and the overtones of a truck driver, was that it thrilled the women, but, more important, young men in the audience could feel that there was a guy up there like them. We could then play the role as a kind of subliminal spoof.'

But not everyone was convinced.

'Oh, disaster, disaster, disaster!' said Terence Young when he heard Broccoli and Saltzman had agreed terms with Connery.

United Artists, too, were unenthused and told Broccoli so in no uncertain terms after they'd seen test footage of Connery. 'New York did not care for Connery. Feel we can do better,' Broccoli cabled Saltzman when he heard United Artists' reaction.

Ian Fleming also took some convincing. Sir John Morgan, who was present when Sean Connery was introduced to Ian Fleming at 16 Victoria Square, recalls: 'Afterwards, Ian said to me, "That couldn't be further from *my* idea of James Bond. Everything was wrong: the face, the accent, the hair." It was a thousand miles away from his idea of James Bond.' (See Appendix 1: 'Ian Fleming Remembered'.)

Broccoli and Saltzman stood by their choice, however, instructing United Artists that they were going ahead with Connery and would not look any further. They were, of course, vindicated and, within four years, Sean Connery was the number one box-office draw in the world.

'It was a bit of a joke around town that I was chosen for Bond,' Connery said many years later. 'The character is not really me at all. But I'd always had a terrible fight to get work in Britain on account of my Edinburgh accent.'

Filming on *Dr. No* was scheduled to begin in January 1962 in Jamaica. Just prior to flying out to begin work on the film, Connery told the *Sunday Express*: 'Like some other people in Northern Countries,

James Bond is very much for breaking the rules. He enjoys freedoms that the normal person doesn't get. He likes to eat. He likes to drink. He likes his girls. He is rather cruel. Sadistic. And I have no compunction at all admitting that I like to eat. I like to drink. And I like girls.'

Sean Connery could not know when he gave that interview how his own personality would soon be indistinguishable from that of James Bond in the minds of millions of moviegoers worldwide.

Nor was he aware of the extent to which he would come to despise the image of 007.

005: Sadism for the Family

'Every man wants to be a superman, to make love to anything that walks, and call on the army, navy and air force if he gets into trouble. With a Bond movie, the guy in the audience pays his three shillings and sixpence and buys a dream.'

Harry Saltzman, 1966

By lunchtime on 16 January 1962, the first shot of *Dr. No* was in the can. Filmed at the international airport in Kingston, Jamaica, the shot was number 39 in the final shooting script. It read:

39. AIR TERMINAL. CUSTOMS BUILDING. DAY

BOND indicates his luggage to a PORTER and moves towards the exit. As he does so he notices a PRETTY CHINESE GIRL in the act of sighting her Press Speed Graphic at him. His reaction is instinctive. He whips off his hat as if to greet somebody, covering his face with it in a perfectly natural gesture. As GIRL is winding frantically on he moves to exit, smiling at her in passing.

Finally, after all the false starts and the horrendous problems with Kevin McClory over THUNDERBALL, Ian Fleming had got what he wanted. The first James Bond film was up and running.

At the urging of Broccoli and Saltzman, Richard Maibaum had rewritten the script, bringing it more or less back in line with Fleming's original book. The spider monkey was gone and Dr No was rightly returned as the villain of the film. Maibaum's script did make some deviations, however. Dr No became an associate of SPECTRE; two minor villains were introduced in the form of Miss Taro (who has a walk-on role in the book) and Professor Dent; Bond's CIA buddy Felix Leiter was included, although he had not appeared in the DR. NO novel; and the climax lurched into science fiction – away from Fleming's Jules Verne-like scrap with the giant squid – by featuring a fight to the death between Bond and Dr No in No's nuclear laboratory.

When Wolf Mankowitz read the final script – which was also worked on by Terence Young's script associate, Joanna Harwood, and Berkely Mather – he insisted his name be taken off the credits: Mankowitz was convinced the whole thing would be an embarrassing disaster and he wanted no further part of it. Cubby Broccoli asked if Mankowitz would prefer to wait until he saw the final picture before making his decision. But Mankowitz was adamant.

'I want my name off it. I don't want my name on a piece of crap, and that script's a piece of crap,' he said. He insisted Broccoli even put it in writing that his, Mankowitz's, name wasn't to be credited.

When he saw the final cut of the picture, Wolf Mankowitz changed his mind and asked Broccoli to have his name put back on the credits. But by then it was too late: the titles and posters were already done and it would cost a fortune to change them.

Many years later, Mankowitz, who died in 1998, tried to rewrite history somewhat by giving a differing version of events, in which he claimed,

I originally wrote *Dr. No.* And Maibaum doctored it. But I fell out with Broccoli and Saltzman and removed my credit. I had a deal to do the rest of the things, but I didn't want to go on working with them and they paid me out on the whole thing – after a bit of argy-bargy – and that was the end of that. I was offered a percentage of Eon if I would go on acting as principal writer and script editor on the other Bonds. But working on with them just seemed like entrapment.

Despite his initial misgivings over the casting of Sean Connery, the director Terence Young had worked hard with his new star, grooming him to be Bond.

The production designer Ken Adam, whose outstanding work on *Dr. No* and six other Bond films has led to his becoming, arguably, the most famous production designer in the industry, recalls, 'You have to remember that Sean was a pretty rough diamond at that time. Terence taught him everything he knew. He had a tremendous influence on creating James Bond in the person of Sean Connery.'

'Terence took me in hand and knocked me into shape,' acknowledges Connery. 'He took me to his tailor and his shirtmakers, Turnbull and Asser.' Young even insisted on one occasion that Connery sleep in one of his Bond suits to get the feel of it. So well made was the suit that, next morning, it did not have a single crease in it.

Young's grooming of Sean Connery certainly paid off. If there was, perhaps, a lingering air of uncouthness about Connery's persona in *Dr. No*, it was certainly pretty well disguised for the most part, and had been eradicated by the time of the second Bond film, *From Russia With Love*, a year later. Sean Connery thrived under Terence Young's tutelage, and, for the most part, he carried off the deception that he had worn Bond's clothes, and lived Bond's lifestyle, all his life.

With Sean Connery signed as Bond, Broccoli and Saltzman and Young concentrated on casting the other roles in *Dr. No*. For the titular villain himself, Noël Coward's name was mentioned as a possibility. Trading on their long friendship, Ian Fleming wired Coward on behalf of Eon Productions, asking if he would be interested in the role. Coward's reply was as succinct as it was witty: 'My dear Ian, the answer to *Dr. No* is No, No, No, No!' Instead, Eon cast the veteran stage actor Joseph Wiseman as Dr No. Wiseman was not very like Fleming's version visually, yet somehow managed to capture something of the essence of the literary Dr No. Realising, correctly, that the metal pincers Fleming's Dr No used in place of his lost hands would look absurd on screen, the filmmakers gave No black metal hands instead. Wiseman was to 'play' another Bond villain three years later when he provided the voice of Ernst Stavro Blofeld in *Thunderball* (Blofeld's face is not seen in that film).

Other roles were filled quickly. The American actor Jack Lord, later to find enduring international fame as the lead in *Hawaii Five-0*, was somewhat miscast as a humourless Felix Leiter; Anthony Dawson, a favourite actor of Terence Young, was cast as the corrupt associate of Dr No, Professor Dent; and the black actor John Kitzmuller was a good choice for Bond's Cayman Islander ally, Quarrel.

One role, however, proved rather more troublesome: that of the 'Girl Friday' Honey Ryder (the name slightly changed from Fleming's original Honeychile Rider). Fleming's description of Honeychile when Bond first encounters her in DR. NO is of 'Botticelli's Venus, seen from behind'. It was a tough image to live up to and finding the right actress was imperative. Additionally, Honey does not appear in the movie until well over halfway through, and, when Bond first sees her, she is emerging from the sea in a bikini. Whoever played Honey, therefore, had to have great screen presence. And Broccoli and Saltzman, poring over thousands of photographs of potential Honey Ryders, still hadn't found her up to within two weeks of the start of principal photography on *Dr. No*. That was until Cubby Broccoli saw a picture of Ursula Andress on top of the pile of photographs on his desk one day. The photograph was, according to Broccoli, 'a publicity still of her in a pose that became a photographic cliché. She was emerging from the water, her clinging wet T-shirt emphasising the perfect moulding of her breasts.' Without knowing it, the photographer – her husband, John Derek – had made Andress strike a pose *exactly* as the *Dr. No* script portrayed Honey Ryder. Broccoli knew he had found the right girl.

Broccoli contacted a casting director in Hollywood he'd worked with previously – Max Arnow – and asked if he knew Ursula Andress. Arnow said that he did and, when Broccoli asked if she really was as beautiful as the photograph, he added, quite rightly, that no photograph could ever quite match her beauty.

Broccoli asked if she could act. Arnow replied that she had a voice 'like a Dutch comic'. But when Broccoli described the character of Honey Ryder and, in particular, her entrance, emerging from the sea, Arnow said that he could think of no one more perfect than Ursula Andress. That was enough for Broccoli, who sent the script to Andress without seeing her. Broccoli knew that Andress's voice was not a problem: it could be overdubbed later (which it was, by the actress Monica Van der Syl).

Cubby Broccoli wrote in his autobiography that Terence Young was annoyed at having Andress foisted on him. But, many years later,

Young claimed the credit for discovering the photograph of Andress in the clinging wet T-shirt in Darryl F Zanuck's office at Twentieth Century-Fox. According to Young's version of events, he 'gave the photograph to Cubby and Harry and they liked it. You couldn't not like it. She looked marvellous. We had lots of other pictures there. Harry and Cubby shared a big desk and every morning I used to go by their office on the way to my office and put Ursula's picture on the top.'

Given that Terence Young had a propensity in later years to be selective in his Bondian memories, the authors of this book are inclined to believe Broccoli's version of events. But, whatever the truth about the casting of Ursula Andress, there is no doubt that her first appearance in *Dr. No* was destined to become one of *the* enduring iconic images of 1960s cinema. 'I tell you, it's a mystery,' she says. 'All I did was wear this bikini in *Dr. No*, not even a small one, and Whoosh! Overnight, I made it.'

The *Dr. No* cast and crew arrived in Jamaica on Sunday, 14 January 1962, and, for the first and only time, the literary and cinematic sides of the Bond empire collided in the same place: while *Dr. No* was being filmed in Jamaica, Ian Fleming was at Goldeneye writing what, for the authors of this book at least, is the very best of the James Bond novels – ON HER MAJESTY'S SECRET SERVICE.

Despite all 1961's problems – the injunction against THUNDERBALL and his massive heart attack – Ian Fleming had ended 1961 and begun 1962 in high spirits professionally. This certainly showed in his writing: prior to beginning work on ON HER MAJESTY'S SECRET SERVICE, Fleming had completed what may very well be his best short story, 'The Living Daylights'.

'The Living Daylights' was written specifically for the launch of the *Sunday Times* colour supplement, scheduled for February 1962. Bond is sent by M to Berlin; his mission is to protect British agent No. 272 as he makes a dash to the West from East Berlin. Agent 272 is bringing with him Soviet nuclear secrets and consequently he's got virtually the whole of the KGB on his trail.

The KGB know where and when 272 will try to cross over and plan to shoot him. Bond must act as a sniper and kill the KGB sniper to protect 272. During the long wait for 272's bid for freedom, Bond spies a beautiful girl in the Soviet sector through the lens of his Sniperscope. She is carrying a cello case and Bond speculates privately about her life.

There is one terrific moment in the story that reveals a great deal about Bond's character and attitude to his work. Just prior to 272's making a run for it, Bond ignores the rules and pours himself a large whisky. Captain Sender, a stiff, by-the-rules representative from the West Berlin station who accompanies Bond, threatens to report him. Bond's weary reply is Fleming at his best.

Reminding Sender that he, Bond – not Sender – has to commit murder that night, he tells Sender to 'stuff it'. Bond asks Sender if he really believes Bond likes the job as a Double-0 and then admits that he'd be perfectly happy if Sender's report resulted in his being sacked from the Double-0 section. He could then 'settle down and make a snug nest of papers as an ordinary staffer'.

When 272 dashes to freedom, Bond spots the KGB sniper and recognises her as the blonde girl with the cello he'd fantasised about earlier. Bond disobeys orders and doesn't kill her: he shoots her hand instead. Sender, who witnessed Bond changing his aim at the last second, tells Bond he will report it.

'Okay,' says Bond. 'With any luck it'll cost me my Double-0 number.'

'The Living Daylights' is a near-perfect short story. Taut, compelling, splendidly structured and telling us more about the character of James Bond than is to be found in the full-length DIAMONDS ARE FOREVER.

'The Living Daylights' was published in the *Sunday Times Magazine* on 4 February 1962 and immediately caused a row. Max Beaverbrook, owner of the *Daily Express*, which had a deal to serialise the Bond novels and was then partway through serialising THUNDERBALL, was furious and ordered that the James Bond cartoon strip be ended immediately. Bemused *Express* readers were presented with one final strip in which THUNDERBALL was abruptly curtailed. The paragraph read, 'Giuseppe flies the stolen atom bomber to the Bahamas and the bombs are hidden in the sea. SPECTRE's ultimatum is sent to the British and US governments – "£100,000,000 in gold or we explode the bombs in your countries." Every agent, including Bond, searches for the bombs. Bond finds them and the world is saved.'

It took many months and a somewhat grovelling letter from Fleming to Beaverbrook to smooth things over. Eventually, the *Daily Express* resumed the James Bond strip – it had been under considerable pressure to do so from readers – and the next book to be serialised was ON HER MAJESTY'S SECRET SERVICE, since THE SPY WHO LOVED ME was rejected by the *Express* as being unsuitable.

If 'The Living Daylights' was one of the best Ian Fleming short stories, ON HER MAJESTY'S SECRET SERVICE is the perfect James Bond novel. Epic in scope, liberally sprinkled with action, violence and humour, and with a romantic subplot that rivals that of CASINO ROYALE as the best in the series.

Frustrated by M's obsession with finding Ernst Stavro Blofeld to the detriment of everything else, Bond actually composes his letter of resignation from the British Secret Service in his head while driving his old Continental Bentley on a dull stretch of road between Abbeville and Montreuil one September. These thoughts are banished, however, when Tracy overtakes him in her Lancia Flaminia Zagato Spyder.

Tracy is, as Bond eventually discovers, no ordinary girl. She is, in fact, La Comtesse Teresa di Vicenzo, daughter of an English governess and Marc-Ange Draco, head of the Union Corse – 'more deadly and perhaps even older than the Unione Siciliano, the Mafia', according to Fleming.

Tracy is on the edge. As her driving proves – she outruns Bond's Bentley – she is living dangerously and recklessly. Bond next encounters her over the gaming tables at Royale. Since this was the tenth anniversary of Fleming's starting to write the Bond books, it was a clever move to open ON HER MAJESTY'S SECRET SERVICE at the scene of CASINO ROYALE's action and to have Bond reminisce about his battle with Le Chiffre. Fleming reveals that, for Bond, there had been 'a drama and a poignancy about that particular adventure' that drew him every year back to Royale. We are also told that, during these annual retreats, Bond always visits the local church and the granite cross in the little graveyard that reads, 'Vesper Lynd RIP'.

Tracy gambles recklessly at Royale and when she inevitably loses she reveals she has no money. Bond saves her reputation by bailing her out. They spend the night together, after which Tracy throws him out.

But Marc-Ange Draco, Tracy's father, believes Bond is just the right man to straighten Tracy out. Bond isn't convinced, so Draco offers him one million pounds in gold bullion as a dowry if he will marry Tracy. Bond turns the offer down, insisting that what Tracy needs is a doctor. He concedes he will do all he can for her and will see her again, but only if she seeks professional help. Draco accepts Bond's terms reluctantly and insists on helping Bond in any way he can. Bond asks for any information on the whereabouts of Ernst Stavro Blofeld.

Draco manages to trace Blofeld to an address in Switzerland, where, it transpires, he is supposedly seeking a cure for allergies in his clinic on top of an alp, Piz Gloria. Not only that, but he is actively seeking recognition of his title as le Comte Balthazar de Bleuville and has asked the Royal College of Arms in London to authenticate his claim. Working with the College of Arms on the case – during which Bond learns that his own family motto is 'The World Is Not Enough' – 007 devises a plan in which he will travel to Piz Gloria disguised as a representative of the college, Sir Hilary Bray (Hilary Bray was, of course, the name of one of Fleming's friends).

Arriving at Piz Gloria just days before Christmas, Bond finds Blofeld's henchwoman, the hideous Irma Bunt, and ten gorgeous English girls who are ostensibly undergoing treatment for allergies. But Blofeld is up to his old tricks. The unwitting girls are being brainwashed into spreading biological warfare agents such as anthrax and foot-and-mouth on their return to England.

His cover blown on Christmas Eve, Bond is forced to escape Piz Gloria on skis, pursued by SPECTRE agents, in one of Ian Fleming's most excitingly written passages. Exhausted and without a weapon, Bond is pursued to a village where a party is in full swung. There seems no escape from the SPECTRE agents until he literally bumps into Tracy, who has been recovering from her depression at a nearby clinic.

Tracy helps Bond escape and he realises he'll never find another girl like her. He proposes marriage and she accepts. Work comes first, however, and Bond and Marc-Ange Draco launch a helicopter assault on Piz Gloria. Blofeld's alpine fortress is destroyed but Blofeld, pursued by Bond in a thrilling bobsleigh chase, escapes.

Bond and Tracy are married on New Year's Day. But Ian Fleming has a superb sting in his tail and, as Mr and Mrs Bond drive to their honeymoon in Tracy's Lancia, a red Maserati containing Blofeld overtakes them. There's the flash of automatic gunfire and Bond ends the novel cradling the dead Tracy in his lap.

Everything about ON HER MAJESTY'S SECRET SERVICE works perfectly and the confidence Ian Fleming was feeling about Bond in those first few months of 1962 comes through clearly in every single page.

There is even a wonderful moment in the novel reflecting when the literary and cinematic worlds of Bond collided in Jamaica. Bond, still undercover as Sir Hilary Bray, is escorted to the public-access area of Piz Gloria by Irma Bunt. This part of Piz Gloria has become very fashionable with the international set, Bunt explains, and she points out the film star, Ursula Andress, to Bond. 'What a wonderful tan she has!' Bunt explains.

This was, perhaps, the most obvious manifestation of Ian Fleming's sense of humour in the entire Bond series. The reason Ursula Andress has a wonderful tan in the novel was because she was filming *Dr. No* in Jamaica: Fleming had written that line after visiting the set and meeting Andress, with whom he was particularly taken, for the first time.

'I remember the first time Ian Fleming came to the set,' Andress recalls. 'He was a fascinating man. So full of information. So full of knowledge. He was a lovely man.' Fleming, accompanied by Noël Coward, Stephen Spender and Peter Quennell, was also present when Ursula Andress's now classic emergence from the sea was filmed. It was a fraught day because Andress had gashed her leg badly on some coral just prior to the shot and her knee had become badly swollen. The filmmakers covered her injuries with makeup and certainly they cannot be seen in the finished film.

Ann Fleming was a less frequent visitor to the *Dr. No* set but she was there with Fleming during the scene in which Dr No's agents rake the beach where Bond, Honey and Quarrel are hiding with machine-gun fire. In a funny letter to Evelyn Waugh, which revealed much of her contempt for James Bond, Ann wrote, 'They were shooting a beach scene, the hero and heroine cowering behind a ridge of sand to escape death from a machine gun mounted on a deep-sea fishing craft borrowed from a neighbouring hotel and manned by communist negroes.' Describing how the sand ridge was 'planted with French letters full of explosive' which were blown up 'by magic mechanism' throwing up the sand in little puffs, Ann then relates how the machine gun made only 'mild pops – but I was assured it will be improved on the soundtrack'. She concludes by saying how it was all in vain because 'unluckily a detachment of the American Navy entered the bay in speed launches and buggered it all up'.

With location filming completed, the *Dr. No* production moved back to Pinewood Studios, just outside London, in late February 1962 where the production designer, Ken Adam, had been overseeing the construction of the sets that would give the film such a distinctive look despite its relatively modest budget.

Final bits of casting were completed as well. Bernard Lee was cast as M; while 35-year-old Lois Maxwell was signed as Miss Moneypenny. Maxwell was desperate for work: her husband, Peter, had suffered a massive heart attack on their son's second birthday and he wasn't expected to survive.

'I called five different people with whom I'd worked,' she recalls. 'Terence Young, Cubby Broccoli and three other directors and producers. I said, "Peter is very ill and I have two little children and I will do anything." It was about the end of January that Terence Young called me. Peter had recovered somewhat but he still wasn't well enough to work or anything. Terence said he wanted me to go and talk to him and Cubby about *Dr. No*. They offered me the choice of playing either Moneypenny or Sylvia, which Eunice Gayson played eventually.

'I said I'd rather play Moneypenny. I remember the scene with Sylvia, she is discovered in Bond's flat in his pyjama top putting a golf ball. Well, I didn't know how to putt a golf ball and I didn't fancy myself in Bond's pyjama top, so I said I would play Moneypenny if they would allow me to give her a background.'

To help her flesh out Moneypenny, Maxwell was able to talk to Fleming himself about the character. 'I only talked to him about three or four times in all,' she recalls. 'But I found myself liking him tremendously. He was very much like my husband. He had this sardonic smile and attitude. I don't think he took Bond very seriously and I think he would have been highly amused if he had thought there would be James Bond fan clubs and that half the world would be absolutely enamoured with this character of his!'

For Bernard Lee, *Dr. No* marked the first of eleven appearances as M; for Maxwell, it was the first of her fourteen outings as Moneypenny.

By the time the cast and crew of *Dr. No* started work at Pinewood, Sean Connery had relaxed noticeably into the role of James Bond and any lingering doubts about his suitability were dispersed for anyone viewing the daily rushes. Connery had been encouraged by the producers and by Terence Young to beef up the humour in his portrayal of Bond in Jamaica and everyone instinctively knew that adding this spin, this self-spoofing dry, dark humour, was what would distinguish *Dr. No* from other standard spy films.

Two early examples of characteristic Bondian humour are the scene in which Bond, arriving at Government House with the dead chauffeur in the back seat, says to the security man, 'Sergeant, make sure he doesn't get away'; and, later, after the hearse that has been trying to force Bond's car off the road plunges into a fiery demise, he quips, 'I think they were on their way to a funeral.'

This humour was truly innovative, as Sean Connery himself now rightly says: 'That dry one-line humour we initiated in *Dr. No* is now all over the movies.'

As Connery's confidence grew, so, too, did the director Terence Young's. By the middle of the shoot, Young truly seems to have got a firm handle on what he wanted and his confidence is never more obvious in the film than the way he filmed the introduction of the James Bond character.

James Bond's first appearance in *Dr. No*, shot at Pinewood, is, arguably, the greatest entrance of any screen hero. It is a scene in which the direction, writing, performances and music combine perfectly – and one that still impresses, no matter how many times one has seen it.

It is set, appropriately enough, in a casino, and Terence Young's camera concentrates on the character of Sylvia Trench (Eunice Gayson), a character created for the film and destined to be 007's first screen conquest. She is sitting opposite a dark-haired man whose face we do not see, duelling with him over *chemin de fer*. Having lost twice to the man, she refuses to be beaten and speaks to the cashier. The dark-haired man takes a cigarette out of his case as Sylvia writes out a cheque.

SYLVIA: I need another thousand.
MAN: I admire your courage, Miss, er . . .?
SYLVIA: Trench. Sylvia Trench. I admire your luck, Mr . . .?
MAN: (*lighting his cigarette*) Bond . . . James Bond . . .

Monty Norman's magnificent theme comes up and we see Connery's face for the first time. The movies were never quite the same ever again.

'The introduction to Bond was a take-off of the star build-up for every picture you've ever seen,' claimed Terence Young. 'Remember how it begins with that gun-metal cigarette case and lighter. Then the hand turning a card, and you see an arm and shoulder, and the woman on the other side. There are at least ten or fifteen different set-ups without seeing Bond: everyone staring in admiration at this man who is winning all the time.

'That was my intention. It was the only way I thought we could make a Bond film. To heat it up a bit. To give it a sense of humour. And to make it as cynical as possible.'

Dr. No wrapped on 30 March 1962 at Pinewood Studios, just days before THE SPY WHO LOVED ME was published to an astoundingly violent reaction. Typical was the article written by Charles Stainsby, editor of the weekly magazine *Today*. The article began by calling the novel 'one of the worst, most boring, badly constructed novels we have read' and then went on to accuse Fleming of producing 'the nastiest and most sadistic writing of our day'. According to Stainsby, THE SPY WHO LOVED ME 'is all part and parcel of the strange nastiness which afflicts many of the Top People in Britain.'

Today, he continued, stood 'firmly against all the things represented by Mr Fleming. We find his writings disgusting drivel. We deplore the manner in which they have been puffed. And we deplore even more the fact that a respectable publisher chooses to put his imprint on them.'

Given that *Today* had actively sought the serialisation rights to THE SPY WHO LOVED ME after the *Daily Express* had turned it down, there was more than a hint of hypocrisy about the article. Negotiations about the serialisation of THE SPY WHO LOVED ME had been ended on Fleming's own instructions, and, looking back now on the article, one is struck by the fact that, if there was, indeed, a 'strange nastiness' afflicting the Top People in Britain in 1962, it had not left *Today* itself untouched.

Fleming believed, arguably with some justification, that *Today* was taking it out on him for his refusing permission for them to serialise THE SPY WHO LOVED ME. Unfortunately, he appeared on the BBC programme *Tonight* and made that very allegation openly. When Stainsby denied Fleming's version of events and started muttering the word 'defamation', Fleming, perhaps mindful of the looming court case with Kevin McClory over THUNDERBALL, backed down and apologised.

Had *Today*'s attack on him been an isolated one, Fleming could have lived with it. But THE SPY WHO LOVED ME incurred the wrath of many reviewers who had previously championed Bond. Curiously, the critics who attacked Fleming most severely for, allegedly, producing a work of pornography were male. Female reviewers, such as Esther Howard in the *Spectator*, were much more positive about the book.

But the rare, brave voices raised in favour of the book were drowned out by the howl of protests from the majority. Of course, there was a sinister undercurrent to all this. Success is always despised in England and Ian Fleming was perceived now as being simply too successful. The testimonial from President Kennedy and the film deal and the bestseller lists meant that even those critics once friendlily disposed towards Ian Fleming had decided it was time to knock him down. That he had written the controversial THE SPY WHO LOVED ME, a book that made this job so much easier for them, was unfortunate.

Ian Fleming knew, deep down, that there was a thinly disguised vein of jealousy running through all the attacks on him when THE SPY WHO LOVED ME was published. But his knowing this hardly helped. The cumulative effect of the controversy was to undermine his confidence and convince him that his experiment with the book had seriously backfired.

Worse, two successive James Bond books in consecutive years – THUNDERBALL and now THE SPY WHO LOVED ME – had caused him real trouble for entirely different reasons. It was a hefty left and right and, after all the excitement of the film *Dr. No* in the first three months of 1962, Fleming was plunged into a kind of despair about Bond again. Ann Fleming noted that he was 'in a decline because of the bad reviews'.

Fleming knew that he'd returned to formula big time in ON HER MAJESTY'S SECRET SERVICE, the first draft of which was complete; but that would not be published until the spring of 1963. All Fleming could do for now was to weather the storm. He asked Jonathan Cape to make sure THE SPY WHO LOVED ME had, in his words, 'as short a life as possible', and requested that there be no reprints or paperback editions. Ann Fleming, displaying, yet again, her contempt for Bond while happily living off the proceeds, wrote to Evelyn Waugh about Fleming's demands on his publishers: 'I am doing my best to reverse this foolish gesture because of the yellow silk for the drawing-room walls,' she wrote caustically.

In the event, THE SPY WHO LOVED ME was banned in several countries for a while; and, although Cape eventually went against Fleming's specific request by bringing out a paperback edition, they did not do so until 1967, three years after his death.

So wounded was Fleming by the critical reaction to THE SPY WHO LOVED ME that he even mentioned the novel in his will. He stipulated that no film be made of it: the title might be used, but no other element from the book was to make it to the screen.

The late spring and summer of 1962 were very important ones in the developing cult of James Bond. For Ian Fleming, this period involved a long trip to Japan to research his next Bond book, YOU ONLY LIVE TWICE. He was also painted by Amherst Villiers and Fleming bought the painting and had it reproduced the following spring in the limited edition of ON HER MAJESTY'S SECRET SERVICE.

A measure of how potent a brand Bond had become was underlined on 29 May 1962, just a day after Fleming's 54th birthday, when the Soviet organ *Izvestia* launched a savage attack on Ian Fleming and James Bond in an editorial. Describing Fleming as 'a tool of American propaganda', *Izvestia* believed America 'must be in a bad way if they need recourse to the help of an English freebooter – a retired spy turned mediocre writer'.

Fleming thought this was hilarious and desperately wanted to use *Izvestia*'s comments on the cover of ON HER MAJESTY'S SECRET SERVICE. Jonathan Cape persuaded him against it.

But the main development of James Bond was taking place in the editing rooms at Pinewood Studios in Buckinghamshire, where Terence Young and the editor Peter Hunt were shaping *Dr. No*.

Dr. No revolutionised film editing and, at first, Peter Hunt was mortified by the cuts Terence Young demanded to give the film its unique internal energy, which made it seem so original on release.

'Nobody ever cut pictures the way we cut the Bond films,' Terence Young said years later. '*Dr. No* and *From Russia With Love* were an absolute breath of fresh air in the cutting rooms.

'Even David Lean, who was a good friend of mine, used to come in and watch *Dr. No* on the moviola while we were cutting it. He was cutting *Lawrence of Arabia* in the next room at the same time, and often used to say he wished we could swop films. "This is fun," he said to me on one occasion, "this is *real* cinema."'

By late July, Terence Young was able to show the film to a select audience whom he had invited to the Travellers Club. The eclectic gathering included, Ian, Ann and Caspar Fleming, the Duke and Duchess of Bedford, Lord and Lady Bessborough and Peter Quennell.

Ann Fleming later called it an 'abominable occasion', even if Mary Crickmere, the Flemings' cook, found the film 'quite gripping'.

'I wish I had,' Ann complained to Evelyn Waugh, 'for our fortune depends on it. There were howls of laughter when the tarantula walks up James Bond's body; it was a close-up of a spider on a piece of anatomy too small to be an arm.'

Fleming, himself, did not enjoy the occasion and, indeed, his approach to the film was always equivocal. In public, he did everything Eon might ask of him by playing the company man.

'Those who've read the book are likely to be disappointed,' he said to *Time* in October 1962, 'but those who haven't will find it a wonderful movie. Audiences laugh in all the right places.' He told Cubby Broccoli and Harry Saltzman that the film was 'wonderful'. And he was generous about *Dr. No*'s leading man: 'Sean Connery was a good choice as James Bond,' he was quoted as saying.

But, privately, Fleming gave the impression to others that he was not satisfied with the film. Alan Barnes and Marcus Hearn, in their book *Kiss Kiss Bang Bang* (B T Batsford, 1997), quote Peter Garnham, who was Fleming's proofreader and research assistant, who accompanied Fleming to another preview screening of *Dr. No* in Leicester Square.

'Ian strode out as the end credits rolled,' recalled Garnham, 'said not a word, hailed a taxi, and sat silently as we were driven back to the pub across from his office. He got out, paid the cab, walked into the pub and ordered a couple of drinks. He took a swig and finally addressed me: "Dreadful. Simply dreadful." We never mentioned the movies after that.' *Dr. No* premiered on 5 October 1962 at the London Pavilion and it could not have been more timely.

'It was all a question of timing,' said Terence Young. 'I think we arrived in not only the right year, but the right week of the right month. We hit audiences at *precisely* the right moment. I think the first Bond picture was the most perfectly timed film ever made.'

In their introduction to *Kiss Kiss Bang Bang*, Barnes and Hearn wrote,

It seems a staggering coincidence that *Dr. No* was unleashed upon the British public in the very same week as both The Beatles' debut 45 *Love Me Do* and snoot-cocking television revue *That Was the Week that Was*. All three have come to be recognised in their respective media; all three are held to have heralded the beginning of a new epoch, to have encapsulated the shiny new freedoms of the sixties. If we must pinpoint the dawning of the modern age, then 5 October 1962 seems as good a date as any.

Something else happened in October 1962 as well. Before the month was out, the world teetered on the brink of all-out nuclear war as President Kennedy and the Soviet premier Khrushchev played nuclear poker for the highest stakes – the future of the entire world – over the siting of Russian nuclear missiles in Cuba. Kennedy called Khrushchev's bluff, Khrushchev blinked first and backed down, and the world breathed a collective sigh of relief.

Dr. No, with its nuclear-powered madman interfering with American interests from a small Caribbean island, was, as Terence Young observed, definitely released in the right month.

Kicked off by Maurice Binder's electric title sequence, including the trademark gun barrel – with James Bond (actually his stunt double Bob Simmons, not Sean Connery, in the first three films) turning to the camera and firing, after which a red curtain of blood seeps down across the screen – and John Barry's pulsating arrangement of Monty Norman's 'James Bond Theme', it's easy to see why, even forty years later, *Dr. No* was such a breath of fresh air in British cinema. As Terence Young rightly pointed out,

> Ian Fleming's stories arrived in a dead, grey period. All the realistic 'kitchen sink' dramas were weighing everything down. London was sinking under the weight of that deadly kitchen sink. It was getting to the point where people couldn't see anything outside their dismal interiors. Then we came along and they found something different. Outside.

Young once said, many years after *Dr. No* had premiered, that the three things that made the film work were 'Sean Connery, Sean Connery and Sean Connery'. While there is more than a grain of truth in this, he was, perhaps modestly, playing down his own contribution to *Dr. No*'s success.

Connery was, without a doubt, a new kind of hero. Utterly classless, the Connery-Bond of *Dr. No* is able to inhabit the elegant Mayfair world of the casino at the start of the film, wearing black tie and oozing *savoir faire*, but he is still Fleming's ruthless 'blunt instrument', never more so than when he shoots Professor Dent in almost cold blood in what remains the series' most violent single act. Connery manages to reconcile these seemingly opposing characteristics so that the join between the inveterate seducer and the ruthless killer can hardly be seen.

But Connery's performance was still in transition. Like everyone else involved in this first Bond film, he was finding his feet and there are undoubtedly moments when the 'rough diamond' Ken Adam has referred to burst from beneath the sheen Terence Young applied to Connery's style. This manifests itself in Bond's being occasionally too harsh towards the other characters. The worst example occurs just after Bond and Quarrel arrive on Crab Key: Bond's curt instruction to Quarrel to 'fetch my shoes' is simply unforgivable.

Moments like this made some critics question whether Broccoli and Saltzman had made the right choice for Bond. Indeed, the critics were divided over Connery. Angela Milne in *Punch* believed, 'Sean Connery is a delightful Bond, stunningly handsome and nicely light-hearted as he pursues the forces of evil from his glossy London world to an even glossier Jamaica.' Although she put her finger precisely on the transitional nature of the performance by adding, 'But his metamorphosis (even his well-known sexual prowess is turned into a joke, a "you know *him*" between film and audience) produces one jarring note and an important one; the callous killings now seem the more callous. That problem will have to be worked out before the Bond image is all set for a series.'

But *Time* magazine was scathing about Connery, suggesting that 'the dark good looks of Scottish actor Sean Connery do not suggest Fleming's tasteful pagan so much as a used-up gigolo.'

Derek Hill in *Scene* accepted that Connery played Bond with 'exactly the right mixture of strong-arm fascist and telly commercial salesman', but deplored the film, claiming 'the skill with which the men behind *Dr. No* present the adventures of their monstrous hero disguises the fact that our applause is invited for jingoism, thuggishness and blind obedience.'

Dr. No was applauded by the popular press but denounced by left-wing critics in supposedly more serious publications. The *Daily Worker* labelled the film as 'vicious hokum, skilfully designed to appeal to the filmgoer's basest feelings' and accused the film of having 'racist implications'; but it was the po-faced *Films and Filming* that missed the joke most of all and, in a remarkably silly critique, went beyond even Paul Johnson's tirade against DR. NO in *The New Statesman*, four years earlier. 'There hasn't been a film like *Dr. No* since . . . when? The Mickey Spillane thrillers of the middle fifties?' bemoaned *Film and Filming*'s Richard Whitehall, who continued:

> *Dr. No* is the headiest box-office concoction of sex and sadism ever brewed in a British studio, strictly bath-tub hooch but a brutally potent intoxicant for all that. Just as Mike Hammer was the softening-up for James Bond, so James Bond is the softening up for . . . what? A fascist cinema uncorrupted by moral scruples? The riot of a completely anarchist cinema? *Dr. No* could be the breakthrough to something . . . but what? At one point Bond nonchalantly fires half a dozen shots [*sic*] into the back of a helpless opponent – the British cinema will never be the same again.

But Whitehall wasn't finished there. Turning his ire next on the then secretary of the British Board of Film Censors, John Trevelyan, who had granted *Dr. No* an 'A' certificate after insisting on just one minor cut, Whitehall raged,

> This is one of the X-iest films imaginable, a monstrously over-blown sex fantasy of nightmarish proportions. Morally the film is indefensible with its lovingly detailed excesses, the contemporary equivalent of watching Christians being fed to the lions, and yet its lascivious dedication to violence is a genuine hypnotic.
>
> Bursting at the seams with violence – the perfect film for a sado-masochistic society – there's never been a British film like *Dr. No* since . . . what?

Whitehall's over-the-top attack on *Dr. No* seems quite absurd today; but, if nothing else, it underlines the precise impact the film had on critics and audiences alike in 1962.

And perhaps critics like Whitehall wrote in despair about a film that, to them at least, eschewed all the liberal and socialist principles they espoused, but one they knew was bound to be a popular hit. Certainly, despite extremely negative reviews like Whitehall's – or, more likely, *because* of them – *Dr. No* became an enormous hit in Britain, earning back the money it had cost in the UK alone, thereby ensuring there would be a second Bond film (Broccoli and Saltzman had already decided that would be *From Russian With Love*).

But, despite the money rolling in, United Artists suffered a bout of nervousness about the movie's potential in the US. Exhibitors had expressed doubts about their ability to sell a film starring an unknown 'limey truck driver'. To the horror and fury of Broccoli and Saltzman, United Artists held back on the American release of *Dr. No* until May 1963, and then released it at an Oklahoma drive-in theatre.

But United Artists' doubts were to be short-lived – and they would never have doubts about the viability of James Bond Stateside ever again. The Oklahoma audience was fantastic, while the reviews were more cinematically intelligent than comparable 'serious' reviews in Britain. *Variety* believed that 'as a screen hero, James Bond is clearly here to stay. He will win no Oscars but a heck of a lot of enthusiastic followers.' While the respected American critic Bosley Crowther found *Dr. No* 'lively and amusing'.

Word of mouth, coupled with good reviews, boosted *Dr. No*'s box office. Costing $1 million to make, the film made back twenty times that sum worldwide. Cubby Broccoli and Harry Saltzman were suddenly very rich men indeed.

Ian Fleming, though, the man who had created it all, was curiously detached from it. James Bond had always been an intensely personal creation; but now the future of James Bond, at least the worldwide branding of the character, was in the hands of others. As John Pearson noted so succinctly, 'His private daydreams had become a world phenomenon, but he had very little contact with it all now.'

In the last weeks of 1962 and the first of 1963, Fleming was feeling melancholic and apprehensive. Largely, this was due to a downturn in his health again and he found writing YOU ONLY LIVE TWICE in the first three months of 1963 at Goldeneye very hard going.

'I'm grinding away at Bond's latest,' he confessed to a friend. 'But the going gets harder and harder and duller and duller and I don't really know what I'm going to do with him. He's become a personal – if not a public – nuisance. Anyway he's had a good run, which is more than most of us can say. Everything seems a lot of trouble these days. Too much trouble.'

Of course, his friends had heard this all before and, again, Fleming's professed boredom with 'grinding away at Bond's latest' is not reflected in the completed book. YOU ONLY LIVE TWICE ranks among the best of the Fleming Bond books and rivals FROM RUSSIA WITH LOVE as the Bond book richest in detail and characterisation. But it is also a strange and bizarre novel and Fleming's increasing obsession with his own mortality and rebirth seeps into every page. Raymond Benson has called it 'haunting and foreboding'.

Having suffered a nervous breakdown following Tracy's murder at the end of ON HER MAJESTY'S SECRET SERVICE, Bond is given one last chance to redeem himself before M kicks him out of the British Secret Service. Stripping him of his 007 number, M sends Bond to Japan on an 'impossible' mission: to persuade Tiger Tanaka, head of the Japanese Secret Service, to let Britain share in Japan's new deciphering system, called Magic 44.

Bond pulls himself together as he and Tiger Tanaka gradually establish a rapport, one that is characterised by a great deal of amusing banter between them. Tiger eventually agrees to let Britain in on Magic 44 – but on one condition. Recently, a Swiss couple, Dr Guntram Shatterhand and Frau Emmy Shatterhand, have moved to Japan and bought a castle on the island of Kyushu. There, the Shatterhands have created a 'garden of death', having stocked the garden with poisonous plants, snakes, scorpions and lethal spiders, and the lakes and streams with poisonous and carnivorous fish. Dr Shatterhand is, Tiger explains, a 'collector of death'. The purpose of the garden is to lure the suicidally inclined members of Japanese society to go out in a blaze of glory.

Shatterhand's lethal garden has become an embarrassment to the Japanese government and they want rid of him. But they do not want to be seen to intervene directly. Therefore, they will give Bond the secrets of Magic 44 – but only if he will infiltrate Shatterhand's castle and assassinate him.

Teamed with Kissy Suzuki, a diving girl and a former Hollywood starlet who is related to the superintendent of police near Shatterhand's castle, Bond's task is to swim the channel to the castle and kill Shatterhand. Bond knows it is a near-impossible feat – he likens it to trying to scale Windsor Castle – but he is given added incentive when he sees pictures of the Shatterhands and recognises them as Ernst Stavro Blofeld and Irma Bunt. Thus, YOU ONLY LIVE TWICE suddenly switches into a story of personal revenge.

Successfully breaking into the castle, Bond is captured by Blofeld and Bunt, but he manages to kill Blofeld and destroy the castle. However Bond is knocked unconscious during his escape and loses his memory.

Missing, presumed dead – his obituary appears in *The Times* – Bond ends the novel cared for by Kissy in her fishing village. Unable to remember anything, Bond knows only what Kissy has told him: that his name is Taro Todoroki, that he is her lover and they make a good life from fishing. Many months pass and there is no sign of Bond's memory returning, until one day he reads about Russia and it triggers a memory. Bond believes Russia has been very important to him in the past and he begs Kissy to help him go there to try to regain his memory. Resigned to losing him, Kissy agrees to help him travel to Russia. She does not tell him she's pregnant with his child.

As a cliffhanger – an amnesiac and vulnerable James Bond travelling naïvely to Russia – YOU ONLY LIVE TWICE's ending couldn't be bettered. Bond's obituary, too, gave Fleming an opportunity to poke some gentle fun at himself. Written by M, the obituary reveals much more about Bond's past than Fleming had hitherto given his readers, and M, while writing that Bond had 'an impetuous strain in his nature, with a streak of the foolhardy', even writes that Bond possessed 'the Nelson Touch'. M goes on to write about Bond's adventures, which attracted publicity in the foreign press and made him 'a public figure against his will'. So much so, writes M, that 'a series of popular books came to be written around him by a personal friend and former colleague'. M dismisses the books as 'high-flown and romanticised caricatures'.

Clearly, Fleming had fun in writing Bond's obituary and the quality of writing in YOU ONLY LIVE TWICE is remarkable for a man who claimed he had no idea what to do with Bond next. Bond's character is developed so well in the novel that, as Raymond Benson points out, 'it marks what might have been a totally new direction for Fleming had he not died in 1964'.

Death, mortality and rebirth are the themes throughout YOU ONLY LIVE TWICE and there are many haunting images that linger in the mind long after one has read the book. No other Bond book quite mirrors Ian Fleming's state of mind at the time he wrote it as YOU ONLY LIVE TWICE does. Even the structure of the book reflects a personal belief of Fleming: it is separated into two halves, Part One called 'It is better to travel hopefully . . .'; Part Two '. . . than to arrive'.

And, when challenged by Tiger Tanaka to compose a traditional Japanese haiku poem, Bond comes up with:

> You only live twice:
> Once when you are born,
> And once when you look death in the face.

As an epitaph for both Fleming and Bond, it could not have been more perfect.

Fleming returned to London with the manuscript of YOU ONLY LIVE TWICE just prior to the beginning of shooting of *From Russia With Love* on 1 April 1963, and the publication of ON HER MAJESTY'S SECRET SERVICE a few days later.

After the traumas of THUNDERBALL and THE SPY WHO LOVED ME, Fleming could relax when ON HER MAJESTY'S SECRET SERVICE became an unqualified success, both critically and commercially. Those critics who had wilfully misinterpreted THE SPY WHO LOVED ME just a year earlier now seemed to have forgiven Fleming for his temerarious success and, collectively, the reviews for ON HER MAJESTY'S SECRET SERVICE were the best he'd enjoyed for years.

Intriguingly, just a month later, in May 1963, Fleming was approached by the Hollywood producer Norman Felton to script a Bond-type series for American television. This series would feature an American agent called Napoleon Solo and eventually reached the screen as *The Man From U.N.C.L.E.* The money was good and Fleming started writing down ideas. But then he had second thoughts. He believed Solo would inevitably be too similar to Bond and that his working on the series would cause 'bad blood' between himself and Eon Productions.

Mindful of the ongoing problems with Kevin McClory, and what he regarded as his shabby treatment over the THUNDERBALL case, Fleming extricated himself utterly but honourably from *The Man From U.N.C.L.E.* In a letter, he assigned to Norman Felton 'all my rights and interest in any material written or contributed by me in connection with an original television series featuring a character named Napoleon Solo.' Fleming acknowledged his receipt of the £1 he had requested in consideration of his assigning his rights in Napoleon Solo to Felton.

Fleming's assessment that his working on *The Man From U.N.C.L.E.* would irritate Eon Productions was probably correct. Eon had worked hard to ensure that *Dr. No* would be a success and now, embarking on *From Russia With Love*, the last thing they needed was Bond's creator working on a series about another secret agent.

Broccoli and Saltzman were determined to make *From Russia With Love* better than *Dr. No* and had been allocated a budget twice that of the first film by United Artists to ensure the new film's success.

'We think it's silly to cut corners,' Broccoli said in an interview. 'We know from *Dr. No* that Bond films are important. They're important because this is the type of entertainment that people prefer. This is what people want to see. Bond is a unique hero. There's none of this rubbish about I won't pull my gun until three seconds after he's pulled his.

'We try to keep the character of Bond as a hard, sometimes cruel man in the films. You might even call it "sadism for the family".'

This ethos permeates *From Russia With Love* but was amended from the next film, *Goldfinger*, onwards: after *From Russia With Love*, the grittiness was replaced by a more stylised violence, which was much more sophisticated but which, for some, inevitably meant an essential element of Bond was lost for ever. That is why some – though by no means all – people associated with the series regard *From Russia With Love* as the best Bond film.

'*Russia* is much more realistic than the others,' Richard Maibaum said. 'We hadn't gone so far yet into the fantastical – it was entirely believable. Real people in real situations.

'*Dr. No* told us what the audience liked, what they sparkled to. So when I wrote *From Russia With Love*, I think we crystallised the kind of thing that the Bond movies should be. That film was the one in which we set the style. It still remains my favourite.'

'*From Russia With Love* is my favourite Bond film and it's the best of the series,' believed Terence Young. 'The tone was set in *Dr. No*, but completed in *From Russia With Love*. After that I think they have been repeating themselves – taking bits from the early movies that were good and using them again and again.

'It's sad really because the series has ended up caricaturing itself. I mean, Bond was already a kind of caricature and to parody himself is asking for trouble. After *Thunderball* the human elements disappeared, too, with gadgets and machines taking the place of people.'

'*From Russia With Love* is my favourite Bond film,' says Sean Connery. 'I liked the story very much and I think it has more credibility than *Goldfinger* or *Thunderball*, which were quite fantastic. As the films got bigger and more expensive, they became more involved with hardware than people.'

Nonetheless, even *From Russia With Love* displayed the producers' penchant for largesse. One set alone – the gigantic room where the chess match is played at the start of the film – cost £150,000, and that for a set in which none of the principal characters appears.

'*From Russia With Love* is a much bigger picture,' boasted Saltzman, showing journalists around the chess-room set. 'Just look at this set. We use 160 extras in this scene. And it's all for one-and-a-half minutes of film. Without Bond . . .'

Many of the talents from both in front of and behind the cameras on *Dr. No* reassembled at Pinewood Studios on 1 April 1963 for the first day of principal photography. Rejoining Sean Connery in his second Bond film were Bernard Lee as M, Lois Maxwell as Moneypenny and Eunice Gayson as Sylvia; even Anthony Dawson, Dr No's hapless lieutenant Professor Dent, returned as Ernst Stavro Blofeld himself, whose face is never seen in the film (the voice was provided by Eric Pohlmann).

Terence Young was back at the helm, Ted Moore was again director of photography, Peter Hunt resumed duties as editor, and John Barry now wrote the entire music score, bar the theme song (crooned over the end credits by Matt Munro), which was written by Lionel Bart.

Ironically, in view of Harry Saltzman's obvious pride over the chess-room set, Ken Adam, production designer of *Dr. No*, whose designs had added so much to the first film, was missing. Stanley Kubrick, having been mightily impressed by *Dr. No*, 'poached' him for *Dr. Strangelove*. Syd Cain took over production design of *From Russia With Love*.

The main title designer Maurice Binder's name was missing from the credits, too. Although his famous gun-barrel sequence still appeared in *From Russia With Love* and *Goldfinger*, he did not return to the series until *Thunderball* in 1965, after which he designed the titles for every subsequent official Bond movie until his death in 1991.

The first day's shooting – on Stage B at Pinewood Studios – was set in M's office. Displaying considerably more faith in the future of James Bond than United Artists initially, Broccoli and Saltzman had had the foresight to retain the set from *Dr. No*. The scene introduced another regular member of the cast – Desmond Llewelyn as Major Boothroyd (Q). Boothroyd had been played, rather blandly, by Peter Burton in *Dr. No*. When Burton was unavailable for *From Russia With Love*, Terence Young cast Llewelyn, with whom he had worked on *They Were Not Divided* in 1950. Boothroyd's character was not defined, however, until the next film, *Goldfinger*, under the director Guy Hamilton. Desmond Llewelyn had no idea that *From Russia With Love* – which was, to him, just another job – would bring him international late-life fame, nor could he know that *From Russia With Love* was to be but the first of his seventeen appearances as Q, up to and including 1999's *The World is Not Enough*.

Other cast members joining *From Russia With Love* were Robert Shaw as Grant, the former model Daniela Bianchi as Tatiana Romanova, Pedro Armendariz (recommended to Terence Young by John Ford, no less) as Kerim Bey and, most incongruously of all, Kurt Weill's widow, Lotte Lenya, as the loathsome Rosa Klebb ('miscasting of the year,' sniffed *Esquire* when she was signed for the part). It was one of the most extraordinary, eclectic and brilliant casts ever assembled for a Bond movie.

Despite its status now as a Bondian classic, *From Russia With Love* could easily have been a disaster. It was plagued by problems on and off set, and one of the fundamental ones was with the script, which was by no means complete even when shooting commenced.

The main problem was the introduction of SPECTRE into the proceedings. Fleming's original novel had had a relatively straight-forward plot to lure James Bond to an ignominious death, which would destroy the reputation of the British Secret Service. But Cubby Broccoli and Harry Saltzman were always keen to keep the Bond films as apolitical as ever, and so Joanna Harwood, who initially adapted the book, and then Richard Maibaum, who wrote the actual screenplay, struggled with the concept of having SPECTRE now playing the British off against the Russians. Thus, Rosa Klebb and Grant are now SPECTRE agents, even though Tatiana, the unwitting lure for Bond, still thinks she is 'doing it all for Mother Russia', as Grant puts it, because she is unaware Klebb has defected from the Russian state police to SPECTRE.

Although the film appears, to a casual observer, to follow Fleming's source novel very closely, SPECTRE's involvement threw the whole script out of kilter from the start. Even the decoding device, the 'McGuffin' of both book and film, had to be renamed: the Spektor from the novel becomes a Lektor in the film, for obvious reasons.

Cinematically, too, it was felt that *From Russia With Love*, with all its Balkan intrigue, would prove to be a much more claustrophobic and confined movie than its predecessor, which had benefited enormously from extensive location work in Jamaica. And again, unlike *Dr. No*'s screenplay, which had been a straightforward action-adventure yarn with sci-fi trappings, *From Russia With Love* was a complex story peopled with exotic, colourful characters.

Broccoli and Saltzman believed, therefore, that the picture needed opening up at the end. Thus the vicious fight between Bond and Grant on board the Orient Express, which forms the real climax of the novel (Bond's 'death' at the feet of Rosa Klebb notwithstanding), is followed in the movie by two well-staged, if somewhat redundant, chase sequences: a helicopter assault on Bond, which owes a huge debt to the crop-duster buzzing Cary Grant in Hitchcock's *North By Northwest*; and a boat chase in the Gulf of Venice (filmed in Scotland when bad weather precluded filming on the proper location).

Another problem facing Maibaum, who tried to remain as close to Fleming's original as he could despite the many chances he was inevitably having to make, was that FROM RUSSIA WITH LOVE featured many violent and overtly sexual scenes that had to be toned down if the film version was to retain an 'A' certificate.

So the fight between the two gypsy girls, a grisly scene in the book, which even Fleming's most robust defenders are forced to admit goes too far, is much tamer in the film; Rosa Klebb's attempted seduction of Tatiana, toe-curlingly overt in the novel, is much more subtle in the film; and the fight to the death between Bond and Grant is much less bloody than Fleming's version, even though it remains one of the finest fights in screen history.

Nevertheless, even the toned-down sequences came dangerously close to falling foul of the censor. 'At one point John Trevelyan, the secretary of the British Board of Film Censors, told me he could see the girls' pubic hair in the catfight,' recalls Peter Hunt. 'I said to him, "I've been watching it frame-by-frame on a Moviola, and *I* can't!" I ended up taking a few frames out here and there. It didn't make any difference really.'

Richard Maibaum was still rewriting scenes when the cast and crew moved from Pinewood Studios to Istanbul, where Ian Fleming joined them. He struck up a deep friendship with Pedro Armendariz, went sightseeing with Cubby Broccoli's wife, Dana, and even made a fleeting, blink-and-you'll-miss-it cameo in the Orient Express sequences.

But script problems were not the only problem Terence Young faced. Pedro Armendariz fell ill in Istanbul. He had terminal cancer and he was fading fast. He pleaded with Cubby Broccoli not to replace him on the film; he knew he was dying and he wanted to leave some money to his wife and children. 'I want to finish this film, Cubby,' he said. 'I *must* finish this film.'

The shooting schedule was altered and the cast and crew returned immediately to Pinewood so that Terence Young could complete Armendariz's scenes in an intense two-week period.

It was horrendous for everyone concerned to watch Armendariz, in obvious pain, struggle to get through his scenes. Towards the end, he was literally having to be propped up. Despite this, Armendariz was determined not to let Broccoli, Saltzman or Young down. He even insisted on doing all his own post-synch work. It's a testament to Armendariz's professionalism that the viewer does not notice his terminal illness at any point during the film.

Once his scenes were completed, Armendariz flew to California and booked himself into the UCLA Medical Center in Los Angeles. Determined not to waste away, he smuggled a gun into his hospital ward and committed suicide.

Everyone involved with *From Russia With Love* was devastated by Armendariz's death and Terence Young had to work hard to motivate his cast and crew. 'Terence's real contribution to the film was a kind of salvage operation,' says Sean Connery. 'He knew we had to get something done and he knew what he wanted. He succeeded remarkably well.'

But Fate still didn't stop tormenting the *From Russia With Love* shoot there. On the morning of 6 July 1963, while preparing to shoot the rescheduled boat chase in Scotland, a helicopter containing Terence Young, a cameraman and the art designer crashed in a loch. The helicopter sank but the passengers and pilot were trapped in an air pocket. Terence Young managed to kick out the door and everyone escaped. Despite his injuries, Young was back on set within thirty minutes of the accident, behaving as though nothing had happened.

Eleven days later, on 17 July, Daniela Bianchi was injured in a car crash on the way to the set. Sean Connery, in a car immediately behind her, dragged her from the wreckage. Bianchi's face was badly swollen and she was unable to film for two weeks.

Connery, too, escaped serious injury or even death when performing his own stunts during the helicopter sequence. At one point, the helicopter, swooping at low level in an attempt to run down James Bond, got just a little too close to Connery for comfort.

'We found out a bit too late to do anything about it that the pilot was not very well trained,' says Connery. 'If you look at the film now you'll see how perilously close that helicopter swoops at me. And let me tell you that was not a camera trick – nor was it planned.'

The accidents and setbacks meant that *From Russia With Love* went over budget and over schedule, and, when the principal photography wrapped in August, with an opening date set at 10 October, Terence Young still had many scenes to reshoot. One of these was the pre-credits sequence – the first of the now obligatory James Bond pre-credits sequences – which showed Grant stalking and then killing 'James Bond'. The victim is, of course, merely target practice for Grant, something that is proved when the SPECTRE trainer Morzeny (Walter Gotell, a series regular as General Gogol between 1977 and 1987) tears off the man's mask. Unfortunately, when viewing the rushes, it was felt that the man playing the victim beneath the mask looked too much like Sean Connery, thus necessitating a reshoot.

Despite all the problems, *From Russia With Love* emerged as a winner. Sean Connery is much more confident as Bond, and certainly more polished; the music by John Barry adds enormously to the atmosphere; the action sequences are particularly well handled (particularly Bond's scrap with Grant on the Orient Express, filmed on

20 and 21 June, with stuntmen doubling Connery and Robert Shaw in just *one* shot); and the essence of Fleming's world is not compromised by the first appearance of gadgets (Bond's briefcase with the exploding talcum powder; Grant's garroting wire in his wristwatch).

Critical reaction to *From Russia With Love* was as polarised in Britain as it had been for *Dr. No*, and there were plenty of killjoys around attempting to rain on Eon's parade.

'We tend to get the movie heroes we deserve,' lamented the *Sunday Express*'s Thomas Wiseman. 'And I suppose nowadays that means James Bond. He is very much a figment of our times, the arch exponent of pop fascism, the parrot-libertine, always ready to seduce a pretty spy for his country.'

Philip Oakes in the *Sunday Telegraph* went much further:

James Bond has already been the subject of much sociological huffing and puffing, and the moral heat generated by his critics must be enough by now to warm a small city. Much of the indignation strikes me as bogus, but what I find extraordinary is that quasi-pornography, which seems to me a fairly clinical description of the Bond dossier, can now be presented as run-of-the-mill entertainment.

Oakes believed *From Russia With Love* was a movie made 'entirely for kicks. Guns go off; girls get undressed; people have sex; people die. Happening succeeds happening, but nothing and no one is of any real significance.' He decried the fact that, in his opinion, 'at no time is character explored, or motive examined. There is no hint of regret for life taken, or life wasted.' The act of love, he argued, 'is reduced to a bedroom workout. Sensation becomes a series of exchanges between a variety of blunt instruments.'

For the *Daily Worker*, the film represented nothing less than the moral bankruptcy of capitalism. 'James Bond: there's a hero for you,' raged Nina Hibbin. 'With one hand holding a gun and the other fondling a girl, dividing his time equally between assassination and fornication! It's fashionable these days to suggest the James Bond approach is only a bit of fun, and mustn't be taken too seriously. *Fun*? That only makes it worse! What sort of people are we becoming if we can accept such perversion as a giggle?'

But the more thoughtful and savvy critics were catching on to what the Bond films were about. 'The Bond films are brilliantly skilful,' wrote Penelope Gilliatt in the *Observer*, and continued,

> Among other things, they seem to have cottoned on to a kind of brutal flippancy that is a voice of the age, the voice of sick jokes about the Bomb and gruesomes about Belsen. Sociologists worry about the seductiveness of the lies in the films, but what audiences surely respond to more is the mockery in the lies. People understand perfectly well that the Bond films are telling them a string of whoppers; this is what makes them laugh.

What no one could fail to notice was that Sean Connery as James Bond was fast becoming a potent box-office force, an inevitable result of the film's box-office-busting performance (it went on to gross almost $80 million worldwide). But, even at this early stage, James Bond was threatening to eclipse not only his creator, but the man who was now 007 personified.

'Sean and I went to America just after *From Russia With Love*,' recalled Terence Young, 'and we sneaked out of the side entrance of the airport.

'There must have been seven or eight hundred people waiting for us out there. There was an old lady there who came through the ring of cops wanting an autograph. I said to Sean, "Sign the bloody thing." So Sean signed it and gave it to her, and she looked horrified. "No, no," she said. "I wanted James Bond." She looked at Sean and he kind of crumpled. It suddenly occurred to him that he was no longer a human being, he was a sex symbol.'

Ian Fleming had attended the premiere of *From Russia With Love* and threw a party for friends at his home in Victoria Square afterwards. But he was unwell and retired to bed soon after arriving home. As John Pearson noted sombrely, 'There was an awful contrast between the virile superhero on the screen and the fading, middle-aged man who had conjured it all up.'

Fleming's failing health was not helped by his looming legal showdown with Kevin McClory, which was scheduled to begin at the High Court on 19 November.

'I'm winding myself up like a toy soldier for this blasted case with

McClory,' he wrote to William Plomer. 'I dare say that a diet of T.N.T. pills and gin will see me through, but it's a bloody nuisance.'

It was to prove to be much more than that.

006: The Bondwagon

'The men and women who allow their talents to be used in the making of films about the exploits of this man are guilty of furthering the shameful aims of Western capitalists.'

Pravda, 30 September, 1965

The THUNDERBALL court case was a dreadful ordeal for Ian Fleming and no one who witnessed him during that time could be under any illusion of the terrible toll it was taking on him.

He was already ill – suffering from angina and a narrowing of the arteries – and his horror of courtrooms added to the strain on him considerably. Even worse was the sense of injustice he felt. As far as Ian Fleming was concerned, he still firmly believed he had done nothing wrong in writing THUNDERBALL. Those closest to him shared that belief but, nonetheless, urged him to settle with McClory because they could see the dreadful, likely irrevocable, damage it was doing to his heart.

'I can't say that the Kevin McClory court case over rights to THUNDERBALL contributed to Ian's death,' says Sir John Morgan, 'because Ian's consumption of whisky and very strong cigarettes, smoked constantly, were the main contributors to that. It would be a big leap to connect the two. But, having said that, the whole affair with McClory devastated Ian. Everyone who knew him well was begging him to settle the thing, myself included, because we could see what it was doing to him. He did settle eventually, but it had gone on too long, and he definitely emerged much battered.' (See Appendix 1: 'Ian Fleming Remembered'.)

Fleming's mood was hardly helped by the news, just three days into the proceedings, that his friend, President Kennedy, had been assassinated in Dallas. Fleming had good reason to thank JFK for the burgeoning success of James Bond in the US, and he had genuinely liked the young president as a man.

Kevin McClory was the sole plaintiff in the THUNDERBALL case because financial problems forced Jack Whittingham to drop out. McClory sued Fleming for plagiarism, breach of copyright and false representation of authorship; he further accused Ivar Bryce, his partner in Xanadu Productions, which was supposed to make the aborted Bond film, of injuring him as a false partner through breach of confidence and breach of contract.

Fleming and Bryce attended the proceedings in the Chancery Division of the High Court every day, which were presided over by Mr Justice Ungoed-Thomas. Fleming had continuously to take nitro-glycerine pills, which had been prescribed to prevent his suffering another heart attack during the stressful hearings.

There was one amusing moment in the opening days of the case when McClory's counsel, Mr Mars-Jones QC attempted to describe James Bond to the judge. 'Bond is an undercover agent in the British Secret Service – tough, hard-hitting, hard-drinking, hard-living and amoral, who at regular annual intervals saves the citizens of this country and the whole free world from the most incredible disasters.'

'Yes, I know,' remarked Mr Justice Ungoed-Thomas, drily. 'I have been saved myself.' Ernest Cuneo, who might be regarded as the *true* begetter of THUNDERBALL, also attended the case. He had flown in from the US to support Fleming and Bryce, both legally and morally, and the court heard about the affidavit in which Fleming acknowledged that Cuneo had 'scribbled off' the basic outline of the film: the draft was dated 28 May 1959. Cuneo had assigned all rights in the draft to Ivar Bryce for $1. As we have seen, Fleming acknowledged Cuneo's contribution by dedicating THUNDERBALL to 'Ernest Cuneo: Muse' – not the action of a plagiarist, we would submit.

The problem was that Kevin McClory undoubtedly had a strong case – and was, perhaps understandably, nursing his own grievances – and his evidence in court was compelling. It was incontrovertible that he had invested time, energy and considerable enthusiasm in the project, so, whatever was the true extent to which Ian Fleming had used Kevin McClory's and Jack Whittingham's ideas in THUNDERBALL – which may or may not have been substantial, depending on one's definition of the word – Fleming could not deny that at least *some* of the copyrighted material from the film scripts had found its way into the novel.

Frankly, once that had been established in court, Fleming and Bryce's defence began to look very weak indeed. It was at this point that Ivar Bryce seriously began to worry about Fleming's health – at least according to his version of events afterwards – and, to prevent his old friend suffering any more, he decided to ask for a settlement with McClory. Since Bryce was funding their defence, Fleming had no option but to agree, albeit bitterly. Privately, Fleming was devastated by what he saw as Bryce's treachery.

The THUNDERBALL settlement was considerably to Ian Fleming's disadvantage and any objective observer, four decades on, might regard it as harsh justice given that Fleming's good faith throughout the affair was acknowledged by the court.

Ian Fleming was forced to acknowledge that all future editions of THUNDERBALL would state that the book was the joint work of Kevin McClory, Jack Whittingham and himself. In exchange for giving up any further claim to the novel, McClory was given the film rights to THUNDERBALL and the 'film scripts' for a consideration paid to Fleming.

At least Fleming did not personally lose much money, apart from his costs, unlike Ivar Bryce, who paid Kevin McClory £35,000 in damages in respect of McClory's claim for infringement of copyright and breach of contract. He also had to meet McClory's costs as well as his own. The estimated total cost of the case was around £80,000, a considerable sum in 1963.

Emerging from the High Court, Fleming was besieged by reporters and did his best to put a brave face on everything. 'I'm glad this whole expensive misunderstanding has now been disposed of,' he told them. 'It's a pity it ever had to come to court.'

Asked if he might use the experience in his next Bond book, Fleming even managed a wintry smile. 'I'm not sure James Bond would feel at home in the Chancery Division,' he remarked.

McClory was understandably triumphant when he emerged from the

High Court. 'I consider it a total victory,' he told the reporters. 'And I'm very happy.'

Immediately after the case, Jack Whittingham sued Ian Fleming for malicious falsehood and libel. But Fleming himself was dead before the case could be heard and Whittingham's case expired.

Ironically, at the same time as the THUNDERBALL case was being heard in the High Court, Fleming himself had been forced to take out an injunction against the *Daily Sketch* newspaper, which had somehow got hold of an advance copy of YOU ONLY LIVE TWICE and revealed in an article dated 15 November 1963, which printed Bond's obituary, that James Bond 'died' at the end of the book. The injunction, more of an irritant to Fleming than anything else, merely added to his weariness.

Indeed, there is nothing more revealing about Ian Fleming's state of mind at this time than an exchange between himself and an old friend. 'What is it like, Ian, what is it really like, to be famous?' asked the friend. 'Ever since I've known you it's what you've really wanted. Are you enjoying it now you've got it?'

'I suppose it was all right for a bit,' replied Fleming. 'Nice being known in restaurants and having people take notice of you. But now, my God! Ashes, dear boy. Just ashes. You've no idea how bored one gets with the whole silly business.'

The truth was, Ian Fleming was utterly destroyed by the THUNDERBALL case, both mentally and physically, and when he went to see a heart specialist in December 1963, a week or so after the settlement, the news was, predictably, not good: he was told he was suffering from coronary and aortic sclerosis, that there were signs of myocarditic damage and definite intermittent coronary insufficiency. The doctor urged him to give up smoking and to take as much rest as possible. Alcohol was not proscribed completely, but the recommended daily amounts were tiny.

Typically, it was a regime Ian Fleming could not adopt for long: 'I must be able to live as I want, with no restrictions, or I don't want to live at all,' he told a friend, defiantly. The problem was, Ian Fleming always wanted to live life as a tough man, but his body simply wasn't up to it any longer.

Friends rallied round Fleming after the THUNDERBALL settlement and it was certainly true that their letters and messages assuaged his despair a little. Typical was John Betjeman, who equated James Bond with

Sherlock Holmes and assured Fleming that he had created a world entirely of his own with his books. 'I think the only other person to have invented a world in our time is Wodehouse,' Betjeman told him. 'This is real art.' The only way to react to the THUNDERBALL case, Betjeman believed, was to 'write on, fight on'.

Fleming was touched by this but replied to Betjeman, 'I am seriously running out of puff and my inventive streak is very nearly worked out.'

Of course, his friends had heard this all before. But, for once, Ian Fleming's inventiveness was waning, probably as a direct result of his failing health coupled with the events of November/December 1963.

THE MAN WITH THE GOLDEN GUN, which Ian Fleming wrote between January and March 1964, is patently the work of a very ill man, a man whose well of inventiveness had finally been drained. It is, by a long way, the weakest James Bond novel he wrote and a desperately sad coda to his glittering career. Able to work on the book for only an hour a day while at Goldeneye, Fleming was never able to revise the book, or to add any of the rich detail that he had made his speciality. Consequently, one might regard the novel as unfinished.

To be fair, Fleming himself wasn't happy with the book even while he was writing it. He told William Plomer that the first draft needed extensive rewriting – rewriting he was ultimately unable to do himself – and that he had not enjoyed writing the book at all.

As a book, THE MAN WITH THE GOLDEN GUN is thin and undernourished. Nonetheless, it remains important not only because it was the last Bond novel Ian Fleming wrote but because it resolves the compelling cliffhanger with which Fleming had ended YOU ONLY LIVE TWICE.

THE MAN WITH THE GOLDEN GUN opens with Bond, having been brainwashed by the Russians, returning from the 'dead' to London, where he attempts – and fails – to assassinate M with a cyanide pistol. Brainwashed by the British to counter the Russians' brainwashing (how much brainwashing can one man take?), Bond is more or less back to normal and sent by M to Jamaica to kill Scaramanga, a freelance assassin used by the KGB in the Caribbean. Scaramanga is known as 'the Man with the Golden Gun' because he uses a gold-plated Colt .45.

Bond ingratiates himself into Scaramanga's setup ridiculously easily and is hired as a bodyguard at a conference Scaramanga's hosting for various gangsters (a direct steal of the 'hoods' convention' in GOLDFINGER). His cover blown during a train ride (a reworking of the railroad section in DIAMONDS ARE FOREVER), Bond eventually kills Scaramanga in a duel in the swamp.

What undermines THE MAN WITH THE GOLDEN GUN, apart from Fleming's inability to work his customary detail into the narrative, is the weakness of the characterisation. Bond is like cardboard; Scaramanga is a painfully inadequate villain and a relatively unintelligent one at that; while Mary Goodnight, Bond's secretary in the previous couple of Bond books, is a disappointing heroine who makes so few appearances in the text she barely registers at all.

Raymond Benson wrote that THE MAN WITH THE GOLDEN GUN 'comes off as what it is – a first draft'. Kingsley Amis agreed, writing in his review in the *New Statesman*, 'Scaramanga is just a dandy with a special (and ineffective) gun, a stock of outdated American slang, and a third nipple on his left breast. We hear a lot about him early on in the ten-page dossier M consults, including mentions of homosexuality and pistol-fetishism, but these aren't followed up anywhere.'

Intriguingly, Amis's review went on to speculate that Fleming possibly intended to develop a theme where Scaramanga is sexually attracted to Bond and his theory certainly isn't ridiculous. For one thing, it would explain the ease with which Bond infiltrates Scaramanga's organisation. As Amis wrote,

> Scaramanga hires him after a few minutes' conversation in the bar of a brothel. (At this stage he has no idea that there's a British agent within a hundred miles, so he can't be hiring him to keep him under his eye.) Bond wonders what Scaramanga wants with him: 'it was odd, to say the least of it . . . the strong smell of a trap.' This hefty hint of a concealed motive on Scaramanga's part is never taken up. Why not?

Fleming had certainly written about gay and lesbian characters before – Wint and Kidd in DIAMONDS ARE FOREVER, Rosa Klebb in FROM RUSSIA WITH LOVE, Pussy Galore in GOLDFINGER – and the dossier M has on Scaramanga, to which Amis refers, mentions the possibility that the assassin has homosexual tendencies: this despite his being 'an insatiable but indiscriminate womaniser who invariably has sexual intercourse shortly before killing in the belief that it improves the "eye"'; and the Voodoo belief that his third nipple grants him 'great sexual prowess'.

So, if Fleming *had* intended to develop THE MAN WITH THE GOLDEN GUN along the lines Amis suggested, it might well have proved to be one of the more interesting Ian Fleming novels. As it is, it remains the weakest, albeit for understandable reasons.

While Fleming struggled to give birth to James Bond one last time in Jamaica, the movie cult of 007 was gathering momentum fast. Cubby Broccoli and Harry Saltzman were well advanced in their plans to bring *Goldfinger*, their third Bond film, to cinemas in the autumn of 1964, while Kevin McClory had wasted no time after securing the film rights to THUNDERBALL in starting work on the film version.

THUNDERBALL had been included in the original option deal Saltzman had made with Ian Fleming, but that had been made before the court case. Now the film rights were owned by McClory and there wasn't a thing Broccoli and Saltzman could do about it. Naturally, they were concerned about a rival Bond film but all they could do was to concentrate on their plans for *Goldfinger*, for which United Artists had agreed an increased budget of $3.5 million.

The *Daily Mail*, a newspaper that never misses an opportunity to create controversy where none exists, tried to mix it between Eon Productions and Kevin McClory from the outset. 'Albert Broccoli and Harry Saltzman are following their two earlier Bond thrillers with *Goldfinger*, in which Bond plays a life-or-death golf match,' the paper wrote on 8 January 1964. 'Kevin McClory is making *Thunderball* in which a madman steals an H-bomb and holds the world to ransom.'

But McClory had one fundamental problem and he knew it. Sean Connery was firmly established as the cinematic James Bond. He was one of *the* leading pop icons of the age. Broccoli and Saltzman had Connery – he was contracted to make a Bond a year – and McClory didn't.

Initially, McClory was bullish, telling the *Daily Mail* that he had a shortlist of three actors in mind for Bond: he refused to name all three but admitted Laurence Harvey was one (Richard Burton topped his list he revealed much later). 'All I will say is that the man chosen will not be an American actor,' McClory said. 'But you can take it from me that my Bond will be a big "animal type" actor.'

But finding an actor to compete directly with Sean Connery's Bond in 1964 would ultimately defeat McClory. And it's not difficult to understand why because, as the Bond editor Peter Hunt put it, 'Sean really was a very sexy man. There are very few film stars who had that sort of quality. He could virtually walk into a room and fuck anybody.'

Guy Hamilton stepped in to direct *Goldfinger* after Terence Young, who had begun preproduction work on it, left to direct another film. Hamilton, whom Broccoli and Saltzman had approached to direct *Dr. No* before Terence Young, was the perfect choice for *Goldfinger*. Born in 1922, he ignored his father's wish that he should pursue a diplomatic career – 'In those days the idea of being a film director was rather like wanting to run a brothel and I was soundly spanked' – and he rose through the ranks of the British film industry, assisting Carol Reed on *The Third Man* in 1949, and John Huston on *The African Queen* in 1951, before making his directorial debut with *The Ringer* in 1952.

As a director, Hamilton is extremely polished and his unique flair for comedy underpinned *Goldfinger* perfectly and created the template of savage, satirical insouciance that characterised the very best Bond films that followed it.

It also helped that he'd known Sean Connery long before he was cast as James Bond. Connery, in Hollywood making *Marnie* for Alfred Hitchcock at the start of 1964, was reportedly showing the first signs of being bored with playing James Bond and was unhappy when he learned Terence Young would not be directing the next film. Connery's friendship with Hamilton assuaged his unhappiness and their existing rapport was to prove a huge asset to *Goldfinger*: 'Guy evoked from Sean an even surer, brisker, more sardonic Bond than in the earlier films,' said the screenwriter Richard Maibaum. 'The effect was to make him more perversely attractive.'

Maibaum was spot on in his assessment. *Goldfinger* showcases Sean Connery's best performance as James Bond: arguably, and no doubt to his chagrin, the best performance of his career. As Raymond Benson has rightly noted, Connery is a pleasure to watch in *Goldfinger*. The embodiment of sixties 'cool', Benson believes Connery is 'totally relaxed, yet able to take command of any situation. He retains the tough persona but reveals an even more sophisticated wit than Bond had had in previous films.'

Terence Young had understood Ian Fleming's books but hadn't really respected them; Guy Hamilton not only understood and respected Fleming's world, but also knew how the original books should be adapted for the screen.

As we explained in Chapter 3, *Goldfinger* remains the definitive James Bond film and the elements that made the film so memorable were all to be found in the source novel. Hamilton, working closely with the screenwriters Richard Maibaum and Paul Dehn, was keen to incorporate as much of Fleming's original as possible, but then to give it some spin. This was because he not only understood what Bond was all about but also recognised what was already happening to the character and the franchise.

'*Goldfinger* was a bit of a challenge because I sensed Bond was becoming a bit of a superman,' he says. 'But using the things that had worked so well in the first two, it was easy to have a target and know what I wanted to do.

'I knew right from the start that the standards had to go higher and higher because each Bond film has to surpass its predecessor. The films offer escapism so we have to endeavour to capture our audience at the very start, get them involved in the problems, and then take them off on a wild and glorious ride to the finish. The important thing is for everyone – the audience and James Bond himself – to have a lot of fun.'

Hamilton stamped his authority on *Goldfinger* right from the start: by comparing the pre-credits sequences of *From Russia With Love* and *Goldfinger* one can immediately see what Hamilton brought to the Bonds. Robert Shaw stalking and killing the bogus 'James Bond' in *From Russia With Love* was an undeniably effective means of opening that film; but the mini-adventure, wholly unrelated to the rest of the film, with which Hamilton opens *Goldfinger* is simply in a different class.

'It seemed to me that if I could do the pre-credits sequence – which is a wonderful piece of nonsense where Bond goes swimming with a seagull on top of his head and unzips his wetsuit and has a white dinner-jacket underneath – and it makes you laugh,' says Hamilton, 'well then after the credits I could take them all for a great big ride and we could all have fun.

'If you believe a man can steal all the gold in the world, monkeys can fly. So you've got to take it all with a pinch of salt. My approach to the audience was, we're going to take you to wonderful places; we're going to show you beautiful girls; we're going to have some suspense; and we're going to have some laughs. So let's enjoy it!'

Hamilton also refined the relationship between the regular characters. Taking his cue from Fleming's GOLDFINGER, in which M is particularly tetchy with Bond, Hamilton beefed up the antagonism between Bond and M in the film. He also changed the relationship fundamentally between Bond and Q, thereby securing Desmond Llewelyn's place in cinematic history.

'At the rehearsals I was working at a desk,' recalled Llewelyn. 'Bond came in and I got up to greet him. Guy said, "No, no, no! You don't take any notice of this man. You don't like him." I thought, but this is James Bond. Q's just a civil servant and he must admire him, like everyone else. But Guy was having none of it. "No, of course you don't like him," he said. "He doesn't show your gadgets any respect at all."'

Hamilton, like Broccoli and Saltzman, also understood the appeal of Bond's gadgets for the audience, which is why he developed Llewelyn's role. Bond's briefcase in *From Russia With Love* had opened the floodgates but *Goldfinger* went much further with gadgetry. This was epitomised with Bond's Aston Martin DB5, which is now known as 'the most famous car in the world'.

Fleming had given Bond an Aston Martin DB III in the original novel, which had included its own hidden extras, such as switches to alter the shape and colour of Bond's front and rear lights if he was being followed at night; reinforced steel bumpers for ramming other cars; a long-barrelled Colt .45 in a hidden compartment under the driving seat; and a pickup receiver in the dashboard to receive signals from a homer. Taking their cue from Fleming's original, the filmmakers gave the DB5 even more fabulous extras: machine guns concealed behind the indicator lights; a bulletproof shield; revolving number plates; an oil jet; a nail dispenser; rear smoke screen; revolving tyre scythe; and an ejector seat operated by a little red button concealed in the gear lever.

The Aston Martin became the trademark gadget of the film and, in a way, of the entire series. The Aston Martin epitomised the stylistic changes made in *Goldfinger* – and highlighted the future direction the film series was to take.

'I think the minute Sean Connery pressed the button on the ejector seat in *Goldfinger* and the audience roared, the series turned around,' says Tom Mankiewicz, screenwriter of *Live And Let Die*, and co-writer of *Diamonds Are Forever* and *The Man with the Golden Gun*. 'The audiences saw outlandish things they had never seen before and the natural response of anybody – writer, filmmaker, producer – is to give them more: more of what they want. And there's a constant pressure as the films gross a great deal of money to make each one bigger, and "more" than the last.

'Take *You Only Live Twice*. Once you have a helicopter come by with a giant magnet and pick a car up off the road, and dump it out in the ocean, well, that's a staggering thing to look at. What you're saying to an audience is, "All's fair; we can do that"; but it's awful tough to keep a serious plot line going.

'You have so many tools available, so many outlandish things which an audience is not only used to but they want to see. They got indoctrinated into it, and that moment when Sean pressed the ejector seat in *Goldfinger* is when I say Bond became Disney in a certain way. It became entertainment; it became an afternoon out, where for two hours you were going to see stuff you never saw before.

'The feeling of Cubby and Harry, and of United Artists, was that if you pulled your horns in and made a smaller picture, the audience would be disappointed.'

Not everyone was happy with the car and its effect on the Bond series. Sean Connery has always given the impression of being ambivalent about the Aston Martin: 'It was an elegant-looking car,' he concedes. 'And when I drove it round Switzerland it impressed a lot of people. But I think its role in the film gave it a more unique quality than the car actually possessed.

'What's amusing is that there must be fifty Aston Martin DB5s around the world claiming to be our original. And people keep paying to see them!'

Terence Young, who returned to the series to direct *Thunderball* after *Goldfinger*, was also unimpressed with the DB5, blaming it – like Tom Mankiewicz – for the series becoming more and more dependent on gimmickry after *Goldfinger*.

'All the human elements disappeared once the gadgets took over,' he complained. 'The gadgets and machines took the place of people. I told them after *Thunderball*, "I think you don't want a director any more, you want an MIT graduate to handle all the machines."'

And John Brosnan, in his excellent *James Bond in the Cinema* (Tantivy, 1972), lamented the influence of the gadgets ushered in by the Aston Martin DB5. Claiming that *Goldfinger* marked a major turning point in the evolution of the Bond films, Brosnan accused the producers of concentrating on the gadgets, gimmicks and sets, thereby neglecting the essential qualities of Ian Fleming's fictional world – especially James Bond himself.

Brosnan argued that the result was the depersonalisation of James Bond as a character, so that he was turned into a 'bland dummy whose only function was to manipulate the various gadgets and act as a catalyst to keep the whole show moving'. And, according to Brosnan, as James Bond 'became less and less a real person it became more difficult to remain involved with what happened to him'.

Was James Bond ever a 'real' person? Even in Ian Fleming's books? It's a moot point. But whichever viewpoint one takes about the introduction of gadgetry in *Goldfinger* – and one must remember the filmmakers took their cue from Fleming's original novel in devising much of the hardware – the fact is that voices like Terence Young's and John Brosnan's were very much in the minority at the time. The gadgetry in *Goldfinger* is clever, fresh and used both wittily and intelligently. It never quite takes over from Bond and audiences lapped it up.

Cubby Broccoli and Harry Saltzman – and Broccoli more than Saltzman, if we're honest – both understood their audience when it came to Bond's gadgetry, and Guy Hamilton admits Cubby Broccoli taught him an important lesson during the filming of the scene in which Q demonstrates the Aston Martin's capabilities to Bond.

Hamilton's intention had been to cut away from the explanation *before* Q could mention the ejector seat so that when Bond pressed the button and the enemy agent went rocketing through the roof, it would be a surprise for the audience. Broccoli, on set during the shooting of the scene, instructed Hamilton that Q must explain every feature.

'I thought that was crass,' says Hamilton, 'because it would spoil the surprise for the audience. But the audience reaction proved Cubby was absolutely right. "Tell them what you're going to do and then do it," is what he told me. He taught me a great lesson and I've always been grateful to him.'

Goldfinger follows Ian Fleming's novel reasonably faithfully, but screenwriters Richard Maibaum and Paul Dehn made some important changes which, for the only time in the entire film series, resulted in the film version actually being better than Fleming's original.

The biggest change was Auric Goldfinger's motivation. In the novel, Goldfinger brings a 'clean' nuclear bomb to Kentucky to blow off the doors of Fort Knox and then steal all the gold (a logistical impossibility); in the film, Goldfinger actually breaks into the vault using a laser, where he plants a 'particularly dirty' nuclear device (with Bond handcuffed to it) with the intention of irradiating all the gold, thus destroying the American economy and ensuring the value of his own gold increases many times.

The writers also make other subtle changes by downgrading Pussy Galore's overt lesbianism in the novel to a more ambiguous sexuality in the film; reducing the role of Tilly Masterson (Masterton in the novel) and increasing Pussy Galore's screentime; and having Bond actually witness the death-by-gold-paint suffered by Jill Masterson (Shirley Eaton in the Bond series' most iconic scene) rather than hear about it second-hand, as in the novel.

Maibaum and Dehn also put a great deal of stylish spin on the dialogue, ensuring that their script for *Goldfinger* established the perfect balance between realism and fantasy, seriousness and humour: a balance that had eluded the first two films and which, perhaps, only *On Her Majesty's Secret Service* (1969), *The Spy Who Loved Me* (1977) and *GoldenEye* (1995) have matched subsequently.

Nowhere is their skill more apparent than in the barn scene where Bond seduces Pussy. Bond is a prisoner of Goldfinger. Goldfinger has told Bond of his plans to detonate the nuclear device inside Fort Knox and of his intention to kill thousands of innocent people around the gold depository by spraying deadly nerve gas in the air prior to the raid. The nerve gas is to be dispersed by the female pilots of Pussy Galore's Flying Circus from their planes. Bond's only hope is to seduce Pussy and persuade her to switch the gas canisters on the planes. The problem is, Pussy doesn't like men . . . does she? The economy with which Maibaum and Dehn resolve this scene is an object lesson in pop screenwriting.

BOND: What would it take for you to see things my way?
PUSSY: A lot more than you've got.

BOND: How d'you know?

PUSSY: I don't want to know.

BOND: (*Grabbing her arm*) Isn't it customary to grant the condemned man his last request?

PUSSY: You've asked for this . . .

Pussy, the judo expert, then floors Bond. A brief tussle follows which ends with Bond on top. Pussy resists but Bond forces himself on her (presumably inspired by the very last line in Fleming's novel: 'His mouth came ruthlessly down on hers.') and she begins to relent.

Honor Blackman was cast as Pussy Galore – something which Guy Hamilton had wanted from the moment he joined the film.

'There was hardly anyone else about who was right for Pussy,' recalls Honor Blackman, 'because I was having great success as Cathy Gale in *The Avengers*. I was coming to the end of my two-year stint and so, since Pussy's character demanded a knowledge of judo, and I was a hot property at that point, it seemed right.'

Indeed, it is impossible to think of anyone else who *could* have played Pussy since Mrs Catherine Gale, John Steed's leather-wearing partner in *The Avengers* 1962–4, was television's first truly liberated female character. As Blackman herself had told reporters in September 1962: 'I'm a first for television. The first feminist to come into a television series; the first woman to fight back. Cathy is all anthropologist, an academic, all brain, and what she doesn't have in the way of brawn, she makes up for in motorbikes, black boots, leather combat suits and judo. I had enormous problems with rewrites at the beginning. Cathy was so wet I had to say, "Look, write my part as if I were a man and I'll turn it into a woman's part."'

Blackman established the connection between *The Avengers* and James Bond. Her successor as Steed's partner, Diana Rigg (Emma Peel), left *The Avengers* to star in *On Her Majesty's Secret Service*; while Steed himself, Patrick Macnee, starred in Roger Moore's Bondian swansong, *A View To A Kill* in 1985. Joanna Lumley travelled in the opposite direction: appearing in *On Her Majesty's Secret Service* before becoming Purdey in the somewhat lacklustre *The New Avengers* in the mid-1970s.

Honor Blackman, though, is unique among *all* Bond girls: she is the only actress playing the female lead in the series who was actually older than the actor playing Bond. Maybe that's why, when Felix Leiter asks Bond why Pussy switched sides, Bond replies with mock-innocence, 'Perhaps I appealed to her maternal instincts?'

Pussy's name caused consternation prior to the film's release. Pussy Galore *is* an outrageous name and shows Ian Fleming's humour at its broadest. United Artists were nervous about getting it past the censor and with some justification: the American censor told Cubby Broccoli bluntly that he would not allow the name to pass. A rather absurd suggestion was that Pussy Galore be renamed Kitty Galore.

'If anyone's so po-faced to take it seriously, then bad luck,' says Honor Blackman. 'But I was shocked anyone was shocked by it. So I used to use her name deliberately in interviews.'

In the event, it was Prince Philip who ensured Pussy retained her name in America. Honor Blackman was introduced to the Prince at *Goldfinger*'s London premiere. Next day, predictably, the headlines were a variation of 'Pussy and the Prince' or 'The Prince meets Pussy'. Broccoli showed the clippings to the American censor and told him bluntly: 'Look at these. If the picture is good enough for Prince Philip and the people of London to see, that ought to be all right over here. Look at those headlines. There's obviously nothing wrong with the word "Pussy" – that's her name! It's been accepted in England and, dammit, if it's OK with them, what are you worried about?'

Pussy got to keep her name in America after that.

Theodore Bikel was originally approached to play Auric Goldfinger but his rather dull screen test precluded his opportunity to play the master villain. Instead, German actor Gert Frobe landed the role. Frobe's command of English might have been shaky – he was ultimately dubbed – but he was well cast as Goldfinger: rarely has one of Fleming's creations been so perfectly realised on film.

Shirley Eaton was cast as the ill-fated Jill; Tania Mallet as Jill's equally ill-fated sister, Tilly; and wrestler Harold Sakata as Oddjob. And what Sakata lacked in acting experience, he more than made up for in incredible screen presence.

Solid, inscrutable, yet slyly humorous, Sakata's performance as the deadly bowler-hatted mute handyman virtually steals the entire picture. The climatic fight between Bond and Oddjob in the vault of Fort Knox – a fantastic set by Ken Adam – remains one of the absolute pinnacles of the Bond series (as John Brosnan noted wryly, no other hero in the history of cinema has ever been in such an outlandish situation: manacled to a ticking nuclear bomb inside Fort Knox while a Korean martial arts expert menaces him).

'The very nature of a gold depository is dull,' says Ken Adam, who was allowed to view the outside of Fort Knox but had to imagine what the interior looked like. 'You can't stack gold very high because of weight problems and questions of transportation. The ingots would be stored in small chambers which would be situated along narrow tunnels. And there's simply no drama in a series of little rooms. In my case, I stacked gold bars forty feet high, under a gigantic roof. I wanted a cathedral of gold. I had a whole crew of men polishing the metal work so that it would shine when we turned the lights on. It was the perfect place to stage the last battle with Oddjob. It was like a golden arena and Bond was able to use gold bars as weapons.'

A welcome visitor to Pinewood in March 1964 was Ian Fleming. With the THUNDERBALL case finally resolved and YOU ONLY LIVE TWICE about to be published, Fleming should have been content. But everyone who saw him when he chatted with Sean Connery and Shirley Eaton on Pinewood's D Stage could see the change in him from the man who had visited the set of *From Russia With Love*. Fleming was clearly very ill indeed. Nonetheless, no one could have known that this would be the last time Ian Fleming would ever visit the set of a James Bond film: still less that he would not even live to see *Goldfinger* completed.

YOU ONLY LIVE TWICE received good reviews and went straight to the top of the bestseller lists (it had 62,000 advance orders, which was a 50 per cent increase over ON HER MAJESTY'S SECRET SERVICE just a year earlier). As usual, Fleming sent an inscribed copy of the book to the Kennedys in the US. Robert Kennedy sent him a black-edged thank-you card which read 'I wish someone else could read it also.'

The following month, *From Russia With Love* premiered in the US and earned excellent reviews and even better box office returns. *Life* ran a feature about the film as well as a profile of Sean Connery, whose burgeoning career – boosted in the US by his starring in Hitchcock's shamefully underrated *Marnie* – was propelling him to international superstardom.

But, as always, life had played one of its dirty tricks on Ian Fleming. In March, aware his health was deteriorating badly, Fleming sold 51 per cent of Glidrose to Bookers, the company owned by his friend, Sir Jock

Left: Less dapper than usual, Roger Moore's 007 takes aim in *The Man With The Golden Gun* (1974).

Below: Steely, determined and cool, Timothy Dalton was the personification of Ian Fleming's 007 in his two Bond movies.

Above: Not MI6, but the real headquarters of James Bond's world: the London offices of Eon Productions at 138 Piccadilly.

Left: The most successful Bond, Pierce Brosnan, gives Michelle Yeoh the ride of her life in one of the finest Bond movies, *Tomorrow Never Dies* (1997).

Right: Number 16 Victoria Square. Ian Fleming's London home from 1952 until his death in 1964.

Above: Richard ('Jaws') Kiel towers over legendary Bond producer Cubby Broccoli.

Below: Eon Production's original London base at 3 South Audley Street.

George Lazenby, whose performance in *On Her Majesty's Secret Service* (1969) remains one of the most underrated in movie history.

Above: David Niven camps it up as Sir James Bond in *Casino Royale* (1967).

Right: Birth of a cinematic icon: Sean Connery as James Bond 007.

Above: For the man who has everything. James Bond's rocket-firing autogyro, 'Little Nellie' draws the crowds on the Isle of Wight in the summer of 1967.

Below: The suitably Gothic 22b Ebury Street, where Ian Fleming lived in the 1930s.

Ian Fleming in May 1962, outwardly unmoved by the terrible reviews for the recently published *The Spy Who Loved Me*.

Campbell. Fleming's success, ironically, had meant it was impossible to keep Glidrose Publications as a private company without Fleming himself being hammered by punitive supertax. His accountants had advised him to sell part of the company, which would provide him with a sizeable tax-free capital sum. The deal eventually worked out was that Bookers paid £100,000 for their share in the company – precisely the same sum his estate paid in death duties after his death just six months later. And the irony was completed when the Bond bonanza began in earnest with the release of *Goldfinger* a month after Fleming's death: it was Bookers, not Ian Fleming, who really benefited from the incredible success of James Bond after March 1964.

There was a further, bitter, irony. Shortly after the deal with Bookers had been concluded, Fleming succumbed to pleurisy, brought on by his insisting on playing a round of golf in the pouring rain with friends. After spending a fortnight in bed, during which time he suffered terrible chest pains, Fleming was admitted to the King Edward VII Hospital for Officers, where he was diagnosed as having a pulmonary embolism. His refusal to quit smoking and drinking had finally caught up with him: blood clots were gathering in his lungs.

In July, Fleming went to recuperate in Hove, staying at the Dudley Hotel. He was in very poor health and utterly exhausted: even meeting people tired him out. Eating little but smoking constantly, Fleming spent his days staring out to sea.

Less than a mile away, at the Metropole Hotel in Brighton, his mother, very old now and extremely frail, was also dying. Theirs had been a difficult relationship and fate had now brought them together. He had not chosen Hove to be near his dying mother; she had not chosen Brighton to comfort her dying son. It was just how things worked out.

Fleming's mother died on 27 July 1964. He ignored medical advice and attended the funeral. On his mother's death, Fleming – like his brothers – finally inherited his substantial share of his father's will. 'What use is it to me now?' he said to Ann bitterly on their way back from the funeral.

His mother's death convinced Fleming that he 'must get back to life, or else' and he again ignored all advice and abandoned his recuperation in Hove to return home to Victoria Square in London. From there he intended to spend all of August at the Guildford Hotel in Sandwich – his favourite hotel – because he had been elected the next captain of the

Royal St George's golf club and he was determined nothing was going to keep him from taking up his position.

Fleming was desperately ill when he attended a committee meeting on 11 August, although he somehow managed to get back to the hotel afterwards to dine with an old friend. But it was too much. He collapsed and was rushed to the Kent and Canterbury Hospital. He was quite calm during the journey to the hospital and apologised to the paramedics. 'I am sorry to trouble you chaps,' he said. His ever-inquiring mind even kicked in and he told them, 'I don't know how you get along so fast with the traffic on the roads these days.'

The ambulance got Ian Fleming to the hospital just after 9.30 p.m. and the medical staff fought for three hours to save his life. But not even James Bond could have saved Ian Fleming this time and he was dead shortly after 1 a.m. on 12 August. It was his son Caspar's twelfth birthday.

Ian Fleming had written James Bond's obituary the previous year. But Bond, of course, always lived twice. Not so Fleming: there was no coming back from the obituaries that appeared for him in the days following 12 August. Had he been able to read them, Fleming would have presumably been satisfied that most – if not all – were reverential and generous.

Fleming was a wealthy man when he died but he was not rich. James Bond had been successful up to August 1964 – after a very slow start – but the worldwide cult that spawned an unprecedented merchandising boom did not truly begin until a month or so after Fleming's death. When Fleming died, his books had sold an estimated forty million copies; the following year alone – 1965 – would see sales increase by a further 27 million.

What truly kickstarted the Bond phenomenon was the release of *Goldfinger* on 17 September 1964 – five weeks and one day after Ian Fleming died. The critics were, with few exceptions, ecstatic. The consensus was that Cubby Broccoli and Harry Saltzman had pulled off a near-impossible feat by improving on *From Russia With Love*.

Penelope Gilliatt, who had accurately put her finger on what made *From Russia With Love* compelling for audiences the previous year, now identified why *Goldfinger* worked so well: 'In all his adventures, sexual and lethal, Bond is a kind of joke Superman, as preposterously resilient as one of those cartoon cats. It may be Paul Dehn's collaboration on the script which here gives new finesse to the jokes; or it may simply be a growing confidence on the part of everyone concerned, and most notably of Sean Connery himself. *Goldfinger* really is a dazzling object lesson in the principle that nothing succeeds like excess.'

Goldfinger is, indeed, the truly definitive James Bond film, without necessarily being the best. Everything works beautifully: the pre-credits sequence; Shirley Bassey belting out the John Barry/Leslie Bricusse/ Anthony Newley theme song; Shirley Eaton painted in gold; the Aston Martin; Bond's near-castration with a laser; Auric Goldfinger; Oddjob; Pussy Galore; and the assault on Fort Knox. Best of all is the new sense of confidence, which is all down to Guy Hamilton's direction. *Goldfinger* is *the* pop art film of the 1960s.

Goldfinger also captured the prevailing public mood in the Western world like no other film before or since, as Pierce Brosnan recalls: 'As a boy in 1964 after leaving Ireland, it was the first film I ever saw in London and it was unbelievable. A naked lady covered in gold paint. Oddjob with that hat. It was just magic. Sheer sophistication. Life changed for me.'

Goldfinger launched Bond frenzy worldwide and smashed international box-office records. It earned back its production costs in just two weeks, gaining a place in the *Guiness Book of Records* as the fastest-grossing film of all time. It also triggered the huge Bond merchandising industry which meant one was unable to avoid the 007 logo. Sales of Fleming's books soared; the *Goldfinger* soundtrack was a chart success; the first Corgi model version of the Aston Martin sold two million units worldwide; there were James Bond toys, games, toiletries, bubble-gum cards, playing cards, even dolls. Anything associated with James Bond was guaranteed to sell: even CHITTY CHITTY BANG BANG, the children's story Ian Fleming had written in 1961 while recuperating from his first heart attack, was a huge hit when it was published in October 1964.

But the unprecedented success of *Goldfinger* created a huge headache for Kevin McClory, who had been trying to put *Thunderball* together ever since acquiring the film rights in his court case with Fleming the previous year. By September 1964, McClory knew that there was no way he could compete with Broccoli and Saltzman's series and, displaying an intelligent pragmatism, he approached them with a proposition just before *Goldfinger* opened: he suggested they co-produce *Thunderball* as the next film in the series.

Broccoli flew to Dublin to meet McClory and struck a deal with him at the airport. Kevin McClory would produce the film for Eon Productions, with Broccoli and Saltzman. This deal required a swift change to *Goldfinger*'s end credits. Originally they had been printed to tell the audience that James Bond would return in *On Her Majesty's Secret Service*, Eon's next planned Bond film: now they had to be changed to say he would be back in *Thunderball*.

Inevitably, Guy Hamilton was first choice to direct *Thunderball* but he declined, claiming *Goldfinger* had drained him of all ideas. Broccoli, Saltzman and McClory then asked Terence Young to direct the picture. Richard Maibaum – who had, of course, already written a screenplay of *Thunderball* for Eon in 1961 – wrote the screenplay with the British writer John Hopkins.

Given the success of *Goldfinger*, United Artists granted *Thunderball* a budget of $5.6 million – more than five times the amount they had allocated *Dr. No* just three years earlier. This vastly increased budget meant that *Thunderball* would be the most lavish Bond film yet, with expansive location filming in the Bahamas and truly innovative underwater work.

Casting on *Thunderball* took on a decidedly Continental feel with a former Miss France, Claudine Auger, cast as Domino (after Julie Christie, Raquel Welch and Faye Dunaway had been considered); Adolfo Celi, an Italian actor who had enjoyed a stage career in Brazil, landing the role of villain Emilio Largo; and the stunning red-headed Italian actress Luciana Paluzzi chosen to play the SPECTRE assassin Fiona Volpe.

Thunderball's eighteen-week schedule began in March 1965 with a Christmas release scheduled. It was a long schedule and this was one of the reasons why Sean Connery was tiring of his commitment to Bond. He was also worried about becoming typecast and extremely frustrated by how Sean Connery and James Bond were becoming indistinguishable in the public consciousness. Nevertheless, Connery was equally aware that Bond had propelled him into a stardom he could scarcely have imagined just three years earlier. Bond had been good to him and he went into *Thunderball* as professionally as ever. But he made it plain in the interviews he granted that he was looking to a future beyond Bond.

'*Thunderball* is the best story of them all really,' he told Roderick

Mann just prior to starting work on the film. 'There are wonderful underwater sequences in the Bahamas and the premise is wildly exciting. I think it could be even better than the last one. But I can't see the cycle going on past that, although I am signed up to do two more – *On Her Majesty's Secret Service* and one other. But who knows? America seems to lap them up.

'My only grumble about Bond films is that they don't tax one as an actor. All one really needs is the constitution of a rugby player to get through eighteen weeks of swimming, slugging and necking. I'd like to see someone else tackle Bond, I must say. Though I think they'd be crazy to do it. There was talk of Richard Burton doing one, and I said he must be out of his mind. It would be like putting his head on a chopping block. Whatever he did he couldn't make the films more successful than they are. Even if Sam Spiegel and David Lean made one, there's no guarantee it would do any better.'

Matters weren't helped by the fact that the pressure of the Bond films had created problems in Connery's marriage to his then wife, Diane Cilento. When the press began speculating about the state of their sex lives during the shoot, Connery was understandably furious. Particularly irksome to him was the way the press reported the story as though Cilento was married to James Bond, not Sean Connery. 'I find that fame tends to turn one from an actor and a human being into a piece of merchandise, a public institution,' he complained to *Playboy* magazine. 'Well, I don't intend to undergo that metamorphosis.

'Let me straighten you out on this. The problem with interviews of this sort is to get across the fact, without breaking your arse, that one is *not* Bond, that one was functioning reasonably well *before* Bond, and that one is going to function reasonably well *after* Bond.'

By comparing Connery's interview with Roderick Mann conducted prior to his commencing work on *Thunderball* and the *Playboy* interview, which occurred during the shoot, one can see vividly how Connery's frustrations about Bond – the length of time it actually took to make a Bond movie, the press intrusion, the eclipsing of Sean Connery the actor by James Bond the icon – crystallised during the making of the film in 1965.

Playing James Bond may have meant Sean Connery edged out John Wayne as the world's favourite film star, but he was convinced the part was also diminishing him as a man and an actor. The problem was that the world was James Bond crazy in 1965: the cult was unstoppable and there wasn't a thing Sean Connery could do to stop the Bondwagon.

Except to get off.

Ian Fleming's last Bond novel, the pitifully undernourished THE MAN WITH THE GOLDEN GUN, was published a month into *Thunderball*'s shoot. Despite poor reviews, it went straight to the top of the bestseller lists and stayed there for weeks. A month later, Kingsley Amis's collection of essays about Bond, *The James Bond Dossier*, was published and followed THE MAN WITH THE GOLDEN GUN up the bestseller list. Nothing could dent Bond's popularity in 1965.

Time, which had featured Shirley Eaton covered in gold paint from *Goldfinger* on its cover just six months earlier, returned to Bondage in a feature titled 'Bondomania' in June 1965. It remains perhaps the most concise and brilliant assessment of the zenith of James Bond mania at that time:

> There seems to be no geographical limit to the appeal of sex, violence and snobbery with which Ian Fleming endowed his British secret agent, James Bond. In Tokyo, for instance, the queue for *Goldfinger*, the third Bond film, stretches half a mile. In Brazil, where the second, *From Russia With Love*, broke all Rio and San Paulo records, one unemployed TV actor had only to change his name to Jaime Bonde to be swamped with offers. In Beirut, where *Goldfinger* outdrew *My Fair Lady*, even Goldfinger's hat-hurling bodyguard, Oddjob, has become a minor hero.
>
> And in New York, the ads and marquees scream: 'JAMES BOND IS BACK . . . TO BACK!' The first movies, *Dr. No* and *From Russia With Love*, both less than three years old, are being double-billed here and all across the US. In the New York area, they jammed 26 theatres and grossed $650,000 for the week. The same crowds, the same large grosses in Boston, Buffalo, Chicago, Los Angeles and Washington; at the drive-ins, traffic rivalled the commuting hour.
>
> What makes the box-office figures that more astonishing is that both films are grossing nearly as much the second time around as the first. Sparking the revival is the success of *Goldfinger*, still finishing its first run and heading for a gross that now seems likely to reach $30 million.

Nor is Bondomania restricted to the US. In England, all three films broke box-office records, and Ian Fleming's last book, THE MAN WITH THE GOLDEN GUN, has already climbed to the top of the bestseller list.

To date, in hard cover and paperbacks, Bond books have been read by some 30 million people, and United Artists estimate that 25 million have seen Bond in reel life. By the time all three current Bond films have been milked dry, the take may top $100 million.

But, just as Fleming's increased book sales had led to his facing a backlash in Britain when DR. NO was published in 1958, so now the Bond movie cult also attracted negative comment – albeit on a much grander scale.

The Vatican deplored Bond in its official newspaper, while Malcolm Muggeridge, whom Ian Fleming had regarded as a friend, weighed in by penning an article in which he opined,

Insofar as one can focus on so shadowy and unreal a character, he is utterly despicable: obsequious to his superiors, pretentious in his tastes, callous and brutal in his ways, with strong undertones of sadism, and an unspeakable cad in his relations with women, toward whom sexual appetite represents the only approach.

The East German newspaper *Neues Deutschland* believed,

The Bond films and books contain all the obvious and ridiculous rubbish of reactionary doctrine. Socialism is synonymous with crime. Unions are fifth columns of the Soviet Union. Slavs are killers and sneaks. Scientists are amoral eggheads. Negroes are superstitious, murderous lackeys. Persons of mixed race are trash.

But it was, perhaps, the article that appeared on 30 September 1965 in *Pravda* (the newspaper founded by Lenin in May 1912) that is a measure of just how Bond's cultural status was reverberating around the globe. Under the heading PREACHING A LICENCE TO KILL, *Pravda* stated,

James Bond lives in a nightmarish world where laws are written at the point of a gun, where coercion and rape is considered valour and murder is a funny trick. All this is invested to teach people to accept the antics of American marines somewhere in the Mekong Delta in Vietnam and Her Majesty's Intelligence agents in Hong Kong and Aden.

Bond's job is to guard the interests of the property class, and he is no better than the youths Hitler boasted he would bring up like wild beasts to be able to kill without thinking.

His creator is Ian Fleming, who posed as *The Times* correspondent in Russia in 1939 but was in truth a spy for the capitalist nations. Although he is now dead, James Bond cannot be allowed to die because he reaches those sent to kill in Vietnam, the Congo, the Dominican Republic and many other places.

It is no accident that sham agents of the Soviet counter-intelligence, represented in caricature form, invariably figure in the role of Bond's opponents, because Bond kills right and left the men Fleming wanted to kill – Russians, Reds and Yellows. Bond is portrayed as a sort of white archangel, destroying the impure races.

The Bond cult started in 1963 [*sic*] when the American leader, President Kennedy, unsuspecting that some American hero with the right to kill would shoot him, too, declared that Fleming's books were his bedside reading. As if by magic wand, everything changed. The mighty forces of reaction immediately gave the green light to Fleming. And in James Bond he has created a symbol of the civilisation which has used bombs to drown the voice of conscience.

The men and women who allow their talents to be used in the making of films about the exploits of this man are also guilty of furthering the shameful aims of the Western capitalists.

Thunderball opened in the UK and US simultaneously on 29 December 1965 and was an immediate success. It went on to gross $141 million worldwide and was supported by a frenzied array of tie-ins and merchandising that made the marketing of *Goldfinger* the previous year seem positively restrained.

Artistically, however, *Thunderball* is a disappointment. Easily the least inspired of the Eon–Connery Bonds, the film is overlong, underpowered and, frankly, in some stretches it is one of only two official Bond movies actually to be boring. While some scenes work extremely well – SPECTRE's hijacking of the Vulcan bomber being the highlight – the film has remarkably little suspense. This is a fatal flaw in a movie in which Bond is supposedly searching for stolen nuclear bombs against the clock.

On the plus side, Sean Connery looks good throughout the movie while Luciana Paluzzi is fantastic as Fiona – the film only ever comes to life when she is on screen. Sadly, however, Claudine Auger is an insipid Domino and Adolfo Celi a very dull villain.

After all the legal wrangles, then, *Thunderball* was a letdown. But not for Eon Productions and United Artists' accountants, who saw the film appear on *Variety*'s chart of the top ten highest-grossing films of all time.

Thunderball was Terence Young's swansong as a Bond director. Frankly, much of the disappointment with the film can be laid at his feet: after Guy Hamilton's inspired and stylised direction of *Goldfinger*, Young's direction of *Thunderball* is often flat and banal. In fairness, he himself recognised the film's shortcomings and there was no doubting his own disappointment with it.

'Although *Thunderball* was an enormous success, I don't really like it,' he admitted some years later. 'To my mind all that underwater stuff was anti-James Bond, because it was slow motion. People swim slowly and you couldn't have them going very fast; we undercranked some of the shots and they looked ridiculous – the water was wobbling around so much it suddenly became stupid.'

Mediocre though *Thunderball* is, the film underlined in the clearest possible way that the global market for Bond was huge. This was not lost on other studios and other producers.

Cubby Broccoli and Harry Saltzman did not mind competition and, given the massive success of their four Bond films thus far, they expected it. But, as *Thunderball* raked in the dollars and the pounds and the yen around the world, they became uncomfortably aware that they would face competition at the box office from a rival Bond movie before their fifth Bond movie premiered. And there was a further uncertainty.

They may still have Sean Connery. But for how much longer?

007: Live and Let Spy

> 'It became a terrible pressure, like living in a goldfish bowl. That was part of the reason why I wanted to be finished with Bond. Also I had become completely identified with it, and it became very wearing and boring.'
>
> Sean Connery, 1974

By the time *Thunderball* was on general release and breaking box-office records around the world at the start of 1966, the 'spy boom' in cinemas and on television had reached its peak. Spies were in, and the Eon Bond series was copied, parodied and ripped off everywhere.

Every major Hollywood studio attempted to jump on the Bondwagon by producing its own superspy and, more often than not, actually trying to launch its own franchises. The Matt Helm series, starring Dean Martin, ran to four films – *The Silencers* (1966), *Murderers Row* (1966), *The Ambushers* (1967) and *The Wrecking Crew* (1968); the Harry Palmer series, based on Len Deighton's books and produced by Harry Saltzman himself, ran to three – *The Ipcress File* (1964), *Funeral In Berlin* (1966) and *Billion Dollar Brain* (1968); and the Derek Flint series, starring James Coburn, managed two – *Our Man Flint* (1966) and *In Like Flint* (1967). All of these series started well but quickly petered out because, unlike the Bond films, their producers cashed in on their initial success and compromised with the sequels. Even Harry Saltzman had not learned this lesson from the Bond series and the third Harry Palmer film was a disaster.

Nonetheless, *The Silencers*, *Our Man Flint*, *The Ipcress File* and *Funeral In Berlin* are all excellent films in their own right. The first Matt Helm and Derek Flint films are particularly funny and the heroine's name in *The Silencers*, Lovey Kravezit, is a fabulous twist on Pussy Galore.

There were also eight *Man From U.N.C.L.E.* films released by MGM (who would distribute the official Bond films from 1983 onwards) in cinemas between 1964 and 1968. The first *U.N.C.L.E.* cinematic release was *To Trap a Spy* which, in reality, was the pilot for the *Man From U.N.C.L.E.* TV series, with a few new scenes shot. The other *U.N.C.L.E.* films all originated as two-part TV episodes spliced together and released as films outside the US.

Joseph Losey directed *Modesty Blaise* in 1966, competing with Stanley Donan's *Arabesque* the same year. Losey's film was a bizarre comic strip, which was a whole lot less funny than its makers thought it was, but *Arabesque*, while nowhere near as good as Donan's 1963 classic *Charade* (which had the sublime casting of Cary Grant and Audrey Hepburn), was good fun.

Bulldog Drummond, whose exploits in the pages of H C (Sapper) McNeile's books predated Fleming's Bond and whose first cinematic appearance in the silent *Bulldog Drummond* came exactly forty years before *Dr. No*, was dusted down and given a Bondian makeover in *Deadlier Than the Male* (1967) and *Some Girls Do* (1970). Richard Johnson, Terence Young's preferred choice as the first Bond before Sean Connery was cast, was an inappropriate Drummond.

John Le Carré, whose espionage books are about as far removed from Ian Fleming's as it is possible to imagine, also benefited from the cinematic spy boom when two of his books were filmed: *The Spy Who Came In From The Cold* (1965) and *The Looking Glass War* (1969). This windfall from the Bondwagon did nothing to endear Bond to Le Carré, who has always been critical of Fleming. In the mid-1980s, at the height of the renewed Cold War, Le Carré visited Russia and told the Soviet press that Fleming's Bond novels were 'cultural pornography'. He also said he despised Bond, a 'Superman figure who is "ennobled" by some sort of misty, patriotic ideas and who can commit any crime and break any law in the name of his own society'.

There was even a cheap Italian spy film called *Operation Kid Brother*, which starred none other than Sean Connery's younger brother, Neil.

Bernard Lee and Lois Maxwell were also persuaded to appear, something that caused tensions between them and Sean Connery during the shooting of *You Only Live Twice*.

And, of course, the Carry On team jumped onto the spy boom with *Carry On Spying* in 1964. Filmed at Pinewood Studios on many of the same stages as Eon's Bond series, *Carry On Spying* may not have been the best of the series, but it had some very funny sequences and saw the Carry On debut of Barbara Windsor.

On television, the list of spy series is headed, naturally enough, by *The Avengers*. Although the series actually began before *Dr. No*, it was a fairly standard thriller series to begin with – intended as a vehicle for Ian Hendry – with Patrick Macnee's legendary John Steed merely a secondary character. It took the Bond films to define *The Avengers*, as Patrick Macnee admits: 'We started shooting before the first Bond film came out, though not, of course, before the books came out. I think, if I were really honest, that *The Avengers* owes a very strong debt to the Ian Fleming books, and in fact when I was approached to do the part I was advised to read them. I took the veneer of Bond for Steed without using the core. In other words, what I left out were the words "licence to kill". I had no licence to kill. All I really had as Steed was a will to bring the enemy to book and I like to feel I could go out without a gun and use whatever was to hand.

'Steed's umbrella was simply a symbol: not of authority or the mighty power of a gun, but as a means of concealing gadgets – which again, of course, was pure Bond.'

Other memorable spy series, on both sides of the Atlantic, were *The Man From U.N.C.L.E.* (its companion series, *The Girl From U.N.C.L.E.*, starring Stefanie Powers, was much less successful), *Mission: Impossible*, which has recently been turned into a successful movie franchise for Tom Cruise, and *Dangerman*, starring Patrick McGoohan as the squeaky-clean John Drake.

Characters like *The Avengers'* John Steed and Napoleon Solo from *The Man From U.N.C.L.E.* (the latter, of course, having been partly devised by Ian Fleming himself) are undoubtedly memorable, but the spy boom did not produce a character who came close to emulating the iconic status James Bond had now acquired.

That was why Glidrose Publications published OCTOPUSSY in 1966, a slim volume containing two of Fleming's short stories, 'Octopussy' and 'The Living Daylights' (a third Fleming short story, 'The Property of a Lady', a trite tale he had written for Sotheby's yearbook in 1963, was added for the paperback run); and why Eon Productions were pushing ahead with plans for their fifth Bond film, which had been intended to be *On Her Majesty's Secret Service* but was now changed to *You Only Live Twice*.

Whatever competition Eon faced at the box office, they had the ace: James Bond. But there was one Ian Fleming property they had not been able to option: CASINO ROYALE. Ian Fleming had sold the film rights to Gregory Ratoff in 1955 and Ratoff's widow had sold them to the producer Charles K Feldman, whose impressive credits included *To Have and Have Not*, *The Big Sleep*, *Red River*, *A Streetcar Named Desire*, *The Seven Year Itch* and the madcap but hugely successful *What's New Pussycat?*.

By 1965, Feldman knew the film rights to CASINO ROYALE were a potential goldmine. But, like Kevin McClory before him, he also knew there was a stumbling block: Sean Connery. How could anyone make a serious Bond film in 1965 without Sean Connery?

Connery may be tiring of Bond – this was no secret in the industry and Broccoli and Saltzman released Connery from his one-picture-a-year commitment to Bond after *Thunderball* and signed him on a one-picture contract for *You Only Live Twice* – but this did not deter Feldman, who approached Connery.

'Charlie Feldman rang me up and asked if I'd be interested,' Connery said. 'I told him "Only for a million dollars," and he said the budget wouldn't run to that. Some time later I ran into him in a London nightclub. By that time the film had already cost millions and he was up to his neck in it. "Y'know something," he told me, "at a million dollars for you I'd've got off lightly."'

Interestingly, Wolf Mankowitz, who had, of course, written the first draft of *Dr. No* with Richard Maibaum for Broccoli and Saltzman, and who was just one of the writers on *Casino Royale*, told a different story, claiming Feldman had turned Connery down from the outset. Notwithstanding Connery's own memories of Feldman having approached him, this would be unlikely: no producer with any commercial nous – and, until *Casino Royale*, Feldman was certainly that – would have dismissed Sean Connery out of hand in the mid-1960s. As the posters proclaimed, 'Sean Connery *is* James Bond!'

Feldman then approached Broccoli and Saltzman with a view to co-producing *Casino Royale*, much the same way as they had reached agreement with Kevin McClory to co-produce *Thunderball*. But Feldman's terms – he wanted 75 per cent of the profits for himself, 25 per cent for Broccoli, Saltzman and United Artists – were impossible for them even to consider, and they told him they weren't interested.

At that point, Columbia Pictures, who'd tried and failed to persuade Broccoli and Saltzman to sell their stake in the Bond empire, stepped in and offered to finance *Casino Royale* for Feldman. They were not to know that the chaotic film would end up costing a then staggering $12 million, far more than the budget United Artists allocated *You Only Live Twice*.

Feldman decided that without Sean Connery, and being in direct competition with the Eon series, the only way to produce *Casino Royale* was as a gigantic spoof in the style of *What's New Pussycat?*, with which he had enjoyed great success in 1965. Significantly, Peter Sellers, Ursula Andress and Woody Allen, who had appeared in *Pussycat*, were all signed for *Casino Royale*. David Niven, a friend of Ian Fleming's and an original contender for 007, was cast as Sir James Bond.

But *Casino Royale* was an unhappy and troubled production. It was scheduled for a Christmas 1966 release, and production began on 8 December 1965, but shooting did not finish until November 1966, by which time *Casino Royale* was way over schedule and hugely over budget. It was released four months late, in April 1967, just two months before *You Only Live Twice*.

Casino Royale has five credited directors – John Huston, Ken Hughes, Val Guest, Robert Parrish and Joe McGrath – and three credited writers – Wolf Mankowitz, John Law and Michael Sayers. In reality, far more people had an input into the script: Ben Hecht, whose screen credits included *Wuthering Heights* and Hitchcock's superb *Notorious*; Joseph Heller; Terry Southern, an associate of Stanley Kubrick; Val Guest; John Huston; Woody Allen, who loathed the film and demanded his name be removed from the writing credit; and Peter Sellers.

With his production spiralling out of control and the industry word of mouth disastrous, an increasingly beleaguered Charles Feldman tried to justify the number of directors. 'Although our screenplay basically follows the book,' he told *Variety*, 'the story breaks into various sequences and we've been trying to find the ideal director to match the mood of each.

'This is the age of specialization. Our concept for this film includes not only multiple stars, such as Peter Sellers, Ursula Andress and Orson Welles among others, but also multiple directors.'

But the input of so many people made it impossible to maintain any sense of coherent plotline for *Casino Royale*, prompting Wolf Mankowitz's caustic comment when he resigned from the picture: 'When I started on it it was a serious business. When I finished, the whole thing was a comedy. Actually, I think it's a new concept in films, the movie version of a four-ring circus.'

Casino Royale's stars were equally at sea. '*Casino* is a madhouse,' wrote Woody Allen to Richard O'Brien. 'I haven't begun filming yet but saw the sets for my scenes. They are the height of bad pop-art expensive vulgarity. My part changes every day as new stars fall in. I think the film stinks, as does my role.'

'I'm in a daze,' Ursula Andress complained to the *Sun*. 'I don't know what I'm supposed to say. I don't know what I'm not supposed to say. I don't know which script, which director, which producer, which scene. It's a confusion.'

'First there was just one James Bond, who is now Sir James Bond,' Wolf Mankowitz told Barry Norman, explaining the 'serious' origins of the *Casino Royale* script. 'He struck such terror into the hearts of the opposition that thereafter the British Secret Service called *all* its agents James Bond to confuse everyone. I saw the story as a kind of Trials of Hercules. Each task Bond faced needed a different talent so someone with that talent was recruited and called James Bond to deal with it. This way everyone who sees the picture will find at least one Bond with whom he can identify.'

The kernel of Ian Fleming's original novel – Bond's battle with Le Chiffre – was used in the Peter Sellers segment. Sellers played Evelyn Tremble (recruited to the Secret Service, called James Bond 007 etc.) who is trained by Vesper Lynd (Ursula Andress) to take on Le Chiffre. But the film veers wildly into repeated absurdities. M (John Huston wearing a silly red wig) is blown up when Sir James's house is destroyed; Sir James delivers M's hairpiece, the only thing of him to survive, to his widow Lady Fiona (Deborah Kerr), only to discover, in an utterly unwatchable sequence, that Lady Fiona is bogus and her castle stuffed full of beautiful SMERSH agents; it's revealed Sir James has a daughter, Mata Bond, the result of a relationship with Mata Hari; a SMERSH flying saucer lands in Trafalgar Square; and Dr Noah (Woody Allen), Sir James's nephew, plans to wipe out all men taller than he is with a virus and replace every world leader with a robot facsimile.

Central to *Casino Royale*'s problems was Peter Sellers, not the least erratic, demanding or difficult of actors. He demanded script changes and insisted one set be torn down because he didn't like it. And then he started arriving late on set – or not arriving at all.

'Peter was having problems with Britt Ekland, his wife at that time,' says Joe McGrath, who was directing Sellers' segment in *Casino Royale*. 'She'd gone back to Sweden and Peter was telephoning her, and nipping across to see her at weekends. Peter was late on a few occasions, and Feldman was getting very annoyed. He told the associate producer John Dark to get Peter to arrive on time. John couldn't do this because Peter wouldn't pay any attention to him. Feldman then called me and said, "You're the director – tell him to get there on time." I refused, saying "No, I'm the director. When Peter's here I'll direct him. When he's not here we'll do something else. You're paying him, Charlie – *you* get him there on time."

'Peter got to hear about this and asked to talk to me in his caravan. He said "Why are you on their side, and what the hell's going on?" I told him I wasn't on anybody's side, and he said, "You should be on *my* side." The problem was that they saw me as a friend of Peter's, and they were asking me, as his friend, to get him there on time. I wasn't going to do that. I told him, "If you want to behave like a naughty schoolboy, get on with it." Then he tried to hit me.'

Worse was to come when Sellers refused to appear on set with Orson Welles, who had been cast as Le Chiffre. 'You can't make a $10-million film, the high point of which is a card duel between two men, if those two men never appear together,' McGrath argued with Sellers. But Sellers, fearing that Welles, a notorious scene-stealer, would eclipse him, refused to budge and the scene eventually had to be shot with stand-ins substituting for each star on alternate days.

'For five days Peter simply didn't turn up while Orson was on set,' says McGrath. 'So for five days I had to shoot on Orson. If I hadn't it would have been five days with nothing done. Peter just wasn't around.

'Eventually he disappeared. No one knew where he was, or would tell Feldman where he was. We couldn't do anything. It destroyed the film.'

Peter Sellers never completed his role in *Casino Royale*, something that the capricious star blamed on the producers. On 15 April 1966, the *Evening Standard* reported that Sellers's connection with *Casino Royale* 'has ended without his part being completed'. Sellers's own version of events was somewhat at odds with how Feldman and everyone else associated with the picture remembered things: 'I was approached by the producer and asked if I would be prepared to continue and make what they called "a gesture". I was naturally anxious to see my part finished, as I have helped to write it and will be getting an author's screen credit [*sic*].

'So I told them, "All right, but we've got to get on with it." We were about to begin one week's extra work when they decided not to continue. It's all very strange. A gigantic puzzle, the whole film.'

Sellers's behaviour merely added to the bad word of mouth about *Casino Royale* in the industry and the press, but its horrendous problems were not greeted with any pleasure by Eon Productions. At the press conference held at the Tokyo Hilton prior to the start of location filming in Japan for *You Only Live Twice*, Sean Connery was asked about *Casino Royale* and whether he thought it would damage the official film.

'I don't think it'll make any difference,' he replied, 'because there have been countless other spy-type films and they haven't made any difference. And I don't see why *Casino Royale* should make any difference.'

But he tried to be positive about the rival movie, adding, 'I hope it makes a lot of money – because it's cost a lot of money!'

Cubby Broccoli was gently dismissive when asked the same question, anticipating 'a sort of enlarged *What's New Pussycat?*, just a harmless spoof', which would do nothing to harm *You Only Live Twice*. In private, Broccoli was worried by the toll *Casino Royale* was having on Charles Feldman, a man he had known for many years, first as an agent and then a producer. 'I liked Charlie,' Broccoli was to say later, 'because he was a straight shooter and was afraid of no one.' But those who knew and liked Feldman, like Broccoli, could not fail to notice how *Casino Royale* was destroying his health. Their fears were horribly realised almost exactly a year after *Casino Royale* opened when he died in May 1968 at the age of 63. Just prior to his death, Feldman told Joe McGrath, 'I think *Casino Royale* drove me crazy. I didn't know what had been shot and what hadn't been shot. I just lost control.'

You Only Live Twice was a very different film from *Casino Royale* in content, although, in its own way, it was every bit as expansive and outlandish. The fantastic success of *Thunderball*, not to mention the first three films, ensured that money was no object in bringing *You Only Live Twice* to the screen: United Artists allocated Eon a budget of $9.5 million.

But the massive success of the first four films had brought with it creative problems. By now, Broccoli and Saltzman knew what the public liked about the Bond movies. The audience for Bond films had certain expectations. *Goldfinger*, in particular, had created a template, a formula, for James Bond films – a cinematic formula that had been refined from Ian Fleming's own unique literary formula.

But Fleming's YOU ONLY LIVE TWICE, brilliant though it is, is an atypical Bond novel. Moreover, apart, perhaps, from Bond's climactic meeting with Blofeld in his nemesis's Japanese castle, the novel is resolutely uncinematic: cinema audiences did not expect, still less want, James Bond recovering from a nervous breakdown at the start of the film, nor ending it as an amnesiac believing himself to be a humble Japanese fisherman at the climax. Thus, Broccoli and Saltzman decided, for reasons of commercial expediency, to discard almost all of Fleming's original novel. The Japanese setting was retained, as were a few characters; otherwise the filmmakers created an entirely new plot.

To realise the new film, Broccoli and Saltzman brought in a new director, Lewis Gilbert, and a new writer, Roald Dahl, both of whose input ensured that *You Only Live Twice* was the biggest Bond epic yet.

Gilbert had such classic films as *Reach for the Sky*, *Sink the Bismark* and *The Greengage Summer* to his credit, and was still basking in the international acclaim for *Alfie* when he began work on *You Only Live Twice*. The Bond film was a challenge he relished:

I enjoy shooting action films tremendously. I suppose they bring out the child in us. You have a scene in which a guy edges round a street corner, there's a burst of gunfire, the guy staggers out clutching his stomach and falls into the gutter. They're marvellous scenes to shoot; if you ask yourself why you enjoy them you realise it's because you remember doing exactly the same things when you were playing as a youngster.

The Bond films actually don't need as much direction as ordinary films because the characters are so well defined. To be fair, I think you have to say it was really Terence Young and Sean that really made the series. Whatever happened afterwards, whether it was by luck or fluke or design, the pattern was essentially laid down in those early pictures. So with the exception of making up jokes and actually doing the action things, a director doesn't have to discuss who his father was and what his relationship with him was like, and all those aspects that are important in a serious film.

Nobody's worried about what Bond did as a child or how his mother treated him. That's not what the Bond films are about. They're all action and fun.

Gilbert has also credited the producers – particularly Cubby Broccoli – for their input into the films. Speaking just after *You Only Live Twice* had premiered in June 1967, he paid tribute to them:

Cubby and Harry are brilliant producers. Success hasn't changed them. I've made about 25 films, so I've worked with quite a few producers in my time. Cubby and Harry are the only two who have definitely contributed towards their film.

In some mysterious way they know the common denominator for what the people want to see – in Tokyo, Berlin, Rome, Paris, Bury or Bolton. And all this is very difficult for a director to know. Directing is very national. You tend to think only in terms of what will go in Britain, among your own contemporaries, your own circle. You're not practised into thinking what will go in Cambodia and Hong Kong.

But Cubby and Harry know. They've seen it happen on other films and they've become experts. They're the only producers who really *know* their audience.

For instance, I remember Cubby saying to me, 'We always have two or three endings to a Bond film.' My natural instinct was to say, 'Oh, look, everybody will reach for their hats and walk out at the first ending.' But Cubby insisted, 'No,' he said. 'They always wait. They know there's going to be some funny extra ending.' So I agreed. And that's what we did.

Came the premiere. Well, the Queen was there, so I knew the audience wouldn't start walking out early. But last week I looked in at the Odeon Leicester Square in London's West End, at 1 p.m. on a Monday afternoon. Full house! Packed! Very thrilling, I must say. I stood at the back to see this ending; I couldn't believe that all these people weren't going to go the minute it seemed to be over. But they didn't. Not one person left until the tag-line joke and THE END came up. Cubby was right. They know these two. Because they have learned this particular field and exploit it.

Gilbert also explains how the 'writing by committee' of *You Only Live Twice*, a process that became increasingly common on the Bond films, actually worked:

The first time we went to Japan, Harry had got an American TV writer called Harold Jack Bloom. We tried to do a story with him but it didn't work out. When we got back to England, someone suggested Roald Dahl, which I thought was a good idea because he'd got that strange offbeat style of writing.

We went on a second recce with Ken Adam, Freddie Young (the director of photography), Cubby and myself – just the four of us – and we flew all over Japan looking for locations. One day, we were flying over an extinct volcano with a lake in its centre and I remember saying, 'God, that would be a good place where the villain could hide.' Ken took that up and he said, 'I could do a wonderful set in there.' And that's how it all started.

When we got back to England we had no idea what the story was going to be about, other than the fact it surrounded a volcano and there was a rocket in it. That much we'd all contributed to on this recce.

So I was closeted in South Audley Street, which was then Eon's London office, with Roald Dahl and we cobbled together a story, and then everybody came in and made their suggestions. That's how it came about really. It was very much a committee-oriented film in that sense. You never know who's made what suggestion and why – but it works in some crazy way.

Of course, there was no American involvement in those days. United Artists put the money up but never came near it really. Cubby and Harry were the prime movers.

Typical of this way of writing the script was the involvement of 'Little Nellie', the tiny but lethal autogyro that Bond uses in a spectacular dogfight with four SPECTRE helicopters. Harry Saltzman had spotted the invention, created by Wing Commander Ken Wallis at his base in Norfolk, and wanted it in the film. By a curious twist of fate, Ken Adam heard a radio interview with Wallis at the same time and also brought up the idea of using the autogyro in the film.

The resulting aerial chase, which replaced a somewhat banal car chase in the script, remains a highlight of the Bond series. Wing Commander Wallis doubled for Sean Connery in the sequence and 'Little Nellie' is one of the all-time great James Bond gadgets.

As Lewis Gilbert knew he would, Roald Dahl, who had been a close friend of Ian Fleming's, brought a dark edge to the *You Only Live Twice* script – a script that, for all the commercial emphasis on gadgets and hardware, remains one of the most underrated of the Bond series. In an amusing, if rather flip, article for *Playboy* to promote the film, Dahl recalled his brief from the producers:

'You can come up with anything you like so far as the story goes,' they told me, 'but there are two things you mustn't mess about with. The first is the character of Bond. That's fixed. The second is the girl formula. That is also fixed.' 'What's the girl formula?' I asked.

'There's nothing to it. You use three different girls and Bond has them all.' 'Separately or *en masse*?' One of them took a deep breath and let it out slowly. 'How many Bond films have you seen?' he asked. 'Just one. The one with the crazy motor-car.' 'You'd better see the others right away. We'll send them round to your house with a projector and someone to work it.' This was the first small hint I was to get of the swift, efficient, expansive way in which the Bond producers operated. Nobody else does things quite like them.

'So you put in three girls. No more and no less. Girl number one is pro-Bond. She stays around roughly through the first reel of the picture. Then she is bumped off by the enemy, preferably in Bond's arms.' 'In bed or not in bed?' I asked. 'Wherever you like, so long as it's in good taste. Girl number two is anti-Bond. She works for the enemy and stays around throughout the middle third of the picture. She must capture Bond, and Bond must save himself by bowling her over with sheer sexual magnetism. This girl should also be bumped off, preferably in an original fashion.' 'There aren't too many of those left,' I said. 'We'll find one,' they answered. 'Girl number three is violently pro-Bond. She occupies the final third of the picture, and she must on no account be killed. Nor must she permit Bond to take lecherous liberties with her until the very end of the story. We keep that for the fade-out.'

In Dahl's final screenplay, Ernst Stavro Blofeld, backed financially by Red China, is launching rockets from his hollowed-out volcano base in a remote part of Japan to intercept American and Soviet space capsules. The idea is that America and Russia will blame each other, eventually leading to World War Three, and, when they have annihilated each other, a new world order, led by China, will emerge.

As a plot, it is utterly absurd, but Dahl wrote it in such a grand, epic style that, somehow, he and the filmmakers pull off the whole ridiculous notion beautifully. Although not everyone agrees with that sentiment. John Brosnan in *James Bond in the Cinema* argued that *You Only Live Twice*'s plot is 'the plot from *Dr. No* with a mysterious island being run by SPECTRE to interfere with American space vehicles and which is eventually blown up by Bond'. But we submit that that, and other criticisms of *You Only Live Twice*, are massively unfair. Frankly, *Twice*'s screenplay is a definite improvement over *Thunderball*'s. It is tighter, more inventive and fairly taut. And it contains some beautiful moments, such as the sequence when Bond, disguised as a fisherman (a lingering idea from the novel) 'marries' Kissy Suzuki.

The true star of *You Only Live Twice*, however, is the full-scale interior of Blofeld's volcano, complete with a fully operational monorail, which Ken Adam built at Pinewood. It was then, and remains, the greatest achievement in the history of motion-picture art design.

The set was designed to match the exteriors, shot at Mount Shinmoe in Japan, and its construction statistics are truly awesome. Built at a cost of $1 million – more or less the cost of the entire first film, *Dr. No*, less than five years earlier – the set soared above Pinewood's backlot at a height of 126 feet (38 metres). Two hundred miles of tubular steel were used in its construction – enough to stretch from London to Manchester and more than was used in the building of the London Hilton; over 700 tons of structural steel; half a million tubular couplings; and 200 tons of plasterwork. It was so vast that, when it was foggy outside, the mist would form *inside* the set as well.

'Filming on this set is the biggest challenge that could happen to a director,' said Lewis Gilbert at the time. 'No film of my knowledge has ever had a set this large, with so many mechanical devices, with so much to film in one place. Every time I look at the set, I'm left with a determination not to waste one inch of all that marvellous space.'

For Ken Adam, however, his triumph was peppered with uncertainties:

The volcanoes in Japan immediately stimulated me. But the pressure was enormous on all of us because Cubby and Harry had committed to a release date. So when I came back to Pinewood I started scribbling immediately. Cubby said, 'How much is it going to cost?' I had no idea, so I said, 'It could cost a million dollars.' Cubby said, 'Well, if you can do it for a million dollars – go ahead.' And in 1966 a million dollars was a great deal of money.

Later on, when I saw the size of it and all the logistical problems, I thought I must have been crazy because if you can do it for a million dollars and everything works, you're a hero; but if something collapsed or went wrong, I'd never work in the film industry again.

The nightmare comes from suddenly realizing that you have designed something that has never been done before in films and that is bigger than any set ever used before. You wake up at night wondering whether or not the whole thing will work. There were times on the volcano set when I was breaking out in eczema and itching all over. I saw a specialist who told me to take some valium. It was all nerves because I had to ask myself, finally, was I crazy? What had I done?

You can surround yourself with the best possible construction engineers, but they can't help. They may be qualified to build the Empire State Building or the Eiffel Tower – buildings which follow normal construction techniques – but we were building a structure for which there were no previous terms of reference and with which no one had had any experience. I mean, who had ever built a 60-foot diameter [18-metre] sliding lake 120 feet [37 metres] up at an angle before?

But the set was also a designer's dream. To be given the freedom to plan such a complicated structure is a challenge no artist could resist. And seeing your drawings and ideas taking shape and becoming reality in steel and concrete and plaster is most satisfying. It is like seeing your own baby grow and become a super man.

The volcano set was the most visible sign of the confidence of Cubby Broccoli and Harry Saltzman. The success of the Bonds had, by 1966, made them two of the most important film producers in the world. But, already, tensions were showing in their partnership: tensions that would escalate over the course of the next four Bond movies.

Once Bond was up and running, the restless Saltzman was always looking for other projects, new business ventures to become involved in. Broccoli, on the other hand, was content to concentrate on Bond. Once he had produced *Dr. No* in 1962, Broccoli produced only two other non-Bond films until his death in 1996 – *Call Me Bwana*, a disappointing Bob Hope vehicle he co-produced, reluctantly, in 1963 with Saltzman, and the splendid screen version of Ian Fleming's CHITTY CHITTY BANG BANG in 1968.

The tension between the two men was obvious to everyone. 'Harry had quite a shock when Cubby said yes to a million dollars for the volcano set,' recalls Ken Adam, who continues,

But Cubby was more of a gambler in that sense. There was always a certain amount of friction between them. Harry was more of an ideas man. He was brought up in the circus and that never left him. He may have come up with nineteen bad ideas but the twentieth was wonderful.

Cubby was much more one of the boys. He had more experience in film production. Harry was much more volatile. He would explode every two minutes and then Cubby would collect the wreckage and come over to me or whoever it was and say, 'Don't worry. You know he doesn't mean it.' But I got so used to working with them and their idiosyncrasies that it didn't really worry me too much.

The problem was that I was on a very friendly personal basis with both of them and I began to feel like an unfaithful mistress because one didn't like the other. And that also became more apparent when they started making separate pictures and both wanted me: Cubby for *Chitty Chitty Bang Bang* and Harry for *The Battle of Britain*. You can't do everything, which meant there was always one of them who wouldn't talk to you for some time.

The friction between Broccoli and Saltzman was compounded on *You Only Live Twice* by Sean Connery's hardening attitude to the films. Broccoli was particularly upset by comments attributed to Connery: 'Money gives you freedom and power. I want to use that power I now have as a producer. What I'm really tired of is a lot of fat-slob producers living off the backs of lean actors.'

The relationship between Connery and Saltzman in particular had deteriorated to the point where Connery reportedly threatened to walk off set occasionally if Saltzman was present. Whatever the truth of those rumours, Saltzman shrugged off the stories of any bad feelings between them when questioned on television by Alan Whicker in a *Whicker's World* special on the making of *You Only Live Twice*, broadcast in March 1967. 'No stars are easy,' said Saltzman. 'But he's all right. We have our differences but the pictures get made.'

Of course Connery, renowned as a consummate professional in the industry, was as dedicated as ever once filming began on *You Only Live Twice* but he made it plain to everyone who would listen that it would definitely be his last Bond film. Cubby Broccoli knew he meant it and, during his interview with Alan Whicker, he was already looking ahead to continuing the series without Connery.

'*You Only Live Twice* won't be the last one under any circumstances. With all due respect to Sean, who I think has been the best actor to play this part, we will in our own way try to continue the Bond series for the audience. And, if Sean doesn't want to do it, if he doesn't agree with our arrangements or whatever, we can't force him to do it. I can't say that he's right or wrong – that's up to him.

'Everything is a headache in making a picture. But you have to be determined to find a way. And if Sean doesn't want to do it – and he has a right not to do it – then that won't stop us from making another Bond, because the audience out there want to see it. We'll present what we have for their approval.'

If Sean Connery had had any lingering doubts about ending his association with the Bond movies, *You Only Live Twice*'s long, arduous shoot, coupled with the incessant press and public attention, convinced him he was right. An intensely private man, he lamented his loss of privacy in interviews: 'I live in Acton and we have a marvellous house in a wonderful situation. Unfortunately, it's too accessible. It means people can come right up to the front gate and get in. It's the only house in the street, in a cul-de-sac right by a park – a perfect situation. But they just come up and sit on top of the cars, or come in at the gate and knock at the door. You get some real headcases that come round and have the most absurd requests like, "It would be marvellous to come and have tea", or, "Could I sign on your wall?" Juvenile, insane ideas. It's an invasion of one's privacy.

'I have no publicity agent, I have no personal manager. Consequently, one goes to the barbers and reads absolute shit written about one that some tinhead has put up.'

At one point during filming in Japan, Cubby Broccoli was forced to plead with photographers to leave his star alone when Connery retreated to his hotel suite. 'He hasn't even had his lunch yet,' Broccoli told them. 'He had to go back up to his room because he didn't have the privacy of having a little lunch. He's an actor. He's here to do a job. He's not just a publicity idol. Now he's here and he's not been given the privilege and respect of Japan for a certain amount of privacy. Today he is supposed to rest – under my orders. If you promise to leave him alone for the rest of the afternoon, *perhaps* I can persuade him to let you take some pictures.'

'Sometimes I think he's quicker-tempered because of all the pressures,' said Connery's wife, Diane Cilento, during filming. 'Like being followed to the lavatory by photographers.

'I think he's tried beyond normal limits. Everywhere you go you can't be by yourself at all, really, because there's always someone coming out from behind a tree.'

'I've never known it like this before,' Connery commented on his hounding by the press in Japan during the *You Only Live Twice* shoot. 'I knew Bond was popular all over the world and he's done a lot for me.

But I created a Frankenstein monster when the series began and now I've had enough.

'None of us could have foreseen how it would catch on. I admit it's done more for me than any other character has done for an actor in history. But if you'd been asked the same questions day after day for four years, how would you feel? Everyone says the same thing. No one seems to think of anything else.

'It's been a lot of fun, particularly in the beginning. But this is the last James Bond for me.'

Eight years later, the fraught memories of filming *You Only Live Twice* were still raw. Speaking in 1974, Connery recalled, 'When we went to Japan, and then to Bangkok and Hong Kong, there were people crowded into the hotel lobbies and on street corners, just waiting to look at me. It became a terrible pressure, like living in a goldfish bowl. That was part of the reason why I wanted to be finished with Bond.

'Also I had become completely identified with it, and it became very wearing and boring. The trouble was the films were getting progressively longer to make and that made it more difficult to even consider other work. And it *is* important for any actor to play diverse roles. *You Only Live Twice* was the last straw. That took six months of my time – and that on top of two or three postponements. I could never give a firm date to anyone else and that meant I missed out on other parts I wanted to do, all because of Bond.'

When principal photography ended on *You Only Live Twice* in December 1966, Connery's decision never to play James Bond again seemed final. No one, including Connery himself, knew that he would ultimately play the role twice more – albeit once in a very controversial Bond film, which was not produced by Eon.

Finding a replacement for Connery for the next film, *On Her Majesty's Secret Service*, would be hard, but Broccoli and Saltzman had another, more immediate, problem to contend with. *Casino Royale*, way behind schedule, was now going to open just two months before *You Only Live Twice*. Whatever its artistic merits, or otherwise, *Casino Royale* had the potential to act as a spoiler, which would harm the box office of *You Only Live Twice*.

In the event, *Casino Royale* just about scraped enough money to cover its negative costs – which was something of a relief to Columbia – but it attracted some of the worst reviews in movie history. One reviewer called it 'sheer, unadulterated hell', while Leslie Halliwell, doyen of British film buffs, believed *Casino Royale* to be 'one of the most shameless wastes of time and talent in screen history'.

Actually, this is unfair. Like *The Avengers* (1998), a film whose reviews rivalled *Casino Royale*'s in opprobrium and in which, ironically, Sean Connery played the villain, *Casino Royale* is nowhere near as bad as legend suggests. It is certainly more enjoyable than *Never Say Never Again*, the 1983 renegade remake of *Thunderball*, as we shall see.

Casino Royale may be a mess, but there are also some scenes to cherish. The take-off of Q-Branch (situated underneath Harrods) is hilarious, while David Niven's Sir James Bond – who believes 'a good spy is a pure spy – inside and out' – has a certainly nobility. This is a Bond, 'the greatest spy in history', who 'stands on his head a lot' and 'eats royal jelly', who grows roses and plays Debussy 'every afternoon until it's too late to read the music', and who 'lets his intestines down and washes them by hand'. He also despises modern-day espionage, as he explains to the international Secret Service chiefs M (John Huston), Ransome (William Holden), Le Grand (Charles Boyer) and Smernov (Kurt Kasznar):

> BOND: In my day spying was an alternative to war. The spy was a member of a select and immaculate priesthood, vocationally devoted, sublimely disinterested. Hardly a description of that sexual acrobat who leaves a trail of beautiful dead women like blown roses behind him.
>
> M: You mean, er . . .?
>
> BOND: You know very well who I mean. That bounder to whom you gave my name and number.
>
> M: My dear James, when you left us we were a small service, underfinanced, ludicrously ill equipped – it was essential your legend be maintained. Without a James Bond, Oh-Oh-Seven, no one would respect us.
>
> BOND: Him and his wretched gadgets.
>
> LE GRAND: Well, we must make use of the weapons of our time.
>
> BOND: So I observe. You, Ransome, with your trick carnation that spits cyanide, you ought to be ashamed.
>
> RANSOME: The Russians started it . . .

BOND: And you, Smernov, with an armoury concealed in your grotesque boots. Listen to them tinkle. And you, Le Grand, with different deadly poisons in each of your fly buttons. And you, M, with your flame-throwing fountain pens. You're joke shop spies, gentlemen.

Such exchanges, rare though they are, make *Casino Royale* a pleasure to watch, albeit only in scattered sections. Best of all is the score by Burt Bacharach, which includes the sublime song, *The Look of Love*, performed on the soundtrack by Dusty Springfield. Bacharach's Bond score is magnificent and, given that John Barry composed one of his finest scores for *You Only Live Twice*, 1967 was definitely a good year for Bond soundtracks.

If the reviews for *Casino Royale* had been horrendous, the reviews for *You Only Live Twice* were also more mixed than Cubby Broccoli and Harry Saltzman were used to when their film premiered at the Odeon Leicester Square, on Monday, 12 June 1967. There was a general feeling that the cinematic spy boom was starting to wane and, mindful of that, many critics were harsher on *You Only Live Twice* than they had been on *Thunderball* eighteen months earlier, even though, in retrospect, *Twice* is clearly the better film. It is a sharp, wild fantasy, which has all the sparkling virtues of *Goldfinger*, on a much bigger budget, with none of the lazy, flabby vices of *Thunderball*.

In the event, *You Only Live Twice* was a massive hit at the box office but, at $111.6 million, its worldwide grosses were some $30 million lower than the $141.2 million enjoyed by *Thunderball*. Even more significant was the drop at the US box office – from $77.6 million for *Thunderball* to $68.5 million for *Twice*.

Time commented, 'the Bonds are losing their value' in their review of *You Only Live Twice*. Maybe that wasn't true artistically, but financially Broccoli and Saltzman were aware that the Bond stock had declined for the first time since they'd started producing the series.

They went into 1968 aware that not only was the spy boom over, but the 007 franchise itself might be on the wane.

Not only that, but they were faced with the headache of finding a new James Bond.

008: A New Bond?

'This never happened to the other fella . . .'

George Lazenby, *On Her Majesty's Secret Service*, 1969

In 1967, two names were synonymous with James Bond in the public consciousness: Ian Fleming and Sean Connery. But, in 1968, two unfamiliar names joined them to carry on the Bond tradition: Robert Markham and George Lazenby.

Robert Markham was the author whose name appeared on the cover of the first non-Fleming James Bond novel, COLONEL SUN, which Glidrose commissioned in 1967 and which was published by Jonathan Cape in the spring of 1968. But Robert Markham did not exist. The name was, in fact, a pseudonym used by Kingsley Amis, who had been Ian Fleming's most vigorous defender and who had published the seminal *The James Bond Dossier* in 1965.

'The use of a pseudonym was agreed by myself and the publisher and Glidrose,' Amis said. 'It was partly for my convenience – because it set that apart from my other novels – but mostly it was because it was considered possible that other writers might like to have a crack at writing a Bond novel. And so it would be less confusing if they all had the same pseudonym. There would be no attempt to dupe the public into believing it was the same man, but it would be more convenient to market the books and so on.'

To those who questioned his motives for accepting Glidrose's offer to write COLONEL SUN, Amis was cheerfully honest. 'Why do it?' he wrote. '[Because] I expect to make quite a lot of money out of the venture and jolly good luck to me. [And] what at the outset was an unimportant motive but has since developed into a major fringe benefit, is the thought of how cross with me the intellectual left will get.'

One of the enduring myths about COLONEL SUN is that Amis based the book on drafts and plans Ian Fleming left behind when he died. Amis considered that a compliment because it implied that COLONEL SUN was a worthy successor to Ian Fleming's series, but the truth was that he started the book from scratch and had himself met Fleming only twice.

'The first time was at a party,' Amis recalled. 'I said to him, "Mr Fleming, it is very rare to meet an author to whom you can honestly say, 'I've read all your books and I enjoy them very much.'" And he said, "That's very kind of you. Of course, you know they're all true."

'The second time was when I let him see the typescripts of *The James Bond Dossier* before I sent it to the publishers for his comments. He kindly took me out to lunch – it was nice, quite expensive – and he had nothing to say on any of the critical things I made. He just had points of accuracy he wanted to put me right about.'

COLONEL SUN is an excellent James Bond novel in its own right. Easily better than some of Fleming's lesser works, like DIAMONDS ARE FOREVER and THE MAN WITH THE GOLDEN GUN, Amis's Bond is largely the same character as Fleming's. It is, as one critic wrote, 'an extremely efficient job of resurrection'.

Pitting Bond against Red China for the first time, COLONEL SUN sees Bond lured to Greece in search of the kidnapped M. The purpose behind the Red Chinese plot, which is led by Colonel Sun Liang-tan, is to bomb an important Russian summit conference and to leave the bodies of Bond and M at the scene, thereby implicating the British. While the book is more sexually explicit than anything Ian Fleming ever wrote and is, perhaps, more violent than any previous Bond book save for CASINO ROYALE, COLONEL SUN succeeds admirably in its core objective of taking over where Fleming left off.

COLONEL SUN was popular with Bond fans at the time – and its reputation has deservedly increased since – but reviewers were harsh, with few exceptions. And Ian Fleming's widow, Ann, loathed the whole idea of continuing the literary Bond after Fleming's death and she wrote scathingly of her 'distaste' for the 'counterfeit Bond'. She added, 'I think Amis should publish under his own name and show the world that his left-wing intellectual pretensions were easily turned to money grubbing – like everyone else.'

Invited by the *Sunday Telegraph* to review the book, Ann wrote,

> Since the exploiters hope COLONEL SUN will be the first of a new and successful series, they may find themselves exploited. Amis will slip 'Lucky Jim' into Bond's clothing, we shall have a petit bourgeois red-brick Bond, he will resent the authority of M, then the discipline of the Secret Service, and end as a Philby Bond selling his country to SPECTRE. James to Jim to Kim.

The *Sunday Telegraph* never published her review, fearing libel.

Whatever controversies COLONEL SUN was making in the literary world, they were overshadowed by Eon Productions' search for a James Bond to replace Sean Connery. The search had begun in earnest in October 1967, and several names were mentioned in the press. Richard Burton was considered, as was Adam West (TV's Batman). A young actor who was just making a name for himself was also seen by Cubby Broccoli. At the age of 21, Timothy Dalton was far too young to play Bond, as he, himself, pointed out to Broccoli. But Broccoli never forgot that meeting – nor did he forget Dalton. Roger Moore, who had been near the top of the list in 1962, was also considered but he was still making *The Saint* and too firmly identified with the role of Simon Templar.

Peter Hunt, promoted from editor and second-unit director to direct *On Her Majesty's Secret Service*, began testing and interviewing scores of actors who were potential James Bonds. At the same time there was a debate among the production team about just what kind of Bond they were looking for. Should he be more modern? Younger? Less formal? 'A great deal of time, days and perhaps weeks, were spent in discussing the sort of character that we would get as a new Bond,' said Peter Hunt. 'These discussions were between United Artists, Broccoli, Saltzman, myself, and everyone else involved because we said to ourselves, "Okay, maybe now this is the opportunity to get a younger, more modern man. Perhaps he should have longer hair or be more hippy." But it was eventually resolved that we would try as hard as we could to find a physical replica of Sean Connery – and that was what we looked for.'

'We had had this plastic surgery idea,' admitted the screenwriter Richard Maibaum many years later. 'Bond had to have plastic surgery because he was being recognised by all his country's enemies. But we thought that was awful and threw it out.'

So, in the end, the decision was unanimous: what they needed was another Sean Connery. Ideally, an *unknown* Sean Connery. But, as Harry Saltzman noted, 'Finding good, undiscovered actors of thirty is not too easy.'

A shortlist of hopefuls was drawn up from the hundreds of submissions from agents, suggestions from other directors or producers, or direct applications. From this shortlist, Peter Hunt intended to film exhaustive screen tests, which could then be submitted to United Artists for approval. On the shortlist was George Lazenby, a 28-year-old Australian former car-salesman and model who was best known on television from the Fry's Chocolate advertisements but who had no acting experience.

Having been advised by an agent that he had the necessary looks and arrogance for Bond, Lazenby had done his homework to get on that shortlist. He had gone to Sean Connery's tailor to get a suit like Connery's, and then went to the famous Kurt's barber's shop at the Dorchester Hotel in Mayfair to get his hair cut like Connery's. Coincidentally, Cubby Broccoli was in the next chair. 'That guy would make a good James Bond,' Broccoli commented when Lazenby left. 'But he is probably a very successful businessman and wouldn't be interested.'

'That was how the story started that Cubby Broccoli discovered me in a barber's shop,' says George Lazenby.

Now looking like James Bond, Lazenby went to Eon's offices at 3 South Audley Street, London. 'I paced up and down outside on the pavement outside,' recalls Lazenby. 'When the receptionist bent down behind the desk, I dashed in and upstairs where the casting was going on. I found myself in Harry Saltzman's office. Harry had his feet on the desk, no shoes on, leaning back and talking on the phone. He pointed at the chair and growled "Siddown . . ." I thought, I'm not sitting down there while your feet are up there, so I went and looked out the window. So he put his feet down, straightened himself up and said, "Have a seat." I got respect straight away.'

Both Broccoli (who *did* remember Lazenby from the barber's shop) and Saltzman liked Lazenby's look. They liked the way he moved – like Connery, he moved extremely well on his feet for a tall man – and Broccoli particularly noted the admiring looks of Eon's female staff when Lazenby walked through the office.

Lazenby had been an Ian Fleming fan for years but he initially believed his lack of acting experience precluded any chance of his actually being offered the part of Bond. 'I'd read all the Bond books,' he says. 'I'd even read CASINO ROYALE before I saw a Bond movie. Every man wants to have characteristics like Bond. Wouldn't it be great to enter a casino, get the best-looking girl, win all the money and go back to your hotel room and punch out the toughest guy around? And then get laid by a beautiful woman and have champagne and caviar.

'As a Bond fan you get illusions – or delusions – that you can play it better than anyone else. I had tough shoes to fill. That didn't bother me, however, because I had nothing to lose.

'But I didn't think I had much of a shot to begin with. As time went by and I saw people drop by the wayside I thought I had as good a chance as anybody. I knew the director, Peter Hunt, was on my side and as it turned out he got what he wanted.

'He said he had more footage of me testing than he had of me in the film. I was tested with all the other actors. If they had another actor for any other role and they needed some screen time to check him out, they used me in the Bond role. I recall playing Bond in a scene with Diana Rigg, who was being tested for the role of Tracy.'

It was during another screen test that Lazenby learned Broccoli and Saltzman had decided he was their man. Unused to the technique of screen fighting, Lazenby had mistimed a punch and accidentally broken the nose of the Russian wrestler Yuri Borienko (who plays Grunther in the movie). Saltzman calmly stepped over the bloodied Borienko and said to Lazenby, 'We're going with you.'

George Lazenby was announced as the new James Bond on 7 October 1968 at a press conference held at the Dorchester Hotel in London. A week later, Lazenby's co-stars – Diana Rigg, who was to play Tracy, the future Mrs Bond, and Telly Savalas, cast as Blofeld – were introduced with Lazenby at another reception.

A week after that, principal photography began at the summit of Mount Schiltorn in the Bernese Oberland district of Switzerland. There, the producers had found a revolving restaurant, which was a perfect match for Blofeld's Piz Gloria mountain-top lair as described by Ian Fleming in ON HER MAJESTY'S SECRET SERVICE.

Although construction had begun in 1961, the restaurant still wasn't completed but, for Eon, it had everything Fleming's novel – and Richard Maibaum's extremely faithful screenplay adaptation – demanded: it was almost 10,000 feet (3,050 metres) above sea level; had excellent ski runs all around for the extensive planned ski chases; and it even had its own cable-car system.

To begin with, the Swiss government weren't keen on the alterations that the *On Her Majesty's Secret Service* production designer Syd Cain wanted to make to the restaurant and refused planning permission. But when Eon promised not only to pay for an entire refit to the interior but also to build a permanent helicopter pad, which could aid mountain rescue services after filming was complete, the Swiss authorities relented.

The final bill to Eon was a relatively modest $60,000 – considerably less than Blofeld's volcano at Pinewood had cost two years earlier. The restaurant was renamed Piz Gloria and retains the name to this day. Despite considerable modifications during the 1980s, it is still recognisably much the same as when the *On Her Majesty's Secret Service* cast and crew departed.

Filming commenced with a shot of George Lazenby as Bond, in full Scottish regalia, entering Piz Gloria's restaurant, where he encounters Blofeld's Angels of Death – the twelve beautiful girls brainwashed into spreading biological warfare – for the first time. In Fleming's novel Blofeld had intended to wage biological warfare only against England, and so the girls came from various parts of England. Maibaum's script globalises the threat, however, so that now the girls are drawn from every continent, although Maibaum retains the Lancastrian Ruby (played by Angela Scoular) from Fleming's original. Among the girls are Jenny Hanley, playing the Irish Girl, Catherine Schell (Nancy) and Joanna Lumley as the haughty English Girl. Writing in the *Sunday Times* in 1987, Lumley dismissed the film: 'We were the Bond girls of '68. Picked like nuggets of gold from the great sieve of Saltzman and Broccoli. We did what we were required to do: namely simper, pose, pout and giggle.'

Ms Lumley presumably kept such thoughts to herself when Messrs Saltzman and Broccoli were actually paying her wages.

Relations on set quickly soured, however, and rumours of feuds and fights were to dog the lengthy production: shooting from 21 October 1968 to 23 June 1969 made *On Her Majesty's Secret Service* the longest official Bond production ever. The rumours majored on two areas: George Lazenby's alleged boorish behaviour and the nature of the apparently frosty relationship between Lazenby and Rigg.

'We all make mistakes,' Lazenby says. 'And I made mine. But I had no idea of the kind of exposure to expect. The press wanted me to be Bond morning, afternoon and night and so I lived Bond *out* of the studios as well as in. I had to have a Rolls-Royce to go around in and women just threw themselves at me if I stepped into a night club. I couldn't count the parade that passed through my bedroom. I became hot-headed, greedy and big-headed.'

At the start of shooting, Saltzman had told the crew in front of Lazenby that the new Bond was the star of the picture and must be treated as a star. But, when Lazenby referred to himself as a star on a later occasion, Cubby Broccoli slapped him down with, 'Listen George, you're not a star – yet. You're not a star just because you call yourself a star. You're not a star just because I call you a star, or the publicity people call you a star, or the director calls you a star. You're only a star when the public says so. And this we will have to see.'

Telly Savalas concurred, pulling Lazenby aside one day and telling him, 'Why are you being so difficult, George? Most actors would give their back teeth to get this kind of a break. You should be paying Cubby, not the other way around, so why don't you cool it?'

According to Broccoli's wife, Dana, Lazenby seemed to be 'at odds with almost everyone'. But what everyone had miscalculated was the strain a new actor, *any* actor, would face stepping into Sean Connery's shoes. In the 1960s it was the equivalent of someone having to replace Paul McCartney or John Lennon in the Beatles – and, if that person wasn't a trained musician, as Lazenby wasn't a trained actor, problems would have been inevitable.

If the Beatles were, as John Lennon claimed, 'bigger than Jesus' in the 1960s, James Bond wasn't far behind. Every lad wanted to be Bond; every dad thought he was. In 1967, the posters had screamed, 'Sean Connery *is* James Bond'. But in 1968 he wasn't. George Lazenby was. And the press seemed to resent him for that.

One incident at Pinewood underlined the frustrations facing

Lazenby. 'When I turned up for my first day's work at Pinewood the man on the gate wouldn't let me in,' Lazenby related in November 1968. 'He didn't know who I was. When I told him I was the new James Bond he didn't believe me. He had to phone through to someone to confirm that this feller named George Lazenby was playing James Bond.'

Particularly frustrating for Lazenby seemed to be the way Peter Hunt had *apparently* abandoned him once shooting had commenced. Hunt had been Lazenby's champion from the start but once filming got under way, Lazenby felt Hunt wasn't guiding him enough.

In part, this was a deliberate strategy of Hunt's: he wanted to keep Lazenby on edge before each take to get the best out of him. But partly this was because Hunt, making his directorial debut with the film, simply could not concentrate on Lazenby the whole time. The logistics of making any feature film are always a headache, but on an epic like a Bond film – particularly with the logistical challenges of filming an actor on top of a Swiss Alp – they are all-consuming. Peter Hunt did not have the time, even if he had the inclination, to nurse Lazenby through his scenes every day. Never having acted before and therefore having nothing to compare *On Her Majesty's Secret Service* to, Lazenby did not appreciate this.

The supposed feud between Lazenby and Diana Rigg is more difficult to explain, since Diana Rigg has barely spoken of it since the film. Certainly, though, most of it seems to have been blown up out of all proportion by the press.

'It was a load of crap,' says Lazenby. 'We didn't get along that badly. I was like the cheeky young kid on the block, and she was like the old hand who knew all the tricks. I wasn't listening to her and it pissed her off. She felt I could have been a lot more clever at it, and she was probably right.'

In one famous incident, the press gleefully reported that Diana Rigg had deliberately eaten garlic before shooting the scene in which Bond proposes to Tracy at Pinewood Studios. The source of that story was, in reality, quite innocent.

'What happened was, she was having lunch a few tables away from me,' says Lazenby. 'Because of all the press, she yelled across the room, "Hey, George! I'm having garlic for lunch, I hope you are!" The press blew that up to "DIANA RIGG EATS GARLIC BEFORE LOVE SCENE WITH LAZENBY!" But we were actually getting along well that day.'

Intriguingly, Alan Barnes and Marcus Hearn's endlessly fascinating book, *Kiss Kiss Bang Bang* (B T Batsford, 1997) quotes Lois Maxwell as saying,

> George Lazenby told me that he and Diana were emotionally involved, but he kept chasing other women as well and she didn't like that at all, so by the time they got to Portugal [to film] they weren't speaking to each other.
>
> Of course, the London press got this and said they hated each other and there was a sort of battle. Diana would say something to one reporter and he would say something to another reporter and churn up the whole mess. But according to George Lazenby, when the film was finished, he went off to the coast of Naples with a couple of pals to relax in the sun and swim, and Diana joined him about a week later.

'I don't recall the petty grievances or paranoid statements Diana accused me of,' Lazenby said in the early 1980s. 'What may have been petty to her was much bigger to me because I was only a beginner. And as for paranoid statements they were all part of somebody desperately trying to co-operate and become a good actor.

'Her parting words to me were: "One day we will sit down and talk about it all." What she meant was when I had grown up. After that, I believe I did.'

Worse than all the on-set tensions as far as Broccoli and Saltzman were concerned was the fact – incredible though it seems – that, more than three months into the shoot, George Lazenby had still not signed a contract. He had signed a letter of intent but not the contract United Artists wanted him to sign for a seven-picture deal. This was a matter of mounting concern and, according to Lazenby, not only did Harry Saltzman offer him money under the counter to sign but United Artists offered him any picture they owned, which he could do between Bonds *provided* he signed the deal to make seven Bond pictures.

Alas, Lazenby had fallen under the influence of Ronan O'Reilly, the owner of the pirate radio station Radio Caroline, who had also managed the Beatles for a week after Brian Epstein died. Instead of listening to Cubby Broccoli's sage advice that he wasn't a star until the public said so, Lazenby listened to O'Reilly, who said he must move on to avoid being typecast.

'I felt he knew more about life and the world than I did,' says Lazenby. 'He told me it wasn't a good idea for me to do another James Bond movie. He felt James Bond was over. He said there was a new era coming. "Look at all the hippies," he said. "They aren't interested in conservative people like James Bond. They're more into *Easy Rider*."

'So I was convinced it was Connery's gig and not mine, and now I was famous, I was better off not doing Bond, and going off on my own and doing other films. Halfway through filming I told them I wasn't going to do another one. I was professional about it and told them I'd be there at all the occasions, but I wasn't going to do another Bond film.

'I don't think they believed me until they sent me the cheque for *Diamonds Are Forever* and I returned it. I thought I knew better. I thought I could make my name with the one film and then be taken up by other producers. That way I wouldn't get locked into the Bond image.

'It was a crazy decision. Things didn't work out that way, and what made it worse was that people thought I'd been kicked out and were reluctant to use me. There was a vendetta against me. In some places, there still is.'

Two months over schedule and with the taint of an unhappy production lingering, critics' knives were sharpened when the film premiered on both sides of the Atlantic on 18 December 1969. George Lazenby, sporting a beard and long hair (much to the annoyance of Broccoli and Saltzman), accompanied Diana Rigg to the London premiere, giving the lie to the supposed feud between them. But no amount of posing for the cameras could spare Lazenby from the disgracefully unfair onslaught his performance received from the critics.

Scenting blood in their belief that *On Her Majesty's Secret Service* might, just *might*, prove to be the end of the Bond franchise, many critics left objectivity behind in their determination to be the one who might legitimately claim Bond's scalp. The result of this collective feeding frenzy is that *On Her Majesty's Secret Service* is still tainted with failure: even now, people who have never seen the film will tell one with absolute confidence that it is the worst James Bond movie ever. And all because of its reputation.

In fairness, it must be pointed out that not every critic followed the slavish pack instinct. Alexander Walker in the *Evening Standard* believed Lazenby 'could pass for the other fellow's twin on the shady side of the casino', while *Variety* claimed Lazenby was 'pleasant, capable and attractive in the role'. And John Gordon in the *Sunday Express* attacked his fellow critics' rubbishing of the film in general, and Lazenby's performance in particular. Praising *On Her Majesty's Secret Service* as 'first class, and full of tension and excitement', Gordon said Lazenby was as good a Bond as Connery and added, 'What's wrong with critics that their views rarely agree with most other people's? Do they just write for each other?'

Financially, too, the widely held believe that *On Her Majesty's Secret Service* flopped is also a myth. Initially, it made financial headlines because of the amount of money it was making. '*On Her Majesty's Secret Service* is the first film to take $1 million gross – about £416,000 – during a single week in America,' reported the *Daily Mirror*. 'And in London it broke the box-office record at the Odeon Leicester Square by taking £22,800 in its second week.'

'*On Her Majesty's Secret Service* has broken records in Britain and America,' said Lazenby when he heard the news. 'This makes my knockers look like idiots. I'm not saying I'm a great actor, but it proves that the fans have accepted me as James Bond.'

In the long run, though, *On Her Majesty's Secret Service*'s worldwide gross proved to be slightly disappointing, compared with the heights scaled by *Thunderball*. Despite its being the most successful movie at the British box office in 1970 – something the film's critics always conveniently forget – the worldwide gross was $80 million, which, compared with the $111.6 million earned by *You Only Live Twice*, was undoubtedly a marked drop. However, *On Her Majesty's Secret Service* was a much longer film – 140 minutes compared with 116 minutes for *You Only Live Twice* or 111 minutes for *Goldfinger* – which necessarily restricted the number of times the film could be shown in any one day, and this had an inevitable knock-on effect on the box office. Nevertheless, no film costing $7 million that earns $80 million could ever be regarded as a flop.

Artistically, *On Her Majesty's Secret Service* is a triumph. Far from being the worst film of the series, the authors of this book have no hesitation in naming it as the best James Bond film. Peter Hunt's insistence on jettisoning gadgets and gimmicks to concentrate on Ian Fleming's novel pays off beautifully. No Bond film, not even *From*

Russia With Love, adheres to its source novel as closely as *On Her Majesty's Secret Service*, and certainly no Bond film captures Fleming's world as perfectly as this one does.

On Her Majesty's Secret Service scores in every department. It is fast, furious and fun. The absurd biological-warfare plot contrasts superbly, as in the book, with the truly believable love-story subplot. The action sequences – two ski chases, a stock-car rally-cum-chase on ice, a beachside scrap in the pre-credits, a helicopter assault on Piz Gloria and a thrilling bobsleigh chase finale – remain some of the most accomplished in the series more than three decades on. The performances – particularly Diana Rigg as the spirited, troubled and ultimately tragic Tracy, Ilse Steppat as the loathsome Irma Bunt, and Telly Savalas's definitive Blofeld – are uniformly excellent. Peter Hunt's taut direction is complemented perfectly by John Glen's editing (Glen would subsequently direct five Bond movies). And John Barry composes what may or may not be his best Bond score (it vies with *You Only Live Twice* for that honour): he certainly gives the series its finest song in this film – 'We Have All the Time in the World', sung by Louis Armstrong.

Best of all, though, is George Lazenby. Has ever a performance been so underrated in movie history? *On Her Majesty's Secret Service* works *because* of – not in spite of – George Lazenby's James Bond. Sean Connery's insouciant invincibility – so perfect in *Goldfinger* or *You Only Live Twice* – may have marred, and certainly would have weakened, the essential humanity of *On Her Majesty's Secret Service*. This is the one film where James Bond could not – and should not – be a superman.

Lazenby, having never acted before and with no formal training to fall back on, was forced to act on instinct throughout *On Her Majesty's Secret Service*. He would be the first to admit that his behaviour on set might be described as arrogance coupled with uncertainty, but that was *precisely* what was required for Bond in this episode where 007's sexual self-assurance is undermined by his falling in love, properly, for the first time. Seen in this light, Lazenby's essential spontaneity fits the James Bond of *On Her Majesty's Secret Service* perfectly. This is a Bond more impulsive and vulnerable than we have seen hitherto; a Bond who, beneath the *savoir faire*, is unsettled and thrown off kilter by his emotions.

George Lazenby's Bond has been described as 'the Human Bond'. It is an apposite title, as the last scene demonstrates, where, as in the novel, Tracy is shot dead by Blofeld and Irma Bunt just after she has married Bond. The way Lazenby breaks down as Bond cradles the dead Tracy in the Aston Martin is breathtakingly effective.

'This never happened to the other fella,' Lazenby smirks in the pre-credits sequence; nor, we submit, did the other fella – or any of the succeeding other fellas – ever do anything quite as moving as this finale.

Had Lazenby signed for another Bond – or indeed another six, as United Artists wanted – it would have been fascinating to see how he might have grown into the role. Alas, it wasn't to happen and, when *Diamonds Are Forever* premiered in December 1971, it starred a very familiar face: Sean Connery.

Eon Productions and United Artists played very safe with *Diamonds Are Forever*, something that, sadly, altered the course of the Bond series as a whole and was detrimental to *Diamonds Are Forever* in particular.

On Her Majesty's Secret Service was not a failure. Far from it. But the truth was that it just didn't do the kind of business Eon and United Artists had been used to. And the uncomfortable prospect facing Cubby Broccoli and Harry Saltzman was that maybe Ronan O'Reilly had been right all along when he told George Lazenby that James Bond was over in 1970. That certainly seemed to be the prevailing view of many in the industry.

That there would *be* another James Bond movie after *On Her Majesty's Secret Service* was never in doubt. *Diamonds Are Forever* had been announced as the next film in the end credits of *On Her Majesty's Secret Service* and both Eon Productions and United Artists were determined a seventh James Bond movie would be released in 1971. But what *kind* of James Bond movie would that be?

It was a period of uncertainty in the franchise, not helped by the continued fracturing of the relationship between Cubby Broccoli and Harry Saltzman. Broccoli, with the exception of producing the screen version of Fleming's CHITTY CHITTY BANG BANG in 1968, was focused on Bond, but Saltzman was not; indeed, his interest in Bond had been noticeably waning since the release of *Goldfinger*, six years earlier. Keen to expand still further, Saltzman used the success of Bond to underwrite his other ventures. Sadly, no other film Saltzman produced achieved anything like the level of success of the Bonds. Even his admirable, all-star *The Battle of Britain* in 1969 had been a financial disappointment. It was obvious to everyone that Harry Saltzman was overreaching himself in his other business ventures. He was painting himself into a corner financially and this, in turn, fuelled the tensions between Broccoli and Saltzman. By 1971, things had become so strained between them that they began alternating responsibilities on their remaining three Bonds together. Broccoli oversaw *Diamonds Are Forever*; Saltzman *Live And Let Die*; Broccoli *The Man with the Golden Gun*.

Nevertheless, they were both united in their desire and need to see the Bonds continue successfully and, at the many inquests into the disappointing returns of *On Her Majesty's Secret Service*, they did ask themselves the dreaded question as to whether James Bond was old-fashioned in the 1970s. And, if so, what could they do about it?

In their hearts, Broccoli and Saltzman did not believe James Bond was past his sell-by date. They preferred to believe that it was *On Her Majesty's Secret Service* itself that had been at fault by moving too far away from their established 007 formula. Peter Hunt had insisted on adhering to Fleming's novel and had eschewed gadgetry and gimmicks: all Q had supplied George Lazenby's Bond with was a safe-cracking device, although he had tried to demonstrate radioactive lint to an unimpressed M.

The producers were convinced that audiences – and American audiences specifically – had not only missed Sean Connery, which was something they couldn't have helped in *On Her Majesty's Secret Service*, but also the outlandish self-mockery of *Goldfinger*, *Thunderball* and *You Only Live Twice*. They felt that the humour had been downplayed too much by Peter Hunt. And they believed that *On Her Majesty's Secret Service*, set almost entirely in Switzerland and Portugal, had been much too European for American audiences: there was nary an American character heard in the movie.

All that was going to be rectified, the producers decided. Guy Hamilton, who had been instrumental in *Goldfinger*'s success, was brought back to direct, and Ken Adam was back as production designer. Meanwhile, Richard Maibaum, who had scripted or co-scripted every Bond film bar *You Only Live Twice* and whose script for *On Her Majesty's Secret Service* was undoubtedly his finest, was encouraged to return to the fantastical style of before. What Cubby Broccoli and Harry Saltzman really wanted was another *Goldfinger* – something that was

evidenced when Shirley Bassey was hired to sing the theme song for
Diamonds Are Forever.

Maibaum duly obliged. His first draft – which jettisoned much of
Fleming's DIAMONDS ARE FOREVER, save for a few characters (Tiffany
Case, the gay henchmen Wint and Kidd, Felix Leiter and Shady Tree)
and fewer still situations – had Auric Goldfinger's twin brother holding
the world to ransom with a laser weapon mounted on the bows of a giant
supertanker. The diamond-smuggling pipeline that was essential to
Fleming's original plot became the means by which Goldfinger
obtained the diamonds through which his laser was generated. 'We
were going to approach Gert Frobe again,' Maibaum recalled in 1983,
'but it didn't work out.'

Instead, Maibaum's original idea was altered through script
discussions so that Ernst Stavro Blofeld, yet again, became Bond's
chief protagonist. The laser-weapon idea was retained but became a
lethal diamond-encrusted satellite instead of an oil tanker (the oil-tanker
idea was recycled for 1977's *The Spy Who Loved Me*).

Another major change occurred after Cubby Broccoli had a dream
about his old friend, the billionaire Howard Hughes. In the dream
Broccoli approached Hughes in his penthouse but, when the man he
thought was Hughes turned round, it was an imposter. When Broccoli
told him about the dream, Maibaum turned this round in the script so
that Willard Whyte, a reclusive billionaire, among whose many
business interests is building satellites for the US government, is
kidnapped by Blofeld. Whyte is kept under house arrest out in the
Nevada Desert while Blofeld himself operates undetected out of
Whyte's penthouse office/apartment in Las Vegas. Since no one has
seen Willard Whyte in public for five years, it's easy for Blofeld to
control Whyte's vast empire with impunity.

Broccoli and Saltzman were reasonably satisfied with Maibaum's
script. It was certainly fantastic and, with space technology, returned the
series to the outlandishness of *You Only Live Twice*. But there was still
a prevailing mood both at Eon and United Artists of a need to
Americanise James Bond, and also make him more relevant to the
1970s.

Plans were made to make *Diamonds Are Forever* at a Hollywood
studio and, with George Lazenby out of the picture, Eon and United
Artists considered using American actors such as Burt Reynolds and

Clint Eastwood to play Bond, although Roger Moore was again considered, only to be ruled out because he had signed to make a TV series, *The Persuaders!*, with Tony Curtis, for Lew Grade.

Eventually, even Cubby Broccoli was prepared to bend his hitherto cast-iron rule that James Bond must always be played by a British actor, and the 42-year-old American actor John Gavin was signed to play James Bond in *Diamonds Are Forever*. Despite notable performances in Hitchcock's *Psycho* and Stanley Kubrick's *Spartacus*, Gavin was not terribly well known and his casting was a surprise to many in the industry.

At the same time, United Artists suggested Maibaum's script be reworked by a young American writer named Tom Mankiewicz. Twenty-eight-year-old Mankiewicz rewrote much of Maibaum's script and there's no question that he added some bitingly funny one-liners. Indeed, thanks to Mankiewicz, *Diamonds Are Forever* has, arguably, the wittiest script of any Bond film.

Sadly, though, while the one-liners are undoubtedly a highlight of *Diamonds Are Forever*, the flipside is that the concentration on humour – some of it very camp humour, too – comes at the expense of a credible storyline.

In a knee-jerk reaction – we are tempted to write 'an almost panicky knee-jerk reaction' – to the *perceived* mistake of making *On Her Majesty's Secret Service* too realistic and believable, *Diamonds Are Forever* lurches too far into ludicrous humour and outlandish situations. Certainly the trend for everything in Bond movies to be played for laughs – which many believe, incorrectly, began with the Roger Moore era and prevailed throughout the 1970s – actually began in Tom Mankiewicz's rewrites of *Diamonds Are Forever*.

Even so, despite being satisfied with a screenplay that played safe by relying on easy, perhaps *too* easy, laughs, United Artists were still nervous about launching John Gavin as the new James Bond. And United Artists' president, David Picker, for one, was convinced that Sean Connery could be lured back to the role of Bond, given the right package.

Despite his being a fine actor, Sean Connery's films since he left Bondage had done good business but none had exactly set the world alight. What Sean Connery needed was a massive hit. And what United Artists felt they needed was Sean Connery back as James Bond. The conditions were therefore set fair for a deal.

And what a deal!

United Artists' offer to Sean Connery became the talk of Hollywood. They offered him a fee of $1.25 million plus a percentage of the profits; *plus* the funding by United Artists of two films of Connery's choice (although, in the event, only one, *The Offence*, was made, in 1972). The deal even took into account one of Connery's complaints about making Bond movies: the length of time they took to shoot and the fact that they invariably went over schedule. The deal guaranteed Connery an additional $10,000 for every week that the film went over its scheduled eighteen-week shoot. When the film wrapped, on schedule, on the Friday night of the eighteenth week of production, Connery remarked to one journalist, 'It can be done, you see, if there's money at stake.'

Connery considered the offer for a week before saying yes. The publicity machine then went into overdrive to announce that Sean Connery was playing James Bond one more – one last? – time and John Gavin was paid off. Gavin continued acting before becoming the US Ambassador to Mexico between 1981 and 1986.

Sean Connery cheerfully admitted in interviews that United Artists had bribed him back into Bondage, but his motives for accepting the fantastic deal were not personal greed. He donated his entire fee to a charity he had recently set up, the Scottish International Education Trust. 'With the money from *Diamonds Are Forever* I could launch the Trust with enough money for there never to be an excuse for it not succeeding,' said Connery at the time.

In his autobiography, *When the Snow Melts*, Cubby Broccoli suggests that both he and Harry Saltzman had misgivings over having Connery back as Bond, but that they were overruled by United Artists. But Broccoli also admits that, whatever tensions might have existed between the producers and their returning star, Connery was as professional as ever while making *Diamonds Are Forever*.

With Connery on board, the Americanisation of Bond was played down, although, since *Diamonds Are Forever* would be set largely in Las Vegas and off the coast of California, there would still be much for American audiences to identify with. Plans to film in a Hollywood studio were dropped and Pinewood Studios became the production base once again because Connery's massive salary could be all but paid for by the Eady Levy subsidy from which the film would benefit by being based in the UK.

Diamonds Are Forever premiered in December 1971 and was an immediate hit at the box office. With a worldwide gross of $116 million, it not only made far more than *On Her Majesty's Secret Service* but also pipped *You Only Live Twice*'s gross of $111.6 million. The film's success convinced Broccoli and Saltzman and United Artists not only that Bond was *not* out of date in the 1970s, but that their decision to inject much more humour into the film was correct. As far as the producers were concerned, *Diamonds Are Forever* had not only re-established the viability of the franchise after the box-office disappointment of *On Her Majesty's Secret Service* but it had created a new template for Bond to which they would adhere in future.

Sean Connery clearly enjoyed making *Diamonds Are Forever* and it shows in his performance, which is his most relaxed and effective as Bond since *Goldfinger*, a significant fact given that Guy Hamilton was the director of both films. Connery also liked the screenplay, commenting in one televised interview, 'I think it's the best script we've had, certainly construction-wise. It's very good.'

'Peter, there's a lot more to you than I had expected,' purrs Jill St John as Tiffany Case in one of the film's more obvious double entendres when Bond, masquerading as a diamond smuggler, Peter Franks, undresses in front of her in her Las Vegas hotel suite. And there's a lot more of Mr Connery than we're used to seeing in *Diamonds Are Forever*, for he is undeniably heavier than last seen as Bond in *You Only Live Twice*. Indeed, his weight seems to fluctuate noticeably throughout the picture. But Connery still dominates *Diamonds Are Forever* with a confidence and self-mockery that transcends the lingering air of his being slightly out of condition. It's hard to disagree with Tom Mankiewicz's assessment that 'it was the first time in any of his films that he looked mature and there was now an old pro's grace about him'.

Other plus points in the film are the sensational Jill St John as the wisecracking Tiffany; the fight – arguably the best fight of the series – between the real Peter Franks (Joe Robinson) and Bond in an Amsterdam elevator; Bruce Glover and Putter Smith as the campily gay, murderous Wint and Kidd (perfectly described by Alan Barnes and Marcus Hearn as 'a sadistic Laurel and Hardy'); a genuine moment of how-does-he-get-out-of-that? when Wint and Kidd shove an unconscious Bond into a coffin and launch it into the fiery ovens of a crematorium; and perhaps *the* most perfect moment of Connery-Bond élan when Bond, dressed in a dinner jacket, calmly steps out on to the roof of an outside elevator at the Whyte House casino-cum-hotel in Las Vegas and rides to the penthouse, where he expects to find Willard Whyte and instead discovers Blofeld (the wonderful Charles Gray camping up the role something rotten).

Sadly, *Diamonds Are Forever*'s weaknesses undermine all the good work and ideas. The script is so confusing and muddled that, halfway though, one begins to suspect that Guy Hamilton has filmed only every other page of the screenplay; Norman Burton is horrendously miscast as Felix Leiter; there's an extremely silly moon-buggy chase, which is juvenile in the extreme; not to mention a tired car chase through Las Vegas; Las Vegas just does not have the class to feature in a Bond movie (just as it didn't in Fleming's original novel); and the film simply runs out of steam twenty minutes from the end with a tiresome denouement on Blofeld's oil rig, which is a very boring base compared with his Piz Gloria in *On Her Majesty's Secret Service* or the volcano in *You Only Live Twice*.

The laser satellite with which Blofeld threatens the world is particularly silly. We know from Bond's own lips that it is about eight feet tall, so the laser beam we see it emit must be about the same width as a pencil. We're sorry to be SPECTREs at the feast but pencil-thin laser beams cannot cause nuclear missiles or submarines to self-combust, let alone destroy whole cities (just *how* is it going to do that?). The actors don't – can't – take Blofeld's threat to destroy Washington, DC, with the laser seriously, and so nor can we, the audience. Consequently, there's a going-through-the-motions weariness through-out the last twenty minutes of *Diamonds Are Forever* and it very nearly ruins the film.

'The picture isn't bad, it's merely tired,' wrote Pauline Kael in the *New Yorker*:

> And it's often noisy when it's meant to be exciting. What's missing may be linked to the absence of Peter Hunt, who worked on the action sequences of all the earlier Bonds, and who directed the last one; perhaps it was he who gave the series its distinctive quality of aestheticised thrills. The daring seemed beautiful in the earlier films – precariousness glorified. This time, even when a sequence works, it lacks elegance and visual opulence; it looks

like a sequence of the same kind in the Bond imitations. No doubt those of us who love the Bond pictures are spoiled, but really we've come to expect more than a comic car chase.

But Kael's opinion was something of a lone voice at the time. More typical was the *New York Times*'s belief that *Diamonds Are Forever* 'is great absurd fun and Connery's return is enough to make one weep with gratitude', while *Village Voice* believed '*Diamonds* deserves to make a billion dollars.'

Time has been much less kind to *Diamonds Are Forever*, however. In 1971, it was lauded at the expense of *On Her Majesty's Secret Service*; more than thirty years later, the reverse is generally true, with *Diamonds Are Forever* usually languishing near the foot of any poll taken among Bond fans to determine which is the best Bond movie. Nevertheless, *Diamonds Are Forever* did at least accomplish what Eon Productions and United Artists asked of it: it reversed the decline at the box office for Bond films and ensured the franchise would survive well into the 1970s.

But the films would have to continue without Sean Connery. Although United Artists approached him to play James Bond again in *Live And Let Die*, it was pretty obvious that Connery would not come back a second time. 'Of course the films will go on,' he told a journalist during the filming of *Diamonds Are Forever*. 'But who'll play me I just don't know and can't guess.'

In the event, the search for the new James Bond, which began in earnest in the first months of 1972 while *Diamonds Are Forever* was still glittering at the box office, was relatively short this time round. Despite pressure, again, from United Artists for Eon to consider American actors such as Burt Reynolds, Clint Eastwood and Steve McQueen, Cubby Broccoli returned to the man who had been on their first shortlist for *Dr. No*; the man who had been on *Ian Fleming*'s shortlist for Bond; and the man whose commitments to the TV series *The Saint* and then *The Persuaders!* had precluded their using him as Bond before: Roger Moore.

Having had his doubts about Roger Moore when casting *Dr. No* in 1961, Broccoli was convinced in 1972 that he was the only actor who could take over the role successfully. But getting United Artists – who were still looking for a big-name American actor to play Bond – to accept Moore was a struggle.

'I kept telling them, "The man *has* to be British",' said Broccoli many years later. 'My partner Harry Saltzman liked Roger, but he preferred a couple of other people. But Harry agreed with me that Roger was right and we put up a fight for him.'

In casting Roger Moore, Broccoli and Saltzman were determined not to repeat what they believed had been their fundamental mistake with *On Her Majesty's Secret Service*. Then they had resolved that what they were looking for was a replica Sean Connery. This time, they believed that the new Bond should have clear blue water between himself and Connery and that the way Bond is depicted in the movie should work towards that. Thus, throughout *Live And Let Die*, many of the associations with Connery's Bond are downplayed: Bond is never seen in a dinner jacket; he does not order a vodka martini, shaken *or* stirred; he does not appear in M's office (M and Moneypenny visit him in his mews flat instead); and poor Desmond Llewelyn, with whom Sean Connery had established something of a screen double act, does not appear at all.

Born on 14 October 1927, Moore had begun his screen career as an extra in *Caesar and Cleopatra* in 1944, and then went to the Royal Academy of Dramatic Art for three years. Upon graduating, he struggled for a while, supplementing his meagre earnings from the few acting jobs he secured with jobs as a waiter, a salesman and, most famously, as a model.

Married in 1946 to the ice-skater Doorn van Steyn, he was divorced when he met and fell in love with Dorothy Squires, one of Britain's most famous singers, whom he married in 1953.

Gradually, Moore's career began to take off. He appeared in *The Last Time I Saw Paris* with Elizabeth Taylor in 1954, *Interrupted Melody* in 1955, and with David Niven in a dire picture called *The King's Thief*, also in 1955. His long television career began with *Ivanhoe* in Britain in 1956, which he then followed up by playing Beau Maverick in the perennial US favourite, *Maverick*.

From 1962 until 1968, Moore became a TV superstar on both sides of the Atlantic, playing Simon Templar in Lew Grade's long-running series, *The Saint*, which was based on the books by Leslie Charteris. His *Saint* contract had precluded his playing James Bond in *Dr. No*, and the first episode of *The Saint* was transmitted in May 1962, just six months before the big-screen debut of James Bond.

'I think it's unfair to speculate what the Bond films might have been like if I'd taken the role in *Dr. No*,' says Moore. 'Sean's pictures were very, very successful so you can't say what would have happened. I think he was absolutely right for the part at that time.'

Success on the small screen seemed to preclude Roger Moore finding it on the big screen, and the two films he made between the end of *The Saint* and his signing as James Bond in 1972 – *Crossplot* (1969) and *The Man Who Haunted Himself* (1970) – were hardly blockbusters. This is a shame, because Moore gives an excellent performance in the latter film, a psychological horror movie, directed by Basil Dearden, about an urbane businessman haunted by an evil *doppelgänger*.

Had *The Persuaders!* been a success, Moore's contract with Lew Grade, which took him up to 1977, would have precluded, yet again, his starring as James Bond in *Live And Let Die*. In fact, the series *was* a success of sorts. Sold to every country in the world except Russia, China and Albania, the likeable partnership between Roger Moore and Tony Curtis was actually seen in more countries than *The Saint*. In Europe, the series was a smash hit; but in the all-important American market it simply died after being used, stupidly, in a ratings battle with the juggernaut that was *Mission: Impossible*.

The Persuaders! did not even complete its run in the US, being taken off after only twenty of its scheduled twenty-four episodes had been screened. It being a hugely expensive series to produce, there was no way Lew Grade could finance a second series of *The Persuaders!* without selling it to America. And America didn't want to know.

But Lew Grade's loss was Cubby Broccoli and Harry Saltzman's gain, and Roger Moore was announced as the new James Bond at a press conference at the Dorchester Hotel on 1 August 1972. Moore, photographed smoking a cigar and sipping a vodka martini, was sporting longish hair and was still carrying the weight he had noticeably gained during *The Persuaders!*. By the time principal photography began on *Live And Let Die* on 13 October 1972 in New Orleans, Moore had slimmed down considerably and his hair was cropped short. It was a leaner, meaner look for the new James Bond and one that belied Moore's 45 years.

Tom Mankiewicz wrote the screenplay of *Live And Let Die* alone and his brief was simple: to introduce the new James Bond in a spectacular, action-packed film. Mankiewicz rose to the challenge well, for it can be said that the streamlined script of *Live And Let Die* is an improvement over that of *Diamonds Are Forever*.

As usual, much of Fleming's original novel was jettisoned. While there had, perhaps, been an argument for doing this with *You Only Live Twice*, given that Fleming's superb, dark novel was resolutely uncinematic, and with *Diamonds Are Forever*, where Fleming's original novel had been one of his weakest, there was no excuse in the case of *Live And Let Die*. While Fleming's LIVE AND LET DIE had undoubtedly dated in the eighteen years since it had been published – particularly in its treatment of the black characters – it was still a brilliant Bond book, which would have served as the basis of a wonderful debut for Moore's Bond. Several sequences from the book that did not make it into Mankiewicz's screenplay but which were used in subsequent Bond movies (the keel-hauling sequences in *For Your Eyes Only* in 1981, and Felix Leiter being fed to the shark in *Licence To Kill* in 1989) prove this.

Still, Mankiewicz's screenplay retains the characters of the black gangster Mr Big (who is also the alter ego of Dr Kananga, the prime minister of a Caribbean island called San Monique); the virginal, psychic Solitaire; the henchman Tee-Hee; and the sinister voodoo backdrop that was so essential to Fleming's novel. Mankiewicz also keeps the story to much the same locations as Fleming's novel – New York, the Caribbean – although New Orleans is used in the film instead of Florida in the book.

Mankiewicz also creates a fabulous character of his own: the red-necked Sheriff J W Pepper, who is played brilliantly by Clifton James and provides some wonderful comic relief in *Live And Let Die*'s lengthy, showstopping speedboat chase through the Louisiana bayous. Sheriff Pepper proved so popular that he was brought back, to much less effect, in the next Bond picture, *The Man with the Golden Gun*.

In place of Mr Big's salvaging of pirate treasure in the Caribbean to finance SMERSH operations in the US, as in Fleming's novel, in the film Mr Big plans to flood the US with free heroin, which is cultivated on San Monique. By distributing the heroin free, Mr Big will drive rival drug dealers out of business, leaving him with a monopoly, a monopoly he intends to exploit by making the heroin very expensive indeed once the number of addicts has doubled.

It's an inspired plot, devious in its simplicity, and Mankiewicz's screenplay is executed well by the director Guy Hamilton, who delivers some truly stand-out sequences. Best of all is the electrifying moment when Tee-Hee deliberately maroons Bond on a bed-sized island in the middle of a pool of crocodiles: Bond's escape by using the crocodiles' backs as stepping stones to safety is wonderful.

The casting in *Live And Let Die* is intelligent, too. Yaphet Kotto, a very powerful actor, underplays his Mr Big/Kananga character beautifully, suggesting a seething violence beneath an urbane veneer; Jane Seymour conveys Solitaire's virginal naïveté well; Julius Harris titters his way malevolently through the film as Tee-Hee, complete with metal arm; Geoffrey Holder haunts the movie as the voodoo god Baron Samedi, 'the man who cannot die'; and David Hedison is the series' best Felix Leiter (he reprised the role in 1989's *Licence To Kill*). Interestingly, in Tom Mankiewicz's first draft of the screenplay, Solitaire was black, but United Artists, already jittery at launching Roger Moore as James Bond, vetoed the idea. A pity.

But *Live And Let Die* was always going to live or die on Roger Moore's performance as Bond – and the public acceptance of it. And despite the bullish publicity campaign, which stressed throughout the shoot and the lead-up to the premiere that Moore was much closer to Ian Fleming's original concept of Bond than Sean Connery, there were doubts about Moore right up until the box-office receipts came in.

Even Moore, who kept a frank diary throughout the production – later published by Pan Books – admitted his own nervousness, as he revealed in his account of meeting Guy Hamilton prior to the film:

We met at Scott's in Mayfair, in true Bond style, over a dozen oysters and martinis. I confessed to Guy that in reading the script I could only ever hear Sean's voice saying, 'My name is Bond, James Bond.' In fact, as I vocalized to myself I found I was giving it a Scottish accent. Guy said, 'Look, Sean was Sean and you are you and that is how it is going to be.'

In the event, Moore's first stab at Bond was a pretty impressive affair. It was a harder, more cynical Bond than he was later to evolve into, but the building blocks of Moore's Bond were, at least, put in place. While there is much in the critic Alexander Walker's assessment that having Roger Moore replace Sean Connery was like the head prefect taking over from the school bully, Moore manages, even in his first attempt, to step out of Connery's shadow. The Bond of *Live And Let Die* is a sharply dressed, deceptively callous, humorous man, who thinks nothing of deflowering the virginal Solitaire to further his investigation, who makes love to the duplicitous CIA agent Rosie Carver (Gloria Hendry) *before* he lets on he knows she's a traitor, and whose seeming adherence to the Queensbury Rules wrong-foots his opponents (witness his demolition of two of Mr Big's lieutenants in the grimy New York alley early in the picture).

Live And Let Die had respectable reviews, although most critics reserved judgment on Roger Moore. But backed by a massive, slick marketing campaign and aided by a superb theme song composed by Paul and Linda McCartney and performed by Paul McCartney and Wings – which was a massive chart hit on both sides of the Atlantic and was nominated for an Oscar – *Live And Let Die* was the hit of the summer of 1973.

A new era had begun. The world had a new James Bond.

009: Licence Revoked?

'We were filming in the Gulf of Siam and you could tell whether it was high tide or low tide by how fat or thin the dead dog in the river was.'

Roger Moore, 1974

With an international gross of $161 million, *Live And Let Die* exceeded *Diamonds Are Forever*'s worldwide gross of $116 million considerably. This confounded those critics who had doubted whether Roger Moore could succeed Sean Connery in the role of James Bond.

Cubby Broccoli and Harry Saltzman could breathe sighs of relief – at least from the point of view of the films. It had been a turbulent five years, in which they had had three actors playing James Bond. But now Roger Moore was established and the films were back at the top. To consolidate Moore's success, they decided to press on with the next film, *The Man with the Golden Gun*, as quickly as possible. Tom Mankiewicz was hired to write a script in the summer of 1973 even as *Live And Let Die* was causing a stir at the box office.

But not even *Live And Let Die*'s success could disguise the ever-worsening relationship between Broccoli and Saltzman. Sean Connery had remarked caustically in 1971, 'They're both sitting on fifty million dollars and looking across the desk at each other and thinking, "That bugger's got half of what should all be mine." ' Connery's ambivalent feelings towards the producers notwithstanding – perhaps not so ambivalent in the case of Saltzman – his remark came as no surprise to many in the industry.

While still careful not to row in public, Broccoli and Saltzman themselves no longer bothered to hide their differences. They even admitted to their strained relationship in interviews. What was not helping the situation was that Harry Saltzman was devoting more and more time to his outside business operations. He had good reason to do so because he had not always invested wisely and some of his business decisions were now beginning to cost him dearly. Harry Saltzman was up to his neck and starting to drown in his debts.

Given their different dispositions, it is remarkable that their partnership survived for any length of time at all, never mind thirteen years. But the end was coming and *The Man with the Golden Gun* was the last film they were to produce together.

Ian Fleming's last novel, THE MAN WITH THE GOLDEN GUN, was a desperately thin book and, for once, the filmmakers were correct in throwing out all but the essentials. They retained the character of Scaramanga, the assassin with the golden gun, and Mary Goodnight as Bond's main squeeze – although both characters differed from the source novel – but even the location of the story was shifted from the Caribbean, which had been used in *Live And Let Die* anyhow, to the Far East (Iran had been considered and then rejected in the earliest stages of preproduction).

Tom Mankiewicz envisaged *The Man with the Golden Gun* as a reworking of the 1953 western *Shane*, which would build up to a duel between Bond and Scaramanga, who, in Mankiewicz's first draft, was an assassin every bit as civilised, accomplished and ruthless as Bond – he was the dark side of Bond. Since *Shane* was the inspiration for the screenplay, Cubby Broccoli even approached Jack Palance, who had appeared in *Shane* opposite Alan Ladd, to see if he would be interested in playing Scaramanga.

But as preproduction continued on *The Man with the Golden Gun* the tensions between Broccoli and Saltzman seemed to spread to other people in the franchise. Guy Hamilton, who had been asked to direct this his fourth Bond picture – and third consecutive one – began disagreeing profoundly with Tom Mankiewicz about the direction and style the picture should take. Their disagreements became so heated that Mankiewicz eventually told Broccoli he wanted to resign from *The Man with the Golden Gun.*

Broccoli then asked Richard Maibaum to work on Mankiewicz's script with Guy Hamilton. This was not as straightforward as it might seem because Maibaum had a fraught relationship with Harry Saltzman by this stage. Moreover, he had not exactly been impressed by *Live And Let Die* (he called it 'a lousy cooking-some-dope-somewhere-in-the-jungle movie'). He had been particularly disparaging about Roger Moore's Bond, and seemed genuinely unhappy about the direction in which the entire series seemed to be heading. Nevertheless, Maibaum reluctantly agreed to work on *The Man with the Golden Gun.*

Maibaum downplayed Mankiewicz's theme of the duel between Bond and Scaramanga, although he did not eliminate it entirely, and introduced the theme of the energy crisis, which was then global news, as the major background to the storyline. In Maibaum's version, Bond's search for a missing solex agitator, *the* essential component of a solar power station that enables the sun's rays to be converted into electricity, is interrupted when a golden bullet engraved with a '007' is sent to MI6 headquarters. This is Scaramanga's calling card and M deduces that someone has paid Scaramanga a million dollars – his usual fee – to assassinate Bond.

Believing the search for the solex agitator to be too important to risk Scaramanga 'popping up' to put a bullet in Bond, M takes Bond off the case but agrees to his taking a leave of absence to track down Scaramanga with a view to killing him.

Bond's search eventually brings him to Scaramanga's mistress, Andrea, when he discovers that it was *she* who sent Bond the bullet. Scaramanga doesn't have a contract on Bond at all. Andrea just wanted to lure Bond to kill Scaramanga to release her from her sexual slavery. Scaramanga, who retains his third nipple from Fleming's novel, uses her to make love to before he kills.

Andrea has an ace up her sleeve. Scaramanga has also been searching for, and has found, the solex agitator (a coincidence that completely undermines the movie's credibility), which he intends using in his solar-energy station hidden away on his private island in Red Chinese waters. Thus Bond's search for the solex and Scaramanga converge in the screenplay, albeit awkwardly.

Compared with his screenplays for, say, *From Russia With Love* and *On Her Majesty's Secret Service*, not to mention some of the work he would do on later Bonds, Maibaum's script for *The Man with the Golden Gun* is tired and uninspired. Perhaps it reflects the simmering resentments and problems that were ongoing between Broccoli and Saltzman at the time. The Bond films had always been collaborative pictures, written by committee, particularly from *You Only Live Twice* onwards. But the prevailing mood at Eon in 1973 and 1974 was not exactly conducive to creative movie-making.

Whatever the reason, *The Man with the Golden Gun* never ignites properly. The introduction of the energy crisis dated the film almost immediately while the inclusion of both Sheriff Pepper, who had proved a hit in *Live And Let Die*, and martial-arts fighting, then big box office thanks to Bruce Lee et al., betrays a lack of confidence and a craving to play safe. Even Guy Hamilton's direction, inspired in *Goldfinger* a decade earlier, seems flat.

One of the most curious aspects of *The Man with the Golden Gun*'s screenplay is that the character of Scaramanga is particularly well written at the expense of Bond. Indeed, in a strange twist, Scaramanga is one of the Bond series' best villains, second, perhaps, only to Auric Goldfinger himself, even though the film itself is generally regarded as the weakest of the official series. Even Cubby Broccoli, when asked about the series, commented, 'I can't say there is a single one I'd want to re-do, although there are parts of *The Man with the Golden Gun* I'd change.'

The success of Scaramanga as a character belongs as much to the script as it does to the superb Christopher Lee (a distant cousin of Ian Fleming), who plays him. In contrast, Bond's character is completely underwritten in the film and only Roger Moore's performance (much better in retrospect than contemporary critics allowed) prevents the film from being even more disappointing than it is.

Scaramanga's explanation of his motivation to Bond, when they first meet at a kick-boxing match, is one of the series' best and is delivered with real feeling by Lee. Brought up in a circus, Scaramanga explains how his only real friend was a magnificent African bull elephant. The elephant went berserk one day when mistreated by his handler, who then shot him in the eye with his gun. Scaramanga retaliated by emptying his stage pistol into the trainer's eye and inadvertently found his true vocation. 'You see, Mr Bond,' he says, 'I always thought I liked animals. Then I discovered I liked killing people even more.'

Later, when Scaramanga wines and dines Bond and Mary Goodnight in his magnificent dining room on his remote island – reminiscent of *Dr. No* in setting, if nothing else – there is another splendid exchange:

BOND: You live well, Scaramanga.

SCARAMANGA: At a million dollars a contract I can afford to, Mr Bond. You work for peanuts. A hearty 'well done' from Her Majesty the Queen and a pittance of a pension. Apart from that, we are the same. (*Raises his glass*) To us, Mr Bond. *We* are the best.

BOND: There's a useful four-letter word. And you're full of it. When I kill it's on the specific orders of my government. And those I kill are themselves killers.

SCARAMANGA: Come, come, Mr Bond. You disappoint me. You get as much fulfilment out of killing as I do, so why don't you admit it?

BOND: I admit killing you *would* be a pleasure.

SCARAMANGA: You should have done that when you first saw me. But then, of course, the English don't consider it sporting to kill in cold blood, do they?

BOND: Don't count on that.

Had the rest of *The Man with the Golden Gun* screenplay matched moments like these (there are, sadly, only a couple more like them in the entire picture), Eon's ninth James Bond film might have been much more exciting. As it is, apart from a couple of neat touches, the film resolutely fails to come to life. Compared with many action films of the era, *The Man with the Golden Gun* still fares pretty well: but as a Bond movie it commits the cardinal sin, like *Thunderball* nine years earlier, of actually being boring in places. Worse, Britt Ekland's Mary Goodnight is, with the possible exception of Tanya Roberts in *A View To A Kill*, the most irritating Bond girl of the entire series. Her ineptness is meant to be amusing. It isn't.

Among the film's meagre highlights are the 360-degree jump Bond performs in an AMC Hornet Hatchback between two ends of a broken bridge; Scaramanga's ingenious golden gun, which is assembled from seemingly innocent components (a cigarette case, lighter, fountain pen and cufflink); the return of Desmond Llewelyn's Q after his absence from *Live And Let Die*; and Maud Adams's performance as Andrea, Scaramanga's tragic lover. Like Luciana Paluzzi in *Thunderball*, Maud Adams is the best thing in *The Man with the Golden Gun* and the film simply shifts into a different class when she is on screen.

And at least the locations are interesting in the film. Extensive use was made of Macau, Hong Kong and Thailand, and Scaramanga's fabulous island was shot on Thailand's island of Phuket. Now a thriving tourist centre, Phuket was so remote when *The Man with the Golden Gun* was filmed there in 1974 that there were very real fears about attacks on the cast and crew by local pirates.

Fears of pirate attacks apart, *The Man with the Golden Gun* was made remarkably smoothly considering the tensions behind the cameras between Broccoli and Saltzman, although conditions were not always what major stars were used to.

'We were shooting in the Gulf of Siam,' said Moore, 'and you could tell whether it was high or low tide by how fat or thin the dead dog in the river was. I fell in a couple of times. We all did. In the morning you could see the women cleaning their teeth in the river, washing their hair, disappearing right into the water to do the other thing. The hum off the river in the morning was amazing.'

The Man with the Golden Gun premiered at the Odeon Leicester Square, in London, as usual, on 18 December 1974, and went on general release on both sides of the Atlantic the following day. The reviews were mostly negative, the consensus being that the film was stale and that the series had probably run its course. Typical was the *New Yorker*'s opinion that 'the script lacks satiric insolence and the picture grinds on humourlessly'.

Initially, the negative reviews did not appear to have hit the box office, since the film seemed to be on course to be another Bond blockbuster. But audiences tailed off quickly and the movie's international gross of $98 million, impressive by other films' standards, signified a huge drop compared with *Live And Let Die*. Of particular concern to Eon Productions and United Artists was the drop in interest in the US market, where the film grossed an extremely disappointing $21 million.

As usual, *The Man with the Golden Gun*'s end credits had promised 'James Bond will return . . .', this time in *The Spy Who Loved Me*. But in 1975 there were many in the industry who wondered if he really would.

This feeling was reinforced by upheavals at Eon when Harry Saltzman, in desperate need of raising capital, put up 100 per cent of their Swiss holding company, Danjaq, to cover his liabilities of some $20 million. But under the terms of their original partnership in 1961 neither Broccoli nor Saltzman could pledge 100 per cent of the company without the other's approval.

'I don't think Harry ever consciously set out to bring me down,' said Broccoli. 'The plain fact was he was in a corner with his back against the wall, and he wanted to get out of it by using me and Dana – our money – to pay the banks.'

The Swiss banks, from whom Saltzman had borrowed, believed their loans were secured by Danjaq and they were determined to get it. Cubby Broccoli was suddenly fighting to preserve everything he and Dana had worked for. Dana's son, Michael Wilson, now a formidable lawyer, came into his own, fighting on the Broccolis' behalf.

The legal wrangling dragged on for many months, making any preparation of *The Spy Who Loved Me* impossible while the very future of the company was in doubt. This frustrated not only Cubby Broccoli but Arthur Krim, head of United Artists, and both men were determined to put James Bond back on top after the relative artistic and commercial disappointment of *The Man with the Golden Gun*.

In the event, the affair was finally settled in December 1975, when Arthur Krim bought out Saltzman's share of Danjaq for $20 million. Thus Cubby Broccoli became the sole producer of the James Bond series.

But, given the relative public apathy towards *The Man with the Golden Gun*, was there anything really left to produce?

Cubby Broccoli was convinced that there was.

0010: Licence Renewed

'I think that the mere fact that we were lucky enough to stumble upon Ian Fleming and James Bond was a bit of good fortune. The rest was all hard work.'

Cubby Broccoli, 1976

It will never be known if *The Spy Who Loved Me* saved Eon Productions' James Bond franchise. No one can know for sure what would have happened to the series had its box-office returns been as disappointing as those for *The Man with the Golden Gun*.

What we can be sure of is that with an international gross of $185 million (including a US gross of $47 million, which was $26 million more than *Golden Gun*'s US gross), which made it one of the biggest blockbusters of the summer of 1977 – the summer of *Star Wars* – *The Spy Who Loved Me* reinvigorated the Bond series.

The Spy Who Loved Me was also an artistic triumph. For many, it remains a highlight of the entire series, on a par with *Goldfinger* and *On Her Majesty's Secret Service*, as well as being *the* definitive Roger Moore Bond film. Some regard it as the best Bond film of all.

But bringing *The Spy Who Loved Me* to the screen was not easy. Even after Cubby Broccoli had resolved his bitter dispute with Harry Saltzman and assumed sole control of the franchise, he faced formidable hurdles, some of which were personal ones.

With *The Spy Who Loved Me*, Broccoli was not just making another movie, still less just another Bond movie. He was simultaneously having to prove to the industry that he could, indeed, go it alone without Harry Saltzman *and* put the Bond movies back on top.

In interviews, Broccoli was bullish. 'People kept asking me what it's like to be going solo,' he told one interviewer. 'Well, I always thought I was solo. I still control the Bond enterprise. Nobody gazumps me! United Artists put up 100 per cent financing and that gives them sole rights to distribute the films. My function is to deliver the films.'

In private, though, Broccoli knew that *The Spy Who Loved Me* would probably be make-or-break time for the series.

'For Cubby it was a huge undertaking in the sense that he had to prove something,' says Lewis Gilbert. 'He was on his own, and if the film were a disaster people would say that he couldn't do it without Harry Saltzman. I think Cubby was conscious of that and worked very hard on *The Spy Who Loved Me*, probably more than he did on any other film.'

Cubby Broccoli was nothing if not a shrewd gambler, and he gambled everything on his belief that the way to challenge the relative failure of *The Man with the Golden Gun* was not to pull in his horns, to think smaller, but to think big, to be bold. *The Spy Who Loved Me* would be the tenth Bond movie and would mark the fifteenth anniversary of the release of *Dr. No*. He was determined, therefore, to make *The Spy Who Loved Me* the most lavish and outrageous Bond film yet. In this, he was supported not only by his wife, Dana, and stepson Michael Wilson, who had been invaluable in the legal battles with Harry Saltzman and his creditors, but United Artists themselves, who, in a unique display of confidence, *doubled* the budget of *The Man with the Golden Gun* for the new film: *The Spy Who Loved Me* would cost $13.5 million.

The concept for the film was fairly straightforward. Nuclear submarines are gobbled up by a supertanker (a throwback to Richard Maibaum's original idea of having the villain mount the laser cannon on a supertanker in *Diamonds Are Forever*) so that their warheads might be appropriated. This plotline had nothing whatsoever to do with Ian Fleming's source novel but, for once, Broccoli had no choice but to jettison Fleming's entire novel: Fleming's will had stipulated that only the title of his controversial novel THE SPY WHO LOVED ME could be used in any film. Eon could use no incident or character, other than James Bond, from the book.

Despite the simplicity of the concept, the script of the film proved troublesome. No fewer than fourteen accomplished writers, including John Landis, Anthony Burgess, Stirling Silliphant, Cary Bates and Anthony Barwick, submitted screenplays but none of them satisfied Broccoli, who felt that the problem each of them had was to lock themselves into a straitjacket by creating set-pieces at the expense of a strong storyline.

From the outset, the idea was to reintroduce Blofeld and SPECTRE after a two-film break. Richard Maibaum, brought in to work on the script, had the brilliant notion of having the SPECTRE old guard, including Blofeld himself, kicked out and taken over by an alliance of terrorist factions drawn from real-life groups such as the Red Brigade.

Although he liked Maibaum's script, Broccoli balked at using real-life terrorist groups in a Bond picture. It was, he felt, much too political: one of the things that had ensured the Bonds' global success had been their apolitical villains (even if it had been suggested Red China backed Auric Goldfinger's assault on Fort Knox and Blofeld's scheme in *You Only Live Twice*).

Lewis Gilbert, who joined the production as director after Guy Hamilton left, introduced the writer Christopher Wood to Broccoli, and Wood was hired to rework Maibaum's script. Out went Maibaum's politicised SPECTRE in favour of a more traditional Bondian setup. The screenplay is credited jointly to Richard Maibaum and Christopher Wood.

One thing Broccoli had impressed on all the writers who worked on the film was the need to redefine the role of the Bond girl. Feminism had redrawn the rules throughout the 1970s and the Bond movies had come in for much criticism from women's groups, although many of their complaints were unfair. While some female characters in the Bond movies had been nothing more than 'eye candy', characters such as Pussy Galore in *Goldfinger*, Fiona in *Thunderball* and Tracy in *On Her Majesty's Secret Service* were rounded parts played by exceptional actresses and were far stronger roles than in comparable action-adventure movies.

Nevertheless, Broccoli knew that negative criticism is hard to counteract in the media and he had concluded that the heroine of *The*

Spy Who Loved Me had to reflect changing social mores. He was also keen to address the détente between America and Russia and so conceived the main female role in *The Spy Who Loved Me* as Russia's top agent, who teams up with Bond to search for the missing submarines – only to discover it was Bond who killed her lover, which makes her swear revenge.

The result was the character of Major Anya Amasova, Agent XXX (well, this *is* a Bond film), who was easily the most important female role written for a Bond film since Tracy in *On Her Majesty's Secret Service*. Barbara Bach, a former model who would later marry the former Beatle Ringo Starr, was cast as Anya and she relished the changing face of Bond girls.

'Well, first of all she's a spy and a serious spy,' she said during filming. 'And she's not really one of Bond's girls, so to speak. She's in the film doing her own bit and she meets up with Bond and it's only almost at the end of the film that there's any kind of attraction between the two of them, other than, let's say, professional competition. So it's quite different. Most of the girls in the Bond films have just been merely beautiful girls that have small parts and come and go. Anya stays from the beginning to the end.'

'In the early days, Bond came into a room, the girl fell, was plundered and you never saw her again,' said Lewis Gilbert. 'We're still pressing for beauty – people expect beautiful women around Bond – but now we must show a lot more of women intellectually. This, of course, has presented us with the biggest challenge the series has faced so far: portraying intellectual qualities while presenting *Playboy*-type visuals.'

Cubby Broccoli was delighted with the character of Anya and very pleased with the casting of Barbara Bach, then a relative unknown. With the exception of Honor Blackman, Diana Rigg, Jill St John and, possibly, Britt Ekland, all of whom were established names, Broccoli's preferred policy was to cast lesser-known actresses in Bond films, as he explained during the filming of *The Spy Who Loved Me*.

'Barbara's a very beautiful girl,' he said. 'And she's comparatively unknown, which I think brings a certain freshness to a Bond film. We've explored getting various well-known ladies, high-priced ladies, to bring in, but in my humble opinion, there's no lady today who contributes that much success if she's high-priced or otherwise, unless we like what she does. I don't think there's any actress today that can support a picture box-office-wise with the possible exception of Barbra Streisand.

'But the price doesn't distinguish the girl in our film from the success of a Bond picture. I mean, we've explored a certain lady in Hollywood who commands a $500,000 wage and that blew her right out of the box for me because she'd contribute no more than Barbara Bach will.'

With the relationship between Bond and Anya established, and the central submarine-stealing plots taking shape in Christopher Wood's shooting script, preproduction on *The Spy Who Loved Me* progressed relatively smoothly throughout the early summer of 1976 until a potentially major problem came from an unexpected source: Kevin McClory.

When McClory had struck the deal to co-produce *Thunderball* with Broccoli and Saltzman in 1965, he'd agreed not to assert his rights in the property for ten years. That agreement ended in January 1976 and, in May 1976, *Variety* announced that McClory and the novelist Len Deighton were collaborating with none other than Sean Connery, albeit in a writing capacity initially, on a rival James Bond project called, variously, *James Bond of the Secret Service* or *Warhead*. The project was being rather grandly referred to in Hollywood as '*Star Wars* Under Water'.

'Kevin McClory came to see me in January 1976,' explains Connery. 'He said he had the rights to do another story on a similar theme to *Thunderball*. I told him I wasn't interested in playing Bond again, but when he said would I co-operate in some way because of the experience I'd had, I thought about it and agreed. I was also intrigued because Len Deighton was going to work on the script and I have a lot of respect for him.

'Well, the three of us did a screenplay and put in all sorts of exotic things in it. We had SPECTRE being responsible for all the aircraft that were disappearing over the Bermuda Triangle. There was going to be an attack on the financial nerve centre of New York by going through the sewers right into Wall Street, which you *can* do. There were going to be mechanical sharks in the bay, a take-over of the Statue of Liberty and the main line of troops on Ellis Island.'

Naturally, the press licked their lips at the prospect of a battle of the Bonds, particularly since *James Bond of the Secret Service* or *Warhead,* or whatever McClory's film was going to be called, involved Sean Connery – even if no one seriously believed he would ever actually play Bond again.

Not for the last time in the Bond saga, it was the lawyers who got rich when McClory took out an injunction to prevent work on *The Spy Who Loved Me* from starting. He claimed the film infringed his copyright by using SPECTRE and the character of Blofeld.

Given that *The Spy Who Loved Me* had already been delayed, Broccoli was keen to press on with the film and he instructed Christopher Wood to eliminate any mention of SPECTRE or Blofeld from the script. Thus the villain became Karl Stromberg, an insanely wealthy and utterly mad shipping magnate – played somewhat lazily by the veteran actor Curt Jurgens, the weakest link in the movie – who steals nuclear submarines to initiate World War Three. This, he believes, will lead to the utter destruction of the world and allow him to set up an underwater colony (couldn't he do that without blowing the rest of us to bits?). Despite the name change, Blofeld-like characteristics can be discerned in Stromberg, even if the character he most resembled was Captain Nemo, the commander of the Nautilus – and prototype Bond villain – in Jules Verne's *Twenty Thousand Leagues Under the Sea* (although giving him webbed hands was a suitably chilling nautical touch worthy of Ian Fleming himself).

Denied the chance to delay *The Spy Who Loved Me*, McClory pressed on with his own Bond project. But Broccoli and the trustees of Ian Fleming took their own action against McClory's film, which prevented its happening – at least until 1982.

Production on *The Spy Who Loved Me* finally began on 31 August 1976 at Pinewood Studios, where Ken Adam, back after a two-film break, had constructed his most lavish Bond sets since *You Only Live Twice*. Indeed, with Lewis Gilbert back directing ten years after he had directed *You Only Live Twice*, *The Spy Who Loved Me* might be regarded as the 1970s equivalent of *You Only Live Twice*.

Some have gone further, claiming *Spy* is nothing more than a remake of *Twice*, but this is unfair. Despite some similarities in narrative – Stromberg's tanker gobbles up the nuclear submarines in much the same way as Blofeld's rocket snatches American and Russian space capsules in *You Only Live Twice*; and the climactic battles in the volcano and the belly of the tanker *do* bear a passing resemblance – the dynamics of the plot, particularly Bond's teaming up with Anya and the whole subtext of their relationship, are utterly different.

Others have accused the film of merely recycling incidents from the previous nine films. Alan Barnes and Marcus Hearn call *The Spy Who Loved Me* 'a vacuous "greatest hits" package' in their book *Kiss Kiss Bang Bang*, while the *Monthly Film Bulletin* complained on its release: 'The film, bearing no relation to its nominal source, seems to do nothing more than anthologize its forerunners.' John Brosnan is even more specific in his criticisms in his book *James Bond in the Cinema*. Stating that *The Spy Who Loved Me* is nothing more than 'an anthology of all the Bond films that have gone before', Brosnan accuses Broccoli of deliberately remaking – albeit more lavishly and spectacularly – some of the most memorable set-pieces from the previous nine Bond films. He claims the skiing scenes in the pre-credits sequence come from *On Her Majesty's Secret Service*; that the fight on the train is a steal from *From Russia With Love* and *Live And Let Die*; that the motorcycle assassin and his rocket-powered sidecar is inspired by Fiona's rocket-firing motorbike in *Thunderball*; that the 'gimmicked-up Lotus Esprit' Bond drives in *Spy* is a repeat of the Aston Martin in *Goldfinger*; that the underwater battles are copied from *Thunderball*; and that 'the basic plot, together with the final climactic scenes in the tanker, are from *You Only Live Twice*'.

These criticisms, which are not actually without some basis in fact, are nonetheless deeply unfair because they ignore the limiting realities of commercial creativity.

All long-running series eventually feed off themselves. *Coronation Street* does it. So does *EastEnders*. *Doctor Who* did it all the time. Even Shakespeare and Dickens were known to repeat certain themes over the course of their careers. And Fleming himself had certainly done it, particularly in THUNDERBALL, which recycled incidents and situations from the previous eight Bond books. Why anyone should imagine Eon Productions' Bond films would be immune from this creative inevitability is difficult to grasp.

The reality is that Cubby Broccoli was *bound* to play safe to a degree in *The Spy Who Loved Me*. His job, in the real world, was to put Bond back on top and if that meant pleasing the *general* cinema-going audience, who are any producer's bread-and-butter, by giving them more of what they'd enjoyed most about the so-called classic Bonds like *Goldfinger* and *You Only Live Twice*, then so be it. *The Spy Who Loved*

Me was not a film with which Cubby Broccoli felt free to tamper with the Bond formula: quite the reverse.

What is amazing, therefore, is that, given those constraints, *The Spy Who Loved Me* is a film bursting with confidence and chutzpah and innovation. And, if it recycles successful elements from previous Bonds, who cares? At least it does so with a freshness that all but disguises the sources. And for that, Cubby Broccoli should be congratulated, not condemned.

Yes, Bond's fabulous Lotus Esprit, which converts into a submarine, is a throwback to the Aston Martin in *Goldfinger*; and, yes, Jaws, the seven-foot-two henchman with steel teeth, played with humorous implacable menace by Richard Kiel, is another Oddjob. But for the vast majority of Bond fans, not to mention the general audience whose opinions are the only ones that really matter, this simply isn't a problem.

Live And Let Die and *The Man with the Golden Gun* had placed Bond against a rather modest canvas. *The Spy Who Loved Me* redresses that. Bond literally saves the world from Stromberg's madness.

Controlled largesse permeated the entire production, as Christopher Wood explains: 'I've worked on films in which producers have said to me, "Chris, baby, it doesn't matter. The sky's the limit. You want to shoot this in Saudi Arabia, shoot it in Saudi Arabia, we don't care. Have as many people as you like, just don't feel there are any constraints." So I write it and then they come back and say, "Why have we got two rooms here? Couldn't she be his wife at the same time? I mean, we'd save money on casting . . ."

'With a Bond film, you do know that with anything you write, money is no restraint.'

Returning to Bondage after ten years, the director Lewis Gilbert proved an ideal choice to ensure *The Spy Who Loved Me* – perhaps the most important film in maintaining the continuation of the franchise, at least until 1995's *GoldenEye* – hit every target in the bull's-eye. He understood exactly the point of evolution the Bond films had reached in 1976.

'Most of the things in Bond films today have kind of grown up with the picture,' he said during filming. 'They tend to keep it to the pattern they've had all along. For instance, they have an unknown leading lady. They don't like to change all the people who are well known, like M and Miss Moneypenny and Q. And there's no way in which they could be changed now because the public really wants to see them.

'The audience likes the pattern, the formula. I think that part of the charm of a Bond picture is you know what you're going to get. Audiences for a Bond film aren't looking for great acting. They want to be overwhelmed by physical things.

'The character of Bond you can't change fundamentally. But you can change his attitude to a certain extent. He doesn't find the girl in this picture so easy, such a pushover as the other girls have been. So in that sense you can change it slightly.

'But it's very well laid down, the law of Bond and people want you to abide by it. Bond films are very different from any other kind of film made. They've disproved every law in the cinema. They've done everything wrong and they're huge successes. I mean in story elements, in characterisation elements, the anticlimactic bit they always have at the end – which you wouldn't dare do in other pictures – where they have a huge big ending and then suddenly the film starts up again: many things they do wrong.'

One of Lewis Gilbert's greatest achievements in *The Spy Who Loved Me* was to concentrate on finally defining Roger Moore's portrayal of Bond.

'The problem was trying to get the image of Sean Connery out of the picture, because if you haven't got Sean, there's no use having his image,' Gilbert said after *The Spy Who Loved Me* premiered. 'We had to do something to make Roger's films distinct. Roger is a totally different person from Sean. As a type and as an actor.

'What Sean did, really, was to make Bond in his own image, because he was not the Bond of the books. Of course, he was a very sexy, attractive, macho man: he still is. He also gave Bond a cynical edge. When Sean Connery killed someone in a Bond film, they were really dead, but with Roger, somehow, because of his sense of humour, you don't quite believe it. Roger gets along on a great deal of charm and friendliness. I don't think audiences ever believe Roger *really* kills anyone.

'So I went more for Roger's humour, because Roger is a wonderful light comedian, which is very rare today. So we changed Bond to fit Roger.

'It was a very difficult thing for Roger to take over that role, and I'm not sure that he was particularly successful in the first two, *Live And Let Die* and *The Man with the Golden Gun*. In fact, *The Man with the*

Golden Gun was right down in America and didn't do very well, but *The Spy Who Loved Me* was right up, because then he ceased to be Sean Connery.

'If I had anything to do with it, I think my contribution was that it was quite wrong for Roger to continue to be Sean, because he wasn't Sean, and now I think Roger is more acceptable than Sean around the world because new generations have come up that didn't know Sean, but who know Roger. And to them he *is* James Bond now.'

It's clear Gilbert perfectly understood Moore's own approach to playing Bond. Moore admitted he based almost his entire characterisation on the opening page of Fleming's GOLDFINGER, when Bond is reflecting on his killing a Mexican bandit while waiting in the final departure lounge at Miami Airport.

'I played Bond differently from Sean,' Moore admits. 'A little lighter, a little more tongue-in-cheek. Maybe if Sean had continued after the first six, he'd have sent it up too.

'I always played it with a certain reluctance to kill. It's very difficult to get in touch with the character by reading Fleming because there's very little about Bond – about the person that he is, only what he's doing. I found him to be a curiously unemotional man but then emotion isn't called for in an action-adventure film. I did a quick sort of sifting through all the books to try and find out what he was like when I started. I only found one thing and that was that he had a scar on his cheek and looked like Hoagy Carmichael.

'And the only other key to the character was that he had come back from Mexico where he had eliminated somebody. He didn't particularly like killing, but he took pride in doing his job well. That was the only thing I could find out about Bond.

'That was my key to it: I didn't like killing but I was pleased I did it well.'

While Moore's performance in *The Man with the Golden Gun* had certainly been more assured than in *Live And Let Die*, the general weakness of that film had largely undermined his good work. But Moore thrived in *The Spy Who Loved Me* and it's easy to see why he regards it as his favourite among his own Bond films. 'It was filled with fun, glamorous lunacy and incredibly ingenious spectacles,' he says. 'Its story worked the best. We reached the right level of humour and all the right elements came together.'

Just as Sean Connery's best performance as Bond came in his third 007 picture, *Goldfinger*, so Roger Moore's third stab at the role in *The Spy Who Loved Me* was not to be bettered by the actor in his remaining four Bond films. Moore commands *The Spy Who Loved Me* without dominating it; his performance is perfectly judged and he clearly relishes Lewis Gilbert's direction.

Despite his assertion that emotion is not required in a Bond film, Moore is called upon to display genuine emotion, albeit briefly, in two key scenes, and he does so with assurance. In the first, at an Egyptian nightclub, where he encounters Anya, all is light-hearted one-upmanship between them – until Anya mentions Bond's wife, Tracy (the series' first reference to her since *On Her Majesty's Secret Service*):

> BOND: Buy you a drink, Major Amasova? Or may I call you Triple X . . .?
> ANYA: So you know who I am?
> BOND: You made quite an impression.
> BARMAN: Yes, sir . . .?
> BOND: The lady'll have a Bacardi on the rocks.
> ANYA: For the gentleman, vodka martini, shaken, not stirred.
> BOND: *Touché*.
> ANYA: Commander James Bond. Recruited to the British Secret Service from the Royal Navy. Licensed to kill, and has done so on numerous occasions. Many lady friends, but married only once. Wife killed—
> BOND: All right, you've made your point.
> ANYA: You're sensitive, Mr Bond.
> BOND: About certain things, yes.

The shadow that crosses Bond's face when Anya mentions Tracy negates all those critics' allegations of Moore's inability to act and this sequence remains one of the best moments of Moore's career in Bondage. He has another equally impressive moment later in the film when Anya, who is becoming closer to Bond as their joint mission progresses, suddenly realises Bond probably killed her lover. When she challenges him, Moore is required to provide one of those moments of introspection, rare in film series but frequent in the novels, with which Ian Fleming humanised 007:

BOND: When someone's behind you on skis at forty miles an hour trying to put a bullet in your back, you don't always have time to remember a face. In our business, Anya, people get killed. We both know that. So did he. It was either him or me. The answer to the question is, yes, I *did* kill him.

Moore plays this dead straight and, for once, despite what Lewis Gilbert says, we really believe he has killed the man. No wonder Roger Moore likes this film better than any other of his Bond films.

The Spy Who Loved Me also remains the favourite of the production designer Ken Adam. *Diamonds Are Forever* had been something of a disappointment after his *tour de force* on *You Only Live Twice*, although, in fairness, the prosaic setting of an oil rig as Blofeld's base gave Adam little scope to match or surpass his hollowed-out volcano. But Stromberg's submarine-gobbling supertanker, not to mention his marine headquarters Atlantis, gave free rein to Adam's imagination.

'In terms of design, my favourite was *The Spy Who Loved Me*,' Adam says. 'I started by experimenting with new shapes and new forms for Atlantis and the interior of the supertanker.

'I decided not to make the same error as on the volcano in *You Only Live Twice* when I did all the structural work, and then it had to be pulled down because from the exterior it didn't look very attractive to the locals. So on *The Spy Who Loved Me*, I built this stage at the same time as I built the set for the interior of the *Liparus* supertanker with the nuclear submarines.

'The stage has been, I think, one of the most successful investments by United Artists because, even though it wasn't a soundstage, it was so big it was used by all the big American productions that came to Europe.'

The stage – named the '007 Stage' – was a vast hangar-like structure that was required when Adam told Cubby Broccoli that there was no soundstage in the world that could house the set he had devised for the interior of the *Liparus*. Not even alternatives, such as the former airship hangars at Cardington – once the home of the ill-fated R101 – which Adam and his team had investigated as a possible site, were big enough. Broccoli's answer when Ken Adam informed him there was no stage anywhere in the world big enough to house his set was simple: 'Then build it!'

The dimensions of the new stage at Pinewood, built at a cost of $1 million, were staggering: 374 feet (114 metres) long (with an exterior tank adding another 38 feet, or 11.6 metres), 160 feet (49 metres) wide and 53 feet (16 metres) high. The stage was awesome: a state-of-the-art complex that was the envy of every studio in the world. Officially opened by the former British prime minister Harold Wilson, the 007 Stage was also the most visible sign of Cubby Broccoli's optimism about the future of James Bond 007.

The Spy Who Loved Me premiered in London on 7 July 1977 and in the US just under a month later on 3 August. It was an immediate hit and, for once, the majority of critics received the film well.

The Spy Who Loved Me succeeds on every level. From the pre-credits sequence, arguably the series' best with Bond skiing off a 3,000-foot (915-metre) cliff and being saved by his Union Flag parachute (a stunt performed by Rick Sylvester and overseen by the second-unit director and editor John Glen), the incomparable theme song 'Nobody Does It Better', written by Marvin Hamlisch and performed by Carly Simon, right through to Bond's cheeky last line about 'keeping the British end up', the film achieves the perfect balance between humour and excitement, fantasy and realism.

There is real tension, overt but controlled laughter, some wonderful gadgetry and gimmickry, and, best of all, a much more comfortable and relaxed Roger Moore at its heart. As Lewis Gilbert said at the time, 'It's the most ambitious Bond film ever made. We've pulled out all the stops. We're proving that not only is Bond alive and kicking in the 1970s, but is ready to continue successfully into the 1980s.'

What even Lewis Gilbert could not have known was that *The Spy Who Loved Me*'s success helped ensure that the franchise would still be thriving in the twenty-first century.

With *The Spy Who Loved Me* in the can, Roger Moore's three-picture contract, which he had signed in 1972, was complete. Given that the success of the film established Moore firmly as one of the top box-office stars of 1977 and finally confirmed him as the established 007, Cubby Broccoli was naturally anxious to sign Moore to another three-picture deal.

'When Connery quit we were sure there would be no more Bonds,' Broccoli said. 'But the public would not let us stop making them. The demand is greater than ever. And with Roger taking over the role in such style, we've gone from strength to strength.'

But Moore knew that *The Spy Who Loved Me* had strengthened his hand considerably. 'I didn't think I would go beyond two Bond films,' Moore once confessed. 'I figured the films would have run their course by then.'

The Spy Who Loved Me changed all that. Bond was going on, seemingly stronger in 1977 than at any time since the mid-1960s. And Roger Moore shrewdly decided to negotiate for future Bond films on a one-picture basis. Nevertheless, he told Cubby Broccoli at the premiere of *The Spy Who Loved Me* that he would play Bond in the next film, which was scheduled to be *For Your Eyes Only*.

Successful though *The Spy Who Loved Me* was, the true cinematic phenomenon of 1977 was *Star Wars*, which triggered a science-fiction boom throughout 1978 and 1979. Suddenly every major Hollywood studio was climbing aboard the space bandwagon: the inevitable *Star Wars* sequel was planned; *Star Trek: The Motion Picture* was green-lit; Steven Spielberg's *Close Encounters of the Third Kind* caused a sensation in 1978; and countless other big-budget – and sometimes not-so-big-budget – science-fiction films were rushed into production.

Eager to consolidate the box office after *The Spy Who Loved Me*'s success, Broccoli and United Artists decided to embrace the science-fiction boom by sending James Bond into space in the next film. Thus plans to film *For Your Eyes Only* were shelved and *Moonraker*, the only available Ian Fleming title left that could accommodate a space theme, was announced as the eleventh James Bond film instead.

The irony of the Bond team jumping on to the space bandwagon in the wake of *Star Wars* cannot be overstressed. Twelve years previously, the huge global success of the Bond films had created their own bandwagon: every studio and producer scrambled to get aboard the Bondwagon to try to emulate the success of Broccoli and Saltzman's series.

The Bonds had redefined the action-adventure genre and Cubby Broccoli was surely right in the mid-1980s when he claimed, 'I consider *Raiders of the Lost Ark* an imitator of our Bond series. I'm sure there wouldn't have been an Indiana Jones if there hadn't been a James Bond.' And, indeed, both Steven Spielberg and George Lucas have generously credited the influence of the early Bond movies on them when both were growing up.

But, where the Bond series once set trends, it now slavishly followed them with *Moonraker*. From a commercial standpoint this undoubtedly made sense. Movie budgets were getting higher all the time and *Moonraker*, costing $30 million, twice as much as *The Spy Who Loved Me* and thirty times as much as *Dr. No*, was a huge investment on the part of United Artists.

The expediency – some even claimed the cynicism – with which *Moonraker* was conceived goes a long way to explain its artistic disappointment when the film was released in June 1979. Many Bond fans – particularly those whose interest in the character centres on the Fleming novels – loathe *Moonraker* and cite it as the worst-ever Bond film, worse even than *The Man with the Golden Gun* or *Never Say Never Again*. Yet it *is* possible to find Bond fans who name it as the *best* Bond film; and, with an international gross of $203 million, it was to remain Eon's highest-grossing Bond film until *GoldenEye*'s $351 million in 1995, something that was to put Cubby Broccoli in a dilemma about the future direction of the series.

Despite its then mammoth budget, the Draconian taxation policies of Britain's Labour government at the time forced Broccoli to make *Moonraker* not at Pinewood but at three major studios in France – Boulogne, Epinay and Billancourt. Only Derek Medding's extensive, Oscar-nominated special effects were filmed at 007's traditional Pinewood home.

Moonraker is really nothing more than *The Spy Who Loved Me* in space. Instead of Stromberg hijacking nuclear submarines as a prelude to destroying the world so he can establish an underwater city, *Moonraker*'s insane billionaire Hugo Drax hijacks a space shuttle on loan to the British from NASA as a prelude to destroying the world so he can establish a city in space. Drax even hires Jaws, who survived *The Spy Who Loved Me*, as his henchman in the second half of the film.

Broccoli and Michael Wilson, now acting as executive producer, again hired Lewis Gilbert to direct; Ken Adam as production designer; and Christopher Wood to write the shooting script, although an uncredited Tom Mankiewicz devised the story with Lewis Gilbert. John Barry was also brought back to write the score (one of his best), and even Shirley Bassey sang the theme song, after Frank Sinatra, Kate Bush and Johnny Mathis had been considered.

On a purely professional level, *Moonraker* is magnificent. Cubby Broccoli often claimed that he put every penny of the budget up on screen in his films and, in *Moonraker*, it's no idle boast. *Moonraker* is an epic in every sense. On a visual level it is probably unsurpassed in the entire Bond series: if nothing else, *Moonraker* is often a very beautiful film to look at.

It also moves quickly from California, to Venice and Rio de Janeiro, and to outer space for Bond's final showdown with Drax aboard his space station. But the problem is that the movie's very expediency undermines it at every turn.

It can be argued that Eon had been playing safe with the Bond films ever since *Diamonds Are Forever*: bringing back Sheriff J W Pepper for *The Man with the Golden Gun* after he'd proved popular in *Live And Let Die* is an obvious example. But with *Moonraker* this tendency goes into overdrive. The return of Jaws, reduced to a cartoon-like shadow of the funny but menacing character he had been in *The Spy Who Loved Me*, is the clearest indication of what is wrong about *Moonraker*.

The Bond films have been self-spoofing since *Dr. No* but *Moonraker* parodies *everything*: itself, the previous Bond films, and other films such as *The Magnificent Seven* and *Close Encounters of the Third Kind*. Worse, the film rarely takes itself seriously, with the result that the humour, so balanced in *The Spy Who Loved Me*, frequently regresses into slapstick.

Everything in *Moonraker* goes too far. A prime example is the pre-credits sequence, which could have been the best in the series. When the space shuttle is hijacked while being ferried to Britain on the back of a 747 (a tremendous sequence), Bond is recalled from an African job. The pilot of the private plane bringing him back to London turns nasty, shoots out the controls and prepares to jump out of the aircraft with his parachute, leaving Bond to his fate (why didn't he just shoot Bond?).

A fight ensues during which the emergency door is opened and Bond is nearly pushed out by the pilot. Bond hangs on and kicks the pilot away into midair. As Bond clings to the door frame, struggling not to be sucked out of the plane, Jaws suddenly appears behind him and pushes him out.

Using freefall techniques, the parachute-less Bond flies through the air like Superman, catches up with the pilot and fights him for possession of the man's parachute. Naturally, Bond relieves the man of his parachute and kicks the man away into the ether. This is wonderful stuff and had the sequence ended there it would have been a Bondian classic.

But no: Jaws, also skydiving, appears behind Bond and a chase through the air ensues. Bond pulls his ripcord and his parachute opens. Jaws pulls his and it snaps because of his strength. His parachute failing to open, Jaws flaps his arms, stupidly, like a bird and plummets to earth. He is saved by falling on top of a circus big top.

Thus, a carefully conceived, brilliantly executed opening stunt is negated by a silly gag. This is *Moonraker*'s tragedy throughout: a promising, if outlandish, Bond film lies buried beneath stupidity.

That is not to say that *Moonraker* is wholly disappointing. There *are* some enjoyable scenes, some of the gags *do* elicit laughter, the locations are gorgeous and the cast is good. Dr Holly Goodhead (a name almost as outrageous as Pussy Galore), the NASA-trained astronaut, is a splendidly accomplished and liberated heroine, although she is played somewhat haughtily by Lois Chiles; and the French actor Michael Lonsdale's Hugo Drax is one of the drollest Bond villains – 'Look after Mr Bond. See that some harm comes to him,' he purrs menacingly in the best line since Auric Goldfinger said, 'No, Mr Bond, I expect you to *die*.'

Drax's French chateau in the Californian desert, 'every stone brought from France', is a wonderful conceit, and Bond's ordeal in the centrifuge trainer when he is almost spun to death is exceptionally well done, even if it is a reworking of the traction-machine sequence in *Thunderball*.

Best of all is the encounter between Bond and Drax at the pheasant shoot, when the filmmakers cleverly have Bond reflect Ian Fleming's own ambivalence about blood sports. Prior to leaving the chateau, Bond goes to say farewell to Drax, who is shooting pheasants, seemingly unaware that Drax has set up a sniper to shoot him from the trees.

DRAX: A pity you leave us. Such good sport.
BOND: Unless you're a pheasant.
DRAX: Oh, really, Mr Bond. Take my gun. A stray bird may fly
   over. Come now . . . (*He hands Bond a shotgun*)
BOND: I doubt I'm in your class.
DRAX: You're too modest, Mr Bond. (*Spots a couple of
   pheasants*) Over there . . .! (*Bond fires but the birds fly on*) You
   missed, Mr Bond . . . (*Whereupon the sniper falls dead from the
   trees*)

BOND: Did I? As you said, such good sport . . . (*Hands back the shotgun*)

When *Moonraker* does get it right, as it does so in this sequence, it succeeds splendidly. And at least it is never boring, unlike *Thunderball* or *The Man with the Golden Gun*. But the film is let down by its script and few could seriously argue with *Sight and Sound*'s assessment that the film has 'conspicuously expensive production values but an unmistakably cut-price plot'.

Interestingly, Lois Maxwell revealed in an interview in the 1980s that Cubby Broccoli himself was dissatisfied with Christopher Wood's shooting script. 'I remember saying to Cubby several years ago while working on *Moonraker* that I didn't like the script much,' she recalled. 'He was inclined to agree with me, but he said the Bond films now have to compete with films like *Star Wars*.'

Diehard Bond fans did not agree when the film was released in June 1979, and Broccoli was inundated with complaints from them. But it is worth remembering that the general audience enjoyed the film enormously and even the reviews, mixed though they were, were often very positive. Dilys Powell, for years the doyenne of British film critics, enjoyed the film, and yet was still able to pinpoint its faults in her review for *Punch*:

Little by little the gadgets have been winning. With *Moonraker* they have taken over; *Moonraker* is the adventure not of Agent 007 but of rear-activated speedboat torpedoes and a handy little wrist-attached exterminator.

Most of the action depends on the impossible. The audience doesn't believe that James Bond can float to earth without a parachute, and laughs because it doesn't have to believe. And the impossible comes every ten minutes. *Moonraker* takes in two continents, moving from Californian nuclear-plant [*sic*] to Venetian glass-factory and back across the Atlantic to Carnival in Rio de Janeiro.

Its two hours could be divided into independent episodes: Bond at the pigeon-shoot [*sic*], Bond in the velocity-test, Bond attacked from a canal-hearse, or acrobatic in a cable-car, or resourceful with a tropical reptile. In fact, *Moonraker* is a serial; it would gratify the desire, common in the silent days, to see all the episodes in one go. It was startling therefore to find myself, towards the end, reflecting that something was a bit tedious.

I know why. The last part of *Moonraker* is space-adventure. The insecure assembly of wire and what-not assumed by sci-fi to be capable of whizzing through space, the long bare corridors which make up the architecture of a sci-fi metropolis – it is all here, and once too often. Sci-fi repeats itself, feeds on itself. The sameness of these eternal space-ships is driving me nuts. Return Bond to earth!'

Powell's plea was not a lone voice. *Moonraker* had left nowhere else for the Bond films to go: it was the furthest into fantasy Eon Productions could launch their hero. The only thing left open to Cubby Broccoli and his team, *Moonraker*'s fabulous grosses notwithstanding, was to get back to basics. Back to Ian Fleming.

But would Roger Moore, who celebrated his 52nd birthday a couple of months after *Moonraker* premiered, be back for the next film, which was confirmed as *For Your Eyes Only* in *Moonraker*'s end credits?

Moore had not enjoyed *Moonraker* as much as *The Spy Who Loved Me*. The punishing 28-week schedule had given him just three days off and in January 1979 he had collapsed in Paris from the pain of a kidney stone while on his way to the Rio de Janeiro location.

His discomfort was compounded during the South American location work by an exhausting daily trek, undertaken in intense heat and humidity, to the Iguacu waterfalls on the Brazil–Argentine border where Drax's jungle hideaway and secret space-shuttle launching pad were situated.

Echoing Sean Connery's complaints about the length of time it took to complete a Bond picture, not to mention the attentions of the press, he gave notice that *Moonraker* might be his swansong as James Bond.

'I did 388 interviews on *Moonraker*, all of them as "in-depth, personal chats," which, of course, was impossible. It got to the point at one stage where I literally had to excuse myself from writers and TV crews to go and do the next scene. The Bonds are a bloody circus – they wheel 'em in and wheel 'em out.

'All the Bond films are intensely physical but there's never been one like *Moonraker*. I really don't want to find myself ever again up the

Amazon climbing up and down waterfalls or struggling through the jungle for five kilometres – and on foot – to get to the next location. If you worked a horse that hard, you'd be prosecuted.'

As the 1970s gave way to the 1980s, so James Bond entered his fourth decade. But in 1980 Cubby Broccoli and Michael Wilson were faced not only with finding a new direction for 007, but the possibility of finding a fourth actor to play him.

0011: Battle of
the Bonds

'Roger plays Bond his way and I play him my way. One newspaper ran a comparison and was particularly flattering to me and unjust to Roger. I don't appreciate that kind of flattery.'

Sean Connery, 1983

Moonraker's success put Eon Productions in something of a quandary. The film may have been condemned by hard-core Fleming fans but it was embraced by the cinema audience, particularly the 15–24-year-olds who comprised the largest part of Eon's most important market – North America. This generation of filmgoers was too young to remember the early Sean Connery pictures: some of them weren't even born when *Dr. No* and *From Russia With Love* were playing in cinemas.

So any return to basics with *For Your Eyes Only* was fraught with peril. What if the audience didn't like it? After all, diehard Fleming devotees made up only a tiny part of the Bond series' audience: most of the people who paid to watch a Bond movie in 1979 had probably never heard of Ian Fleming, let alone read one of his books.

Nevertheless, Cubby Broccoli and Michael Wilson, who was executive producer on the new film as well as co-writer of the script with Richard Maibaum, were convinced that the time was right to return to a grittier Bond.

'We decided the time had come to humanise Bond and make him less dependent on electronic hardware,' says Michael Wilson. 'If he was in a jam, he had to rely more on his wits to get him out of trouble. It makes him much more interesting.'

It was a change the new director John Glen embraced. Having served as editor and second-unit director on *On Her Majesty's Secret Service*, *The Spy Who Loved Me* and *Moonraker*, Glen had experience of Bond films from opposite ends of the spectrum – *OHMSS* and *Moonraker* – and he left no one in any doubt as to which he preferred:

We decided it was time for the films to return to the style of the first Bond pictures. When they were straightforward thrillers. We wanted to put the emphasis back on *people* rather than gadgets and sets – though keeping the extravagance, the action, and, of course, the Bond girls. It was a decision which appealed to me because *From Russia With Love* has always been a favourite of mine.

After *Moonraker* we'd really gone about as far as Bond could go in that direction. Everyone agreed we'd got all the mileage possible out of the plots about guys trying to blow up the world. The Bond pictures have always prided themselves on being the originators of certain styles in the cinema, and although *Moonraker* appeared before the American space shuttle had flown, once the space programme was underway, we knew it was time to get away from the hardware.

The solution was to base the script of *For Your Eyes Only* on two of Ian Fleming's short stories – 'For Your Eyes Only' and 'Risico' – which had been published in 1960, as well as taking a sequence from Fleming's second novel, LIVE AND LET DIE – where Bond and Solitaire are keel-hauled behind Mr Big's yacht – which had not been used in the film version.

Searching for the missing ATAC transmitter, which can render Britain's Polaris fleet useless and which has been lost off the Albanian coast – the British agent and marine archaeologist Sir Timothy Havelock is murdered alongside his wife by a Cuban hit man, Hector Gonzales. The Havelocks' daughter, Melina, swears revenge.

Assigned to find the ATAC, Bond attempts to question Gonzales but is captured by him. Bond makes his escape in the confusion when Melina shoots Gonzales in the back with a crossbow. Her quest for revenge not satiated – she wants to kill whoever paid Gonzales to murder her parents – Melina reluctantly agrees to wait until Bond can find the ATAC.

Bond's quest takes him to Emile Leopold Loque, an enforcer in the Brussels underworld, who, according to Bond's informant, Aris Kristatos, a respected businessman, works for a notorious Greek smuggler, Milos Columbo.

Captured by Columbo, Bond learns that it is Kristatos who is the true villain of the piece. Kristatos lets Bond and Melina retrieve the ATAC from the ocean bed before trying to kill them. Surviving their keel-hauling ordeal, Bond, Melina and Columbo go after Kristatos, tracing him to an abandoned monastery high in the Meteora mountains in Greece. Bond destroys the ATAC to prevent Kristatos from selling it to the KGB and talks Melina out of killing Kristatos simply out of revenge (Columbo saves her the job, anyway).

Compared with Christopher Wood's often inane script for *Moonraker*, the *For Your Eyes Only* screenplay is in a different class altogether. It contains the most original Fleming material in a Bond screenplay since *On Her Majesty's Secret Service*, written twelve years earlier, and, in many ways, can be regarded as the direct sequel to the Lazenby film. This is reinforced by the very first scene in *For Your Eyes Only*'s pre-credits sequence, which opens in an English country churchyard with Bond putting flowers on Tracy's grave – the headstone reads 'Teresa Bond. 1943–1969. Beloved wife of James Bond. "We Have All The Time In The World".' This is the prelude to an ordeal by helicopter, orchestrated by a bald-headed, white-cat-stroking, wheelchair-bound villain, who, of course, is absolutely not Ernst Stavro Blofeld (because of the legal disputes over ownership of the character) but who just happens to look like Telly Savalas's Blofeld at the climax of *On Her Majesty's Secret Service*, right down to the neck brace.

In reality, that scene was written to introduce any new actor who might be playing Bond, to give the series a sense of continuity, because in August 1980, with *For Your Eyes Only* scheduled to start shooting on 15 September, Roger Moore had still not signed for his fifth Bond film and possible successors were being screen-tested frantically.

'There was some talk that Roger wouldn't do *For Your Eyes Only*,' says John Glen. 'So we had to be prepared to break in the new Bond. So opening in the churchyard was my idea, to keep the continuity of the character and reveal the new Bond in an exciting situation.'

There was every reason to believe that Roger Moore was out of Bondage for good. He'd told journalists quite firmly at the press launch of his film *The Sea Wolves* in July 1980 that he had played James Bond for the last time. 'I don't want to take another six months out of my life playing James Bond again,' he said.

Other actors were screen-tested, including Timothy Dalton, who had been approached for *On Her Majesty's Secret Service*. 'There was a time when Sean Connery gave up when I was approached,' he says. 'I was very flattered but I think anyone would have been off their head to take over from Connery. I was also too young. Bond should be a man in his mid-thirties, at least. A mature adult who's been around.

'I wasn't approached for *Live And Let Die*, but there was a time when Roger may not have done *For Your Eyes Only*. They were looking around then and I went to see Cubby Broccoli in Los Angeles. At that time they didn't have a script finished but, to be honest, the way the Bond movies had gone, they weren't my idea of Bond movies, although they were fun and entertaining. They had become a completely different entity.'

Ultimately, the cat-and-mouse game between Cubby Broccoli and Roger Moore was settled when Moore signed for *For Your Eyes Only* for a reported seven-figure fee. Moore's astute decision not to sign another three-picture contract after *The Spy Who Loved Me* was paying rich dividends.

For Your Eyes Only began shooting, as planned, on 15 September 1980, with Roger Moore making his fifth appearance as 007. The opening in the graveyard, devised for any new James Bond, was retained because everyone believed it was a strong opening to the new film, as, indeed, it proved to be.

While *For Your Eyes Only* was in the planning stages, the directors of Glidrose Publications, the James Bond copyright holders, decided that the time was ripe for the return of James Bond in a new series of novels. It was thirteen years since Kingsley Amis's COLONEL SUN, a book that had proved a James Bond novel was viable if not written by Ian Fleming; and the success of Christopher Wood's novelisations of the scripts of *The Spy Who Loved Me* in 1977 and *Moonraker* in 1979 was further proof that there was still a literary market as well as a cinematic one for James Bond.

In the event, Glidrose commissioned John Gardner to write three new James Bond adventures. The first was to be published in the spring of 1981, just weeks before the release of *For Your Eyes Only*.

Gardner, who was born in 1926, had been writing thrillers since the early 1960s. Among his international bestsellers were *The Nostradamus Traitor*, *The Garden of Weapons* and *The Dancing Dodo*, the last of these being described by the *Guardian* as 'an expertly crafted thriller which produces a frisson of excitement and fear'. He was also the creator of the cowardly Boycie Oakes, an eliminator of security risks for the Secret Service. Oakes had even turned up in a film, *The Liquidator*, starring Rod Taylor and Jill St John, which had been one of the numerous James Bond spoofs made at the height of Bond mania in 1966.

Thus Gardner seemed the ideal man to take the literary James Bond into the 1980s and his first Bond book, LICENCE RENEWED, promised much.

Dedicating the book to the memory of Ian Lancaster Fleming, Gardner wrote in his introduction to the book,

> We have become so used to James Bond gadgets which boggle the mind that I would like to point out to any unbelievers that all the 'hardware' used by Mr Bond in this story is genuine. Everything provided by Q Branch and carried by Bond – even the modifications to Mr Bond's Saab – is obtainable on either the open, or clandestine, markets.

Ian Fleming had always liked to anchor the exploits of Commander Bond in some kind of reality, so Gardner's approach augured well. And, in the first book at least, Gardner's James Bond was recognisable as Fleming's Bond, with remarkably few signs of ageing. He may have moderated his alcohol intake; his cigarettes, still custom-made by Morelands of Grosvenor Street, may be milder; and there are minute flecks of grey showing at the temples; but he's still slipping into worsted navy slacks and a Sea Island cotton shirt off duty, and still wearing the Rolex Oyster Perpetual on his wrist.

Unfortunately, he has forsaken his Bentley for a Saab 900 Turbo, a horrendous mistake on Gardner's part since it is difficult to think of a less-Bondian car than a Saab. That apart, the Bond of LICENCE RENEWED is pretty much the same Bond as the later Fleming novels – ON HER MAJESTY'S SECRET SERVICE, say. The cover, designed by Mon Mohan using a commissioned watercolour by Richard Chopping of a Browning 9mm gun, evoked particular memories of the Fleming books.

As a novel, LICENCE RENEWED is fun, but it's a romp that owes more to Cubby Broccoli than to Ian Fleming. Many of the incidents in the book are reminiscent of the Eon films, which is disappointing, while the main plot – the phony Laird Anton Murik plans to trigger meltdowns in six nuclear power stations if his demands aren't met – is, as Raymond Benson rightly points out, clearly inspired by *The China Syndrome*.

Quibbles apart, LICENCE RENEWED was a noble first effort and was fairly well received by reviewers. *The Times* believed that 'Gardner's James Bond captures that high old tone and discreetly updates it,' while the *Daily Telegraph* thought LICENCE RENEWED was 'constructed, scrutinised and checked with immense care – Ian Fleming would not be displeased.' The *Financial Times* was even more thrilled: 'No fan will fail to be caught up in the world-scale adventure of LICENCE RENEWED. The dear old formula of the Mad Scientist is also renewed, with great success; and the Girl – with a splendidly improbable name of course – is a worthy addition to the famous gallery of Bond's beauties.'

But it was left to Philip Larkin, who called Bond 'the latest – perhaps the last – of the Byronic heroes', when reviewing LICENCE RENEWED for *The Times Literary Supplement*, to put his finger most accurately on what the novel wasn't – and could never hope to be:

The trouble is that to resurrect Bond you have to be Ian Fleming. For he was his creator in a way that Tarzan or Sherlock Holmes or Billy Bunter clearly weren't theirs. It was Fleming who smoked seventy cigarettes a day, who wore dark blue Sea Island cotton shirts and loved scrambled eggs and double portions of orange juice for breakfast; Bond was a kind of *doppelgänger* sent out to enact what Fleming himself had never achieved.

The ease with which Bond appeared suggests the tapping of deep imaginative springs. And the novels that succeeded them drew on the same dark source: 'The next volume of my autobiography,' he would call the book currently in progress, masking his personal involvement by mocking it.

Since [the books] were instinct with a personality much more complex, much more intelligent, much more imaginative than Bond's – the personality of Fleming himself – they remain alive in a way that COLONEL SUN and now LICENCE RENEWED cannot hope to do so.

LICENCE RENEWED was an immediate bestseller on both sides of the Atlantic, helped, no doubt, by the anticipation of *For Your Eyes Only*, which was due to open in the UK on 24 June 1981 and in the US two days later, and was being widely trailed as a return to Bondian basics.

Sadly, not even the prospect of a new Bond blockbuster could save United Artists, which had been fatally holed beneath the waterline by the horrendous failure of Michael Cimino's wandering-but-underrated western, *Heaven's Gate*. On 21 May, United Artists was sold to MGM for $380 million. James Bond had a new home.

For many Bond fans, *For Your Eyes Only* was a breath of fresh air, which reinvigorated the franchise and vindicated Cubby Broccoli and Michael Wilson's decision to forsake the fantastic science fiction of *Moonraker* for a return to Fleming. 'We're concentrating on the character,' Broccoli told reporters, adding, in a *volte-face* from two years previously, 'We don't need to compete with *Star Wars*. This is a story where the character shines through.'

Broccoli was right. For the first time since *On Her Majesty's Secret Service*, here was a Bond film where the people mattered more than the gimmicks. The film is a tough, exciting thriller in its own right with a credible plot and even more credible characters. Unlike LICENCE RENEWED, in which John Gardner had gamely attempted to update Fleming's James Bond to the 1980s – with only partial success – *For Your Eyes Only* is a 1980s Bond film imbued with Flemingian style.

Best of all, Roger Moore plays Bond much more seriously: the wit and style of his Bond persona, perfected in *The Spy Who Loved Me*, is retained but in this film it is underpinned with serious intent at the expense of levity. Bond goes through hell in this movie: he's beaten up, attacked by ice-hockey players, keel-hauled through sharks and, best of all, kicked off a mountain in Greece and left dangling by the most slender of ropes.

On a sad note, *For Your Eyes Only* marked the first Bond without an appearance by Bernard Lee as M. He had been noticeably more frail in *Moonraker* but had managed to turn up for work on *For Your Eyes Only*. However, he found it impossible to remember his lines and M's scenes had to be hurriedly rewritten, substituting the Chief of Staff (played by James Villiers) for M. Lee died in January 1981 while *For Your Eyes Only* was still being shot.

Much of the credit for the success of the film must go to its director John Glen. *For Your Eyes Only* was his directorial debut but was so successful that he directed the next four Bond films – *Octopussy, A View To A Kill, The Living Daylights* and *Licence To Kill* – making him the only director to date to direct five consecutive Bond movies.

Cubby Broccoli had been impressed with Glen's work on *On Her Majesty's Secret Service, The Spy Who Loved Me* and *Moonraker* and showed enormous faith in him by giving him his directing debut on such a prestigious film. To begin with, though, some wondered if Broccoli had made a mistake, as Glen himself recalls:

I had an horrendous first week on a beach in Greece with everything getting stuck in the sand, and I got three days behind schedule. To make matters worse, it seemed as though all the top men at United Artists were sitting around on the beach watching me fall behind and calculating that by the end of the second week I'd be six days behind and at that rate it'd take a year to complete the movie.

But Cubby was a rock. He told them to count to ten and give me a chance. He was such a good guy. He backed me up so strongly that we were all busting a gut to keep the thing on the rails so as not to embarrass him. In the end, we kept within budget, although we went over schedule by a few days.

Broccoli's faith in Glen was well rewarded when *Variety* said *For Your Eyes Only* was:

one of the most thoroughly enjoyable of the twelve Bond pictures despite the fact that many of the usual ingredients in the successful 007 formula are missing. The entire film is probably the best directed on all levels since *On Her Majesty's Secret Service*, as

John Glen, moving into the director's chair after a long service as second-unit director and editor, displays a fine eye and as often as not keeps more than one thing happening in his shots.

Most reasonable critics agreed, and greeted *For Your Eyes Only* with good notices. There were, as ever, some dissenting voices, most noticeably in the British broadsheets, whose critics, wilfully or otherwise, never seemed to 'get' the appeal of the cinematic Bond.

Many fans and critics alike praised the toughening up of Moore's Bond. This was ironic, since Moore himself had taken considerable persuading that this was the right decision. Nowhere was this more obvious than in the stand-out scene when Bond confronts the henchman Locque's car. Bond stands his ground as Locque deliberately drives at him and, as he gets in range, shoots, hitting Locque in the shoulder. Locque's car spins out of control and comes to rest, precariously, on the edge of a precipitous drop. The car is slipping and Locque scarcely dare breathe for fear of sending it toppling over.

Bond approaches slowly and Locque's eyes silently plead with Bond to help. Bond gently reminds Locque of the man he has killed, a friend and colleague of Bond's, and then viciously lashes out with his foot, kicking the car and Locque over the edge. This is totally in character for Ian Fleming's James Bond but Moore felt it was out of character for *his* Bond. 'It's not me,' he argued. 'I don't do that sort of thing.'

John Glen persisted, arguing that it was entirely within character, and Moore reluctantly agreed to shoot the scene as written. The result is one of his very best moments as 007.

For Your Eyes Only grossed $195 million worldwide. This was slightly down on *Moonraker*'s record, but only just, and in Britain the film beat *Raiders of the Lost Ark* to be the top box-office movie of 1981. Buoyed by the film's success, Eon announced that *Octopussy* would be their next Bond film, to be released in the summer of 1983.

The spring of 1982 saw a flurry of activity in the James Bond story. At that year's Oscars ceremony, on 29 March, Cubby Broccoli was awarded the Irving G Thalberg Award, the highest honour that can be granted by the Academy of Motion Picture Arts and Sciences. The award, which is not made every year, is given to any producer whose work reflects a consistently high standard. Previous recipients had included Cecil B De Mille, Walt Disney and Alfred Hitchcock.

The award was presented to him on the stage at the Dorothy Chandler Pavilion by Roger Moore. At that time, protracted negotiations were taking place as to whether Moore would strap on Bond's shoulder holster for a sixth time. The American actor James Brolin was screen-tested and was regarded as a frontrunner should Moore not sign: Brolin's screen test – a re-creation of Bond's seduction of Tatiana Romanova in *From Russia With Love*, which he performed with Maud Adams playing Tatiana – was excellent. But, in July, Moore agreed to play Bond in *Octopussy* for a reported $4 million and a percentage of the profits.

Broccoli and MGM/UA were, by that time, keener than ever to retain the services of Moore, whose box-office appeal as Bond had been proven by three straight blockbusters in a row. The reason for this was that Kevin McClory, who had been trying, unsuccessfully, to make a James Bond film since 1976, had finally had a breakthrough.

In the summer of 1981, Jack Schwartzman, a former tax lawyer who had been an executive vice-president at Lorimar and was now working as an independent producer, bought the rights to make one James Bond film based on McClory's film rights to THUNDERBALL. McClory thus became executive producer of the proposed new film.

Having secured foreign distribution rights, Schwartzman got financial backing from Warner Brothers and then secured his biggest coup of all: getting Sean Connery interested in playing James Bond once more.

By all accounts, Connery took some persuading. Having collaborated with McClory and Len Deighton on the proposed *James Bond of the Secret Service/Warhead* script in 1976, Connery seemed to have lost interest by 1980. This was partly due to the lawsuits that had been flying around ever since McClory's project was first announced and he was cautious about entering into Bondage again.

'I thought about it for a long time,' he admits. 'Then I talked it over with my wife, Micheline. She encouraged me and said, "Why not? What would you risk? After all these years it might be interesting." And the more I thought about it, the more I felt she was right.

'Micheline also came up with the title, *Never Say Never Again*. I liked it immediately. It was romantic and pre-empted all the bullshit I knew would be written about my coming back to Bond.'

But Connery's appearance in the film came with some understandable conditions in addition to his reported $3 million salary and share of the profits. He insisted he be 'indemnified against the lawsuits that were flying around, and then on the creative side I wanted to be totally protected and I wanted the best cast possible.'

Connery had script approval, casting approval, director approval, even lighting-cameraman approval. Having decided to return to Bondage, Connery was taking an active role in all aspects of the production. Unfortunately, if things went wrong – and they certainly went wrong during production of *Never Say Never Again* – it meant he would have to shoulder much of the responsibility of actually getting the picture finished.

Cubby Broccoli and the trustees of Ian Fleming's estate did not take the threat of *Never Say Never Again* lying down. Broccoli took out an injunction against the rival production, claiming that it would be trading on Eon's success and would be milking ideas from previous Eon Bond films, particularly *Thunderball*, because *Never Say Never Again* was, basically, a remake of *Thunderball*. This application for an injunction failed because the judge felt Schwartzman's production was too far advanced for it to be fair to stop.

The legal rumblings did not end there, and some considerable doubt arose as to what Schwartzman could actually use in his rival Bond picture. 'I saw Sean and his wife at Norman Jewison's house,' says Lois Maxwell. 'I said, "I hear you're doing a remake of *Thunderball*," and he said, "That's right." I said, "Why don't you give me a part?" and Sean said, "I'm sorry but I'm not allowed to use the characters of M, Q or Moneypenny. I can only use Bond."' But, in the event, M, Q and Moneypenny all feature in *Never Say Never Again*.

Interestingly, in the midst of all the legal wranglings, John Gardner's second Bond novel, FOR SPECIAL SERVICES, was published in May 1982. This introduced a revamped SPECTRE under the control of one Nena Blofeld, Ernst Stavro's daughter. It is a novel about daughters because Bond's main squeeze in the book is none other than Cedar Leiter, Felix's daughter.

FOR SPECIAL SERVICES is an interesting book and the *Sunday Times* believed it was 'much better nonsense than the previous Gardner resurrection of James Bond', but, already, Gardner was starting to tamper with the Bond formula, which irritated many Ian Fleming fans: for instance, Fleming had never mentioned that either Blofeld or Leiter had a daughter and, given that Fleming's Blofeld was supposedly asexual, the existence of one is somewhat unlikely. Kingsley Amis, in particular, was scathing about the book, calling it 'hesitant and obscure – hopeless!'

Warner Brothers announced that *Never Say Never Again* would be released in the summer of 1983, in direct competition with Eon's *Octopussy*. This was a crass decision, which would have been to the detriment of both films. When Broccoli heard the news, he retorted, 'If they're going to release their film at the same time as ours, then I'm going to re-release the first three Bond films at the same time, so that the public will be able to compare the slender, handsome, good-looking Sean Connery.'

Of course, as soon as it was confirmed Sean Connery was, indeed, returning to Bondage, the press had a field day in promoting the Battle of the Bonds and, in particular, they attempted to stoke the competition between Connery and Moore. This was not something that the two men, friends for many years, welcomed and they deliberately met up to have a drink while filming their respective movies.

'I met Roger in London while I was making *Never Say Never Again* and suggested we squash the rumours and speculation about rivalry by posing together and issuing a statement,' said Connery some time after completing the film. 'He naturally agreed. After all, we're friends.

'In a sense though, it's a no-win situation, because we both lose because we're being set up against each other. There have been a lot of unfair comparisons but I don't want to make them. Roger plays Bond his way and I play him my way. One newspaper ran a comparison and was particularly flattering to me and unjust to Roger. I don't appreciate that kind of flattery.'

Nevertheless, the press built up the rivalry between the two productions, with Connery's comeback getting favourable coverage at the expense of Moore's. Indeed, the consensus was that Connery's film was going to wipe the floor with Moore's: Connery would show Moore how it should be done. Battle was joined when *Octopussy* began shooting on 10 August 1982 in Berlin and *Never Say Never Again* started work on the French Riviera just over a month later on 27 September.

Octopussy used material from Ian Fleming's two short stories 'Octopussy' and 'The Property of a Lady' in its screenplay, written by Richard Maibaum, Michael Wilson and George MacDonald Fraser.

Assigned to discover why fake Fabergé eggs have turned up at auction in London – it may be an attempt by the Russians to raise funds for covert operations – Bond travels to India to investigate Kamal Khan, an exiled Afghan prince who is somehow involved in the scheme. Bond discovers that Khan is in cahoots with the mysterious and beautiful Octopussy, a woman whose many business interests include a travelling circus. They have been smuggling the real Russian treasures across borders, using the circus as a cover.

Octopussy is the daughter of Major Dexter Smythe, a disgraced British agent whom Bond had once investigated and allowed to fall on his sword rather than face the disgrace of a court martial. For this, Octopussy thanks Bond and they fall in love.

Also involved in the smuggling scheme is General Orlov, a renegade member of the Soviet government who disapproves of disarmament talks with the West. Bond discovers that Orlov and Khan have double-crossed Octopussy: the next smuggling trip of the travelling circus will take her to a USAF base in West Germany. Orlov and Khan substitute a nuclear bomb for the smuggled Russian treasures. Orlov reasons that exploding the bomb on the base will make it look as though an American bomb has detonated accidentally. This will cause groups like CND in the West to demand unilateral nuclear disarmament (a scenario Fleming first aired in YOU ONLY LIVE TWICE), leaving the Soviet Union as the world's dominant nuclear force.

Octopussy is a superb James Bond film, arguably second only to *The Spy Who Loved Me* as Roger Moore's best. It is exciting, funny and exotic, and the production values are very high throughout. The cast is quite wonderful, too. Maud Adams, who had previously appeared in *The Man with the Golden Gun*, was cast as Octopussy (after Faye Dunaway had been strongly rumoured to play the part); the veteran actor Louis Jourdan was signed as Kamal Khan; and Steven Berkoff was an inspired choice to play General Orlov.

As for Roger Moore himself, he was, perhaps, beginning to show his age more in *Octopussy*, and ten years on from his first appearance as 007 in *Live And Let Die* the rigours of shooting in the intense heat of India did take their toll.

'A lot of location work means a lot of travelling,' he said during filming. 'And the hazards of the places where you are shooting, like India, where it can affect the stomach and you've still got to work.

'And when you're on location it's a six-day week. And, as Bond, I'm an idiot running around in a black tie and dinner jacket while everybody else is in a sari. Tearing around in that heat is arduous; we have laughs but it's a slog.'

While acknowledging what Bond had done for him, Moore also expressed some frustration with the limitations of being known as Bond, just as Sean Connery had done so before him:

'The real drawback to acting Bond is that it's not acting. You are just a comic-strip hero, the central character around which the action and the gadgets revolve. Bond is exactly the same in the last scene as he is in the first. I'm not saying I'm the world's greatest actor, far from it, but I do enjoy acting.

'It just so happens that I am offered, in the main, derring-do heroes. There's an attitude among the people who put up money for films and they say, "No, we know that in that type of film we will get our money back. We may be taking a risk if we use him in something else." But it's better to be a highly paid personality than an out-of-work actor.'

Nevertheless, despite his looking older than previously, Moore looks good in *Octopussy*. And, despite what he said about Bond making few demands on him as an actor, the film *does* demand some serious acting from Moore, even though the director John Glen allows a little more of Moore's characteristic humour to come through than he had in *For Your Eyes Only*. The best dramatic moment comes when Bond – Moore holding his own admirably in a scene with the extraordinary Steven Berkoff – confronts General Orlov about exploding the nuclear bomb on the USAF airbase:

BOND: You surely can't be inviting a full-scale nuclear war? What happens when the US retaliates?
ORLOV: Against *whom* . . .?
BOND: My God, of course. Our early-warning system will rule out the possibility of that bomb having been launched from Russia or anywhere else. Everyone will assume – *incorrectly* – that it was an American bomb triggered accidentally.
ORLOV: That would be the most plausible explanation.
BOND: Europe will insist on unilateral disarmament, leaving every border undefended for you to walk across at will. And it doesn't matter a *damn* to you, I suppose, that thousands of

innocent people will be killed in that 'accident' of yours?

ORLOV: Better than letting a handful of old men in Moscow
   bargain away our advantage in disarmament talks.

When *Octopussy* premiered in June 1983, the critics, clearly
relishing Sean Connery's comeback, which had been put back to an
October release in the US and a Christmas release in the UK, were
harsher on Moore's film than it deserved.

But the film broke records for a Bond film on its first week on release
and went on to post a worldwide gross of $184 million. Broccoli could
relax a little. Whatever happened when *Never Say Never Again* was
released, *Octopussy* was yet another blockbuster. Better yet, with a $68
million gross in the US, *Octopussy* beat *Moonraker*'s record at the US
box office.

It was a satisfying result for the film, which, in 1983, celebrated the
21st birthday of Eon's Bond series. 'We enjoyed making this one,'
Broccoli said at the London premiere of *Octopussy*. 'We enjoy making
all our Bond pictures. The crew always looks forward to making a Bond
picture. Particularly the English boys who work on them at Pinewood.
They're all very happy pictures.'

After his attempts to have an injunction served on *Never Say Never
Again* had failed, Cubby Broccoli kept his counsel once production on
both films had begun, preferring to concentrate on bringing *Octopussy*
to the screen.

'We're not going out to compete, saying "We're going to be the best
Bond",' he said before *Octopussy* opened. 'The public's going to decide
that anyway. So it always annoys me to see in the press: this Bond is
fighting that Bond. That's really not so. At least as far as we're
concerned.'

However, as shooting progressed on both Bond pictures, Broccoli,
like everyone else, could not help but hear stories coming out about
Never Say Never Again. And the rumours about Sean Connery's
comeback were not good.

When the film finally premiered, it was apparent that the stories were
not just the usual bad-mouthing that always goes on in the industry.

Let's not be ambiguous: *Never Say Never Again* is simply dreadful.

For anyone who believes Ian Fleming was treated harshly in the 1963
THUNDERBALL case, there's a certain poetic justice in the artistic failure

of *Never Say Never Again*. From the outset, the film was characterised by incompetence and misjudgment, despite the undoubted individual skills of everyone involved. It is a Bond film made by people who – on this evidence at least – appear not to have the slightest idea of how to make a Bond film.

Typical of the misjudgment was the director Irvin Kershner's approach to directing Connery's new Bond film.

'I went back and reread Ian Fleming,' he said. 'I also looked at some of the old films and realised which ones I liked and which were not up to par. And then I decided to forget I had seen any of them. So far as I am concerned, there was never a Bond picture before. I'm not trying to copy anything.'

Kershner, whose direction of *The Empire Strikes Back* had been so assured just a couple of years earlier, is a reliable director and his deciding to treat the Bond film as though there had never been a Bond film before *might* have worked had he been introducing a new actor in the role of Bond. But it was an absolutely perverse way to approach *Never Say Never Again*, the film that was trying to reintroduce *the* 1960s cinematic icon – Sean Connery as James Bond – to 1980s cinema audiences.

Never Say Never Again was an unhappy picture. As we have seen, it should have been ready for the summer of 1983, when it was scheduled to go head-to-head with Eon's *Octopussy* at the box office. But Jack Schwartzman had misunderstood the rigours of a Bond shoot and the film went woefully over schedule and massively over budget.

For Sean Connery, *Never Say Never Again* turned into a nightmare that left him disillusioned and disappointed. He had always complained about the length of time it had taken to shoot the Eon Bond films back in the 1960s. Indeed, it was one of the reasons he had given for handing in his licence to kill originally in 1967. But he was still shooting *Never Say Never Again* in the summer of 1983, some nine months after principal photography began on the French Riviera on 27 September 1982 when certain scenes needed reshooting. '*Never Say Never Again* felt longer than my other six Bond pictures put together,' he later complained.

Connery's unhappiness was shared by everyone else on the film. 'Jack Schwartzman was a very good businessman but he didn't have the experience of a film producer,' says Irvin Kershner. 'He and I had divergent views of what the film should be. I tried to maintain what I could of my vision, but you can only do so much when the studio sides with the producer, whether he's right or wrong.

'The film was not a happy film. In fact it was a very unhappy film for most of the people working on it. It was disorganised, totally disorganised. Everyone suffered as a result.'

The unhappiness of the production can be seen etched on the face of Kim Basinger – who plays Domino – throughout *Never Say Never Again*, and she confirmed in an interview in 2001 that Connery himself was miserable throughout the shooting. 'Sean knew it wasn't working,' she said. 'And this wasn't the most pleasant situation for Sean.'

Aware that his return to Bondage was being watched – and judged – by the whole world, Sean Connery was forced to take over much of the production of the film to try to salvage something from the wreckage. But his own disappointment with the final product – not to mention the disappointment of almost every James Bond fan – was hardly worth the effort he had put into the film and he took a lengthy sabbatical once *Never Say Never Again* had premiered.

'I was pretty sickened by the making of the whole movie,' Connery says. 'It wasn't the best experience and I didn't do another film for two, two-and-a-half years.'

Sean Connery's feelings about the film are justified because, frankly, *Never Say Never Again* is a dire mess, less entertaining even than *Casino Royale*. Irvin Kershner's direction is unfocused and pedestrian (he is the only director to render Rowan Atkinson, who plays a bumbling British agent, unfunny); the locations seem dreary and drab; the music score and theme song by Michael Legrand are by far the worst heard in any Bond film; the excellent Klaus Maria Brandauer seems to be acting in another movie altogether; Edward Fox is a horrible M, Pamela Salem an insipid Moneypenny and Alec McCowen's Q just doesn't work; and some of the other performances – particularly Barbara Carrera as the absurd SPECTRE assassin Fatima Blush – are practically unwatchable. Worst of all, *Never Say Never Again* looks cheap: its production values are no better than a routine TV movie, which is simply unforgivable in a Bond film.

Just one sequence – a stylish tango between Bond and Domino, choreographed by Peggy Spencer – gives a hint of what might have been. Otherwise, *Never Say Never Again* is utterly devoid of wit, style or that certain chutzpah that characterises the Eon Bond films. There isn't even any action to speak of, save a limp motorbike chase, which is over all too soon. It really is no exaggeration to say that there's more entertainment, thrills, action and laughs to be found in the pre-credit sequence of *Octopussy* than in the entire running length of *Never Say Never Again*.

The movie's major problem is Lorenzo Semple Jr's emaciated script. Even allowing for the fact that he was limited by legalities to restricting himself to just a remake of *Thunderball* – which had been none too thrilling in 1965 – there is no excuse for the poor apology for a Bond screenplay that *Never Say Never Again* ended up with.

Sean Connery reportedly had reservations about Semple's script – as well he might – and he asked the British TV writers Dick Clement and Ian La Frenais to rework it. Clement and La Frenais, who did not receive a credit because of a bizarre restriction imposed by the Writers' Guild of America, are excellent writers but even they seem uninspired by the material for once. Their most notable contribution to the script and the film's funniest line – when a nurse asks Bond to give a urine sample in a beaker to which he replies 'From here?' – is even recycled from an old episode of their classic Britcom *Porridge*.

Trying to excuse the messy script, Irvin Kershner made a very interesting comment after filming had ended, which Alan Barnes and Marcus Hearn quote in *Kiss Kiss Bang Bang*: 'Of course, we had the problem that I had to shoot a film that didn't impinge on the images or the rights of *Thunderball* the film. I had to stay with the book, but the book was not do-able as a film!'

But, hang on: wasn't the whole basis of the THUNDERBALL case the accusation that Ian Fleming had *supposedly* based the book on the screenplays jointly written by himself, Kevin McClory and Jack Whittingham? Ah well, as Bond himself comments in *Never Say Never Again*, '*C'est la vie* – such is life.'

Never Say Never Again premiered in October 1983 in the US and in London on 14 December 1983. The press build-up was incredible, particularly in the US, where the critic Roger Ebert seemed to speak for everyone: 'There was never a Beatles reunion. Bob Dylan and Joan Baez don't appear on the same stage anymore. But here, by God, is Sean Connery as James Bond.'

Such sentiments – middle-aged critics yearning for their prime in the 1960s – probably explain why *Never Say Never Again* received such positive reviews. Connery's presence alone seemed to blind them to the film's numerous faults, with the result that never before – and never since – had such a dire film had so gentle a ride at the hands of the critics. 'It's the only film I've been criticised for which I wasn't even in,' Roger Moore commented as review after review praised Connery's comeback at the expense of his interpretation of Bond.

Time has proved much less forgiving to *Never Say Never Again*, however. As did cinema audiences in 1983. Despite all the industry talk of how *Never Say Never Again* would blow *Octopussy* – and, with it, Eon's entire franchise – out of the water, the opposite proved to be true. *Octopussy* trounced *Never Say Never Again* at the box office, proving there is justice in the film world after all.

'To judge the success of any film, the box-office receipts are the truest indicator of what the public wants to see,' said a satisfied Cubby Broccoli. 'In all territories of the world, with one exception, *Octopussy* had 20–30 per cent higher attendance figures.'

The one exception – ironically, given Broccoli's heritage – was Italy.

Even before the box-office figures were in, Broccoli demonstrated his faith in Roger Moore by announcing, just prior to *Never Say Never Again*'s London premiere, that Moore would star in Eon's next Bond film, *From A View To A Kill* (later shortened to *A View To A Kill*).

For once, Broccoli and Moore had settled terms quickly. Roger Moore had achieved the seemingly impossible – he had seen off a challenge from Sean Connery – and Broccoli and MGM's acceptance of his terms was a reflection of that. Roger Moore *was* James Bond in the mid-1980s, just as he had been for a decade.

But he would be nearly 57 when *A View To A Kill* opened in 1985. Time stands still for no man. Not even James Bond. Cubby Broccoli and Michael Wilson knew the time was coming when they would have to find a new James Bond.

Once the headache had been to find someone who could fill Sean Connery's shoes. Given Roger Moore's unexpected triumph in the Battle of the Bonds, they knew they now had to find someone who could replace Roger Moore *as well as* Sean Connery.

Finding someone who could satisfy fans of both their very different styles was not going to be easy.

0012: The Bonds Lose Their Value

'Bond is not a paragon of virtue. He's man riddled with vices and weaknesses as well as strengths. But that is the nature of the man, and the nature of the world he lives in.'

Timothy Dalton, 1989

John Gardner's fourth James Bond novel, ROLE OF HONOUR, was published in the spring of 1984. His previous three efforts had been enjoyable hokum, if hardly on a par with Fleming's novels or, indeed, the first non-Fleming Bond novel, COLONEL SUN. The third book, ICEBREAKER, published in the spring of 1983, had been by far and away the best of Gardner's books to date, even if it essentially dealt with the hoary old device of Bond's defeating a neo-Nazi plot to establish a Fourth Reich.

But, starting with ROLE OF HONOUR, Gardner's novels began to disappoint many Bond fans, and devotees' anticipation for the next Gardner Bond each spring lessened as his series progressed.

However, the real anticipation among fans in 1984 was the start of shooting of the fourteenth Bond movie, *A View To A Kill*, in the autumn. Nineteen eighty-three had been a bumper year for the character: no matter how much *Never Say Never Again* had been a letdown, there had still been two Bond films released within six months of each other, which made the wait until the release of *A View To A Kill* in the summer of 1985 seem longer than ever.

Disaster struck the production even before the cameras started rolling when the 007 Stage at Pinewood burned down on 27 June 1984. *A View To A Kill* needed a huge stage to house Peter Lamont's massive climactic mine set and Cubby Broccoli had to decide whether to rebuild the stage at a cost of £1 million or to abandon Pinewood and shoot *A View To A Kill*'s interiors at a Hollywood studio. Broccoli decided on a rebuild and the new stage – renamed 'The Albert R Broccoli 007 Stage' – had risen from the ashes within four months.

With Roger Moore already on board, the screenwriters Michael Wilson, who was now also co-producing the series with his stepfather Cubby Broccoli, and Richard Maibaum came up with a gloriously over-the-top and splendidly spectacular idea for what everyone sensed was going to be Moore's swansong: the villain, Max Zorin, would cause Halley's comet to veer off course and crash into San Francisco's Silicon Valley, thus inflating the value of his microchip-producing company many times.

Despite the obvious similarities with Goldfinger's plan to increase the value of his gold by irradiating the gold held in Fort Knox, this original scenario was a typically bold idea. Sadly, it was dropped in the early stages in favour of having Zorin exploit the San Andreas fault to wash away, literally, Silicon Valley.

'In the end, we decided the Halley's comet idea was just a little *too* fantastic,' said Maibaum. 'So we decided that, as Silicon Valley lies between the Hayward and San Andreas Faults, we would have him create an earthquake that would send the entire Valley into the Pacific instead.'

A pity.

Building the plot around microchips and making Silicon Valley the target was a deliberate attempt by Eon to make *A View To A Kill* as up to date and as relevant as possible to the teens and young adults in their audience. This policy was followed through to the rest of the production as well: Duran Duran, then riding high, were hired to perform John Barry's pulsating theme song (which went to number one in the US and number two in the UK); the Oscar-winning actor Christopher Walken became the youngest Bond villain to date when he signed as Max Zorin (after David Bowie had been approached); and, in the most significant move of all, the striking disco diva Grace Jones was cast as May Day, Zorin's lethal henchwoman and lover.

This repositioning of the dynamics of the franchise was undoubtedly astute and, in a long-running series – the Bonds had now been produced for 23 years – essential. Unfortunately, *A View To A Kill* was the wrong film in which to do it.

The problem with *A View To A Kill* is that Zorin and his organisation are young and vibrant, while the forces ranged against them – the British Secret Service – are ageing or elderly. Never is this more apparent than in the early scenes at Ascot when Bond, Moneypenny, Q, M (played for the second time by Robert Brown after his debut in *Octopussy*) and Bond's ally Sir Godfrey Tibbett (the wonderful Patrick Macnee) observe Zorin and May Day.

The age of the British agents – the actors range from being in their late fifties to their seventies – compares unfavourably with the youthful blond Zorin and the animalistic strength of May Day and it creates a damaging faultline in the picture. One critic remarked of Roger Moore when the film was released, 'He's not only long in the tooth – he's got tusks!' while Tony Bennett and Janet Woollacott in *Bond and Beyond* (Macmillan, 1987) remark that 'May Day sinks the Rolls-Royce containing Bond and Tibbett, packing them off like a couple of old has-beens'.

Not even the most diehard and loyal of Bond's fans could refute that argument, although some of the comments about Roger Moore's age were deeply unfair. Yes, he does look somewhat older in *A View To A Kill* than in *Octopussy*, but physically he's still in great shape as the hot tub scene with Fiona Fullerton, playing the East German agent Pola Ivanova, demonstrates.

But the relative youth of Walken and Jones, not to mention the Bond girl Tanya Roberts – barely adequate as Bond's main conquest, Stacey Sutton – merely accentuates his age. The casting of the slightly more mature Maud Adams as Octopussy in the previous film had toned this down: no attempts were made in *Octopussy* to play down Moore's age and his maturing Bond worked beautifully in that film.

There is also a slight weariness about Moore's performance in *A View To A Kill*. The general consensus is that *Octopussy* should have been his final Bond film and this belief is strengthened by the sense throughout *A View To A Kill* that we are perhaps seeing Moore's Bond just once too often. It's a fading performance.

This sense of weariness with the part came through in some interviews. While acknowledging the need to promote the film, Moore made no secret of his sense of boredom with it all. 'Part of our business is the selling, the advertising,' he told one journalist. 'It's no good Proctor and Gamble producing a new soap and not letting the public know it's in the shops. You have to advertise.

'But I get tired of the tremendous publicity drive one gets with Bond films and I get a little bored talking about myself.'

He also had reservations about the direction in which the series was going. Tony Bennett and Janet Woollacott remarked on the Americanisation of *A View To A Kill* in their book *Bond and Beyond*. Given that half the film takes place in and around San Francisco, there is a certain inevitability of that; nonetheless, the film does seem to be the most American-flavoured of the series to date. This may be because MGM, in a state of internal upheaval at the time, meddled throughout the film's production, unlike United Artists, who had always let Eon get on with it as they wanted.

Moore was also unhappy with the increasing violence in the series. *A View To A Kill* is not a serious Bond film: in many ways, it is the only Bond film produced after 1980 to gaze back yearningly at *Moonraker*'s slapstick excesses. But the violence was upped in the film and there's certainly more blood spilled than is usual in a Bond film. Moore was not happy about this. During filming he had railed against what he disliked to see in films: 'I don't like full frontal nudity. I don't like foul language. And I wouldn't make a film I would be embarrassed about my kids or somebody else's kids seeing.' And Moore did not like some of the things he saw during *A View To A Kill*.

'I was horrified on the last Bond I did,' he said many years later. 'Whole sequences where Christopher Walken was machine-gunning hundreds of people. That wasn't Bond. Those weren't Bond films. It stopped being what they were about. You didn't dwell on the blood and the brains spewing all over the place.'

Perhaps it was the sense of the end of an era that added to Moore's general unhappiness with *A View To A Kill*. Certainly his mood seems to have even temporarily affected his relations with Cubby Broccoli: Broccoli recounts in his autobiography an incident during filming when he reportedly told Moore, 'Quite frankly, Roger, you're being a bigger pain than Sean Connery used to be.' (*When the Snow Melts*, Boxtree, 1998.)

When *A View To A Kill* was released in the early summer of 1985, critics were, at best, lukewarm and this was reflected in a drop at the box office. International grosses were down to $152 million, some $30 million down on *Octopussy*. *A View To A Kill* was hardly a failure but it was still the lowest-grossing Bond since *The Man with the Golden Gun*. The drop in the US box office was even more pronounced.

This sounded alarm bells at Eon and Cubby Broccoli and Michael Wilson knew that a radical rethink was needed for the next film. When it became public knowledge in 1986 that Roger Moore would not be returning to the role, the casting of a new actor gave them the scope and opportunity to make just such a change.

It had been fourteen years since Eon last had to search for a James Bond. There had been times since *Moonraker* when it had looked as though Roger Moore might not play the part again and they had tested other actors. But, each time, Moore had relented and slipped on the shoulder holster again. This time there was no doubt. When *The Living Daylights* premiered in the summer of 1987, there *would* be a new James Bond.

But who? As in 1972, there was no shortage of 'help' or comment from the newspapers. Names such as Mel Gibson, Anthony Andrews, Tom Selleck, Bryan Brown, Nigel Havers and even the England cricketer Ian Botham were tossed around, while one newspaper actually claimed in February 1986 that the American actor John James, one of the stars of *Dynasty*, had been all but signed for the role.

'No, no seven!' complained the late Jean Rook, for years 'the first lady of Fleet Street'. 'I am shaken but not stirred that John James, who plays love-struck Jeff Colby like a calf on Valium, is in line to be the next James Bond,' she fumed in the *Daily Express* on 19 February 1986.

Mr James may be 29, slaughteringly beautiful, tanned, 6ft 3in, with hair like Malibu surf. But he is ALL American, from capped tooth to jogging toe, the definitive Campus Casanova, with a Californian accent like squeezed orange juice. I shudder, and not with ecstasy, to think of him mouthing: 'My name is Barned, James Barned,' through that expensive US bridgework.

'There is no need for Bond to be a British actor,' says a spokesman for the Bond-makers, who are trying to replace the now rather too weather-beaten 57-year-old Roger Moore. Absolute rot. James

Bond, 6ft, 12 stone 7lb, born in Glencoe of a rugged Scot and a glamorous French mother, is the most bristling male chauvinist pig ever to be educated at Fettes – after being chucked out of Eton with a left-over penchant for cold showers.

He is Royal Navy to the hilt, and a crashing snob to hand-made boot, who treats women like gun dogs, and has his gold-banded cigarettes rolled in Grosvenor Square. However they clip Mr James's over-long hair and his accent, he'll never fit the part which is tailored for Anthony Andrews or Nigel Havers with healthier chest measurements.

Mix Mr James into any British house party and the butler would be the first to see through him. Pure canned Coke. Not the real thing.

Journalists though should not have believed what they read in the papers. The real names on Eon's shortlist were Timothy Dalton, Pierce Brosnan, Sam Neill and an actor named Lambert Wilson. Jerry Weintraub, then production head at MGM, tried to interest Broccoli in Mel Gibson and said he could get him for a two-picture deal at a reported fee of $10 million. Broccoli's reply was succinct: 'I had no wish to cast Mel Gibson in the part,' he recorded in his autobiography.

Broccoli had been interested in Dalton since Sean Connery had given up Bond after *You Only Live Twice* but the shooting schedule of *The Living Daylights* clashed with *Brenda Starr*, a film Dalton was already contracted to. Dalton was seemingly out of the picture.

Broccoli liked the unknown Lambert Wilson, who tested well, but Michael Wilson had doubts. Sam Neill also tested well. He was the bookmakers' favourite to become Bond and had the backing of Michael Wilson, Barbara Broccoli (Cubby's daughter and the associate producer) and the director John Glen – but not Cubby Broccoli.

Which left Pierce Brosnan. In his splendid biography, *For My Eyes Only* (B T Batsford, 2001), John Glen recalls how he reminded Cubby Broccoli and Michael Wilson of Brosnan, whom they had first met when he'd accompanied his wife, Cassandra Harris, to Corfu in 1980, where she was playing Lisl for them in *For Your Eyes Only*.

Initially, Broccoli was not convinced Brosnan was right for the kind of James Bond he wanted to see in *The Living Daylights*. Brosnan's screen persona in *Remington Steele* was deceptively lightweight and Broccoli felt that he would probably take Bond along the Roger Moore route rather than return him to the ballsy character both he and Michael Wilson were keen to reintroduce. There was also a lingering problem about Brosnan's youthfulness: despite being 33, he looked much younger.

But MGM were keen because of the popularity of *Remington Steele* in the US, so Broccoli invited Brosnan to Pinewood to make a series of tests. John Glen put Brosnan through his paces in a selection of scenes from *Dr. No* and *From Russia With Love*.

When Brosnan's tests were edited it was obvious that Broccoli's reservations were unfounded. Beneath the patina of lightweight charm, Brosnan's acting style had a deep well of darker emotions, something he displayed in his sinister portrayal as Major Petrovsky in *The Fourth Protocol*, which was being shot in England while Eon's search for the new James Bond continued.

Everyone agreed that Brosnan was perfect. 'Cubby slowly nodded as he watched the test,' says John Glen. And MGM, when they saw the test footage, gave Brosnan their unqualified support.

Eon had their new James Bond.

There was just one problem. *Remington Steele*, which was produced by Mary Tyler Moore Television, had been cancelled by NBC, which screened the show in the US. But Brosnan was still under contract, just, and, when news leaked about his being cast as Bond, NBC abruptly renewed *Remington Steele*. Fierce negotiations broke out between Cubby Broccoli and Mary Tyler Moore Television: Broccoli agreed that Brosnan could make six episodes before starting work on *The Living Daylights*; MTM and NBC wanted him for a full series of 22.

The impasse was not to be breached. Broccoli was adamant that Brosnan could not be James Bond and Remington Steele simultaneously. Alas, Brosnan could not get out of his contract and had to return to *Remington Steele*. He was reportedly gutted, more so when NBC finally cancelled *Remington Steele* for good shortly afterwards.

With the start date on *The Living Daylights* looming, Eon were suddenly without a James Bond again. Eon were committed to delivering the film to MGM for a summer 1987 release and so any delay would be critical. Nevertheless, *The Living Daylights* was postponed for two weeks while Eon tried to find their James Bond.

Although it did not seem so at the time, the delay now worked to Eon's advantage. Having been denied the opportunity to use Timothy

Dalton because of his commitment to *Brenda Starr*, the altered schedule meant that he would now be free, and, on 6 August 1986, Timothy Dalton was confirmed as the new James Bond. 'I finished *Brenda Starr* in America on a Saturday, caught a plane which landed in London on Sunday and started work on the Bond movie on Monday morning,' says Dalton, recalling just how tight the schedule became.

Born in North Wales on 21 March 1946 but brought up in the Derbyshire town of Belper, the classically trained Dalton had enjoyed an excellent stage career since graduating from RADA in 1966. His film career started impressively when he played the young King Philip of France opposite Katherine Hepburn, Peter O'Toole and Anthony Hopkins in the Oscar-winning *The Lion in Winter*, which he followed up with *Cromwell*, *Mary Queen of Scots* and *Wuthering Heights*, in which he stepped into Laurence Olivier's shoes to play a very 1970s Heathcliff.

Robert Fuest, director of *Wuthering Heights*, said of him: 'Tim is no carbon copy of anyone. There was Brando. There was James Dean. Then along came their imitators. But Tim is no imitation of anyone. He is a new original.'

A decade or so later, Sheridan Morley wrote of him in 1982:

> Few actors of thirty-six can look back on a fifteen-year career which has encompassed a film debut at twenty-one in *The Lion In Winter*, a long-standing affair with Vanessa Redgrave, star turns in *Cromwell* and *Wuthering Heights*, a stint in *Charlie's Angels* and a role as the sixth of 91-year-old Mae West's husbands in her farewell movie *Sextette*, to say nothing of three classical years with the Prospect Theatre and another three with the RSC back in the early 1970s.
>
> Like O'Toole who got him the job in *The Lion In Winter* and like Olivier whose *Wuthering Heights* footsteps he followed, Dalton has always lived dangerously on both stage and screen.

Yet, despite his having been described as 'the greatest acting find in the last decade' in the 1970s, and of possessing 'the looks which could well bring back the era of the matinée idol', there was a sense of 'Timothy who?' in the popular press when Dalton was announced as Bond.

Partly, this was because of his love of privacy, which meant that journalists were in the dark as to much of his background.

'I'm a very private person with nothing mysterious to hide, who just likes to do his work and do it well and then get away from it all and go fishing,' he told reporters when he was signed as Bond. 'There is no Pussy Galore, no jet-setting, no champagne or caviar – not even a dry martini, shaken or stirred – in my life!

'But I'm really delighted about it. The joy and excitement James Bond brings to people throughout the world is very, very special. I'm looking forward to the challenge of playing him but I have to say that following in Sean and Roger's footsteps is a daunting task. Especially handling all the publicity.'

Even Sean Connery seemed enthused about Dalton. Asked to comment on the new Bond, Connery said, 'I think they've made a good choice. I haven't worked with Tim but I know him and think he will be good. He's certainly the right age to play Bond.

'I hope he's got a good lawyer and can stamp his personality against the hardware. I hope every success for him.'

With continued uncertainty about just *who* was going to play Bond, Michael Wilson and Richard Maibaum, once again collaborating on the script, had written *The Living Daylights* and particularly Bond's role in a fairly generic way, pulling back from the overt humour of Roger Moore. When Dalton came on board and made clear his desire to return the part to what Ian Fleming had envisaged, Wilson and Maibaum made adjustments to the script, tailoring it to the new star. The result was that *The Living Daylights* screenplay was the best since *On Her Majesty's Secret Service*. Some critics have complained that the story is convoluted though, frankly, one would have to have the attention span of a goldfish to lose the thread.

Using Fleming's best short story, THE LIVING DAYLIGHTS, almost verbatim as their starting point, Wilson and Maibaum have Bond assigned to protect the defecting Russian General Koskov in Bratislava. When Bond spies a pretty sniper preparing to shoot Koskov, he disobeys his specific shoot-to-kill orders and merely shoots the rifle out of her hand instead. When the head of station, Saunders, remonstrates with him, Bond says, 'That girl didn't know one end of a rifle from the other.'

Back in England, Koskov is debriefed by M and reveals that General Pushkin in Moscow has reactivated the old SMERSH directive, '*Smyert Shpionam* – death to spies' (a wonderful throwback to Fleming, this), and a concerted assassination programme of Western agents has begun.

When Koskov is supposedly snatched back by the Russians, M orders Bond to liquidate General Pushkin. Bond, however, is not convinced that Pushkin is behind *Smyert Shpionam* and goes in search of the female sniper in an attempt to get a lead.

The sniper turns out to be the beautiful Kara Milovy, a cellist who is also Koskov's girlfriend. Koskov tricked her into firing blanks at him to make his defection look real. In reality, he was setting her up to be killed by Bond.

Bond catches up with Pushkin in Tangier and it transpires that he has been investigating Koskov, who has been associated with the American arms dealer Brad Whittaker. Koskov has used a great deal of Soviet money to buy arms from Whittaker, arms to supply Russian forces in Afghanistan, but no arms have yet been delivered.

In reality, Koskov and Whittaker have used the money to buy heroin, which they will sell on the streets of the West and turn a huge profit. They will still be left with a fortune when the arms have been delivered. Only Pushkin suspects what they are up to, which is why Koskov has framed him with talk of *Smyert Shpionam* and tricked M into ordering Pushkin's liquidation.

Bond fakes an assassination of Pushkin, after which Koskov abducts Bond, who is taken to Afghanistan with Kara. Koskov delivers Bond and Kara to the Russian authorities and claims he is there on a secret mission. What he's actually there for is to purchase his heroin, which he intends to fly out on a Hercules transporter.

Bond and Kara escape from the Russian airbase where they have been imprisoned and team up with the Western-educated leader of the local mujahedeen, Kamran Shah. With Shah's help, Bond attacks the airbase and he and Kara fly off in the Hercules with Koskov's heroin – but not before Koskov's henchman, Necros, manages to scramble aboard.

A furious fight between Bond and Necros ensues – with Bond and Necros scrapping while clinging to a camouflage net *outside* the back of the airborne Hercules (in one of the series' most thrilling sequences) – before Bond defeats Necros, who falls to his death.

The Hercules and heroin destroyed, Bond confronts and kills Brad Whittaker, while Pushkin arrests Koskov and puts him in 'the diplomatic bag' to be sent back to Moscow.

It's a good story, which is utterly credible, while still allowing for some traditional Bondian touches, and the romantic subplot between Bond and Kara is particularly well handled. It's easily the most believable love affair in the series since Bond fell in love with Tracy in *On Her Majesty's Secret Service*. Bond is virtually a one-woman man in the film, and although this was partly influenced by the prevailing AIDS scare – when monogamy was in and promiscuity briefly unfashionable – it was the demands of the story rather than political correctness that really dictated this change.

Fortunately, in most other respects, *The Living Daylights* sensibly eschews political correctness and it is particularly gratifying to have Bond smoking – absolutely rightly and apparently at Dalton's insistence – throughout the picture, just as he had in Fleming's original books and as Connery had done in the early films.

Other aspects also harked back to the past. Since *The Living Daylights* marked the 25th anniversary of the Eon series, Wilson and Maibaum decided to bring back one or two past favourites to mark the event. Bond is back behind the wheel of an Aston Martin – in this case a souped-up Volante, complete with rockets behind the fog lamps and laser cutters in the hubcaps – and Felix Leiter makes his first appearance since *Live And Let Die* in 1973 (not counting *Never Say Never Again*, which, let's face it, no one ever does).

The Living Daylights seemed like a breath of fresh air in 1987, coming as it did after the appalling *Never Say Never Again* and the generally lacklustre *A View To A Kill*. That is not to say it's a perfect film. The lack of a real villain – Koskov is really nothing more than a likable rogue and Brad Whittaker has too little screen time to make any mark – is a drawback; the use of the Russian invasion of Afghanistan has dated the film horribly (as does the Cold War backdrop to *Octopussy* and the energy-crisis theme of *The Man with the Golden Gun*); and the theme song performed by A-ha is poor (a shame, because John Barry's score – his last for Bond – is one of his best).

But the cast is excellent: Jeroen Krabbe shines as the weaselly Koskov; Maryam d'Abo conveys Kara's innocence beautifully; the always reliable John Rhys-Davies excels as Pushkin; and Art Malik is both sexy and funny as Kamran Shah.

There's even a new Miss Moneypenny. Lois Maxwell retired from the series when Roger Moore left, believing, correctly, that it would look absurd for a new, younger Bond to be flirting with her. Caroline Bliss takes over duties as a younger Moneypenny – who, quite bizarrely, tries to tempt Bond by inviting him to listen to her Barry Manilow collection at one point – but the casting is not terribly successful.

The best casting of all, though, is Timothy Dalton himself. It's difficult to argue with Raymond Benson, who wrote,

> From the first glimpse of him, it is clear Timothy Dalton is a James Bond to be reckoned with. He is marvellously well-cast; for fans of Fleming's novels Dalton is too good to be true. Quite simply, Timothy Dalton's characterisation of James Bond is the most accurate and literal interpretation of the role we've ever seen on screen. Timothy Dalton embodies the man from the novels.

Benson was right. Dalton *is* James Bond, or at least, *Ian Fleming*'s James Bond, something that his many detractors never seem quite able to grasp. It's as though Dalton's critics, programmed for twelve years to accept Roger Moore's amiability, are incapable of recognising just what an outstanding performance he gives in the film. Furthermore, Dalton managed in *The Living Daylights* what both Connery and Moore didn't really accomplish until their third Bond films (*Goldfinger* and *The Spy Who Loved Me* respectively): to define his interpretation right from the outset.

Complaints about his supposed lack of humour (made, naturally enough, by those same critics who'd complained that Moore was *too* humorous) are particularly absurd. Dalton may not be a gag-a-minute performer but his humour is there, in the subtext of his performance: it comes in a look here, a flicker of amusement behind the eyes there. What he does *not* do is send up the character – or the film.

Above all else, this is a James Bond who *thinks*: he is no mere cipher who reacts to events.

To accomplish his remarkable debut as 007, Dalton read and reread the source – Ian Fleming's novels – as he made explicit in every interview he gave:

> Fleming wrote it. Fleming created it. His books gave rise to the movies. Those movies have gone on for 25 years. He must have done something right.

The only way I can work as an actor is to work with the author, to reveal the author's intentions. That doesn't mean to say you can bring all those qualities to all the movies because each movie is different and, anyway, they're not written by Ian Fleming. But certainly they're written of that world. You can't talk about a Bond movie without talking about Ian Fleming.

That's why I went back to the books. The early movies were really quite close in spirit to the books. They weren't really special effects or gadgets movies. They were very popular, imaginative thrillers. They stretched the boundaries of believability but they were still contained within believability.

Fleming made you believe this guy could do these things. And he made you believe in the paradox of Bond. Bond *is* a paradox. He is not a paragon of virtue; he's a man riddled with vices and weaknesses as well as strength. But that is the nature of the man, and the nature of the world he lives in. He's a killer. A murderer. He's a bad lad. But he's also on the side of good. And how does he live with that paradox? That's what's interesting about him.

Bond seemed to me to be so much more human and a real personality – kind of multidimensional – in the books and early movies. One of the problems playing Bond is that he becomes the instrument or vehicle through which a hi-tech adventure story is told. That can be a problem, as it can often mean that the other characters are much better defined. When these movies started, we were in the forefront of innovation. I don't know how old I was when I saw *Dr. No* in 1962. Fifteen or sixteen. But it was splendid. *Dr. No* just came and took cinema by the scruff of the neck and banged it right down into today. It was terrific.

The miracle is that they're still as popular as they ever were. That's because they're hero stories and hero stories have crossed all cultures and all history; people need heroes. But they've always been done bloody well, as well. Mr Broccoli's never attempted to cheaply exploit a previous success. He's always tried to make sure that every single film is done better than the one before. The money is spent. What I believe is that we've got to stay in the forefront, which is tough to do. We've got to have great stories, and Bond has to be fleshed out a bit more.

Aware that taking over Bond was always going to be difficult, Dalton preferred not to talk too much about his predecessors. 'It's a futile exercise,' he said. 'Over 25 years of Bond movies, everyone has their own idea of what a Bond movie is. The fact is that every single movie is different from the others. I mean, how can you compare *From Russia With Love* to *Moonraker*? It's such a different story and such a different style. You can't compare Connery and Moore because they were in such different films.

'Roger's films weren't my idea of Bond movies. They had become a completely different entity. I know Roger and I think he did a fantastic job. He is one of the only people in the world who could be fun in the midst of all that gadgetry.

'It was Mr Broccoli's idea that we move away from that style of movie. The danger, of course, is what if people don't like the style we've gone for? Some people say they prefer Connery's Bonds and others prefer Moore's Bonds – the world is pretty much divided depending on who you grew up with. For me, the personal challenge was to get these movies back into a world that I consider to be James Bond's world.'

Most Ian Fleming fans would agree that Dalton managed exactly that in *The Living Daylights*, and the more perceptive critics concurred. *Newsweek*, while welcoming the fact that the plot was as fast and outlandish as ever, noted that, 'this Bond inhabits a more ambiguous universe than his predecessors – a world where he acts on instincts more than orders. When an officious British agent whom Bond has grown to respect is suddenly killed, 007 actually looks grieved before he turns coldly furious and dashes off to avenge his colleague's death.' *Variety* went further, believing '*Daylights* will be tough to top. Everyone seemed up for this one and it shows.' Intelligent reviews such as that were a vindication of Dalton and Eon's mature approach to the film.

The Living Daylights earned a worldwide gross of $191 million, a considerable improvement over *A View To A Kill*, which, on the face of it, should have cheered Broccoli and Wilson. But the silver cloud had a dark lining: the US market was still soft, something that Eon and MGM couldn't fail to note.

In truth, despite the success of Dalton's debut, Bond was beginning to fall foul of changing social and moral attitudes in Hollywood. The ecology of the entire industry was changing. Formality was out, Bruce

Willis's dirty vest was coming in. The violence quotient in films was being upped considerably. Stars such as Schwarzenegger and Stallone were riding high in mindless action flicks where more was expended on the pyrotechnics than the scripts.

Bond was facing competition from a new breed of action hero, although all of them arguably owed their very existence to Bond: they certainly owed their near universal use of the one-liner to punctuate tension to *Dr. No*.

The director, John Glen, had been aware of the change in Hollywood from the mid-1980s, which was why he'd upped the violence a little, with Eon's blessing, in the Bond series from *A View To A Kill* onwards. Nonetheless, *The Living Daylights* still seemed tame compared with films such as *Lethal Weapon*. And so, as production on the next Bond film, originally called *Licence Revoked*, began, the decision was made to make this, the sixteenth Bond film, the toughest ever.

Capitalising on the audience's acceptance of Timothy Dalton as 'the most dangerous Bond – *ever*', *Licence Revoked* was framed to tackle a theme of uncompromising contemporary relevance, the international drugs trade, and to alter Bond's motivation profoundly: Bond would resign from the British Secret Service to embark on a mission of personal revenge. No longer a blunt instrument of the British government, Bond was transformed into an avenging angel.

Eon's long-held policy of producing 'sadism for the family' was redefined for the new film, as Timothy Dalton told *007 Magazine*:

I'm pleased the movie is more violent. That's the world James Bond must live in and if you don't like it, don't go and see the film. We're not making movies for kids. We're making movies for adults. It's an adult fantasy that kids will enjoy.

I think kids can go and see this and should go and see it. But we're not making the movie for eleven-year-olds. We're making it for the child in all of us. It's a violent world Bond inhabits. Violence is the very nature of a Bond movie.

But whether it's more or less violent is relatively speaking. People getting fed to the sharks, to the piranha fish, people getting set on fire, people being shot with harpoon guns, people being shot with bullets, Bond killing people – they're all classic elements of the genre.

Is this film violent? Yes, it's violent. But you don't see the violence. What the filmmakers do, which is brilliant, is they create the tension of violence, but the violence is all in the mind.

Dalton also defended the film by claiming that *Dr. No* caused a storm when it was first released in 1962 and, in this, he was undoubtedly correct, arguing that,

> *Dr. No* created an outrage. Not only for its violence but for its sex. But there's no sex at all in *Dr. No*, so what were they talking about? What they were actually talking about in '62 – and the sixties didn't really begin until the mid-sixties so '62 was still the fifties – what they were talking about was Ursula Andress coming out of the waves in a bikini. It was the first time we'd seen a bikini. That was an outrage sexually. As for the violence, the film was given an A certificate because Bond gunned down an unarmed, defenceless man. That was considered morally wrong and very violent.

It's impossible to fault Dalton's argument but, on the other hand, there is also no disputing that his second Bond film was conspicuously more violent than any that had gone before. And the humour is mature and dark – and despite what critics say, there *is* plenty of humour in the film, most of it supplied by Desmond Llewelyn's Q, who enjoys more screen time in this Bond film than any other.

It was a bold move to tamper so radically with the formula but it was one that was to make *Licence To Kill* – the title the film was ultimately released under because MGM worried that American audiences wouldn't understand what 'revoked' meant – the most controversial Bond movie of all.

For Philip Lisa and Lee Pfeiffer, authors of *The Incredible World of 007*, *Licence To Kill* was 'simply stated, the best James Bond movie since *The Spy Who Loved Me* and, arguably, since *On Her Majesty's Secret Service*'; but for Alan Barnes and Marcus Hearn, who wrote *Kiss Kiss Bang Bang*, it is, 'not a James Bond picture; devoid of glamour, elegance, élan, it's a *Rambo*, a *Death Wish* – mean-spirited, second-division, conveyor-belt popcorn'.

Frankly, *Licence To Kill* polarises Bond fans, and somewhat confused audiences when it was released in the summer of 1989 (although it scored higher in test screenings in America than any previous Bond movie).

In the film, largely set in a fictional South American country, Bond acts as best man at the wedding of his friend Felix Leiter (David Hedison reprising the role he played in *Live And Let Die*). On their way to the wedding they're interrupted by Felix's partners at the DEA with news that Franz Sanchez, a notorious drug smuggler, has been spotted nearby. Bond accompanies Leiter ('strictly as an observer') as a helicopter takes them to where Sanchez is snatching back his errant girlfriend, Lupe Lamora, from another lover. In the ensuing battle, Sanchez almost gets away in a light aircraft. Bond, Leiter and the DEA men pursue in a helicopter and Bond is winched down onto Sanchez's plane. He attaches a cable and Sanchez is literally reeled in, whereupon Bond and Leiter parachute to Leiter's wedding.

Leiter is betrayed by a corrupt DEA agent named Killifer and Sanchez wreaks revenge on Leiter by having his men burst in on Leiter's honeymoon. Leiter's bride is raped and murdered, while Leiter is taken to a fishery factory owned by Sanchez's associate Milton Krest. There, in a scene lifted directly from Fleming's LIVE AND LET DIE, Leiter is deliberately fed to a shark.

Bond finds Leiter barely alive, having lost half a leg and an arm. Bond goes to Krest's factory and finds Killifer. Killifer falls prey to the shark, thanks to Bond.

M orders Bond to refrain from seeking revenge and to resume duties. Bond refuses and resigns from MI6, whereupon M revokes his licence to kill. Bond goes after Milton Krest and sets him up so that it looks like Krest has been double-crossing Sanchez: something which, ultimately, makes Sanchez take a terrible revenge on Krest. Aided by a CIA agent, Pam Bouvier, and by Q, who flies out to help without M's consent, Bond manages to ingratiate himself into Sanchez's confidence and discovers that Sanchez's scientists have discovered a way of dissolving cocaine into petrol, which makes smuggling it in a fleet of petrol tankers easy. Bond destroys Sanchez's entire operation and kills a petrol-soaked Sanchez by setting him on fire – but not before he's let Sanchez know it has all been because of what he did to Leiter and his wife.

There are those who claim revenge is not a suitable motive for James Bond but these are people who simply do not understand what Ian

Fleming's Bond was all about. When the Robber fed Leiter to the shark in LIVE AND LET DIE, Bond made sure the Robber ended up as the shark's next meal; and in YOU ONLY LIVE TWICE, when Bond learns that Dr Shatterhand and his wife are none other than Ernst Stavro Blofeld and Irma Bunt, his entire motivation becomes one of personal revenge for their murdering Tracy a year before. And have *Licence To Kill*'s critics forgotten the first Bond film, *Dr. No*, in which Bond's reply to Dr No's suggestion that Bond might join SPECTRE is that if he did he'd choose the Revenge Department so he could have revenge on the man (Dr No) who had killed Quarrel and Strangways?

What makes Bond's revenge resonate so well in *Licence To Kill* is the performance of Robert Davi as Franz Sanchez, the object of that revenge. His pet iguana with a diamond-encrusted collar notwithstanding, Sanchez is an all too believable Bond villain. Just as Scaramanga in *The Man with the Golden Gun* is one of the best Bond film villains because he is the 'dark side' of Bond, so too is Sanchez.

Sanchez is a ruthless drugs baron; a murderer who rips out the heart of the man his girlfriend, Lupe, has absconded with to give her a 'Valentine' and who then proceeds to whip her for her 'misdemeanour'. But he is also a man with a strong personal moral code, twisted though it may be, who holds dear the virtue of loyalty: his disappointment is palpable when associates betray him. The contradictions in Sanchez's character are superbly layered in the screenplay, making Sanchez, arguably, the most perversely attractive of Bond villains.

There is a hint of bisexuality in his character, again underplayed beautifully by both actor and script, which has echoes of the literary Scaramanga: Sanchez's embraces of his young hit man, Dario (Benicio Del Toro, making his first mark in the movies), linger just a beat too long not to be significant, and there are even suggestions that Sanchez is attracted to Bond.

The revenge theme is further served by the South American flavour that permeates the whole movie. Mexico was the principal location, with Key West in Florida providing the backdrop to the action in the early part of the film. Interiors were shot at Churubusco Studios in Mexico City – built in the 1940s by Cubby Broccoli's old friend Howard Hughes – rather than Pinewood Studios; it was only the second time that Eon had been forced to abandon Pinewood.

Exactly ten years earlier, in 1978, production on *Moonraker* had been switched to Paris because of the prohibitive tax regime of the then Labour government; now, the overheating British economy, which would crash spectacularly in 1990, the weak dollar and the knock-on effects of the shortsighted abolition of the Eady Levy in the 1985 budget, had all conspired to push up the costs of producing a major film in Britain in 1988–9.

Cubby Broccoli did not want to leave England but, as he himself pointed out, the arithmetic was simply against Pinewood. In the event, the logistical and technical problems encountered in Mexico led to delays and frustrations with the ironic result that *Licence To Kill* ended up costing almost exactly as much as it would have done had Eon stayed at Pinewood.

The pollution and thin air in Mexico City was the source of many problems. Many of the cast and crew found it difficult to work. The conditions took a particular toll on Cubby Broccoli, who became very ill with breathing problems. He had to be rushed back to Los Angeles in a plane fitted with a respirator, leaving production in the hands of Michael Wilson and Barbara Broccoli.

Licence To Kill's problems did not end when principal photography ended. The title change from *Licence Revoked* to *Licence To Kill* meant that MGM's publicity department, which had promoted the original title, now had to alert the public to the new one. Worse, Eon's brilliant promotion campaign concept, which contained some of the best artwork of the entire series, was summarily discarded by MGM. The studio, which was lurching from one crisis to another at the time, substituted a crass campaign, created 'in-house', which was so banal it barely registered even with Bond fans tuned in to the film.

The film also ran into trouble with censors around the world, particularly in Britain. Despite Eon's intention to produce a tougher Bond film, the violence in *Licence To Kill* is justified and never gratuitous. Furthermore, there was little danger of kids copying scenes such as Felix Leiter being fed to a great white shark. There aren't many of those in British suburbs.

That didn't stop the British Board of Film Classification demanding an absurd number of cuts to the film *before* they would grant it a 15 certificate. This higher rating naturally limited the film's potential audience – as well as disappointing those Bond fans too young to see it

– and was demonstrably unfair: the newly introduced British 12 certificate would have been a much fairer rating.

Worst of all, MGM premiered the film at the height of the summer bloodbath at the box office in America. In the summer of 1989, *Licence To Kill* faced competition from *Batman* (according to Broccoli the most hyped film in history), *Lethal Weapon II* (given the same certificate as *Licence To Kill* by the British Board of Film Classification despite being far more violent and containing a plethora of four-letter words), and *Indiana Jones and the Last Crusade*. With its lacklustre promotional campaign, *Licence To Kill* could barely register against competition like that.

The result was that *Licence To Kill*, one of the more interesting and certainly most courageous Bond films, slumped at the US box office. It scraped a disappointing $35 million, which barely covered its costs and was the lowest US gross since *The Man with the Golden Gun*. The film fared slightly better internationally, eventually earning a worldwide gross of $156 million, which was just ahead – by about $4 million – of *A View To A Kill* four years earlier.

So, again, *Licence To Kill* could hardly be regarded as a flop. But there was a perception that the series had run its course, particularly in the US. Eon had made no secret that *Licence To Kill* had been toughened up *specifically* to appeal to the US market. That had backfired.

While many true Bond fans had embraced the return to the Bond of Fleming's novels and the early films, too many in the general audience, seemingly, had not. The net result was that the Bonds had, indeed, lost their value.

Would there ever be a market for James Bond again?

0013: Will James Bond Return?

> 'Pierce was always the favourite. We wanted to give him the
> part in 1986 but he wasn't available. We didn't just give him
> the role now on the flip of a coin.'
>
> Michael Wilson, 1994

Although no one knew it when it was released in the summer of 1989, *Licence To Kill* marked the end of several eras in the Bond franchise. It brought to an end, prematurely in many fans' eyes, Timothy Dalton's brief but interesting tenure as Bond; and was the last film on which Cubby Broccoli had direct involvement.

Licence To Kill was also the last of John Glen's five Bond pictures as director and the last film for which Maurice Binder would supply the credits. The film was also the last to bear Richard Maibaum's name as a screenwriter. Binder and Maibaum both died in 1991.

Maibaum had scripted or co-scripted every Eon Bond film bar *You Only Live Twice*, *Live And Let Die* and *Moonraker*; his name appeared as co-scriptwriter on *Licence To Kill* with Michael Wilson but, in reality, a strike by the Writers' Guild had prevented his working on the script after he had written the treatment with Wilson. Thus, Maibaum had been writing about James Bond for 28 years, more than twice the length of time Ian Fleming wrote the Bond novels, and Maibaum was a major influence in the development of James Bond since 1962. He was also a man of strong opinions, who praised Sean Connery's performance but made no secret of his disappointment with Roger Moore.

'Sean Connery was absolutely perfect,' he said. 'Apart from being a great specimen and good-looking, he had a basic irony about him. Also he was a much better actor than most people thought. You believed all the physical stuff that Sean did.

'As far as I'm concerned, Roger has a dimension of disbelief. He does what I consider to be unforgivable. He spoofs himself and he spoofs the part. When you start doing that, the audience stops laughing.

'That's why I was very pleased to see the move towards more gritty reality with Timothy Dalton. If the actor does not believe what's happening, the audience will not believe it either, and Timothy certainly has the ability to take an audience with him.'

Robert Brown and Caroline Bliss also left the series after *Licence To Kill*. Brown had played M four times – *Octopussy*, *A View To A Kill*, *The Living Daylights* and *Licence To Kill* – but had never managed to eclipse Bernard Lee's memorable interpretation. Caroline Bliss had had an even harder task in trying to eradicate memories of Lois Maxwell's 23-year reign as Miss Moneypenny and, sadly, she was never in danger of doing so, at least on the evidence of her two appearances in *The Living Daylights* and *Licence To Kill*.

Licence To Kill broke the pattern of production that had been established since *Dr. No* in 1962. The longest gap between Bond films had been the 31 months that separated the release of *The Man with the Golden Gun* and that of *The Spy Who Loved Me* (there had been a gap of thirty months between *You Only Live Twice* and *On Her Majesty's Secret Service*). After *Licence To Kill* there would not be another James Bond film for more than six years.

The years 1990–1994 were bleak, barren years for the Bond franchise. With only occasional TV screenings of previous Bond movies, the annual John Gardner novel and an animated children's TV series, *James Bond Junior*, to satisfy fans, the character really did seem to have been exhausted.

Other film series stepped into the vacuum left by the Bond films pretty quickly. The *Die Hard* films were perceived by several critics to be the Bond films of the 1990s. Bruce Willis's dirty white vest may have been far removed from the sartorial splendour of 007's dinner jacket, but Willis's quips and his innovative means of getting out of danger were Bondian in the extreme. And Alan Rickman in the original *Die Hard* was surely the best Bond villain never to appear in a Bond movie.

To the uninformed, the perceived failure of *Licence To Kill* was the cause of the apparent end of the James Bond series, but this wasn't correct. For one thing, *Licence To Kill* was not a commercial failure. It had covered its production costs and made a healthy profit worldwide, which, as Michael Wilson pointed out, was the definition of a successful movie. Furthermore, plans were being made by both MGM and Eon for the next Bond film, the seventeenth in the series, in late 1989 and early 1990 – although there was a recognition that changes would have to be made following the disappointing audience response to *Licence To Kill* in the US. An MGM spokesman told *Variety*, 'There's a desire to get some new people involved and get a fresh slant on the material. It's obvious that the series is a little tired.'

Actually, nothing of the sort was obvious, since *Licence To Kill* had been bold, innovative and a break from the traditional formula, but no film company has ever let the facts get in the way of a good press release. The perception – an unfair one – was, as *Variety* put it, of a 'wilting Broccoli empire', and directors such as Ted Kotcheff and John Landis were suggested as helming the next Bond film.

As 1990 progressed, various other unsubstantiated rumours began to emerge. One was that Cubby Broccoli had hired Alfonso Ruggiero Jr, a writer on *Miami Vice*, to rewrite an original Bond script penned by Michael Wilson, another that Gloria Katz and Willard Huyck (responsible for, heaven help us, *Howard the Duck*) had been asked to write a script. *The Property of a Lady* was mentioned as a possible title, even though Fleming's THE PROPERTY OF A LADY had been used as a source for the *Octopussy* screenplay; but the most intriguing rumour of all was that Imagineering, Walt Disney's effects studio, which created mechanical and electrical devices for Disney theme parks, had been asked by Eon to build the most sophisticated robot ever seen in the movies.

Thus, both Eon and MGM *were* planning a new James Bond film in 1990. MGM, which, as we saw in the last chapter, had been hit by crisis after crisis throughout the late 1980s, really had no other choice: its only other franchise was *Rocky*. And that really *was* looking tired.

Events, however, overtook plans for the new Bond. MGM was sold to the Italian businessman Giancarlo Paretti, whose huge holdings in the US entertainment business were dominated by the giant US subsidiary Pathé Communications. But, as the deal was going through, Cubby Broccoli's lawyers pointed out that the back catalogue of sixteen Bond pictures were being sold off at bargain-basement prices in a number of foreign TV and video licensing deals as an apparent deal-sweetener.

Eon's parent company, Danjaq, which actually held the film rights, filed suit against MGM/UA Communications and Pathé Communications to block these international TV licensing agreements which, it was alleged, would see the Bond films sold in France, Spain, Italy, South Korea and Japan at well below market rates for the rest of the century. Danjaq had not been consulted and, as far as Broccoli and Wilson were concerned, it was not just a matter of breach of contract: it was a fundamental fight for the survival of James Bond. 'If these deals take effect, we're going to be foreclosed for the remainder of this century from exploiting the Bond films,' explained Danjaq's attorney, 'which are the next frontier for exploiting the value of these works.'

Despite what they believed was the absolute rightness of their case, Broccoli and Wilson were in no doubt about the difficulties they faced in taking on MGM/Pathé, particularly since Broccoli's health was beginning to deteriorate. Norman Tyre, Broccoli's friend and personal legal adviser, laid out the realities to him: Broccoli, always the gambler, was ready to play the odds.

'He was confronted with a choice,' Tyre later recalled. 'Accepting a subordinated position for future Bonds, or facing a nasty drawn-out lawsuit.

'He was informed crystally clear that the chances in the lawsuit were less than 50 per cent, and that the cost of litigation would be between three and four million dollars. I asked him for his decision. Without a moment's hesitation he announced loudly and clearly "Let's go for it!" So typical of Cubby.'

The lawsuit filed, the cinematic James Bond then went into a hiatus from the end of 1990 until 1993, when the suit, after delaying tactics by lawyers, was due to be heard.

Curiously, with no prospect of James Bond's returning in the near future – if at all – screen attention switched back to his creator, Ian Fleming, with two TV movies devoted to his life in 1990. Charles

Dance, who had appeared briefly in *For Your Eyes Only* and had been a contender to take over from Roger Moore, played Fleming in Anglia Television's £2 million *Goldeneye*. Handsomely mounted but scrappily scripted by Reg Gadney, *Goldeneye* was baffling to anyone unfamiliar with Fleming's story. Nonetheless, part of it was filmed on location in Jamaica using Fleming's real Goldeneye house, which made it a muted treat for any true Fleming fan.

Charles Dance, who studied Fleming in depth before beginning work on the film, captured the author's mannerisms well, but the script ultimately defeated him. Phyllis Logan played Ann, Patrick Ryecart came off best as Ivar Bryce, while the usually reliable Julian Fellowes (who wrote *Gosford Park*) caricatured Noël Coward disgracefully. Roger Moore's daughter, Deborah Barrymore, had a small part in the film, which gave *Goldeneye* some novelty value.

Almost simultaneously, the American Turner Broadcasting System produced *The Secret Life of Ian Fleming*, which was a highly speculative account of Fleming's early life and career. There was even more novelty value with this TV movie, since Jason Connery, Sean's son, played Fleming. Easily the more enjoyable of the two films, *The Secret Life of Ian Fleming* was written by Robert Avrech, directed by Ferdinand Fairfax and boasted an impressive supporting cast, including Kristin Scott Thomas, Joss Ackland and David Warner.

John Gardner's books continued to be published, one a year, into the 1990s, providing Bond fans, starved of new screen adventures for Commander Bond, with something new. Had the books been better they might have made the interminable wait for a new Bond film bearable, but Gardner's books continued to disappoint many Bond fans. It wasn't that they were badly written, just that the James Bond he was writing about had so little in common with Ian Fleming's James Bond.

Gardner himself was aware of this and in 1989 he wrote, somewhat caustically,

I apologise for not being Ian Fleming, just as I apologise for the reviewer who believes there are no moving parts in a computer, the one who imagines that all cigarettes are white, and the one who thinks the books are sexually tame because his memories of the Fleming novels are that his parents regarded them as dirty books, so he read them in secret. Grow up all of you.

There is a hint, there, of an author who knows he's disappointing some of his readers and so, in fairness, we should point out that Gardner's Bond books *did* occasionally manage to rise above the banal rut he seemed to have got himself into. DEATH IS FOREVER, published in 1992, is one of his most exciting, as well as boasting the best Gardner title apart from NOBODY LIVES FOREVER (1986); but 1991's THE MAN FROM BARBAROSSA is a very dull book indeed. NEVER SEND FLOWERS, published in the spring of 1993, was another disappointment but it causes a ghoulish frisson today because its plot climaxed with the attempted assassination of Princess Diana at EuroDisney in Paris: the princess was killed in Paris just four years later.

Ironically, for a man who professed not to like adapting screenplays, Gardner's books of the films *Licence To Kill* and *GoldenEye* remain among his best Bond novels.

Nineteen ninety-two marked the fortieth anniversary of Ian Fleming's creating James Bond and the thirtieth anniversary of *Dr. No*, but the events passed off relatively unremarked. A CD compilation of James Bond themes to mark the thirtieth anniversary of the Eon series was popular, though, and the use of Louis Armstrong's 'We Have All the Time in the World' from *On Her Majesty's Secret Service* to advertise Guinness some time later indicated that Bond still had cultural relevance.

Despite the legal dispute between Danjaq and MGM, there were signs that the studio, still struggling, was keen to try to reinstate the Bond series. In 1992, *Variety* reported that the studio was actively looking for a new James Bond and had drawn up a list of actors headed by Pierce Brosnan. This story was reported in newspapers around the world, causing Cubby Broccoli to insist that Timothy Dalton should play James Bond in the next film, whenever that might be.

However disappointing the box-office receipts of *Licence To Kill* had been, the James Bond franchise remained the most successful in cinema history and there seems to have been a general realisation at MGM throughout 1992 that they needed Bond and Broccoli back on side. As 1993 dawned, Danjaq's case was about to be heard. It was then that Broccoli learned that MGM wanted to settle.

'We had to fight our way through,' said Michael Wilson some time later. 'It took three years until Paretti was pushed out, clearing the decks for us to go forward again.

'There seemed to be a desire at MGM to get the films out again. I think that when it was all resolved, that was the first order of business.'

As far as Cubby Broccoli was concerned, his gamble had paid off. The settlement was not just satisfactory in monetary terms: Danjaq secured a new and more advantageous arrangement in the production of the Bond pictures.

But who would play James Bond? In August 1993, Timothy Dalton was seemingly happy to resume duties as 007. He'd been contracted for three Bond films and he'd made only two. He told the *Daily Mail*, 'The court case was generally solved earlier this year and now we have a writer – Michael France who wrote Sylvester Stallone's *Cliffhanger* – who is going to come up with a story. When we've all agreed on that, he'll write a script and then we'll look for a director.'

Dalton said that the earliest he expected to begin filming the new Bond film would be in January or February 1994.

Certainly, Michael France, who began work on the script of *GoldenEye* in the late spring of 1993, wrote the script fully expecting Dalton to play Bond. 'We didn't know it would be Pierce when we started,' he said. 'It was sort of generally assumed that it would be Tim. I tried to write it with him in mind. A lot of physical action, some emotional intensity and not a lot of humour.'

But, on 12 April 1994, Timothy Dalton announced his retirement from the role. He explained that his three-picture contract with Eon had expired in 1990 after the preproduction on his third Bond film was halted because of the litigation between Danjaq and MGM.

'Even though the Broccolis have always made it clear to me that they wanted me to resume my role in the next James Bond feature, I have now made this difficult decision,' Dalton said. 'It has now been six years since the last James Bond film and eight years of worldwide identification with the 007 image. As an actor, I believe it is now time to leave that wonderful image behind and accept the challenge of new ones.

'The Broccolis have been good to me as producers. They have been more special as friends.'

Eon's press release reciprocated Dalton's best wishes:

We have been advised by Timothy Dalton that after starring successfully in two James Bond films he has decided that he does not wish to return as the star of the next film of the series.

Over the past eight years we have enjoyed a very happy personal and professional relationship with Timothy. In his portrayal of the James Bond character he made the role his own by bringing Bond back to the hard-edged style of the early Ian Fleming novels to delight audiences around the world.

We regret Timothy's decision. We have never thought of anyone but Timothy as the star of the seventeenth James Bond film. We understand his reasons and will honour his decision. We look forward to announcing our plans for the seventeenth Bond film in the near future.

Naturally, the press speculated on who would succeed Dalton. Pierce Brosnan was the obvious frontrunner – although names like Kenneth Branagh and Hugh Grant were also mentioned – but would he want the part now? Eight years is a long time in anyone's life and a lot had happened to Brosnan in the intervening years, not least his nursing his wife Cassandra through her fatal ovarian cancer, to which she succumbed in 1991.

Furthermore, there was much idle speculation in the press that there was no place for James Bond in the mid-1990s. If a week is a long time in politics, eight years is an aeon in international politics. Since the last Bond film, the Soviet Union had collapsed and a ruthless form of capitalism had filled the vacuum left by the corrupt communism of before. There had been the Gulf War. There was upheaval in the Balkans. The strong Thatcher–Reagan axis, of which the 1980s Bonds had been so much a product, had gone. Britain now had a spineless government, lurching from crisis to crisis and unable to halt the inexorable encroachment of Brussels in national affairs – a government soon to be replaced, perhaps even more damagingly, by one obsessed with spin and presentation to the detriment of everything else.

The world was a very different place, a more confusing place. Spy writers on both sides of the Atlantic were struggling to produce books that remained relevant in the wake of the Soviet Union's demise. 'What place was there for a suave British spy in the 1990s?' asked many columnists. Britain had become an international irrelevance, so why should American audiences care about James Bond any more? The consensus was that it was pointless reviving James Bond and that *GoldenEye* would not do well.

Pierce Brosnan was well aware that, if he did sign on the dotted line as Bond, he might be jumping aboard a sinking ship. As he said at the time he was confirmed as Bond, 'There's a lot at stake.'

Born on 16 May 1953 in County Meath, Ireland, Brosnan moved with his family to London when he was eleven. 'I was one of the lads,' he says. 'I was *sarf London*, y'know. But somehow I felt different. All my mates were going off to be painters or plumbers but I kind of invented myself to be a commercial artist. And then I found acting and I found a certain refuge, a sense of belonging.' He studied acting at the Drama Centre for three years between 1973 and 1976 under the tutelage of the school's co-founder and director, Christopher Fettes.

'You were encouraged to investigate yourself there,' Brosnan says. 'To educate yourself. It was not for the faint-hearted, but if you survived Drama Centre you could survive any ordeals in your career.

'My training gave me my beginning and it gave me the career that I have now, so I'm forever grateful. That time at the Drama Centre was my university, and I found it absolutely intoxicating listening to Chris talk about theatre, about the life of an actor, the guts it takes to be an actor, the responsibility to the text and to what the author puts down.'

In May 1977 Tennessee Williams selected Brosnan to create the role of McCabe in the British premiere of *Red Devil Battery Sign*, which opened at the Round House in Camden Town and transferred to the Phoenix Theatre in the West End. He also starred in other prestigious London stage productions such as *Wait Until Dark* and Franco Zeffirelli's *Filumena*.

His first screen appearance was in an episode of *The Professionals* and he followed this up with an episode of *The Hammer House of Horror*. He made his feature film debut in *The Long Good Friday*, that seminal British gangster flick starring Bob Hoskins and Helen Mirren, in 1980 and also appeared the same year in *The Mirror Crack'd*, an all-star Agatha Christie romp directed by Guy Hamilton.

Brosnan accompanied his wife, Cassandra Harris, to location shooting on Corfu for *For Your Eyes Only*, his introduction to Bondage, the same year and admits that the night he met Cubby Broccoli for the first time, 'I turned to Cassie in this old rent-a-wreck car and joked the whole way home, saying, "My name's Bond, James Bond." I said, "This is it, darling, there's no going back now."'

Next, Brosnan made the thirteen-part *Nancy Astor* for the BBC, which earned him a Golden Globe nomination, and then the acclaimed American mini-series, *The Manions of America*.

The Manions of America was a useful calling card in Los Angeles and Brosnan and Cassandra Harris moved out to LA to try to make more progress in his career. 'My agent in London had got me a list of introductions,' he says, 'and we stayed with another agent in Los Angeles while I did the rounds.'

The result was *Remington Steele*, which catapulted him to international stardom: it was one of the most widely viewed syndicated series of all time and Brosnan was featured on the covers of *Newsweek*, *US*, *People* and *TV Guide* long before he was considered as James Bond in 1986. Brosnan described the character of Steele, the playboy detective who took all the credit for the crimes solved by his partner, played by Stephanie Zimbalist Jr, as 'a cross between John Cleese, Cary Grant and James Bond'.

Subsequent TV mini-series and films followed, including *Around the World in Eighty Days*, *Lawnmower Man*, *Mr. Johnson* and *The Fourth Protocol*. In each performance, he quietly added to his growing reputation as a performer of great depth beneath the impossibly handsome face he'd been born with. One critic even called him 'a Cary Grant for our times', and the comparison is by no means ridiculous since, like Grant, Brosnan possesses a formidable acting talent, not to mention superb comic timing, beneath the patina of the good-looking Hollywood leading man.

He was still not, however, a leading player in Hollywood in 1994. High-profile international television popularity does not always translate into movie stardom and, although Brosnan had appeared in a top Hollywood film, *Mrs. Doubtfire*, he was the second male lead in that.

Thus, playing James Bond in *GoldenEye* was risky. If it succeeded, he knew that he would be made for life. But if it flopped – as many cynics predicted it would – and if he were the last James Bond, the man who ended the series, he could damage his career irreparably. In 1994 there were no guarantees of success.

Brosnan, sporting a beard for another role, was revealed to the world's press as the new James Bond at the beginning of June 1994 in the Drawing Room at London's Regent Hotel. 'To be honest, there was never anybody else in the frame,' *GoldenEye*'s director Martin

Campbell said. 'I saw some people just in case, but I think Pierce is actually much better now than he would have been in '86. I saw the '86 screen tests and he looked unbelievably young.'

'Pierce was always the favourite,' concurred Michael Wilson. 'We wanted to give him the part in 1986 but he wasn't available. We didn't just give him the role now on the flip of a coin.'

'He's perfect,' Barbara Broccoli said. 'He has all the qualities that Bond needs. He is charming. He has bags of charisma and he's sexy. I think I know what's sexy. I've known Pierce for a very long time and know he's a great actor.'

Brosnan made no secret of his delight in finally getting to play the part that had eluded him eight years previously. 'I got the role last Wednesday,' he told reporters, 'and it's been a heady time to say the least. I'd been cautiously optimistic for the last couple of weeks. I'm a little older and a little wiser, and I think it's an appropriate time in my life to be doing this role. It's something that has been part of my life.

'I know it sounds very premature to talk about if I'm going to be different. But there are certain parameters that have to be adhered to. This is a Bond for the nineties. We are really going to try and push the envelope on this and shake it up. He has to go back to being a more kind of flinty character. More humour has got to come in. And also I think it's time to really try and peel back certain layers of his character and see what lies beneath this man. See what demons might be there in his character. I think what is appealing to an audience is to see a character who's very strong and see a certain vulnerability within that character. I don't think it demeans the character. I think it only enhances it.

'But with a piece like this you're dealing with fantasy so I think the political correctness has to be eased up a little. We're going to have a bit more fun with this and not take it so much on the nose.'

Asked about his reaction when the chance to play Bond had been snatched away from him at the eleventh hour in 1986, Brosnan revealed the real depth of his anger. 'I was shocked,' he said. 'I was shocked that the call happened on that particular evening. I was devastated. My late wife and I had put our children back in school in London. We had done five years in Hollywood, thank you very much. It was time to become an international film star now.

'That it didn't happen was shocking. Welcome to the world of business and cold-deal Hollywood. Thank you very much but it ain't going to happen. I got angry when the penny really dropped. I think it was about a couple of months later and I saw Tim Dalton and I wished him well. I thought he was courageous in the choice he took and the road he walked.

'I bore it philosophically for a while. Then about six months later it got to me. I was driving down Pacific Highway and I had to pull over to the kerb and get out of the car and bellow at the ocean. The sheer anger at small people who manipulated my life and career came into full focus. What could have been, should have been, might have been. Then you get over that, you better get over that otherwise it will beat you up, knock you down. It serves no purpose at all so you let it go. You get on with your career.'

While Brosnan was keen on peeling back the layers of Bond in *GoldenEye*, both he and the director Martin Campbell knew they couldn't alter the basic formula too much.

'When you're given the job your first instinct is to say, "Oh, I'll rewrite this whole thing and do it differently",' said Campbell. 'And then you think, "Hold on, this series has been going on for 33 years and it's been a huge success. People will expect certain things." So I went back and watched all the films again, and I realised that those elements, corny lines included, are absolutely terrific. I certainly wouldn't want to tamper with a lot of that.

'So James Bond of the nineties will have a lot of the attributes of the old James Bond. The sense of humour's there; the licence to kill, there's the lethal side to him. What is interesting is words like loyalty, Queen and Country and so forth in the nineties. We're much more cynical about those things now. I think that makes for an interesting side of Bond.

'You could argue in fact that, perhaps, it's not fashionable. But all the attributes in the past that have worked for Bond will remain. And I think Pierce will bring something new to it.'

It was clear from the outset that the cast and crew of *GoldenEye* faced a formidable challenge in resurrecting the cinematic James Bond.

0014: A Sexist, Misogynist Dinosaur

> 'It's a new world. With new enemies. And new threats. But
> you can still depend on one man . . .'
>
> *GoldenEye* trailer, 1995

The cynics were wrong.

GoldenEye did not bomb. On the contrary, with a worldwide gross of
$350 million, it easily broke *Moonraker*'s record gross of $203 million
by a considerable margin. The American market for the film was
particularly strong: within six months of its release, *GoldenEye* had
earned more than $106 million.

Moreover, reviews for *GoldenEye* were, collectively, the best for a
Bond film since *Goldfinger* thirty years earlier. The task facing Eon
with *GoldenEye* was formidable but simple: they had one shot to restart
the Bond series and to introduce Pierce Brosnan as the new 007.

They succeeded beyond anyone's wildest expectation: not only did
GoldenEye completely reinvigorate the franchise, returning Bondmania
to levels it had not enjoyed since the mid-1960s, but Pierce Brosnan, in
his very first shot at the role, established himself as, *at least*, the best
Bond since Connery. And some critics, not to mention many in the
audience, were already wondering if he might not just turn out to be the
very best Bond of all.

How was this possible? How had a film that many in the industry had written off even before principal shooting began on 16 January 1995 turned out to be the most successful of the series so far? How did James Bond, a character perceived to be outdated by countless sneering columnists in 1994, become re-established as *the* leading cinematic icon in 1995?

The answer was straightforward. Far from shying away from the changes in the world since *Licence To Kill*, the producers, Michael Wilson and Barbara Broccoli, the director, Martin Campbell, and the writers, Michael France and Jeffrey Caine, *embraced* them and turned them into an advantage.

The ending of the Cold War and the collapse of communism in the former Soviet Union had not made the world a safer place. The world was a much more dangerous place. Fragmentation of the Soviet Union had seen the former Soviet Bloc replaced by volatile states, some bristling with weapons of mass destruction.

Shifting social mores had also made the world a confusing place, particularly for men. Political correctness was perceived by every sensible person to have gone too far, but it had left both sexes bewildered.

What the producers of *GoldenEye* did was to make Bond a fixed point in the uncertain New World Order. Bond's world, like our own, had changed. Perhaps the most obvious manifestation of that change is that parts of *GoldenEye* were filmed on the streets of St Petersburg. The idea of shooting a Bond film in Russia would have been unthinkable just a decade earlier.

Rather than try to change Bond to adapt to this new order, *GoldenEye* emphasises everything Bond was in his heyday against the backdrop of the new world. We may all be having to adapt to change but Bond, refreshingly, is the man he always was. As the trailers for *GoldenEye* said, 'It's a new world. With new enemies. And new threats. But you can still depend on one man . . .'

'The Cold War had ended, the Berlin Wall had come down,' says Michael Wilson. 'Lots of things had changed and we had to confront some of those changes. We were always contemporary, and we just made another contemporary film in light of the change of circumstances. I think of James Bond as being a pretty consistent character but like anyone who lives in this world, he's not unaffected by it. He's mostly the same character as always, with pretty much the same ideas. The world has changed around him, so it's *how* this character interacts with the present world that is important.'

The intelligence with which Eon repositioned Bond into the present world in *GoldenEye* certainly paid off with the critics. 'No one could say that the plot wasn't forged out of conventional Bond material,' believed the *Guardian* in a typical review. 'Nor that the fantasy hasn't a tinge of realism to give an edge to its absurdity. That's the strength of the movie. It gives its audience what they've always wanted, while obliquely suggesting that Ian Fleming's hero is a bit of a cad by modern standards.'

The biggest personal change in Bond's world was that M was now a woman, played by, arguably, the greatest actress in the world today, Judi Dench. In what is, perhaps, the most important scene in the film, if not the entire series, an exchange between Bond and the new M, the writers define the new Bondian rules perfectly:

> M: You don't like me, Bond. You don't like my methods. You think I'm an accountant. A bean-counter more interested in my numbers than your instincts.
> BOND: The thought had occurred to me.
> M: Good. Because I think you're a sexist, misogynist dinosaur. A relic of the Cold War, whose boyish charm is wasted on me.
> BOND: Point taken.
> M: Not quite, 007. If you think for one moment I don't have the balls to send a man out to die, your instincts are dead wrong. I've no compunction about sending you to your death. But I won't do it on a whim, not even with your cavalier attitude to life.

What this important exchange does is to reintroduce one of the basic tenets of Fleming's world: Bond is once again a blunt instrument wielded by the new M. And this intelligent repositioning of the series, reintroducing essential Flemingian elements into the updated *milieu*, resonates throughout *GoldenEye*. Bond even retains a classic British car for personal use – an Aston Martin DB5 (a lovely reminder of *Goldfinger*) rather than the Bentley from the novels – despite Q issuing him with a BMW Z3 Roadster for 'office' work.

Bond's fundamental beliefs are also examined. In one scene, a reflective Bond is seen brooding on a magnificently photographed beach. Alec Trevelyan, the former 006 and Bond's erstwhile closest colleague, whom Bond believed was killed in 1986 by Soviet General Ouromov, is very much alive and is now Bond's enemy. Trevelyan, the son of Lienz Cossack parents whom the British betrayed after World War Two, is now the head of the Russian Janus crime syndicate and is working in league with Ouromov. Together, they have control of the GoldenEye, a secret Russian satellite capable of creating a radiation surge on earth over a wide area when detonated. Bond knows he must confront Trevelyan at his base in Cuba and kill him.

Moments with Bond reflecting on the nature of his work as a killer exist in Fleming's books but they're extremely rare in the film series and the one in *GoldenEye* stands out. Bond's reflections are interrupted by Natalya Simonova, the beautiful Russian computer programmer with whom he's teamed up. Their exchange is one of the best in the entire Bond series:

NATALYA: He was a friend, Trevelyan. And now he's your
    cnemy and you will kill him. It is that simple.
BOND: In a word, yes.
NATALYA: Unless he kills you first?
BOND: Natalya . . .
NATALYA: You think I'm impressed? All of you, with your
    guns, your killing, your death. For what? So you can be a hero?
    All the heroes I know are dead.
BOND: Listen to me . . .
NATALYA: How can you act like this? How can you be so cold?
BOND: It's what keeps me alive.
NATALYA: No. It's what keeps you alone.

Ian Fleming would not have been displeased.

There's another fabulous exchange later, when Bond has infiltrated Trevelyan's lair and learned that Trevelyan intends to break into the Bank of England electronically to transfer its funds into his own account. This will be followed moments later by his setting off the GoldenEye over London, which will not only hide his crime but create a worldwide financial meltdown. It will also avenge his parents by destroying every electronic record held on every computer in Greater London, thereby returning Britain to the Stone Age. Bond taunts him, saying that, despite the grandiose nature of his scheme, Trevelyan really amounts to nothing more than a bank robber, a common thief:

> BOND: All so mad little Alec can settle a score with the world fifty years on.
> TREVELYAN: Oh, please, James, spare me the Freud. I might as well ask you if all the vodka martinis ever silence the screams of all the men you've killed. Or if you find forgiveness in the arms of all those willing women for all the dead ones you failed to protect.

Moments like this anchor *GoldenEye* in a kind of heightened reality from which its more fantastic elements do not lurch into absurdity. And *GoldenEye does* boast some fantastical elements. Bond's gadgets – the laser beam in the watch, the BMW with Stinger missiles hidden behind the headlights – are all modern twists on past Bondian glories, as is the character of Xenia Onatopp, played with relish by Famke Janssen. Xenia, an ex-Soviet fighter pilot now working for the Janus Syndicate, who kills men by squeezing them between her thighs, is a gleeful throwback to Fiona in *Thunderball* and Helga in *You Only Live Twice*, and is all the better for it (she is also everything *Never Say Never Again*'s disastrous Fatima Blush is *not*).

Casting in *GoldenEye* is nigh-on perfect. As well as Brosnan, Dench and Janssen, the film boasts excellent performances from Sean Bean as Trevelyan, Izabella Scorupco as Natalya, Alan Cumming as nerdish Boris Grishenko, and Robbie Coltrane as Valentin Zukovsky, a Russian villain who is, according to Coltrane, 'more Arthur Daly than the Kray Brothers'. Minnie Driver even makes a cameo as Irina, Zukovsky's girlfriend.

There are also changes at MI6: in addition to Judi Dench's M, Samantha Bond debuts as a splendid Moneypenny and Michael Kitchen plays Bill Tanner, the chief of staff who was Bond's closest friend at MI6 in Fleming's books. To the delight of all Bond fans, one familiar face made a comeback: Desmond Llewelyn as Q.

The action, too, really delivers the goods. The pre-credit sequence alone features two of the best stunts in the series: it begins with Bond bungee-jumping down the face of a dam and concludes with his steering a motorcycle over a sheer cliff from where he skydives after a falling pilotless plane, scrambles into the cockpit and pulls it out of its dive. A tank chase through the streets of St Petersburg is both exciting *and* funny. And Bond's final scrap with Trevelyan on the giant Cuban satellite dish hundreds of feet in the air (in reality the Arecibo observatory in Puerto Rico) makes for a thrilling climax.

Like its predecessor, *GoldenEye* was not filmed at Pinewood Studios, which was too busy to accommodate the production. Instead, Eon built a new studio facility at Leavesdon, an airfield outside London, which included an old Rolls-Royce factory, which Peter Lamont and his team converted into gigantic sound stages. St Petersburg was re-created on the airfield at the site for those destructive parts of the tank chase that obviously could not be shot in the historic areas of the real St Petersburg.

Although Michael Wilson and Barbara Broccoli produced the film, the credits still read, 'Albert R Broccoli presents Pierce Brosnan as Ian Fleming's James Bond 007 in *GoldenEye*.' Despite failing health, Broccoli had taken an active part in the early stages of production but his involvement had been curtailed in June 1994, just days after Pierce Brosnan had been signed as Bond, when a chest X-ray taken as the prelude to routine eye surgery revealed he had an aneurism on the aorta. The aneurism was ready to rupture, perhaps within three months.

Surgery to remove the aneurism and do the necessary triple bypass was possible but fraught with risk. He might die during the operation or, because of the vital nerve centres around the aorta, he might be left paralysed even if the operation were otherwise successful. Do nothing and the ruptured aneurism would kill him.

Cubby Broccoli, the inveterate gambler, had never gambled on odds so high. But, typically, he went for the operation, which took eight hours. He suffered a minor stroke but recovered, although he lost the power of speech. Broccoli, still not a man to be defeated even in his mid-eighties, worked hard with a speech therapist to regain his speech. Ironically, while Broccoli was recovering from his surgery, both Terence Young and Harry Saltzman died during September 1994: Young in hospital in Cannes on the 7th, Saltzman at his home in Paris after a long illness on the 27th. Both were 79.

Broccoli was further saddened that month by news that Herve Villechaize, who'd played Nick Nack in *The Man with the Golden Gun*, had taken his own life on the 4th, and by the tragic news that George Lazenby's son, Zachary, had died of brain cancer at the young age of nineteen on the 24th.

Cubby Broccoli was never well enough to visit the set of *GoldenEye*, but he saw the rushes every day and liked what he saw. The tremendous success of the film thrilled him – not only for himself but for Michael Wilson and Barbara Broccoli, for whom the film was a particular triumph.

With *GoldenEye* established as a blockbuster at the start of 1996, Kevin McClory, of whom relatively little had been heard since *Never Say Never Again* in 1983, announced in a lengthy article in *Variety* that he was planning to produce another remake of *Thunderball*, this time called *Warhead 2000AD*, to rival Eon's eighteenth Bond film, scheduled for a Christmas 1997 release. According to the article, McClory claimed that his reason for working on yet another remake of *Thunderball* was to finance other projects.

To start with, McClory's claims were not taken terribly seriously by many in the industry. He had made similar noises before but these really amounted to little. According to official US court documents (United States Court of Appeals for the Ninth Circuit, 27 August 2001), in 1986 McClory cabled the chairman of MGM/UA to inform them that the Bond pictures infringed upon his rights in *Thunderball*, and in 1987 he filed a correction registration with the US Copyright Office regarding the book THUNDERBALL, listing himself and Jack Whittingham as its co-authors. And in 1988 McClory's company Spectre Associates took out full-page and multipage ads in *Variety*, stating that its 'rights' to James Bond were being infringed upon by MGM/UA and Danjaq.

Despite these occasional flurries of public accusations, McClory had taken no legal action and many believed his announcing *Warhead 2000AD* was but another McClory proclamation that would amount to nothing. Cynics pointed out that McClory did not even disclose any of the fundamental requirements of a production, such as which studio was financing the project, who was going to star in it or, indeed, even if there was a script. But rumours of McClory's plans persisted throughout 1996 and it was claimed it had moved into preproduction by the end of the year, although many in the industry still refused to give the rumours much credence: a fanzine, *Bondmanian News* (Issue 12) even made the extraordinary claim that the telephone number on McClory's official press kit was in fact that of a telephone box outside Boots the Chemist in High Holborn, London. One persistent rumour associated with *Warhead 2000AD* was that McClory had asked Timothy Dalton to star in it.

In the spring of 1996, John Gardner's final James Bond novel, COLD (COLDFALL in the US), was published. Gardner's series had long since run its course with the books petering out into what for some fans was a succession of meaningless and, frankly, boring adventures. There was a feeling that, perhaps, the resurrected literary Bonds should end with Gardner's last effort, but Glidrose made the surprising announcement that the American writer Raymond Benson, author of the highly acclaimed *The James Bond Bedside Companion*, had been commissioned to succeed John Gardner.

'It was important, provided the guy can write – and Raymond can write – to have someone who knew what we want and what the public wants and will get the facts right,' said Peter Janson-Smith of Glidrose. 'Raymond understands Bond. He knows the Fleming books so well. He's not trying to Americanise him. It's not so much a sequel as a new Bond adventure.'

There was much criticism of Glidrose's decision initially: it was difficult to tell quite what his critics thought was Benson's bigger crime – his nationality or the fact that he was a computer-game designer. But Raymond Benson's first book, ZERO MINUS TEN, silenced the doubters when it was published in 1997. More than Kingsley Amis, and certainly more than John Gardner, Raymond Benson's James Bond was almost indistinguishable from the agent created by Ian Fleming. Maybe the book isn't written quite as well as Fleming's series – given Fleming's unique qualities as a writer, that would be asking too much – but Benson's book is still a remarkable debut. And as his series progressed – Benson published THE FACTS OF DEATH in 1998, HIGH TIME TO KILL in 1999, DOUBLESHOT in 2000 and the superb NEVER DREAM OF DYING in 2001, plus skilful novelisations of *Tomorrow Never Dies* and *The World Is Not Enough* – he improved with each book. Benson's latest Bond novel, THE MAN WITH THE RED TATTOO, was published in May 2002.

On 27 June 1996, Albert R (Cubby) Broccoli died peacefully at his home at the age of 87. His funeral was held at the Church of the Good Shepherd in Beverly Hills on 1 July. Timothy Dalton was one of the pallbearers and John Barry helped choose the music for the service.

A memorial service was held in London because, as Dana Broccoli's letter inviting friends and colleagues to attend the informal event stated, Cubby had spent forty years living and working in London.

The service was held at 11 a.m. on the cold, rainy morning of Sunday, 17 November, at the Odeon Leicester Square. It was presented by Iain Johnstone and tributes were made by the Prince of Wales, Robert Wagner, Bryan Forbes, Christopher Lee, Desmond Llewelyn, Guy Hamilton, Lewis Gilbert, John Glen, Jill St John, John Barry, Lois Maxwell, Jane Seymour, Shirley Eaton and Michael Wilson. Roger Moore, Timothy Dalton and Pierce Brosnan all made extraordinarily warm speeches. 'I wanted *GoldenEye* to be great for him,' said an emotional Brosnan. 'And only him. I missed him on *GoldenEye*. And I will miss him throughout the making of number eighteen.'

The service ended with a montage of photographs of Broccoli's private and public moments shown on the screen of the Odeon to the accompaniment of 'We Have All the Time in the World'. Those of us who were there will always recall it as an immensely moving yet uplifting celebration of Broccoli's life.

Sean Connery and George Lazenby did not attend.

Keen to capitalise on the success of *GoldenEye*, MGM were eager to open the eighteenth Bond film, *Tomorrow Never Dies*, in December 1997, and with a February 1997 start date for principal photography that did not leave much room for manoeuvre. But, from the moment *Tomorrow Never Dies* went into preproduction, it was a movie plagued by problems and, allegedly, bad feeling.

A draft script, written by Bruce Feirstein, was delivered to Eon in September 1996, featuring a story said to be inspired by Britain's imminent handover of Hong Kong to China (the same background used in Raymond Benson's ZERO MINUS TEN, incidentally).

Eon then began work on deciding their studio requirements and the expectation was that they would return to the Leavesdon Studio they had created for *GoldenEye*. That was until George Lucas signed to produce his next *Star Wars* movie at Leavesdon, effectively blocking any other major film from being produced there until 1999.

Pinewood was also unavailable, leaving an exasperated Michael Wilson to comment, 'There's now a question of where we can go to film Bond number eighteen. We have made all bar a couple in the UK but somehow everything is just contriving to make keeping that tradition alive difficult.'

In the event, Eon decided to follow the precedent they had set themselves two years earlier: if you can't find a film studio to accommodate your production, build your own! This is what they did, converting an old Kwik Save supermarket depot in St Albans into a state-of-the-art film studio for *Tomorrow Never Dies*; although some scenes *were* shot on the 007 Stage and in the studio tank at Pinewood.

Having sorted out the problem of the studio, Eon were then faced with location problems. The basic story of *Tomorrow Never Dies* sees Bond and a Chinese agent, Wai Lin, teaming up to thwart the mad media mogul Elliott Carver's plan to inaugurate a war between Britain and China to boost the ratings of his satellite news channel. Some of the action is set in Vietnam and Eon believed they had secured permission to film on location in Vietnam. The Vietnamese government reneged on this agreement at the eleventh hour, however, when they decided Bond was much too anti-Communist a character to be seen in their country. A frantic search for a substitute location took Eon eventually to Thailand, where much of *The Man with the Golden Gun* had been shot more than twenty years earlier.

Other problems reported in the press were of rows on set, particularly between the director Roger Spottiswoode and the writer Bruce Feirstein. After Feirstein had delivered his draft script, other writers were brought in to work on the script but Feirstein was reinstated by the producers a few days before shooting started. Feirstein then rewrote the rewritten script, much to Spottiswoode's reported fury. At one point, Spottiswoode was said not to be on speaking terms with Feirstein or the producers.

The rewrites naturally upset the actors, many of whom were reported to be angry at receiving new pages of script on the morning of shooting scenes they had already learned. Furthermore, Teri Hatcher, playing Carver's wife and a former lover of Bond's, became pregnant just prior to shooting, which necessitated all her scenes with Brosnan being brought forward. There were also reports of tension and creative differences between Brosnan and Hatcher – reports that may or may not have been exaggerated in the press, as had been the supposed feud between George Lazenby and Diana Rigg on *On Her Majesty's Secret Service*.

As if all this wasn't bad enough, Pierce Brosnan sustained a nasty facial injury during a fight scene, which required stitches and meant he could be filmed from only one side while his face healed.

With a virtually closed set, unusual for a Bond movie, any news coming out of the *Tomorrow Never Dies* production was invariably bad, often giving rise to speculation that the film was in trouble. Even before principal photography began on 1 April 1997 (second-unit work had filmed much of the pre-credits sequence in the French Pyrenees in January), rumours were circulating in Hollywood that the budget had spiralled to $100 million (twice what *GoldenEye* had cost) and the movie would not be ready in time for its projected release date.

For MGM, who had no other Christmas 1997 release planned apart from *Tomorrow Never Dies*, it was imperative that the Bond film be delivered on time. All the more so since they were looking to Eon to reproduce the success of *GoldenEye* to bolster their planned stock market flotation planned for the same time.

Pierce Brosnan called all the bad stories emerging from *Tomorrow Never Dies* 'rubbish', and, while the tension of being up against the clock throughout must have added to the strains that are inevitable on any major feature film, it certainly seems that many of the horror stories were exaggerated.

One of the authors of this book, Martin Sterling, spent time on the set of *Tomorrow Never Dies* and never once witnessed any incident that remotely resembled anything reported in the press; although Desmond Llewelyn went on record to say, 'Yes, there was a certain amount of friction. I think it was a difficult production because it had to be out by Christmas. I liked the director; as far as I was concerned he was very good. I usually have to have those damn idiot boards up to remember certain things but he wouldn't let me use them. I said all right, but it's going to take a long time. I'm getting old and I can't remember my lines. As a director he was good.'

Despite all the problems, *Tomorrow Never Dies* wrapped in September 1997, leaving three months before its UK premiere on 9 December – a desperately tight postproduction period, but not an impossible one. On a sad note, Princess Diana was scheduled to visit the set the week after she was killed in Paris at the end of August. Her death cast a shadow over the last couple of weeks of shooting.

With *Tomorrow Never Dies* finally in the can, Michael Wilson and Barbara Broccoli should have been able to relax. But then came the realisation that *Tomorrow Never Dies* would open in the US on the same day – 19 December 1997 – as James Cameron's delayed but much-anticipated *Titanic*.

Then, on 14 October 1997, Sony Pictures announced that it had teamed up with Kevin McClory and, using rights to the James Bond character allegedly owned by McClory, intended to produce a rival James Bond series.

'I had several choices of studios with whom to work,' McClory said. 'But Sony Pictures and Columbia stood head and shoulders above the other studios. This is a great opportunity to join old friends in propelling James Bond into the twenty-first century.'

MGM hit back immediately, saying, 'Kevin McClory's claims of ownership of rights to James Bond have been disputed for more than ten years. Any claim that he can create a James Bond franchise is delusional.'

The lawyers were about to get rich again.

0015: The World Can't Get Enough

'Bond is the best at providing that escapism, that entertainment and sheer bravado.'

Pierce Brosnan, January 2002

There was no way *Tomorrow Never Dies* was going to sink *Titanic* at the box office. But, with a worldwide gross of $334 million, *Tomorrow Never Dies* almost matched *GoldenEye*'s mammoth success. In the all-important US market, *Tomorrow Never Dies* actually outstripped its predecessor: with a US gross of $124 million, it earned nearly $20 million more than had *GoldenEye*.

Tomorrow Never Dies is also a cracking Bond film. Fast, funny, tightly scripted and furiously paced, it shows in the final product none of the alleged problems or rows that supposedly plagued the production. The first hour in particular ranks with the very best films in the series and if the pace slackens a little during the second half – particularly when Bond and the Chinese agent Wai Lin board Carver's stealth yacht in the South China Seas for the final showdown – it scarcely matters.

It is also particularly well cast. Pierce Brosnan looks fitter, more muscular than before and is clearly more comfortable in 007's shoes than previously; the splendid Michelle Yeoh, one of the Far East's biggest box-office stars, makes Wai Lin a formidable Bond girl; and

Jonathan Pryce is a splendid villain as Carver (although he confessed to Gary Morecambe in 1999 that he wished Roger Spottiswoode had allowed him to camp up the part a little more).

Teri Hatcher's performance as the tragic Paris Carver, a former lover of Bond's, is less impressive, but she looks stunning and the love scene between Bond and Paris is truly erotic, something of a rarity in the series.

Whatever problems there may or may not have been between Roger Spottiswoode and other members of the production team, Spottiswoode's direction is taut and spare, with the effect that *Tomorrow Never Dies* boasts an internal energy not seen in any Bond film since *Dr. No*. And, in hiring David Arnold to write the score for the film, Eon have at last found a composer for the series who is a fitting successor to John Barry.

Most important of all, *Tomorrow Never Dies* proved *GoldenEye* had been no nostalgia-inspired one-off fluke. After the bleak years of the early 1990s, the series had not only come back with a bang, but the global market for Bond was bigger than ever.

All of which made the possibility of a rival Bond series produced by Sony Pictures galling to MGM. But, by February 1998, the legal battle was poised to go further still. Not content with trying to launch a rival Bond franchise, Sony also claimed they wanted a share of MGM's estimated $3 billion in profits from the eighteen Bond movies produced by Eon/Danjaq.

Sony's argument was that, because of their deal with Kevin McClory, *they* owned part of the James Bond film character. They based this extraordinary claim on McClory's 1963 settlement with Ian Fleming in the THUNDERBALL case. Sony argued that, because McClory had worked with Fleming prior to the production of Eon's movie series, his contributions to the cinematic James Bond character meant that McClory, and now Sony, were owed a percentage of the profits. (As we demonstrated in Chapter 3, however, there seems little doubt that Ian Fleming himself laid the foundations of the *cinematic* James Bond in his seventh novel, GOLDFINGER, which was written *before* Fleming and McClory met.) Reports in the trade press, such as *Variety*, suggested that Sony paid Kevin McClory $2 million to use his claimed rights as the basis for their proposed Bond series with the promise of a further $15 million if the series actually happened.

MGM had not taken Sony's announced intention to launch a Bond series lying down. On 17 November 1997, MGM and Danjaq filed suit against Sony, claiming ownership of the James Bond film franchise. According to a filing by MGM with the Securities and Exchange Commission, dated 16 December 1997, the suit alleged copyright infringement, trademark dilution and unfair competition, among other charges. MGM stated that they were seeking 'various forms of legal relief based on the Company's [MGM] position that the defendants do not have any legal right to produce or distribute a franchise of James Bond films, or any James Bond films, in the USA'.

As a precaution, MGM also purchased the global distribution rights to *Never Say Never Again* from Taliafilm in December 1997. Like a bastard child no one wanted to know, grudgingly admitted into the family, *Never Say Never Again* joined its better, and legitimate, Bondian siblings as an official MGM Bond film.

MGM's suit did not end the war of words in the press, and on 19 May 1998 MGM sought an injunction against Sony, saying it believed production on Sony's first rival James Bond movie was going ahead much faster than MGM anticipated. This was important because Cubby Broccoli's injunction against *Never Say Never Again* in 1982 had been denied only because the judge in that case felt the film was too far advanced to stop. MGM believed that Sony had already begun making the movie – Sony refused to comment on its production status – and asked for an immediate injunction.

The injunction was granted by a US district judge in Los Angeles, a decision that Sony appealed. When the appeal was heard on 22 November 1998, the Appeals Court judge ruled in MGM's favour, saying the injunction preventing Sony developing their Bond film should continue. Nevertheless, the case between MGM and Sony was still set for a trial because, even though the Appeals Court judge affirmed the lower court's decision, he did not rule on the case: he merely ruled on the injunction that prevented Sony from making their movie while the rights were still under litigation.

In the event, the trial did not go ahead because Sony threw in the towel at the end of March 1999. It had been obvious throughout the various legal processes initiated when Sony first announced their intention to create a rival Bond series that the American legal system would prevent it because of copyright and trademark law. The judge in the case had given every indication that MGM would win.

Reality eventually bit and Sony and MGM settled. In the complicated deal, Sony gave up every right to make Bond movies, including that of remaking *Thunderball*. MGM also acquired the rights to *Casino Royale* from Sony, which meant that MGM now owned every Bond movie ever produced.

'We have given up the universal rights to make a James Bond picture,' said Sony's attorney David Steuber. But one man still hadn't given up: Kevin McClory.

Accusing Sony of settling the case from under him, *Variety* reported that McClory stood up at the settlement and told the judge that he did not wish to settle and intended to continue his copyright claim against MGM and Eon/Danjaq. *That* case, he was determined, would come to court.

In June 1999, McClory told *Variety* that he was negotiating with two companies to produce James Bond movies. The first was a 'reworking' of *Thunderball*, which would now be called *Warhead 2001*, and would be set, apparently, in Australia.

MGM reacted with another filing with the Securities and Exchanges Commission. 'Mr McClory did not participate in the settlement,' said MGM, 'and continues to allege that he has certain rights to the Bond films. We contend that the only rights Mr McClory ever had were limited to remaking the movie *Thunderball* and that even those rights have expired.'

McClory's determination to press on with his claim seemed to tax the patience of even some of those who'd taken an even-handed view of the producer's campaign. Typical of their reaction was Desmond Llewelyn, who was quoted as saying, 'I knew Kevin quite well. He was charming when we were making *Thunderball* and there was no friction between them [McClory, Broccoli and Saltzman] at all.

'He's gone a bit mad now. When *Thunderball* was an enormous success he started talking about the films he was going to make; God knows what he wasn't going to do. But nothing ever happened. Then he made *Never Say Never Again* and then he said he was going to make another one. But he sold out his rights to Sony. I think it's all finished now.'

Well, not quite. A trial date was set. Kevin McClory *would* get his day in court, but not before Eon released their nineteenth Bond film, *The World Is Not Enough*, in November 1999.

Directed by Michael Apted from a screenplay by Neal Purvis and Robert Wade, Dana Stevens and Bruce Feirstein, *The World Is Not Enough*, which took its title from Bond's family motto (revealed in Fleming's ON HER MAJESTY'S SECRET SERVICE), began principal photography on 11 January 1999 at Pinewood Studios.

Shot on location in London, Azerbaijan, Turkey, Spain and the French Alps, *The World Is Not Enough* propels Bond into a complex plot about greed, revenge and world domination through the power of oil and hi-tech terrorism, and brings together, arguably, the greatest concentration of talent the Bond series had seen to date. In addition to the series regulars Pierce Brosnan, Judi Dench, Samantha Bond, Michael Kitchen, Desmond Llewelyn and Colin Salmon (who made his series debut as M's assistant in *Tomorrow Never Dies*), *The World Is Not Enough* sees John Cleese making his debut as Q's assistant and Robbie Coltrane reprising his *GoldenEye* role as Valentin Zukovsky. The acclaimed French actress Sophie Marceau also stars as Elektra King, the daughter of a murdered oil tycoon whom Bond is assigned to protect; Robert Carlyle as Renard, a terrorist who has a bullet embedded in his brain, which is slowly killing him but which renders him impervious to pain; and Denise Richards as a somewhat improbable nuclear scientist called Dr Christmas Jones.

Pierce Brosnan was relaxed and happy making *The World Is Not Enough*. 'It's a bit like coming back to family,' he claimed, during shooting. 'Doing this the third time around is comfortable. I actually looked forward to doing it.

'And it *is* like a family. Barbara Broccoli and Michael Wilson have taken over from their father Cubby, who set up a working relationship with people that grew over many years. He got the best out of people and it never ceases to amaze me how wonderful everybody is.'

Admitting he was feeling much more confident in the role, Brosnan added, 'The first one was always going to be the test. If that had been a problem, who knows? The stakes were high and we all worked very hard. You have that little trick of fear in your stomach every day when you are working on something like this. It was very tense to start with, the expectations were so high. There was a desperate need to get it right and make it the best ever. That is an ongoing thing with Bond: we have to be better each time.

'This time, though, because of the success of the previous two, you come in with more confidence, more relaxation. You know what you are doing a bit more, you know what you want to do with it a bit more. But basically it's just the confidence.'

Brosnan relished the challenges of *The World Is Not Enough*'s intelligent screenplay, which pushed Bond's psyche into darker areas than previously. Having fallen in love with Elektra – against orders and his better judgment – whom he believes he is protecting from Renard, Bond begins to suspect, and then must deal with the reality, that she is really his main adversary in league with Renard. The pain on Brosnan's face as he finally does his duty and kills Elektra is one of the best moments in the series, one that encapsulates the moral doubts Ian Fleming's Bond had about being a 'blunt instrument'.

The World Is Not Enough opened in November 1999 and immediately became the most successful Bond film in the US ever. Critics, too, were largely impressed. The leading US critic Roger Ebert called it 'a splendid comic thriller: exciting and graceful, endlessly inventive'. The *San Francisco Chronicle* believed the film was packed with 'chases, gadgets, wet T-shirts, even fine acting – this Bond outing ranks among the best. The result is a thoroughly satisfying, completely entertaining film that's also, rather surprisingly, an emotionally full experience.' *USA Today* called *The World Is Not Enough* 'one of the best post-Sean Connery Bonds and one of the best-cast 007 movies', while the *New York Times* rightly praised Sophie Marceau, who they believed 'does a smashing turn as Elektra in a mischievously sexy performance that manages to make Bond that much more interesting'.

British reviewers were scarcely less enthusiastic. 'Michael Apted's film is a winner of its kind,' said the *Daily Telegraph*. 'It is filled – as it should be – with references to Bond movies past, and yet it is new and exciting in ways of its own. Get to the queue before the queue gets to you.' *BBC Online* called the film 'bigger, bolder, brasher' and went on to say, 'as Bond movies go, *The World Is Not Enough* more than delivers the goods. Brosnan now commands the role with elegant authority, the stunts and action sequences are among the best I've ever seen and the locations are superb.'

The World Is Not Enough, then, was both a critical and commercial smash hit, launching Bond into the twenty-first century with great aplomb. Indeed, by the spring of 2000, Pierce Brosnan's three Bond films had earned, collectively, more than $1 billion – an incredible achievement for a franchise written off by industry cynics in 1994.

For many Bond fans, however, the release of *The World Is Not Enough* was overshadowed by the death of Desmond Llewelyn, who was killed in a car crash on 19 December 1999. 'I'm not ready for retirement yet,' the 84-year-old Llewelyn told reporters on the set of the film. 'The producers have assured me that as long as the Almighty doesn't want me, they do.' Poignant words from a man whose seventeen performances as Q between 1963 and 1999 will never be forgotten.

A memorial service for Llewelyn was held at St Paul's Church, Knightsbridge, on 27 March 2000, and was attended by Dana and Barbara Broccoli, David Arnold, Samantha Bond, Shirley Eaton, Lewis Gilbert, Peter Lamont, Christopher Lee and Lois Maxwell. Roger Moore was the only Bond actor to attend: Pierce Brosnan and Timothy Dalton were both prevented from attending by filming commitments.

Michael Wilson was also prevented from attending by his having to prepare for the legal case in Los Angeles between Danjaq and Kevin McClory, which finally reached court, after several delays, in March 2000.

McClory again claimed that, because of his work on THUNDERBALL and the disputed film scripts, he was partially responsible for the success of *all* future Bond films. Central to his claim was the fact that *Thunderball* was chosen by Cubby Broccoli and Harry Saltzman as Eon's first Bond film in 1961, and Richard Maibaum had written a screenplay based, McClory asserted, on the joint work of himself, Jack Whittingham and Ian Fleming. When THUNDERBALL went into litigation, plans to make *Thunderball* were dropped and Maibaum co-wrote *Dr. No* instead. McClory claimed that copyrighted elements from THUNDERBALL found their way into *Dr. No* and subsequently into the rest of the series. He also alleged that Danjaq had wilfully infringed his copyright.

At the trial itself, heard before Judge Edward Rafeedie, McClory's claims ultimately centred on whether there were laches. 'Laches' is a legal term that refers to unreasonable delay in pursuing a legal remedy, and, if proved, meant that McClory had left it too long before claiming to be the co-creator with Ian Fleming of the cinematic James Bond.

The hearing itself was not without bizarre incident, as official court documents (United States Court of Appeals for the Ninth Circuit) reveal. According to these records,

> Following several delays, the district court held a bench trial on laches. To the apparent surprise of both sides, McClory did not appear. Danjaq moved unsuccessfully to dismiss the case for failure to prosecute, and then put on its sole witness, the company president Michael Wilson, who testified for much of the day. At the end of the day, McClory's attorney informed the court that McClory would be able to testify two days later. The court agreed to the delay, and set a date for a trial on infringement in the event it found no laches. However, two days later McClory again failed to appear. His attorney stated that he had not heard from McClory, and that McClory 'would [not] contribute much more to what is in the record.' With that representation, the court proceeded with closing arguments.

The next morning, Judge Rafeedie dismissed McClory's claims on the grounds of laches: in other words Kevin McClory's failure to bring the case to court at an earlier date had prejudiced Danjaq's defence because nearly all the witnesses who could, in Judge Rafeedie's words, 'untangle McClory's web of allegations and intrigue' were long dead (Ian Fleming, Cubby Broccoli, Harry Saltzman and Richard Maibaum being the principals).

On Danjaq's alleged infringement of McClory's claimed copyright, Rafeedie concluded that McClory had known about the alleged infringement since at least 1961, and that his only suit to enforce any rights against Danjaq was the 1976 litigation (when he sought an injunction against *The Spy Who Loved Me*), which, in any case, was unrelated to the action he was now taking. Thus, Judge Rafeedie decided, there had been a delay of at least 21 years – and more likely 36 years – between McClory's knowledge of the potential claims and the initiation of litigation. According to Rafeedie, Danjaq had presented 'overwhelming and uncontroverted evidence of substantial prejudice due to McClory's delay'.

McClory's defeat in the courts led to headlines around the world that claimed that the forty-year row over the rights to the James Bond franchise was finally over. Even *007 Magazine* managed to bring itself to 'hope that this is truly the end'.

But McClory wasn't finished yet and announced his intention to appeal the verdict, claiming that the judge had erred in concluding both that Danjaq had established the elements of laches and that Danjaq was not guilty of 'naked infringement'.

Ironically, while the future of ownership of the cinematic James Bond was being decided in a Los Angeles court in the spring of 2000, another dispute – just *who* wrote the distinctive 'James Bond Theme' – had to be settled by a British jury in the High Court almost exactly a year later, in March 2001. Ever since *Dr. No* in 1962, Monty Norman had been credited in every official James Bond film as the composer of the 'James Bond Theme'. But in an article in the *Sunday Times* it was suggested that John Barry was brought in to write the theme for £250 on the condition that he wouldn't receive any credit for it. Norman, described in the article as a 'little known London musician' when, in fact, he was an award-winning composer, sued the *Sunday Times* for libel. He was said to be particularly upset by the suggestion that he had been profiting from work he did not write for nearly forty years.

Monty Norman and John Barry both gave evidence in court and sat facing each other as the famous theme was played. After four hours' deliberation, the jury decided that Norman and not Barry had written the theme and awarded Norman £30,000 in damages. Norman told reporters that he felt 'absolutely delighted and vindicated' by the verdict. Given that it had always been understood in the industry and by fans alike that John Barry had *arranged* the 'James Bond Theme' written by Monty Norman, the whole business seemed unnecessary and a sad coda to John Barry's association with the Bond series.

Five months later, in August 2001, Kevin McClory's appeal was heard by the Ninth Circuit Court of Appeals. Upholding the earlier decision, the Appeals Court rejected McClory's lawsuit, thereby ending the long-running dispute over ownership of James Bond.

Writing on behalf of the appeals panel, Judge M Margaret McKeown explained their decision:

> Every so often, the law shakes off its cobwebs to produce a story far too improbable even for the silver screen – too fabulous even for the world of Agent 007. This is one of those occasions, for the

case before us has it all. A hero, seeking to redeem his stolen
fortune. The villainous organization that stands in his way.
Mystery! International intrigue! And now, not least of all, the
dusty corners of the ancient law of equity.

More specifically, this case arises out of an almost forty-year
dispute over the parentage and ownership of a cultural phenomenon:
Bond, James Bond. We are confronted with two competing
narratives, with little in common but their endpoint. All agree that
James Bond – the roguish British secret agent known for martinis
(shaken not stirred), narrow escapes and a fondness for fetching
paramours with risqué sobriquets – is one of the great commercial
successes of the modern cinema. The parties dispute, however, the
source from which Agent 007 sprang.

After considering the history of the case – from the original dispute
with Ian Fleming to Sony's deal with MGM in 1997 – Judge McKeown
went on:

> The suit now pitted McClory against Danjaq. The crux of McClory's
> claim was that certain of the Bond movies released over the past
> thirty-six years infringed on McClory's rights under United States
> copyright law. Because, McClory argued, he possessed the rights to
> both the novel THUNDERBALL and the materials developed during the
> writing of the initial *Thunderball* script, he also possessed the rights
> to certain plot elements that first appeared in those works: namely,
> the 'cinematic James Bond' character, SPECTRE, the villain Ernst
> Stavro Blofeld, and the theme of nuclear blackmail.

But the Appeals Court upheld the earlier court's decision that Kevin
McClory had simply waited too long to bring his case and that the delay
prejudiced Dajaq's defence. The judges pointed out that McClory could
not possibly claim he didn't know about the alleged infringement until
he filed his suit (in 1998). 'This is not a case of some secret computer
code,' wrote Judge McKeown, 'but of eighteen publicly released, widely
distributed movies, beginning some forty years ago.' She went on:

> It is uncontested that many of the key figures in the creation of the
> James Bond movies have died in the intervening forty years.

These include Ian Fleming; Harry Saltzman and Cubby Broccoli, the producers of the Bond movies; Terence Young; Richard Maibaum; and Richard (Jack) Whittingham, the screenwriter hired by McClory to work on *Thunderball*.

At the hearing before the district court, Danjaq's president presented unrebutted testimony that many of the relevant records are missing. The Maibaum scripts for *Thunderball* are gone, as are all but the final draft of the *Dr. No* shooting-script. Moreover, he testified, Danjaq's 'files are incomplete, and we do not know what all the documents are.'

Ruling on McClory's claim that Danjaq wilfully infringed his copyright, the appeals judges affirmed that they were

satisfied that the evidence is insufficient as a matter of law to demonstrate that Danjaq willfully infringed on McClory's rights. The record before us tells the following story:

In the early 1960s, McClory and Fleming were embroiled in a dispute over the rights to the THUNDERBALL novel and the script materials. Danjaq was aware of this dispute and took care not to infringe upon McClory's rights. In the course of purchasing the film rights to Fleming's books, THUNDERBALL was expressly excluded from the deal pending the outcome of the litigation between Fleming and McClory. And when the litigation dragged on too long, Danjaq shelved its efforts to make *Thunderball* and instead went forward with *Dr. No*.

Then, despite McClory's just-concluded struggles with Fleming over the rights to THUNDERBALL, he did not file suit against Danjaq for any purported infringements in *Dr. No* or *From Russia With Love*, nor did he complain about them. Indeed, not only did he fail to sue Danjaq – he went into business with them. In 1965, McClory and Danjaq negotiated a ten-year license, pursuant to which Danjaq released *Thunderball*. This fact, too, suggests that Danjaq had no notice during that period of any copyright claims by McClory vis-a-vis Danjaq properties. And when McClory sued in 1976, alleging, among other things, that the soon-to-be-released movie *The Spy Who Loved Me* infringed upon his rights in *Thunderball*, Danjaq responded by removing the allegedly infringing material.

Danjaq was not on notice before the current litigation that McClory claimed a right in the supposed cinematic iteration of the James Bond character. The Bond character had been developed by Fleming over the course of six years and seven books before McClory came into the picture. Even assuming that McClory reinvented the Bond character in the *Thunderball* script materials, there was simply no way for Danjaq to know that McClory was laying claim to such a property. Given that lack of knowledge, and the absence of evidence of willfulness, a jury could not find willful infringement.

Judge McKeown concluded:

So, like our hero James Bond, exhausted after a long adventure, we reach the end of our story. For the foregoing reasons, we affirm the district court's determination that Danjaq established laches; that, as a matter of law, McClory is unable to establish willful infringement; and that laches bar McClory's claims in their entirety.

McClory's crusade was finally over.

With Eon/Danjaq's complete ownership of James Bond established once and for all, thoughts turned immediately to their next Bond film, *Die Another Day*, to be released in November 2002 – almost exactly forty years since the release of *Dr. No*.

The new Bond film was given a boost on 16 November 2001 when Pierce Brosnan was voted the 'Sexiest Man Alive' by *People* magazine in the USA – proof that he was firmly established as *the* perfect Bond for the twenty-first century.

Die Another Day, Eon's twentieth James Bond film, began principal photography on Monday, 14 January 2002, just one day short of the fiftieth anniversary of the day Ian Fleming sat down at Goldeneye to write the first words of CASINO ROYALE. Quite what Fleming would have made of the fact that the film was costing $100 million we can only speculate.

With a story that begins in the demilitarised zone between North and South Korea with a hovercraft chase and spectacular location shooting in London, Iceland, Hawaii, Spain and the UK, the new film promised fans the most lavish, outrageous and biggest Bond film ever. It also has a cast to die for: the series regulars Judi Dench, Samantha Bond, Colin Salmon and John Cleese (now credited as Q) all rejoin Pierce Brosnan for the new film, and they are joined by Halle Berry, Rosamund Pike and the British actor Toby Stephens.

At a press conference held at Pinewood Studios on Friday, 11 January 2002, Pierce Brosnan, nursing a 'miserable head cold', wrong-footed the industry by announcing that he'd already agreed to make a fifth Bond movie – Bond number 21 – and might possibly do a sixth after that.

'Well, let's just keep it simple and say, yes, I'm keen to do another one after this,' he told reporters. 'I am very proud to be sitting here today. Time has gone by so quickly. It seems like only yesterday I did this for *GoldenEye*. And here I am doing my fourth Bond. It is very much like slipping on an old pair of shoes in some respects.

'Bond is the best at providing that escapism, that entertainment and sheer bravado. The girls. The gadgets. And Bond getting out of tricky situations.

'I do think about retiring from Bond. It's a demanding role. You have to have a lot of stamina for it. I would like to get off the stage with grace when the time is right. I'm honouring my contract with this one but it would be wonderful to do another one. After that, I don't know.'

Halle Berry admitted that it was difficult to establish herself as the new Bond girl after nineteen other movies. 'There are tough images to replace and, to be honest, I don't think it's about replacing them. It's about adding another image to the bevy of the ones before.'

Rosamund Pike, contracted to play Miranda Frost in what is her first movie, agreed. 'It's been an electrifying ride. I feel like I've been picked up in a huge machine and not been put down again. And I won't be put down again until the end of the year or beyond.'

The director Lee Tamahori also revealed that some script changes had been necessary in the wake of the 11 September terrorist outrages in New York: 'There was a mass of destruction in this movie and it involved the death and destruction of a lot of American personnel. When we looked at it, we thought let's just take that out. There is a code of ethics and this film is not rooted in hard-edged reality.'

Tamahori also insisted that although his Bond film would be a state-of-the-art action movie, he would strive to keep Bond as faithful to

Fleming's original concept as possible. 'He will not be turned into a New Age guy who goes around visiting shrinks,' he told reporters. 'Bond may seem anachronistic and antediluvian, but it would be wrong to play around with the character too much.

'It's all very well to reinvent him, but some facets to his character everyone expects. I've been a big fan of the Bond movies most of my life. To me, the Bond film is a kind of impregnable fortress of film-making. It used to be about girls and gadgets and a good-looking spy and then it changed shape and is now about girls, gadgets, a good-looking spy – and big action. It is a timeless thing and it is constantly evolving.'

For Michael Wilson, the longevity of the series is no mystery. 'I'm convinced that the tremendous success of the James Bond series is directly attributed to the quality that the pictures have been able to maintain,' he says. 'Cubby always insisted on the films having high production values, which is no doubt why they continue to be successful. Barbara and I continue to produce the Bond films in the same way and, hopefully, we'll repeat the success of *GoldenEye*, *Tomorrow Never Dies* and *The World Is Not Enough* as the series continues.'

Fifty years on, Ian Fleming would doubtless be very proud of them.

Appendix 1

Ian Fleming Remembered:
A Conversation with
Sir John Morgan KCMG

'I went for a drink with some friends in the autumn of 2001 and, by chance, met Sir John Morgan KCMG, who was also there. Sir John has now retired from Her Majesty's Diplomatic Service. He served in Moscow (twice), Peking and Rio de Janeiro and was British Ambassador in Seoul, Warsaw and Mexico City. I had no idea when I told him about our plans for this book that he had known Ian Fleming so well. He invited me to his home to share his memories of Fleming with us and the resulting appendix is Sir John's fascinating account of the Ian Fleming he knew.'

Gary Morecambe

I first met Ian Fleming when I was working at the embassy in Moscow in the 1950s, where I was third secretary. Ian was the foreign editor of the *Sunday Times* for many years. He was very laid-back. He spent no more time than was needed at his desk. He liked the job because it gave him lots of opportunities for foreign travel; this would be the basis of his book some years later called THRILLING CITIES.

It was the Bond books, of course, that made him his name; and after he married Ann Rothermere, relatively late in life, he decided that what he was going to do was write a novel a year. He claimed it was an offshoot of having married in his forties.

For this purpose, he acquired a house in Jamaica called Goldeneye. After Christmas each year, he would go out there. He had a little pineapple-shape construction at the end of the garden, where he'd sit at his typewriter, and in the space of two or three weeks would produce a novel – one a year, which I believe he did for something like thirteen years running. He took a great deal of trouble over his preparation. He would spend the year getting his thoughts straight, then pop off to seclusion at Goldeneye and write the book up.

When I came back from my stint abroad in 1958, I met up again with Ian and we would get together often for lunch and share a nice old gossip. Then, through a freak chance, totally unconnected with him, I met the person who became Ian's stepdaughter. She was Fionn O'Neill, the daughter of Ann Fleming's first marriage, to Lord O'Neill. Ann would later marry Lord Rothermere, but the marriage would remain childless. With Ian she would produce the one child, Caspar. Fionn became my first wife, so all at once I was Ian Fleming's stepson-in-law!

There was an obituary in *The Times* recently of a man called Edward Crickmere, who had been Ian's butler. It was full of inaccuracies, so I wrote a letter to *The Times*, pointing out things such as the fact that Ian Fleming never referred to him as 'Crick', Ian always being punctilious in calling him Crickmere; his wife, who was cook, was always 'Mrs Crickmere', never Mary. There was also speculation that Crickmere had been a model for a James Bond character, so I wrote in my letter that this was true; that he'd been the model for Oddjob, the Korean bodyguard of Auric Goldfinger. I gave Ian the idea that he should be both Korean and called Oddjob, though I can't recall where that name came from. I had always been interested in Korea, and was later ambassador there.

The obituary had gone on to say that Ian had left the country to live in Jamaica, implying that he become some sort of tax exile. This wasn't true. Ian didn't leave the country: he always lived in England, and died in Canterbury.

After my letter was published in *The Times*, I received a letter from Roy Jenkins saying how pleased he was that I'd written it, and that the piece in *The Times* was so terribly inaccurate. He'd been very annoyed about it all, but apparently my letter had set his mind at rest.

The obituary also wrongly wrote that Ian was a passionate partygoer. It was Ann who adored parties, but Ian would avoid them on the slightest pretext. On many occasions, Ian used me as an escape route – 'Annie is giving one of her parties; see you eight o'clock at Overton's – and we went to eat at Overton's, a very pleasant fish bar, which sadly no longer exists, that stood opposite London's Victoria Station. At that time, Ian was living at Victoria Square, which was just around the corner.

We would often meet there, and Ian would always have the same meal: buckets of Pouilly Fuissé and a lemon sole. We would always sit at the bar, where Ian would then proceed to go through his ideas with me for his future James Bond plots, which was great for me, and something he seemed to enjoy enormously, too.

I think he felt he had an ally in me: not only had I suggested the Oddjob character in the GOLDFINGER novel, but I'd given him some Russian detail for FROM RUSSIA WITH LOVE, and also some background research on Bond's enemy, SMERSH.

He was always concerned with accuracy, and was always very put out if he received letters from anybody pointing out an inaccuracy in his work. There was a letter he received after FROM RUSSIA WITH LOVE had been published. According to the author of the letter, there was a very grievous error in the novel: Ian had described the hiss of hydraulic brakes on the railway train carrying Bond back from Istanbul, but that particular train didn't have hydraulic brakes! Ian told me that was the one occasion when he felt his aim for accuracy had let him down.

I was much involved with YOU ONLY LIVE TWICE, because that was based in Japan, and Ian wasn't completely au fait with the ways of that part of Asia. So it would be back for dinner at Overton's, and he would give me a list of questions about the country. At that time, I was working in the Far Eastern department of the Foreign Office, and one of my mates, Brian Hitch, was a great Japanese expert. Things like the correct name for the Japanese Secret Service, the correct spellings for many different things – all of these would be kindly provided by Brian Hitch, through me, at Overton's.

Another source for research was a splendid man called Dick Hughes, who was the *Sunday Times* correspondent in Hong Kong, a good friend of Ian's, and who would appear as Dikko Henderson in YOU ONLY LIVE TWICE. Dick Hughes took Ian to Macau, off Hong Kong, to research THRILLING CITIES. The name Dikko Henderson in YOU ONLY LIVE TWICE was also a play on Nikko Henderson, a future ambassador to Washington, and another friend of Ian's.

I was posted to Brazil. In the last of Ian's James Bond books there was a sentence with says something like, 'Blofeld has now disappeared, and I expect he will turn up in the Amazon jungle.' And that was the basic plot of what would have been his next novel, had he not died. It was going to have two strands. He was, as aficionados will know, fascinated with voodoo, and in Brazil there is a particularly arcane form of voodoo, which is called macumba. Ian asked me to provide as much information as I could about macumba practices, so I went to quite a lot of macumba christenings, where they would throw girls in long white dresses into the huge waves of Copacabana beach as a form of baptism. And they had very bizarre rites. Outside my house one day, on a manhole cover, there was a dead cockerel and a box of Havana cigars! My wife saw the box of cigars and thought someone had lost it, so brought it into the house. The maid went berserk, saying that as this was a gift to a macumba god, it had to go back straightaway – so I never got my cigars!

Ian naturally loved all this. I wrote him a series of letters, which must still exist somewhere among his papers. He told me that he read them out over dinner, which I was very touched about.

The other strand to this Bond novel he was never to write was a man called Kaiser, who had his own secret empire in the middle of the Amazon jungle, where they mined manganese. But there was no road into this hidden place, and all the workers and all the food were flown in. The idea was the interplay between this extraordinary secret city in the Amazon jungle and macumba. I think his ideas for it were rather better than those he used in what would prove to be his final novel, THE MAN WITH THE GOLDEN GUN, and I know he was working on it with extreme vigour right up to his death.

Talking earlier of Goldeneye, Ian's Jamaican home, makes me think of the time he let Sir Anthony Eden and entourage use the place. Ann Fleming was a friend of Clarissa Eden. Ann had clearly given a totally wrong impression of the luxuries and qualities of their house. After Anthony Eden's virtual breakdown following the Suez crisis, Ann offered Clarissa and Anthony the use of Goldeneye for recuperation. They took her up on the offer, but it was not a success, Anthony Eden being bitterly disappointed with the whole thing. What had been described so eloquently, no doubt, came across as more of a tiny hovel on the beach with no amenities to speak of. And then they had problems organising proper security for him. It was disastrous. But that wasn't Ian's idea at all.

Ann was a difficult person. A very complex character. Quite often horrendous. One only has to read her published letters to see what she thought of me. She uses a Greek word, which I forget, to describe me, which means someone who is trying to marry above his station. She wrote frequently to Evelyn Waugh about it. But nonetheless, when you come to read her letters, one of the most poignant letters of all is the one she wrote to me a few days before Ian died.

Written at Sandwich and dated 8 August 1964, she expresses her gratitude for my reassuring letter to her, and even compliments me by saying it is a model letter to a 'Ma-in-law'. She then tells me that Ian's life 'hangs on a thread' and any possible recovery depends on his exercising self-control with his intake of cigarettes and alcohol. She describes how Ian's doctor had spent the holiday weekend with them and that even he had witnessed the sad change that ill health and drugs had wreaked on Ian. According to Ann, these changes in his character had left him dreadfully unhappy – she refers to him as 'poor old tiger' – the result of which had extinguished all the fun in their lives. She says that Ian nags at her and then at Caspar all the time (something which was out of character for him) and that it has become an anguish to be with him, and quite impossible to make any plans for the immediate future.

She then describes the funeral of Ian's mother just a few days earlier which he had somehow managed to attend. Dubbing it 'Operation Granite', she says it was a 'tearless, musicless, and practically wreathless' affair, proof, she believes, of their being 'a very Scottish family'. She says their wreaths were the diameter of soup plates, making her 'sheaf of arum lilies shockingly conspicuous!' And she notes with distaste how the sons held a conference before the service to decide how much they should give to the old lady's nurse – she believed this was in very bad taste.

Three days after she wrote that letter to me, Ian was dead.

Ann was always moaning about something, which was unfortunate for Ian, who had been told by his doctor that he had to give up the booze and the fags and to avoid tension. But I remember that, despite the doctor's advice, Ann would come into the room and start arguing with him about some insignificant detail, and he would say, '*Pace, pace, pace*' – 'Peace, peace, peace.' Then he'd turn on his heels and go out of the room. He just couldn't stand any of these sorts of tensions by this time. This would take place at the flat at Sandwich, and though it overlooked the beach, it was very small and quite claustrophobic and the atmosphere was always tense. Ian, of course, though no one knew it at the time, was in the very final days of his life. It was from this address he would be rushed to Canterbury Hospital, where he died.

I can't say that the Kevin McClory court case over rights to THUNDERBALL contributed to Ian's death at that time, because Ian's consumption of whisky and very strong cigarettes, smoked constantly, were the main contributors to that. It would be a big leap to connect the two, but, that said, the whole affair with McClory devastated Ian. Everyone who knew him well was begging him to settle the thing, myself included, because we could see what it was doing to him. He did settle eventually, but it had gone on too long, and he definitely emerged much battered.

Ian had few close friends and led a fairly solitary life. But there were one or two. One was called Duff Dunbar, who inherited a Scottish baronetcy late in life. He was an eccentric bachelor who maintained that the only intellectual game in the world was draughts, and he was totally unbeatable. I know that Ian and Duff conferred quite a bit. Another friend was Ivar Bryce. Ivar had a beautiful house in Essex – Moyne's Park. The sad thing was, Ian had made Ivar the godfather to his and Ann's son, Caspar, but, because of a falling out between Ivar and Ann, she would never let him see Caspar. Very painful for Ivar, because he was very conscious of his duties towards the boy. The tragedy of all this was that time was so short: Caspar would commit suicide while still in his youth.

Caspar's mother was a great socialiser: her table was always surrounded by dons and politicians, and society people. She made Caspar's life quite difficult by making him perform for company. In consequence, he had a very stressful childhood. At the same time, James

Bond was becoming more and more well known, and Caspar, rather to show off at Eton, had a collection of guns, one of which was found in his room at the school. Sadly, the headmaster, Chenevix-Trench, expelled him without even beginning to telephone the family. The first Ian and Ann heard was that poor Caspar was on his way back home.

Caspar then had a bad time following this. I helped get him into New College, Oxford, because he was a very keen Egyptologist; he had a very fine collection of Egyptian objects. Then, sadly, he took drugs and dropped out of college. He was a very bright and charming boy – the most wonderful child. I was so very fond of him.

He took an overdose, eventually. He left a suicide note, saying he wished that all his collection of Egyptian figures – Ushabti figures, mainly – to go to the Devizes museum. The ultimate sadness was that the Devizes museum was allowed only to have things found on the territory of Wiltshire. So even his last wish was unfulfilled.

Ian's relationship with Caspar was close; it was with his mother that it remained quite tense. But Ian's own relatively premature death must have pushed Caspar closer to the edge. The mainstay of Caspar's life had been the old family nanny – Nanny Sillick – who had in fact looked after Lord O'Neill and my first wife. She, effectively, brought up Caspar and was his rock.

Ian's pastimes. He was a great bridge player but absolutely hated to lose. I played a lot of bridge with him. I recall one occasion playing a totally irrational game, yet I took Ian to the cleaners because he was completely foxed by this play. I'd never seen him so incandescent. He got up and walked away from the table saying, 'You can't do all these rubbish bids.' I took a nice slice of money off him. But Ian was a good bridge player – and a good backgammon player, too.

Ian was quite keen on casinos – a background theme to many a Bond book and film – and he particularly liked games like *chemin de fer*. He would fly his car over from Lydd to Le Touquet and nip into the casino for the weekend.

One of Ian's greatest interests was his desire to amass a collection of books that contained what he considered 'original thought'. The range was vast. It included a first edition of Lenin's newspaper *Iskra* (*The Spark*) and also Baden Powell's *Scouting for Boys*. There were many volumes. All were placed in beautiful black leather cases and filled two bookcases at Sevenhampton. After his death, Ann sold them all to an

American university – much to Caspar's chagrin. Ian had hoped that this would be his legacy.

Although at heart rather conventional, Ian, from time to time, sought to present himself as something of an eccentric. I recall one occasion in 1962 when we were all spending Christmas together at Shane's Castle, County Antrim, the seat of Ian's stepson, Lord O'Neill. On Boxing Day there was a very traditional shooting party. It had all the old-fashioned trimmings. The positioning of each gun in the various lines was chosen by selecting an exquisite ivory token from an old polished leather case. A game cart drawn by an aged horse was prepared to hang the kill. The beaters were all retainers on the estate. A selected few of the local grandees were invited to participate. All were dressed in the impeccable style for shooting parties established in the nineteenth century. The shotguns were valuable heirlooms. Lord O'Neill lent me a magnificent Purdey for the occasion.

As we set off for the first drive, Ian appeared. He was wearing a beige waterproof jacket and trousers and a Tyrolean hat with a feather. Even more surprising, he had a shotgun with a revolving barrel – something I am sure had never been seen before by the assembled Ulster dignitaries. There was a hush of incredulity and embarrassment, not least from Lord O'Neill himself. We then went off to the first stand with Ann Fleming dutifully following in her husband's wake to position herself behind the eight guns.

As it turned out, all went well. The pheasants were plentiful. Moreover, winter had been particularly harsh and the woodcocks were available in unprecedented numbers, having come down from their usual higher ground. These birds are renowned for jinking down the line making a laughing stock of the best guns in the country. However, on this occasion, in no small measure thanks to Ian's somewhat unorthodox style, Lord O'Neill was able to make an entry in his meticulously kept Game Book. We had achieved the woodcock record – one that, I think, has not yet been equalled to this day.

Many people ask if there was a model for 007. Going a bit into the psychology, I think Ian would have wanted the ego of 007. It is important to remember that in his group there were two people – one was Earl Jellicoe and one was Paddy Leigh-Fermour, both of whom had been in the navy – who had been hugely brave and won Distinguished Service orders and much besides, while Ian was essentially an office wallah in the admiralty, and never saw any action at all. I believe having great heroes for friends did affect him a bit. Bond became an alter ego – or the ego Ian would liked to have owned.

Ian was a generous man with gifts. He particularly liked leather goods. He gave me a set of leather cases for a wedding present. All these leather goods were made by a company called Lansdowne Luggage, which was in Bury Street, London. Ian gave me a copy of the original James Bond briefcase – not with all the gadgets, but identical otherwise. On the back of these gifts he would have engraved, 'To J, from 007'. So, he was then calling himself 007. This was at a time when not one person in ten thousand had ever heard of 007.

I was there when Sean Connery came round to 16 Victoria Square after he'd been selected to play Bond in the first film, *Dr. No*. Afterwards, Ian said to me, 'That couldn't be further from my idea of James Bond. Everything was wrong: the face, the accent, the hair.' It was a thousand miles away from his idea of James Bond.

I asked Ian which actor he envisaged in the role. He replied there was an actor called Edward Underdown, who oddly does appear in one of the Bond films but in a very minor role. So this was Ian Fleming's idea of James Bond. It's interesting to speculate that there is a Sean Connery who has made millions through a film company's decision to go with him, and an Edward Underdown, whose acting career finished early on and, I believe, ended his working life as the clerk of Chepstow Racecourse, never knowing that, if Ian had had his way, he would have become one of the most famous names in the world, and had been within an ace of being the multimillionaire that Sean Connery has become.

Something I am often asked about is the code number 007. It is only speculation, but I give you this theory. In the time of Elizabeth I there was a noted magician and charlatan called John Dee. At one stage of his many-faceted career, John Dee was a spy for Lord Walsingham. His code number was 007, and I think that it is reasonable to suppose that this is why Ian selected that particular number. We shall never know for certain.

Ian was, naturally, delighted that his books had finally begun to be made as films. There was a little private cinema on South Audley Street, and he would give it to me for viewings to my friends. We had a party there for *Dr. No* and *From Russia With Love*. These were the only two films that Ian lived to see: he died during the making of *Goldfinger* in 1964.

What Ian wanted was not so much financial reward as recognition as a serious writer. Possibly the writer he admired most was Raymond Chandler, whose beautifully written books about his private eye, Philip Marlowe, were his ideal. Ian was particularly gratified when Raymond Chandler came to London and asked to see him. The meeting of possibly the two greatest writers of their genre in the twentieth century took place at 16 Victoria Square. Ian was looking forward to it with almost childlike anticipation.

I was there. Raymond Chandler was also a great hero of mine. Sadly, it was a dismal disappointment for Ian and me. Chandler was seriously drunk and they shared no meaningful conversation. I had the task of finding a taxi and, even more difficult, getting Raymond Chandler into it, to set him on his way back to his hotel. I think that his wife, many years older, had suddenly died and he had never really recovered from the shock.

Ian's taste in art was, like so many things about him, unexpected. I do not recall his having any interest in music. I do not think he ever went to the opera. He collected portrait silhouettes and naïve pictures of pirates. He showed little interest in conventional art. I always found this rather surprising, particularly as he and his brothers had been brought up in Turner's house in Cheyne Walk, Chelsea, by their mother, a most extraordinary woman who deserves a biography. Their father, Major Valentine Fleming, won the DSO, and was killed in World War One. His name is commemorated on a plaque in the Travellers' Club, Pall Mall.

Ian's reading was not particularly profound. He always said he needed to keep abreast of the opposition, so read anything that was remotely similar to his own genre. I have mentioned his admiration for Raymond Chandler. I also recall how impressed he was with Len Deighton's first work, *The Ipcress File*. He inscribed a copy for me as a Christmas present – which I still have. His wife was a friend of Evelyn Waugh (their extensive correspondence has been published) but Ian always denigrated his writing. Iris Murdoch was also a frequent attendee at Ann's soirées, but Ian said he never read a word she wrote.

I remember Evelyn Waugh and Iris Murdoch sharing a sofa at Victoria Square. Evelyn Waugh had an antique ear trumpet, and ostentatiously refused to register anything Iris Murdoch said.

Ian became really animated only at a card or gaming table, but GOLDFINGER embraced another great passion of his life, that being golf. He had lived at the Old Bishop's Palace, Bekesbourne, outside Canterbury, very close to the famous Sandwich golf course, which featured in the story. Ann didn't like living at this particular house, as she complained it was too near a railway line, and she insisted they moved to Sevenhampton, near Highworth, Wiltshire. She built a house there out of an existing property.

Ian hated the house, describing it as a canteen for dons, who would come across from Oxford. He would try to avoid going down there. Eventually, there was a compromise: they bought a very small flat at Sandwich.

Though I don't play golf, he used to take me to his matches at St George's. They were quite original in form. There would be a large round table for his golfing mates. The drink would be absolutely prodigious. Then there would be a conversation, which at first I found completely incomprehensible. A number would be said, then they'd say another number. I couldn't work out what they were deciding. It transpired that what they were actually doing was deciding which hole they were going to play, and how much money they were going to have on it. So, it might have been eight and five thousand – we'll play the eighth hole and we'll have five thousand pounds on it.

Ian, at that time, drove an extremely vulgar Thunderbird, an American car, which he lent me to go off on my honeymoon. All these golfing friends, including Ian in his Thunderbird, would drive to the nearest point to the chosen hole and play it. A great deal of money would subsequently change hands. Then it was back to the clubhouse, and back to their wives, where they'd say, 'Gosh I played a very strenuous eighteen holes at the golf course.' Quite amusing, but that was Ian's way of playing golf by the end of his life.

Ian never benefited from all the money that his creation, James Bond, was to bring in. All the really big money came in the years following his death, and continues right through to the present day, though how much goes to the family, I am not sure. He sold 51 per cent of himself to Glidrose for what, today, would be considered peanuts: so Ian, even if he had lived, would not have received anything like the monies he might have done. Lord Campbell of Croy, the head of Eagle Star and Glidrose, was the beneficiary of Ian's decision to sell off Bond.

Ian kindly left my elder children a very small element of the film rights. As he said in the covering letter, it should prove enough to pay for a nanny – which was about what it amounted to.

What I find quite intriguing was the question of the probate of Ian's will. By the time it came to have probate, the value of the film rights had changed dramatically, and so the probate commissioners had to decide what was the value of a particular book on the day that Ian died – in other words before the phenomenon had really taken off. There were two lawyers involved: one was Lord (Arnold) Goodman, the other was Sir Matthew Farrer, the Queen's solicitor. These two great men battled famously over this.

In retrospect, it's intriguing. They valued quite highly Ian's book, THRILLING CITIES, which had never been made into a film, and never made any money at all. And they valued as totally insignificant a book Ian had written as bedtime stories for Caspar, which was CHITTY CHITTY BANG BANG. This, of course, proved to be as big as some of his Bond books, but the commissioners of probate said it was something that had no cinematic potential at all. I believe it was zero-rated. The book was a bestseller, then there was the film and now a West End musical!

The story was based on a real Polish count who lived in a place called Bridge in Kent. He had this car he called Chitty-Chitty-Bang-Bang, which he would drive frantically around the lanes of Kent near Bekesbourne. That's where Ian got the original idea.

The only time in recent years I've come into contact with Bond was when I was ambassador in Mexico in the late eighties, and the Bond production for *Licence To Kill* had based themselves out there. I had all the cast, including the then Bond, Timothy Dalton, and Q, Desmond Llewelyn, to a swimming party of the residence. I arranged an exhibition of my original James Bond attaché case, the one inscribed, 'To J, from 007', which went down well; so did a subsequent trip to the house where Trotsky was murdered.

Wouldn't Ian have been amazed if he could have seen all the fuss that still persists over Bond? I was working in Rio de Janeiro when I heard Ian had died. Of course, Ann had kept me posted of his worsening condition.

Now they are both gone, buried in the churchyard at the end of a tree walk which goes from Sevenhampton Place, where I would spend so much time with them, to the church in Sevenhampton. Some years ago, word got round that Ian had been buried in a golden coffin, so the grave was sadly desecrated. Ian, Ann and Caspar are all buried there. A complete family.

If I had to sum up Ian, I would describe him as one of the most interesting, most stimulating people I have ever met – a completely delightful man. I knew him from before James Bond, then through all the beginnings of his success, and I remained totally devoted to him.

Even now, if I had to choose someone with whom to sit down and enjoy a glass of wine and a lemon sole, Ian would be at the top of the list.

Appendix 2

007: Behind the Scenes

Martin Sterling

(This article is reprinted with the kind permission of the *EDP Magazine*, where it first appeared on 20 November 1999.)

The Caspian Sea is remarkably calm far beneath the rickety wooden steps of the caviar factory I'm climbing. When I reach the main platform which runs all around the fishery itself, I pause and look round. Lights from Baku in Azerbaijan glitter in the distance.

This is a large oil centre and wells – which once supplied the whole of the Soviet Union – are situated off the coast of the Caspian, many of them with long causeways stretching as far as 50 kilometres out to sea.

But all is not what it seems. What, for instance, is a brand new BMW Z8 doing on another platform? Why does that helicopter at the other end of the factory have a lethal buzz-saw where its undercarriage should be? And how come I'm in Azerbaijan when I only turned off the M25 half an hour ago?

My guide turns to me. 'If you've got a mobile phone, can you turn it off, please,' she says. 'It could set off the explosions.'

I'm not in Azerbaijan, of course, but at Pinewood Studios in Buckinghamshire. And where else could I be but on the set of the nineteenth James Bond film, *The World Is Not Enough*?

Set against a background of greed, revenge and world domination through the power of oil and hi-tech terrorism, *The World Is Not Enough* delivers everything audiences have come to expect from the most successful and enduring cinema franchise of all time – and then some.

While the locations – Turkey, Azerbaijan, France, Spain, Scotland and London – are as glamorous as ever, and the stunts even more eye-popping than usual, the script of the last Bond movie of the twentieth century may be remembered as the most engrossing of the series.

The consummate intelligence with which *The World Is Not Enough* has been put together is reflected in the talent both behind and in front of the camera. This Bond film has the most distinguished cast of any series entry. In addition to Pierce Brosnan playing 007 for the third time and Judi Dench and Samantha Bond returning as M and Moneypenny respectively, *The World Is Not Enough* features noted French actress Sophie Marceau; Robert Carlyle as the anarchist, Renard; *Starship Troopers'* Denise Richards as Dr. Christmas Jones; Desmond Llewelyn making his seventeenth appearance as Q; John Cleese as Q's new assistant; musician Goldie as a bodyguard; and Robbie Coltrane reprising the role of Valentin Zukovsky – 'more Arthur Daley than the Krays,' according to Coltrane – the Russian gangster he first played in *GoldenEye*.

For director, the producers Michael Wilson and Barbara Broccoli turned to the distinguished Michael Apted. Apted, until now unknown as an action director, has previously directed films such as *Coal Miner's Daughter*, *Gorky Park* and *Gorillas in the Mist*.

His early television work including working as an investigative reporter on *World in Action* and directing many episodes of *Coronation Street*. Apted is also the creator and director of the engrossing documentary project which began with a group of fourteen British schoolchildren in 1963 and which has revisited them every seven years since. The most recent instalment, *42 Up*, was broadcast by BBC1 in July 1998.

All of which seems a far cry from the explosive world of James Bond. So much so that when Apted first received the call from the Bond producers, he thought it was a joke. 'But I'm thrilled it wasn't,' he admits in a break between scenes. 'Once the job became a possibility, I was desperate to do it. I grew up with the Bond films and, like any young man of my generation, I was permanently influenced by Ursula Andress and her bikini.

'Every film is a worry but with so much expectation riding on a new

Bond film, there's so much more to worry about. I don't want to repeat what others have done but I still want to deliver the things people expect. The action, the stunts, the girls, the gadgets and the locations – you mess with those at your peril.

'So it's a real challenge to make it all fresh and original. We're not only competing with other action films but also with the Bond franchise itself. I'd suggest something and someone would say, "Oh, but we did that on Bond No. 7" – it made my head reel. But I think we did well finding spectacular new twists on a ski chase and the boat chase on the Thames and constructing other sequences that are completely original. This film has the unique Bond stamp, that's for sure.'

Apted is full of praise for Pierce Brosnan and concurs with the general opinion that he is, at the very least, the best Bond since Sean Connery and, arguably, the best Bond of all.

'Pierce brings vulnerability and warmth along with his considerable physical skills,' says Apted. 'He contrasts with Sean, who made Bond much more contained. Pierce looks for relationships and character development and is always asking for "stuff to play", which is music to a director's ears and a life-line to his co-stars.'

This is repeated by Brosnan's co-stars, all of whom have nothing but praise for the Bond star. Dame Judi Dench says Brosnan is a genuinely nice person. 'He takes everything in his stride,' she says. 'He's absolutely perfect as Bond. He's a modern Bond and maybe Sean Connery wouldn't have been that.'

Robert Carlyle agrees: 'Working with him has been a breath of fresh air. I didn't know what to expect but he made me very welcome. He's a terrific actor as well and I think he deserves every credit. It's a very difficult job he does.'

I understand what Carlyle means when I leave the caviar factory set and go to Pinewood's cavernous 007 Stage which was built for *The Spy Who Loved Me* in 1977 and rebuilt for *A View To A Kill* after a disastrous fire in 1984.

Here, production designer Peter Lamont, who has been associated with the Bonds since *Goldfinger* in 1964 and who won an Oscar for designing the sets for James Cameron's *Titanic*, has constructed the massive interior of an oil pipeline.

Pierce Brosnan and Denise Richards are playing out the scene where Bond and Christmas Jones make their escape from the blazing pipeline.

This requires them to stand on a hydraulic platform which propels them 40 feet into the air through the inferno. It's a gruelling scene which requires several takes to complete: and neither Brosnan nor Richards is using a stunt double.

Even so, right to the last take, Brosnan is determined to push his performance to the limit. He and director Michael Apted talk continually, each making suggestions as to how to make the scene more compelling. Brosnan speaks with the quiet authority of a man who has made the part of James Bond his own. And well he might: *GoldenEye* and *Tomorrow Never Dies* made $700 million at the box office, making Brosnan the most successful Bond financially.

I catch up with him at his trailer a few minutes after he's left the 007 Stage. We've met several times since he became Bond but I've never seen him looking as fit as he does now. When I arrive, he's talking to two young French girls who've won a magazine competition to visit the set. They explain, in very broken English, that they had to state James Bond's nationality to win.

'What did you say?' Brosnan asks them.

'English,' the girls chorus.

'They're here under false pretences,' I say.

'Indeed they are,' says Brosnan. 'In Ian Fleming's books, Bond's father was Scottish and his mother Swiss. Bond isn't English at all.'

He leaves it to me to try and explain this to the two, increasingly bewildered, French girls and his famous sense of humour manifests itself in a huge grin as I struggle to make myself understood.

When the girls have gone, I confess to Brosnan that I sneaked into the editing suite earlier where the fabulous ski chase, filmed near Chamonix the previous week, was already being edited.

'I suppose you know Bond's parents were killed in a climbing accident at Chamonix,' he says casually, revealing, yet again, how much he's researched the character of Ian Fleming's 007.

He's called back on-set and we don't meet again for a couple of months. By now it's June. They're into the last week of shooting and Brosnan can't wait for the film to be finished.

'We've only got another week and I can't wait to get away,' he admits. 'It's always like this on a big movie. Everyone feels tired and you just want a holiday. Journalists keep asking me if I'm going to do a fourth Bond. Maybe I shouldn't answer them this week.'

He makes that last comment with a smile which tells me not to take him too seriously.

If he seems particularly tired today, it isn't only the Bond film that is responsible. He's just returned from a flying visit to the States where he saw his remake of *The Thomas Crown Affair* for the first time.

'People tell me how good it is, and what chemistry I have with Rene Russo,' he says. 'But I can't see it myself. I just see this guy up on-screen and think, "who the hell is that?"' His modesty is never far from the surface.

We're sitting in his luxurious dressing room in Pinewood's F-Block. It's more like an hotel suite than a dressing room and comes complete with its own bedroom and kitchen. And yet, when I think of Brosnan alone in this vast space during the inevitable long breaks between scenes, which occur on any major motion picture, it occurs to me for the first time just how lonely the life of an international star can be. Indeed, he told me when I arrived that he was glad of the company.

'I hate days like this,' he says. 'They've either got me dangling from a rope or they're throwing me in the fucking studio tank. Not much acting required.' He flashes that grin again and then says, 'Let's have a cup of tea.'

Brosnan goes to the kitchen, puts tea-bags into a couple of mugs and boils the kettle. To take my mind off the unlikely image of James Bond making me tea, I scan his coffee table and notice a first-edition copy of Ian Fleming's ON HER MAJESTY'S SECRET SERVICE.

Fleming, it seems to me, is never far from Brosnan's mind when he's playing Bond. Maybe that explains why he's so good at it.

I tell him how much I like the title of the new film, *The World Is Not Enough*, which, Fleming revealed in ON HER MAJESTY'S SECRET SERVICE, was the Bond family motto.

'Yes,' he says. 'I like it, too. I've been very lucky with the titles of my Bond films.'

There's no doubt that Pierce Brosnan has enjoyed making his third Bond film more than his first two: 'The first one was always going to be a test. It was very tense to start with because expectations were so high. This time, though, because of the success of *GoldenEye* and *Tomorrow Never Dies*, you come in with more confidence, more relaxation.

'*The World Is Not Enough* has gone very smoothly. Michael Apted is a superb director. I trust him and he listened to what I had to say about

Bond having dialogue you can believe in, and having an emotional base from which I can work off. So I've had the greatest time on this film.'

The assistant director knocks on the door and pops his head in to say that Brosnan is required back on-set.

Pierce Brosnan escorts me out of the dressing-room and we part in the corridor: me to the car park and him to the sound stage.

'Think of me being thrown in that bloody tank again on your way home, won't you?' he grins, as we shake hands.

And then he disappears back into the maelstrom of James Bond, of whom the world can never have enough.

Appendix 3

Words of Bondage

Ian Fleming

'The target of my books lies somewhere between the solar plexus and the upper thigh.'

'James Bond really is a frightful cad. And apart from the fact that he wears the same clothes that I wear, we don't have quite as much in common as some people think. But I do rather envy him, his blondes and his efficiency, although I can't say I much liked the chap at first. In fact, I began by disliking him intensely, but grew fond of him in time. Let's face it, he has been very good to me.'

'I simply wanted to create an interesting character to whom extraordinary things happen, but I never set out to make a paragon or a freak. I wanted him to be entirely anonymous and let the action of the book carry him along. I didn't believe in the heroic Bulldog Drummond types. I felt these types could no longer exist in literature. I wanted my lead character to more or less follow the style of Raymond Chandler and Dashiell Hammet's heroes who are believable people, believable heroes. I was considerably influenced by Chandler and Hammet, and to some extent in my childhood, by E Phillips Oppenheim, and Sax Rohmer.

'Although James Bond is almost entirely a product of my imagination, I used various people I came across during the war – Secret Service men, commandos, newspaper men – as a basis for him. My experiences during the war, and my knowledge of intelligence work, led me to write about them in a highly bowdlerised way, and I simply used Bond as the central figure. He just came out of thin air. There he was – a compound of secret agent and commando types I had met. But although he is a meld of qualities I noted among various people, he remains, of course, a highly romanticised version of the true spy.'

'At first, I didn't even give Bond a complete personality. In my earlier books, you will find a few of his later mannerisms, no real in-depth characterisation of him. I didn't even provide him with a detailed personal appearance. I kept him virtually blank. This was quite deliberate and enabled, I am sure, people to identify themselves with him. People simply put their own overcoats on James Bond and built him into what they admire. But then, as I got to know him better, I filled in mannerisms and characteristics. He started eating those meals of his and dressing a certain way so that he gradually became encrusted with characteristics, although much against my will.'

'It was my determination to make Bond believable that led me to his name. When you think of it, it is a dull name. I could have called him Peregrine Carruthers, or something lush-sounding, but then I would have defeated my aim of making him credible. I wanted the blankest name possible. One of my "bibles" in Jamaica is a book by a distinguished American ornithologist called *Birds of the West Indies* by James Bond. The name sounded just right to me.'

'James Bond is a blunt instrument wielded by a Government department. He's hard, ruthless, sardonic, fatalistic. He likes gambling, golf, fast motor cars. All his movements are relaxed and economical. Bond is permanently in his mid-thirties. I'm in my fifties, so my age takes the edge off his sort of galivanting about. But we do have something in common – golf, love of swimming, and a hatred of office work.'

'I write for warm-blooded heterosexuals in railway trains, aeroplanes, and beds.'

'Bond's a bit of a bastard. He has his vices, and few perceptible virtues, except patriotism and courage, which are probably not virtues anyway. He reads books on golf and so on, when he reads anything, but he is essentially a man of action in a violent age, not a person of much social attractiveness. But then I didn't intend him to be a particularly likeable person. As for his sexual prowess, seduction has to a marked extend replaced courtship. The direct, flat approach is now standard. I wouldn't say he's particularly typical of our times, but he is certainly *of* the times.'

'There are all sorts of popular notions about Bond. There is the business about his being fastidious over clothes. His shoes, for instance. In fact, I've never mentioned them, except to say he doesn't like laces. Any more than he likes buttons. He's fond of black silk knitted ties I agree. But there is no snobbery about his clothes. His suits are Savile Row: mine are from Cork Street – it's slightly cheaper. But Bond and I both wear sea-island cotton. It's very good stuff. In fact, I approve of all the things he uses. We both happen to like short-sleeved shirts. I have done many of the things that he has done, and have been to all the places he has – so I can describe them. We are both Scottish. I suppose, all in all, it's true to say we have a lot in common. Bits of me undoubtedly creep in – quirks and tastes, likes and dislikes, but he's got much more guts than I have, is considerably more handsome, and eats rather more richly than I could possible manage to do. But I admit Bond is very much the Walter Mitty syndrome – the feverish dream of the author of what he might have been – bang, bang, kiss, kiss – that sort of stuff.'

'I've the usual vices myself – selfishness, and so on. But Bond is really a latter-day St George. He does kill wicked dragons after all. The main difference is, I'm not a tough individual. All I ever do is take a little exercise which doesn't compare too well with Bond's usual routine of up at seven, swim a quarter of a mile, an hour's sunbathing, run a mile, swim again, lunch, sleep, sunbathe, hot bath and massage, dinner, and asleep by nine – that is, when he's training.'

'I really don't see why Bond should drink miserable cups of tea and dreary half pints of beer. I insist on seeing that the man enjoys only the best.'

'Bond hasn't got a social life – how can he have? Just a few girlfriends. I'm not a great socialiser either. My wife fully understands my attitude, that I don't care for her parties and literary friends. For one thing, you know, if you are married to a hostess, you find that she will seat the most interesting man next to herself and saddle you with the boring wives. So, whenever possible, I avoid going to my wife's parties.'

'I find the people one meets in the low striptease joints in Hamburg infinitely more interesting than anyone one would meet at a Belgravia dinner party. Give me a cheap joint any day. That Belgravia crowd – you would need a tin-opener to get at them. They may, of course, be just as interesting as anyone else underneath, but it would take years to find out, and then, of course, they might turn out to be as boring underneath as on the surface.'

'I was delighted, but surprised, at Bond's acceptance in America – that an Englishman should have been chosen by them as a popular hero. That is so unusual but, I suppose, he must seem very American in so many ways – his likes and dislikes, and his rather full sex life. I think perhaps that his sort of patriotic derring-do was the reason President Kennedy enjoyed his exploits so much. He was in keeping with President Kennedy's own concept of endurance, courage and grace under pressure. That is why I am sure Bond was his favourite adventure character. Of course, it's very nice to know that a president, Prince Philip and former CIA Chief Alan Dulles enjoy my books. It's also very good for sales.'

'I aim for the total stimulation of the reader all the way through, even to his taste buds, which is why I have Bond skipping from peril to passionate women, to play at the gaming table, and the pleasures of *haute cuisine*. It doesn't hurt to raise the blood pressure of novel readers a little. We could do with a bit of raising. I don't think my books do any harm. It's all good, healthy fun. As a boy I used to read the penny dreadfuls and the blood-and-thunder stuff. Bond is no worse, and has no greater influence on readers. Even Grimm's fairy stories are filled with violence.'

'My plots are bizarre, but are made of real things. I take a lot from life. I always include subjects in which I'm interested, such as sharks. I also always study the best authorities on the particular subject I want for a book. I try to make everything credible, as related to what I know about the rather improbable world of espionage. Glaring inaccuracy, or a stretching of plausibility, would bother me far more than it would any reader. If anyone thinks that Goldfinger's painting his girlfriend all over with gold paint is far-fetched, I would remind them that there was a case of a striptease girl on the Continent who died after being gilded all over. It sealed off all the pores of the skin which needs to "breathe" if the body is to survive.'

'I suppose one always projects one's secret fantasies in my sort of fiction. That I suppose is why male readers like my stories; they express what every man hopes might happen, and jolly well knows it doesn't. The reason women like the stories is because women are all masochistic and I suppose they like the way the female characters are bashed about. Bond is the kind of man every girl secretly dreams of meeting, and leads the life every man would like to live if he dared.'

'James Bond could never be a good husband. I couldn't have him settling down. His wife would be irritated with his constantly going abroad. She would want to change his way of life, and then he'd start worrying about domestic trivialities back home, his own fidelity and, well, he wouldn't be Bond anymore. That's why when in ON HER MAJESTY'S SECRET SERVICE I did marry him off, I speedily wrote off his wife. I killed her. It was the easy way out. I enjoy being able to remove his women whenever I feel like it. He had a secretary named Loelia Ponsonby once, until I got fed up with her because she was so greedy and grasping. I got bored with her. So I sacked her.'

'I greatly enjoy knowing that other people, quite intelligent people, find my books amusing and entertaining. But I'm not really surprised, because they entertain and amuse me, too.'

Raymond Chandler

'Ian Fleming's writing is hard, racy, direct, vivid stuff. A form of writing most suitable for translation into strip form. I often wish I had Ian's virtues.'

'Perhaps James Bond is a little too tough. Bond is a dangerous man. Dangerous to his enemies. Dangerous to himself. In real life, I suppose, Bond would not last more than twelve months. His enemies would combine to see to that. Philip Marlowe, now – he'll probably end his days in a street accident. The American crime syndicate would never really go out of their way to bump him off. He's not dangerous enough to them.'

'Ian Fleming's hard, clean style is unusual in England. There's that difference between American crime stories and British crime stories. The British stories lack pace. But Fleming has got away from the prosy style. He's an exception – he has this pace.'

Sean Connery

'I guess it never came hard to me playing Bond. Ian Fleming and I met several times, but only to talk about Bond. He seemed to live and think Bond. After those meetings we had, Bond seemed to infect me also. When I first met Fleming, there was no dissension between us on how to see Bond. I saw him as a complete sensualist – senses highly tuned, awake to everything, quite amoral. He always does what *he* wants. I particularly like him because he thrives on conflict. Bond lives for the moment, doing a tough job. He may not be around tomorrow, remember.'

'When I was in Jamaica making *Dr. No*, both Ian and Noël Coward were out there. "So you're going to play Bond?" Noël said. "Dreary slob, isn't he?" I said I disagreed, and Noël said, "Ah, such loyalty. You dear, dear boy." Noël asked me if they were going to shave some of the hair off my chest for the film, and I said there had been talk of it. "Be assured they will, dear boy," he said. "Ian will insist; he'll be terribly jealous because he hasn't got any."'

'It is remarkable how the Bond character has burned round the world like a forest fire. He's tough, ruthless, a compulsive killer, and savage with the women he loves – and leaves. But everybody seems to like the guy. I suppose he represents an outlet for our repressions – whatever they are. But I'm not knocking Bond. He's been very good to me.'

George Lazenby

'I regret I turned down *Diamonds Are Forever*. The only silver lining was that I met my wife and had a couple of kids – I wouldn't have done that had I gone on to do another Bond. But my career would have been much better off. I would have been a saleable commodity. As it is now, people can say, "Why didn't you do another one? Didn't they want you?" They actually wanted me to sign for seven years. Seven years to me then was a lifetime. The contract was an inch and a half thick. It covered everything, from how to cut your hair to how to behave in public.'

'I haven't seen any Bond from Roger Moore onwards. I know the formula, I know the format, I know what's going to happen. A lot of gadgets – it doesn't interest me at all. Not at all. And I'm amazed that Bond is still going on.'

Roger Moore

'I always played it with a certain reluctance to kill because my only key to playing Bond from the books was the beginning of one of Fleming's stories where it said that Bond was on his way back from Mexico, where he had eliminated somebody. He didn't like killing particularly, but he took a pride in doing his job well. That's my key to it: I don't like killing.'

'I was horrified on the last Bond I did. Whole slews of sequences where Christopher Walken was machine-gunning hundreds of people. I said, "That wasn't Bond, those weren't Bond films." It stopped being what they were about. You shouldn't dwell on the blood and the brains spewing all over the place.'

Timothy Dalton

'Ian Fleming obviously did something right. His books were great best-sellers and still are. I was astonished to discover just how good a read they are even today. He created the character of James Bond and he did it right.'

Pierce Brosnan

'I didn't have any chances when I started playing Bond. There was a lot at stake. I didn't want to be the man who put the final nail in the coffin. If I screwed up and it hadn't worked, I don't know if the series would have gone on. Tim Dalton gave a wonderful performance, a performance which was very true to what Fleming had put down. But the audience had been conditioned and primed with humour and a kind of sly nod. If you're going to play it dead straight, then it had better be rich in many varying aspects of the character. The audience wants to have fun.'

Michael G Wilson

'Most people in my position would think they wanted to do something different, to expand their horizons. But I go around the world and people say a Bond film was the first their dad took them to, or some old married couple's first date was a Bond film. These films are seen by about 500 million people in their first years. They get two hours of escapist entertainment whatever their problems in life, however dull their jobs are. I can't think of anything I could possibly do that would even come close to that.'

Bibliography

THE JAMES BOND NOVELS
By Ian Fleming
Casino Royale, Jonathan Cape, 1953
Live And Let Die, Jonathan Cape, 1954
Moonraker, Jonathan Cape, 1955
Diamonds Are Forever, Jonathan Cape, 1956
From Russia With Love, Jonathan Cape, 1957
Dr. No, Jonathan Cape, 1958
Goldfinger, Jonathan Cape, 1959
For Your Eyes Only, Jonathan Cape, 1960
Thunderball, Jonathan Cape, 1961
The Spy Who Loved Me, Jonathan Cape, 1962
On Her Majesty's Secret Service, Jonathan Cape, 1963
You Only Live Twice, Jonathan Cape, 1964
The Man with the Golden Gun, Jonathan Cape, 1965
Octopussy and The Living Daylights, Jonathan Cape, 1966

By Robert Markham (Kingsley Amis)
Colonel Sun, Jonathan Cape, 1968

By Christopher Wood
The Spy Who Loved Me (the book of the film), Jonathan Cape, 1977
Moonraker (the book of the film), Jonathan Cape, 1979

By John Gardner

Licence Renewed, Jonathan Cape/Hodder & Stoughton, 1981
For Special Services, Jonathan Cape/Hodder & Stoughton, 1982
Icebreaker, Jonathan Cape/Hodder & Stoughton, 1983
Role of Honour, Jonathan Cape/Hodder & Stoughton, 1984
Nobody Lives Forever, Jonathan Cape/Hodder & Stoughton, 1986
No Deals Mr Bond, Jonathan Cape/Hodder & Stoughton, 1987
Scorpius, Hodder & Stoughton, 1988
Win, Lose or Die, Hodder & Stoughton, 1989
Licence To Kill (based on the screenplay by Michael G Wilson and
    Richard Maibaum), Coronet, 1989
Brokenclaw, Hodder & Stoughton, 1990
The Man From Barbarossa, Hodder & Stoughton, 1991
Death Is Forever, Hodder & Stoughton, 1992
Never Send Flowers, Hodder & Stoughton, 1993
Seafire, Hodder & Stoughton, 1994
GoldenEye (based on the screenplay by Michael France and Jeffrey
    Caine), Hodder & Stoughton, 1995
Cold, Hodder & Stoughton, 1996

By Raymond Benson

Zero Minus Ten, Hodder & Stoughton, 1997
Tomorrow Never Dies (based on the screenplay by Bruce Feirstein),
    Hodder & Stoughton, 1997
The Facts of Death, Hodder & Stoughton, 1998
High Time To Kill, Hodder & Stoughton, 1999
The World Is Not Enough (based on the screenplay by Neal Purvis and
    Robert Wade), Hodder & Stoughton, 1999
Doubleshot, Hodder & Stoughton, 2000
Never Dream of Dying, Hodder & Stoughton, 2001
The Man with the Red Tattoo, Hodder & Stoughton, 2002

RECOMMENDED READING

Kingsley Amis, *The James Bond Dossier*, Jonathan Cape, 1965
Kingsley Amis (under the pseudonym Lt.-Col. William 'Bill' Tanner),
    The Book of Bond (or Every Man His Own 007), Pan Books, 1965
Mark Amory (editor), *The Letters of Ann Fleming*, Collins Harvill, 1985
Alan Barnes and Marcus Hearn, *Kiss Kiss Bang Bang*, B T Batsford, 1997

Tony Bennett and Janet Woollacott, *Bond and Beyond: The Political Career of a Popular Hero*, Macmillan Education, 1987

Raymond Benson, *The James Bond Bedside Companion*, Boxtree, 1984

Albert R Broccoli, *When the Snow Melts*, Boxtree, 1998

John Brosnan, *James Bond in the Cinema*, The Tantivy Press, 1972

Noël Coward, *The Noël Coward Diaries*, edited by Graham Payne and Sheridan Morley, Weidenfeld & Nicholson, 1982

Peter Evans, *Peter Sellers: The Mask Behind the Mask*, Leslie Frewin Publishers, 1969

Ian Fleming, *The Diamond Smugglers*, Jonathan Cape, 1957

Ian Fleming, *Thrilling Cities*, Jonathan Cape, 1963

Richard Gant, *Ian Fleming: The Man with the Golden Pen*, Mayflower-Dell, 1966

John Glen, *For My Eyes Only*, B T Batsford, 2001

Peter Haining, *James Bond: A Celebration*, W H Allen, 1987

Sally Hibbin, *The Official James Bond Movie Book*, Hamlyn, 1987

Sally Hibbin, *The Making of Licence to Kill*, Hamlyn, 1989

Philip Hoare, *Noël Coward*, Sinclair-Stevenson, 1995

Iain Johnstone, *The World Is Not Enough: A Companion*, Boxtree, 1999

Sheldon Lane, *For Bond Lovers Only*, Panther, 1965

Cole Lesley, *The Life of Noël Coward*, Jonathan Cape, 1976

Philip Lisa and Lee Pfeiffer, *The Incredible World of 007*, Boxtree, 1992

Andrew Lycett, *Ian Fleming*, Weidenfeld & Nicholson, 1995

Roger Moore, *Roger Moore As James Bond*, Pan Books, 1973

Gary Morecambe and Martin Sterling, *Cary Grant: In Name Only*, Robson Books, 2001

Graham Payne (with Barry Day), *My Life with Noël Coward*, Applause, 1994

John Pearson, *The Life of Ian Fleming*, Jonathan Cape, 1966

John Pearson, *James Bond: The Authorized Biography*, Sidgwick & Jackson, 1973

Lee Pfeiffer and Dave Worrall, *The Essential Bond*, Boxtree, 1998

Dave Rogers, *The Avengers*, ITV Books and Michael Joseph, 1983

Dave Rogers, *The Avengers Anew*, Michael Joseph, 1985

Steven Jay Rubin, *The James Bond Films*, Talisman Books, 1981

Roger Ryan and Martin Sterling, *Keeping the British End Up*, Coronet Books, 1987

Graham Rye, *The James Bond Girls*, Boxtree, 1999
Bob Simmons (with Kenneth Passingham), *Nobody Does It Better*,
   Javelin Books, 1987
O F Snelling, *James Bond: A Report*, Panther, 1964

007 Magazine is published by the James Bond 007 International Fan
Club and Archive, G3, The Mayford Centre, Smarts Heath Road,
Woking, Surrey, GU22 0PP, England (www.thejamesbondfanclub.com)

Index